HOW TO CONFIGURE AND *EQUIP* YOUR *WAREHOUSE*

TO DOCK — TO DOCK — TO STOCK — AND BACK

 FriesenPress

Suite 300 - 990 Fort St
Victoria, BC, Canada, V8V 3K2
www.friesenpress.com

Copyright © 2016 by Keith MacDonald & John Binns
First Edition — 2016

All rights reserved.

No part of this publication may be reproduced in any form, or by any means, electronic or mechanical, including photocopying, recording, or any information browsing, storage, or retrieval system, without permission in writing from FriesenPress.

ISBN
978-1-4602-7834-5 (Hardcover)
978-1-4602-7835-2 (Paperback)
978-1-4602-7836-9 (eBook)

1. *Business & Economics, Facility Management*

Distributed to the trade by The Ingram Book Company

HOW TO *CONFIGURE* AND *EQUIP* YOUR *WAREHOUSE*

FROM DOCK TO STOCK
AND BACK TO DOCK

Contents

4		ABOUT THIS MANUAL
6		WHY BOTHER?
12		**SECTION ONE** A BUILDING BLOCK METHOD
42		**SECTION TWO** USES OF STORAGE SEGMENTS AND A DATA FORM
110		**SECTION THREE** DOCK EQUIPMENT & PALLETS
124		**SECTION FOUR** SHELVING, CAROUSELS & VERTICAL LIFT MODULES
154		**SECTION FIVE** STORAGE RACKS
192		**SECTION SIX** FORKLIFTS
210		**SECTION SEVEN** FORKLIFTS
246		**SECTION EIGHT** ORDERPICKERS
262		**SECTION NINE** COMBINING EQUIPMENT INTO A SYSTEM
298		**SECTION TEN** ORDER PICKING SYSTEMS
314		**SECTION ELEVEN** GUIDANCE METHODS & AUTOMATED GUIDED VEHICLES - AGVS
322		**SECTION TWELVE** CONCLUSION
324		**SECTION THIRTEEN** TERMINOLOGY

ABOUT THIS MANUAL

This manual is for those who want a *practical* guide for selecting materials handling equipment, handling methods, and layout options to fit an existing building or configure a new facility. Very little theory of materials handling is included as there are a number of good books available for those who want to study this subject.

Determination of the total space requirement in a distribution center falls quite nicely into the time-proven concept of dividing the larger problem into smaller components in order to simplify the questions and answers. These efficiently designed areas are **zones,** which can be regrouped into an overall plan. The answers will lead to selected systems, including equipment combinations, storage height, depth and aisle widths. Keep in mind that efficient use of **cubic space**, not just area, is necessary. The goal for each zone and the completed layout is to obtain superior cube utilization combined with efficient handling.

The needs of most zones are usually not complex, but each will require basic data, estimated if not known. The gathering of data may be time consuming, but it is necessary to make selections from a wide range of products.

The selection of methods and equipment is inseparable from the amount of floor space needed for each zone.

One purpose of this manual is to help you determine what different zones to use; their areas, the method of storage and handling in each. This will allow you to easily try alternate dimensions for each zone to arrive at a layout for a new or existing building.

Some sections contain sketches of a great many types of commonly used warehouse equipment, with some basic specifications, comments pertaining to their best uses and also a few caveats. Use this library as a reference in your selections.

Also included is considerable detail pertaining to dimensioning of equipment, such as racks and forklifts, so they work together as a system without problems. Regardless of building size, the layout is very much a game of inches. An unexpected extra half inch per bay, when multiplied a number of times in a row of racks, can cause an expensive headache. Some of the pitfalls you can avoid were learned the hard way by the authors; sales representatives of materials handling equipment for many years.

A *"building block"* method of quickly estimating space requirements is introduced and carried further to be used for zone dimensioning, spacing of building columns and other data.

Safety tips are included in some explanations. Surprisingly, some of them seem to be little known or used.

Until now you may have been immersed in gathering data to determine what results are wanted from a planned new facility. Depending on size and complexity of the project, you may be using in-house sources, or outside consultants, with extended experience.

Regardless of how it was assembled, when you have enough data as to storage quantities and rotation requirements for each stock keeping unit (sku), it is time to select the handling and storage equipment which will efficiently produce the results wanted.

The selections begin at the receiving dock.

There is a bit of duplication throughout the manual, mostly inserted for the benefit of those who might skip to a section which is of most interest to them.

With the great variety of ever-changing material handling equipment, the use of an industry consultant will usually prove to be a good move, and is recommended.

Even though you may have recommendations as to the *types* of equipment needed, each person involved in the actual selection should have access to the detailed considerations presented here; so all can be literally "on the same page".

This manual is meant to be a guide only, to some methods of space planning and equipment selection. Statements, drawings and dimensions are used to explain concepts and may vary considerably according to each particular situation or equipment combination. The selection options remain the responsibility of the purchaser.

All applicable codes and regulations must be adhered to, and building plans, layouts, sprinklers, clearances, rat-runs etc. should be approved by your insurance underwriter and fire code consultant prior to committing any funding to the project.

The authors have strived in every way to be as accurate and complete as possible in the creation of this book, notwithstanding the fact that they do not warrant or represent at any time that the contents within the book are accurate due to the rapidly changing nature of the subject.

While all attempts have been made to verify every piece of information provided in this publication, the Authors assumes no responsibility for any errors, omissions, or contrary interpretation of the subject matter present in this book.

Note: Conveyors are NOT discussed in any detail within this manual. These and advanced automation are subjects which require their own manuals.

WHY BOTHER?

Why bother to check which equipment combinations and building configurations are most advantageous for **your** mix of products and orders? Why not just do it the way others in the same industry have done it?

Well, perhaps they made mistakes and have problems and inefficiencies with which they are living, but which are an ongoing cost. Maybe a lot of cost, or, perhaps they were just unaware of the great improvements in equipment capabilities.

Whether or not you have well planned systems, using efficient methods and equipment combinations within a suitable building, can mean the difference between saving or spending large amounts of money.

This manual strives to help you accomplish the physical elements of these goals in easy, logical increments.

While there are many things to be considered in planning a warehouse the three which are concentrated on here are, storage and retrieval systems, space, and product movement.

Product movement may be in many mixtures of large or small volumes, requiring different types of equipment with varying lift heights and aisle widths. In some distribution centers space may be sacrificed for ease and speed of throughput. In others, perhaps freezers are a good example, maximizing storage capacity is essential.

To some readers, especially those not previously involved with the details of equipment selection and layouts, we believe the descriptions, drawings and selection criteria will be very informative and save many common and costly mistakes, as well as a lot of time.

To others the concentration on details may become tedious, but hopefully, they will find enough useful information here to continue reading. *Remember, it takes only one useful idea or safety tip to make the effort worthwhile.*

To get an idea of the space saving potential of various storage systems take a look at the drawings and explanations on the next two pages.

SOME EFFECTS ON AREA BY VARYING SYSTEMS.

The sketches on the next page show the effects of some alternate combinations of aisle widths, storage heights and depths on the area needed for 1000 pallet storage slots. *The process of comparing many alternates need not take long because a form is provided later for easy comparisons without any drawings.*

The first area shown on line 1 is for a system using 12' wide aisles to store pallets four high in single-deep (selective) pallet racks, requiring 12,500 sq. ft. for our designated 1000 pallet slots. This is then used as a basis for comparisons with other combinations. Beside it are shown systems with aisles reduced to 8 ½' and 5 ½' while retaining the same height and depth.

Line 2 shows some increased heights along with the same aisle widths. The areas are further reduced.

Line 3 switches from single-deep storage to two-deep, again with a variety of aisle widths and storage heights.

Line 4 tries four-deep with varying heights and aisle widths.

Line 5 shows a comparison of two of the alternates with savings of 5090 sq. ft. *per 1000 slots.*

Line 6 saves almost 7000 sq. ft. compared to our basic area, by using two-deep storage, six high, 8 ½' aisles. Two-deep (also called double-deep) should be looked at very closely. It can often be used very successfully instead of single-deep.

If your building has a yearly cost of $10.00 per sq, ft. this 6950 sq. ft savings obviously amounts to $69,500 per 1000 slots / year. Put a value on your actual cost and number of slots needed.

Selection of storage depths, heights, aisle widths and equipment to suit various situations are covered in considerable detail in this manual.

COMPARISONS OF AREAS REQUIRED FOR 1000 STORAGE SLOTS WHEN USING VARYING COMBINATIONS OF AISLE WIDTHS, STORAGE HEIGHTS AND DEPTHS. BASED ON 48" DEEP X 40" WIDE PALLETS AND AN ESTIMATED ALLOWANCE FOR 12' WIDE ACCESS AISLES.

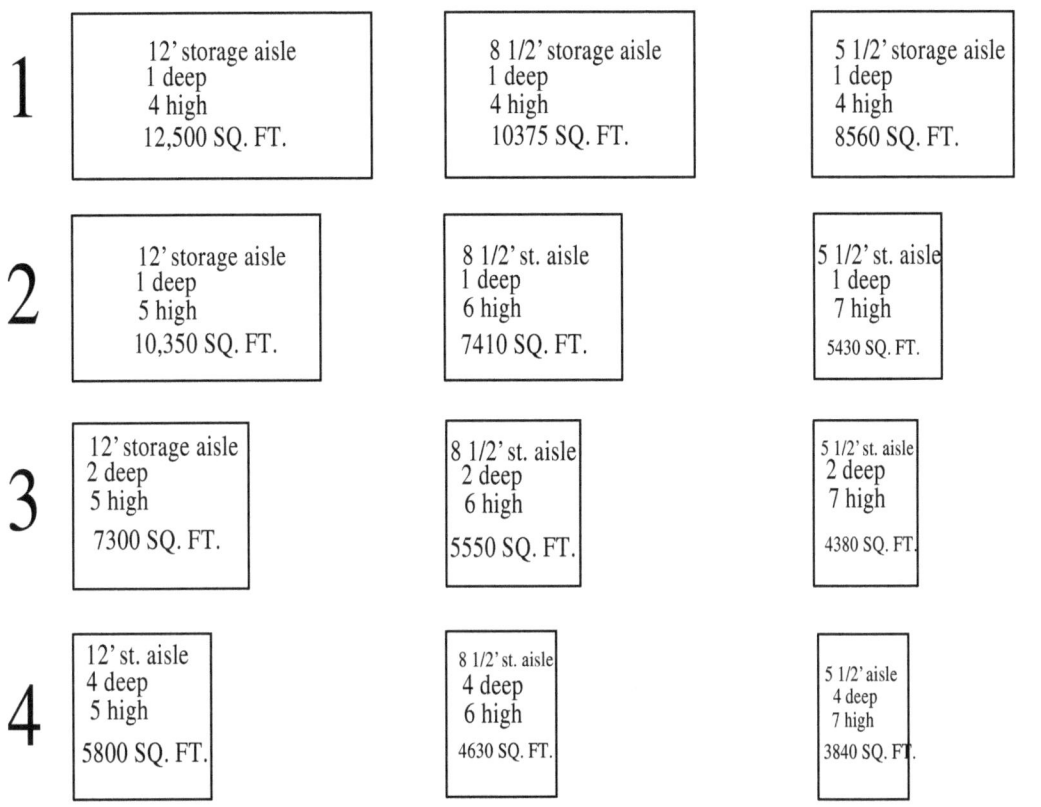

HERE ARE A COUPLE OF COMPARISONS FROM THE ABOVE ARRAY

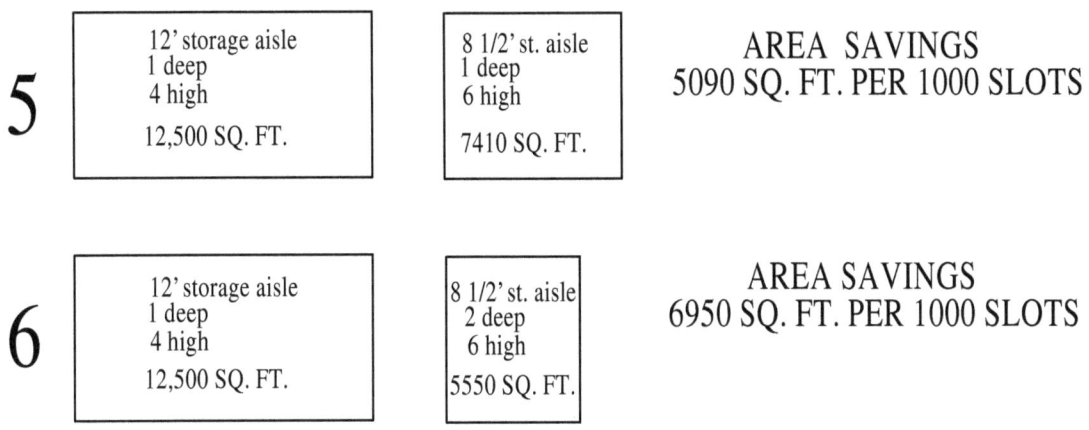

WHY BOTHER?

FUNCTIONS OF A DISTRIBUTION CENTER

Before trying to decide on the size and dimensions of a distribution center it is a good idea to list the activities which must be accommodated. The functions of a distribution center (DC) can vary from a simple few to a great many. The list is intended to make sure no space or equipment needed is overlooked.

MOST* DISTRIBUTION CENTERS HAVE FOUR BASIC PHYSICAL FUNCTIONS:

- RECEIVE
- STORE
- RETRIEVE
- SHIP

ADDITIONAL OPERATIONS NECESSARY TO ACHIEVE THESE BASIC FUNCTIONS WILL INCREASE THE MINIMUM LIST OF ACTIVITIES TO:

- RECEIVE
- TRANSPORT TO STORAGE
- STORE
- RETRIEVE
- TRANSPORT TO SHIPPING
- SHIP

TO THESE YOU CAN ADD ANY OF A LONG LIST OF ACTIVITIES WHICH MAY APPLY, WITH THEIR ADDED SPACE AND HANDLING REQUIREMENTS, THEN THE LIST COULD LOOK LIKE THIS:

- RECEIVE
- SORT AND CHECK
- PALLETIZE
- STAGE PRIOR TO STORAGE
- TRANSPORT TO STORAGE
- STORE IN RESERVE LOCATION
- MOVE FROM RESERVE TO ACTIVE LOCATION
- REPLENISH BROKEN CASE AND OTHER SPECIAL AREAS
- RETRIEVE
- FULL PALLET LOADS
- CASE PICKING
- BROKEN CASE PICKING

HOW TO CONFIGURE AND EQUIP YOUR WAREHOUSE

- MERGE ALL PORTIONS OF EACH ORDER
- CHECK
- PACKAGE
- TRANSPORT TO SHIPPING
- STAGE
- SHIP

You may have many more functions than are shown. In fact some of them may have been in your operations so long that they are forgotten as separate requirements. It is important to have a complete list before planning your space and equipment needs.

* Operations where goods arrive and are then sorted and reshipped have no storage function. These are referred to as CROSS-DOCK operations. An example would be a department store chain which receives a large shipment and, without putting it in storage, sorts it into smaller quantities and ships it to its stores.

SECTION ONE
A BUILDING BLOCK METHOD 1

TO QUICKLY AND EASILY:
Compare Suitability and Space Requirements
of Alternate Equipment Combinations
(STORAGE AND RETRIEVAL SYSTEMS)

WHAT IS A "STORAGE AND RETRIEVAL SYSTEM"?

The word *"system"* is used in this manual to include any combinations of storage and handling equipment along with the methods and aisle widths used to store and retrieve products. These systems have a defined amount of space per pallet and require dimensional compatibility of the different types of equipment, such as racks and forklifts.

These are basically "physical" systems and do not include consideration of software programs to control them, except in a few instances.

Using this restricted definition, three examples are as follows:

1) **A counterbalanced forklift** is used to store and retrieve full pallet loads within drive-in racks. The forklift and racks are a combination of two types of equipment, and the storage and retrieval of full pallet loads is the method of using them as a system. Here it is obvious that the forklift and racks must be dimensioned to allow the forklift to safely enter the racks and be capable of placing a full load on the top storage rail. Additionally, the storage aisle must have sufficient width to allow the forklift to work safely and efficiently.

2) **A stand-on reach truck** is used to load full pallets into selective racks, with low lift pallet trucks used for case picking from the lower levels. When a pallet on one of the lower levels (the pick levels) becomes empty it is replenished from the upper reserve levels by the reach truck. The racks and two types of forklifts are the equipment combination while picking from the lower levels with reserve storage above is the method of use.

3) **High level shelving is hand loaded from an Orderpicker** and orders are assembled by retrieving the stored goods using the same Orderpicker. Here you might want to consider guiding the Orderpicker in the narrowest of aisles to increase safety and efficiency while allowing the picker to easily and safely pick from the shelving on both sides. The guidance becomes an integral part of the system, along with the shelving and Orderpicker, and the hand storage and retrieval on all levels and both sides of the aisle is the method of use.

These are just a few examples of systems. The actual selection and dimensioning of a system must be done with great care if serious and costly errors are to be avoided. Some examples, using much more detail, are included in section 9 and it is recommended that this attention to detail be used for *each* system, regardless of how simple it might appear to be at first glance.

WHAT TO EXPECT IN THIS SECTION

The objective is to help you decide on the preferred storage and retrieval system(s) for *your* operations.

You may need more than one system and there may be advantageous system differences to those of other companies in similar businesses.

In the process of selecting a system you could be interested in some alternate situations:

Trying to get the *maximum storage slots in* ***a pre-determined area.*** This area might have fixed dimensions or might be as you choose. It could be for the planning of a new building or to help in your selection of a lease building. Two very different situations.

Trying to get ***a pre-determined number of slots*** *in the smallest* ***practical*** *area.*

To begin, the number of storage and retrieval activities are listed and it is stated that all of ***the following descriptions and explanations concentrate on a system having full pallets inbound with full pallets and cases outbound,*** using a variety of rack types and forklifts.

Questions that must be answered to decide on the most efficient system of this type are listed. (Other systems with differing storage and retrieval requirements can be planned using the same basic steps.)

Then follows an explanation of a **Building Block Concept** for step-by-step selections to answer these questions, expanding from a basic pallet load to a finished storage layout. THE FIVE BUILDING BLOCKS ARE: STORAGE SLOTS, MODULES, SEGMENTS, ZONES AND SECTIONS. Explanations of these components begin on page 17.

These five building blocks are then explained in great detail, with the use of many drawings. Alternate storage heights and depths, with varying aisle widths, are easily compared. This method will provide the means to assess the suitability of an existing building or help to configure a new one.

A DATAFORM is then introduced in Section 2. This form, simply filled in, provides a number of highly useful estimating tools and a method to try alternate dimensions and configurations in a relatively short time, without drawings. It will be most useful once the building block concept is fully understood.

EQUIPMENT SELECTION FOR *YOUR* WAREHOUSE

THE SELECTION OF METHODS AND EQUIPMENT FOR EACH ZONE IS INSEPARABLE FROM THE AMOUNT OF FLOOR SPACE NEEDED.

A large variety of materials handling equipment will be described in other sections. Selection of the types best suited to your warehouse requires data and decisions based on **what results are wanted.**

A good starting point is to develop a list of activities in your facility and be sure each is included in the final layout.

Storage and retrieval activities may include one or all of the following.

- PALLETS – IN ——— PALLETS – OUT
- PALLETS – IN ——— CASES – OUT / PIECES – OUT
- CASES – IN ——— CASES – OUT / PIECES – OUT
- CASES – IN ——— PIECES – OUT
- PIECES – IN ——— PIECES – OUT

BECAUSE THEY ARE EXTENSIVELY USED, WE WILL CONCENTRATE HERE ON *SYSTEMS FOR FULL PALLETS INBOUND, WITH FULL PALLETS AND/OR CASES OUTBOUND, USING RACKS FOR STORAGE.*

For each differing storage and retrieval **zone** the same questions arise. (Consider a zone to be a portion of the warehouse planned for specific products and/or methods of storage and handling.)

If questions or terms here are not fully understood don't be concerned. All are to be closely looked at, beginning on the next pages.

QUESTIONS:

NUMBER OF SKUs?

QUANTITIES OF EACH SKU? PLANNED MAXIMUMS AND MINIMUMS?

ROTATION REQUIREMENTS?

DAILY THROUGHPUT?

NUMBER OF PICK FACES NEEDED?

NUMBER OF AISLE FACES NEEDED?

TOTAL NUMBER OF PALLET SLOTS NEEDED?

FLOOR STACKING OR RACKS? (RACKS WILL BE USED IN MOST EXAMPLES).

WHAT TYPE OF RACKS?

STORAGE DEPTH?

HOW TO CONFIGURE AND EQUIP YOUR WAREHOUSE

STORAGE HEIGHT?

CASE PICK METHOD?

FORKLIFT TYPE AND AISLE WIDTH?

LENGTH AND WIDTH OF THE ZONE?

The next considerable number of pages in sections 1 and 2 are intended to help answer these difficult questions. It is probably the single most important (and maybe most difficult) section of this manual. But, when fully understood, you will have powerful tools to determine preferred systems types, configure the storage and handling area of a new building, or assess the suitability of any building under consideration.

We will return later in the book to address the above specific questions.

A BUILDING BLOCK METHOD TO DETERMINE PALLET STORAGE SYSTEMS

By using building blocks you start with small increments and progress to zones and sections. The sections are later combined into a completed storage layout.

HERE ARE FIVE EASY PLANNING INCREMENTS, INCREASING IN SCOPE TO ARRIVE AT THE COMPLETED LAYOUT

1) STORAGE SLOT

Contains one pallet load and is the basic increment in this type of system. Dimensioning of a storage slot is easy if the load size is known (length, width and height). If the size is not known it must be determined, at least on a trial basis. Remember the pallet or skid the load is on.

2) STORAGE MODULE

Contains one or more storage slots, all intended to hold the same sku. Module type and size is arrived at by a process involving storage quantities, throughput and rotation.

3) SEGMENT

Contains one or more modules plus an aisle. This is the block which is used for many purposes. A list of segment uses is shown below, each of which will be described in detail, using many drawings.

- **A** A segment is an easy step toward determining square feet per storage slot at the lowest level, with various aisle widths and storage rack types. This figure can be very useful for comparisons. *Does not include allowance for access aisles; add 20% for an estimate.*

- **B** To provide a tool for a quick estimate of the total storage area needed. *Does not include an allowance for access aisles; add about 20%.*

- **C** To easily try alternate combinations of lengths and widths (configurations) for the storage area needed. This can be especially helpful when searching for a lease building or planning a new one. *Includes allowance for access aisles.*

- **D** To estimate optimum spacing of building columns.

- **E** To experiment with possible layouts *within existing column centers*, quickly showing any problem locations.

- **F** To closely estimate the rack components needed for a selected layout.

But to assemble a segment it is necessary to select an aisle; this will lead to a discussion of forklift types and their aisle widths.

STORAGE SLOT

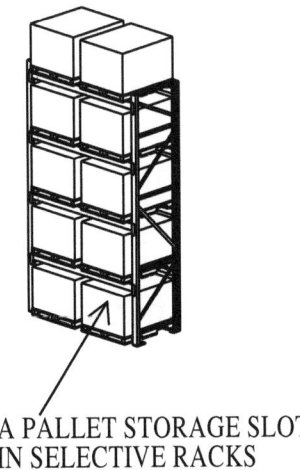

A PALLET STORAGE SLOT
IN SELECTIVE RACKS
THIS IS ALSO A
ONE-PALLET MODULE

STORAGE MODULE IN RACKS

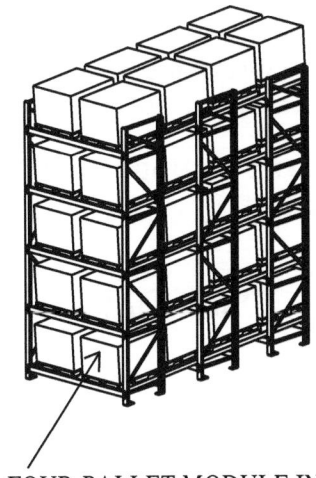

A FOUR-PALLET MODULE IN
PUSH-BACK RACKS
THEY SHOULD ALL BE THE SAME SKU

STORAGE SEGMENT

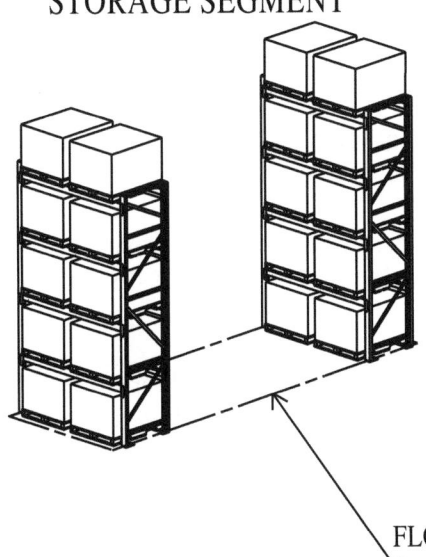

THIS SEGMENT CONSISTS OF TWENTY
ONE-PALLET MODULES AND A STORAGE AISLE

THE DIMENSIONS AND AREA OF THE SEGMENT ARE
KNOWN SO THE TOTAL AREA NEEDED FOR ANY
NUMBER OF SLOTS IS EASY.

FLOOR AREA PER SLOT IS ALSO EASY.

THE SEGMENT DIMENSIONS CAN BE USED TO
ASSEMBLE DIFFERENT CONFIGURATIONS OF
ZONE LENGTHS AND WIDTHS TO DETERMINE THE
BEST ZONE SHAPE FOR YOUR ACTIVITIES OR
BUILDING LIMITATIONS.

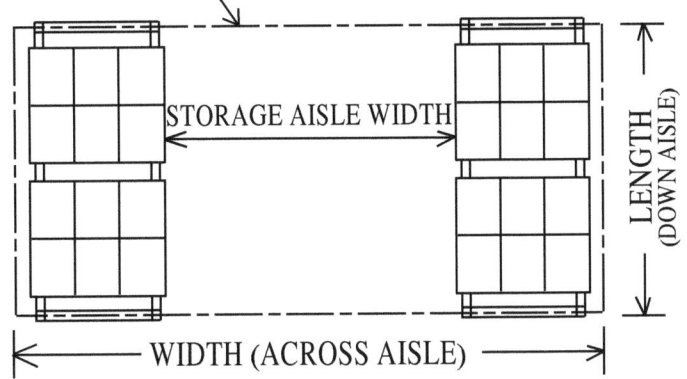

(INCLUDES AISLE-GOODS-FLUE ALLOWANCE)

1 *A BUILDING BLOCK METHOD*

4) **ZONE**
   Contains any quantity of segments to provide the total storage slots needed for a distinct activity. Rearranging the segments easily tests alternate zone dimensions.

5) **SECTION**
   Contains one or more zones grouped together for any reason, such as families of products, sales volume, case picking, security, etc. etc.

SECTIONS ARE THEN ARRANGED IN A COMPLETED LAYOUT TO SUIT YOUR ACTIVITIES AND BUILDING

SUMMARY OF THE FIVE BUILDING BLOCKS

STORAGE SLOT: Contains one pallet & load.

STORAGE MODULE: Contains one or multiple pallets.   Must decide best modules.

SEGMENT: Contains multiple modules plus an aisle. Must decide aisle width and storage depth.

ZONE: Contains multiple segments. Must decide length/width configuration.

SECTION: Contains one or more zones. Combine zones into a warehouse section Then combine sections into a completed layout

The next pages show and explain **pallet slots and storage modules.** They also explain the effects on pallet accessibility and product rotation with the various storage methods.

Understanding modules will allow the selection of the best ones for your activities. **Then, because a segment is assembled by combining modules and an aisle,** a discussion of typical aisle widths for a number of forklift types is included.

Segments will be used to make drawings of different shapes of zones; which are then compared for space efficiency. **Once this method is understood, a form is introduced to quickly compare the space efficiency of differing zone shapes without using any drawings.**

Each zone tried will quickly yield the zone overall dimensions and area as well as some other comparative information.

As the method of using building blocks expands there is some duplication of statements or data for ease of referencing with a minimum of page flipping.

MODULES, SEGMENTS, ZONES AND SECTIONS

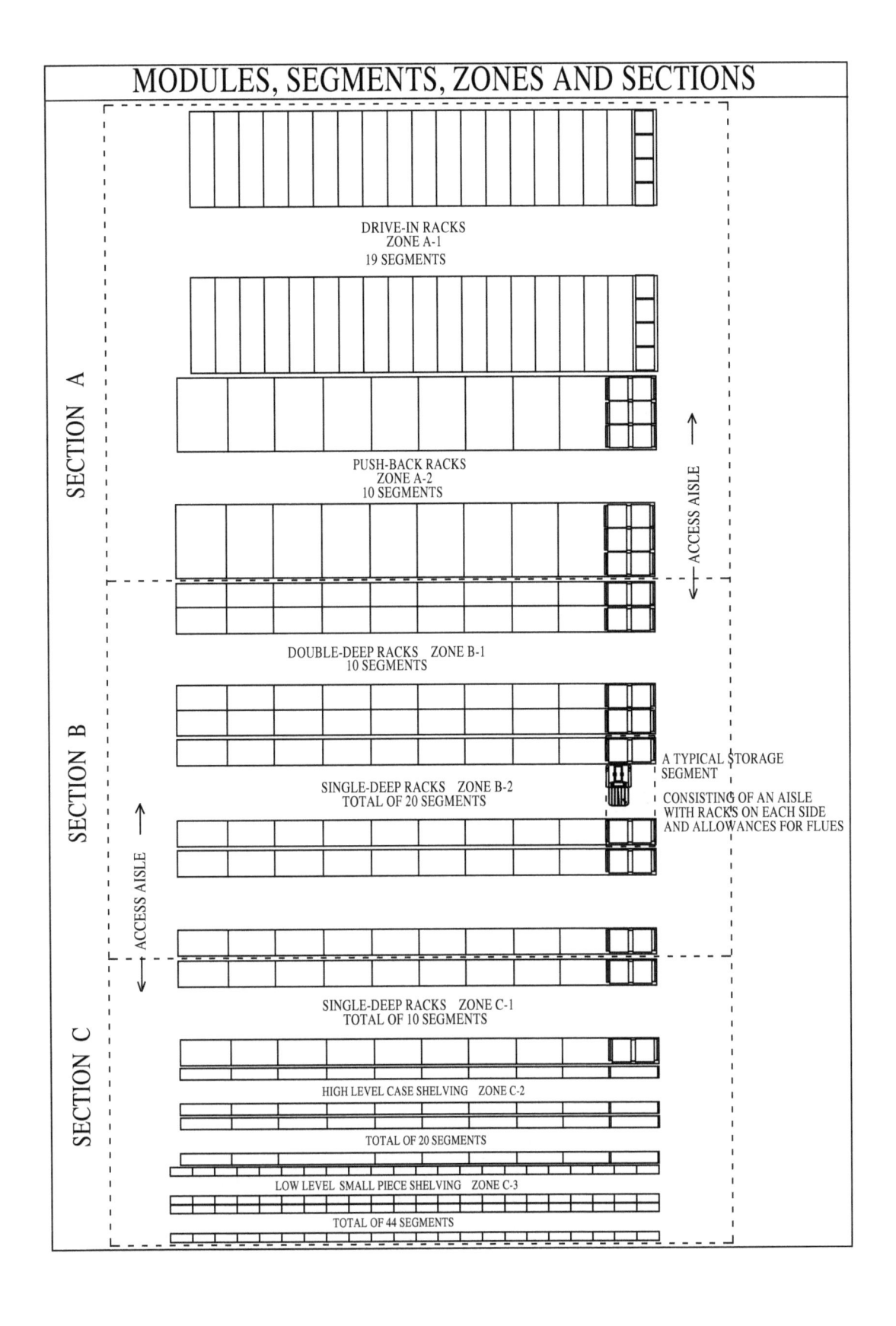

SECTION A

DRIVE-IN RACKS
ZONE A-1
19 SEGMENTS

PUSH-BACK RACKS
ZONE A-2
10 SEGMENTS

← ACCESS AISLE →

SECTION B

DOUBLE-DEEP RACKS   ZONE B-1
10 SEGMENTS

SINGLE-DEEP RACKS   ZONE B-2
TOTAL OF 20 SEGMENTS

A TYPICAL STORAGE SEGMENT CONSISTING OF AN AISLE WITH RACKS ON EACH SIDE AND ALLOWANCES FOR FLUES

← ACCESS AISLE →

SECTION C

SINGLE-DEEP RACKS   ZONE C-1
TOTAL OF 10 SEGMENTS

HIGH LEVEL CASE SHELVING   ZONE C-2
TOTAL OF 20 SEGMENTS

LOW LEVEL SMALL PIECE SHELVING   ZONE C-3
TOTAL OF 44 SEGMENTS

1 *A BUILDING BLOCK METHOD*

1) A PALLET STORAGE SLOT

THIS IS THE FIRST BUILDING BLOCK

In a pallet storage system all dimensions flow from the pallet size, or by load size if it overhangs the pallet. Rack openings and storage height are obviously affected but aisle width and flue size may also be influenced by load overhang.

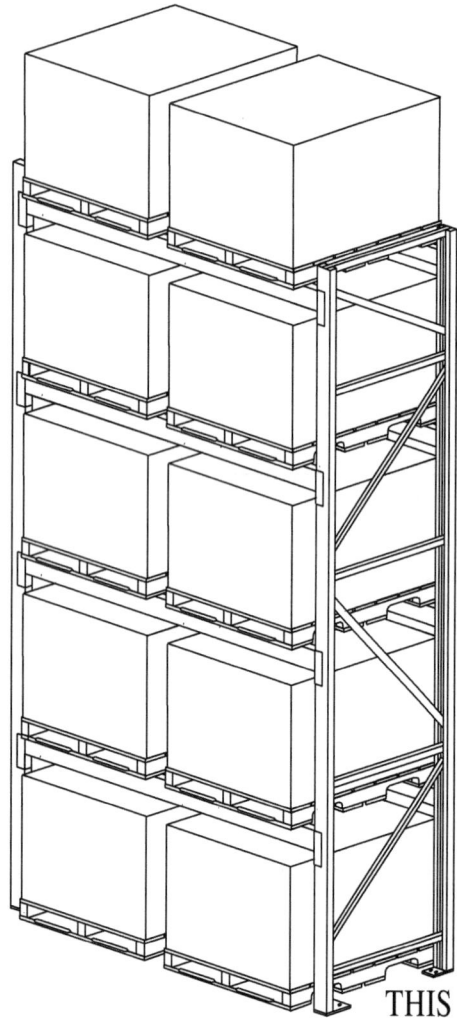

A PALLET STORAGE SLOT IN SELECTIVE RACKS

THIS IS OFTEN REFERRED TO AS A FLOOR-LEVEL SLOT OR A FLOOR SLOT

THE AREA PER FLOOR SLOT, INCLUDING ALLOWANCE FOR THE STORAGE AISLE, CAN BE USED FOR INITIAL AREA CALCULATIONS AND SYSTEM COMPARISONS

2) STORAGE MODULES

THE SECOND BUILDING BLOCK IS A STORAGE MODULE

A PALLET STORAGE MODULE can be thought of as a defined storage location which holds one or more pallets. It is best used to hold only one type of sku, in single or multiple quantities, depending on module depth and height.

A number of rack and floor stack modules are shown on the following pages. They are at the core of each zone, affecting rotation, honeycombing and pick faces as well as zone and area configurations.

It is essential to understand that a slot and a module are different entities. A rack pallet storage slot can hold only one pallet. A rack module may contain one or many pallet slots. Some confusion may take place because a slot is also a one-pallet module. But there is no need to dwell on this, modules will become clear as their uses are explained.

There are two important types of modules, each with a distinct effect on rotation control.

FIFO (FIRST-IN, FIRST-OUT)

Selective and flow-through racks are the only racks which automatically provide fifo, where the first pallet put into the module is automatically the first one to come out of it.

LIFO (LAST-IN, FIRST-OUT)

Here last-in, first-out is mandatory (double-deep, push-back and drive-in racks plus floor stacking). The dangers of honeycombing are greatly increased with the wrong lifo system, especially when the module is too deep.

Although lifo is the most common way of naming this storage method it's possible that FILO would be more descriptive. FIRST-IN, LAST-OUT brings home the realization that some loads are being 'buried' behind others and care must be taken not to overextend the depth.

And then there is the dreaded FISHS: FIRST-IN, STILL HERE SOMEWHERE.

In some instances, where strict fifo rotation is not always needed, active product may be loaded in front of longer term storage. Doing so results in good use of space but will usually result in extra handling. Of course, a satisfactory inventory control system is needed to keep track of stock locations and ages.

The most important fact to realize at this stage is that as module size (especially depth) increases so does the probability of honeycombing and/or product aging. On the other hand modules which are not deep enough will usually mean poor use of space. Keep these contending options in mind as you review the selections available, shown on the following pages.

MODULE DEPTHS

THE SKETCHES WHICH FOLLOW WILL BE USEFUL IN UNDERSTANDING THE ALTERNATES

A one-slot module (or, if you prefer, call it a one-pallet module) is contained in *selective racks*. Every pallet is an aisle face pallet and all can be used as pick faces when employing a high level Orderpicker at the higher levels. *Two-slot modules* could exist in *double-deep* or *push-back racks*. Each level can hold a different sku with one pallet on the aisle face and another behind it.

Three-slot modules could exist in *push-back* and *flow-through racks*. Each level is an independent lane and can hold a different sku, with one pallet on the aisle face and two others behind it.

Modules of four or more storage slots could exist in *push-back* and *flow through racks*. Each level is an independent lane, and can hold a different sku, with one pallet on the aisle face and three or more behind it.

Modules of four or more storage slots could also exist in *drive-in, drive-through and mole-type racks* and also in *floor stacks*. Each bay of drive-in racks and each row of a floor stack is meant to store only identical loads. Mixing sku's in this type of storage will result in extra handling and other rotation problems. Drive-ins are essentially the same storage type as floor stacks but loads can be stacked to higher levels without product crushing.

Drive-through racks are the chameleons of the rack world and would rarely hold only four loads. When the situation warrants it they can be used as drive-ins or even as a combination of drive-ins and selective. Depending on how they are used they may alternate between fifo and lifo.

RACK TYPE	FIFO	LIFO	STORAGE DEPTH ONE SLOT	STORAGE DEPTH TWO SLOTS	STORAGE DEPTH TWO OR MORE SLOTS
SELECTIVE	X		X		
DOUBLE- DEEP		X		X	
PUSH-BACK		X			X
FLOW- THROUGH	X				X
DRIVE-IN		X			X
DRIVE-THROUGH	X*	X*			X
MOLE_TYPE		X			X
FLOOR STACKS		X	X		X

* DRIVE-THROUGH RACKS OFFER A CHOICE OF FIFO OR LIFO

HOW TO CONFIGURE AND EQUIP YOUR WAREHOUSE

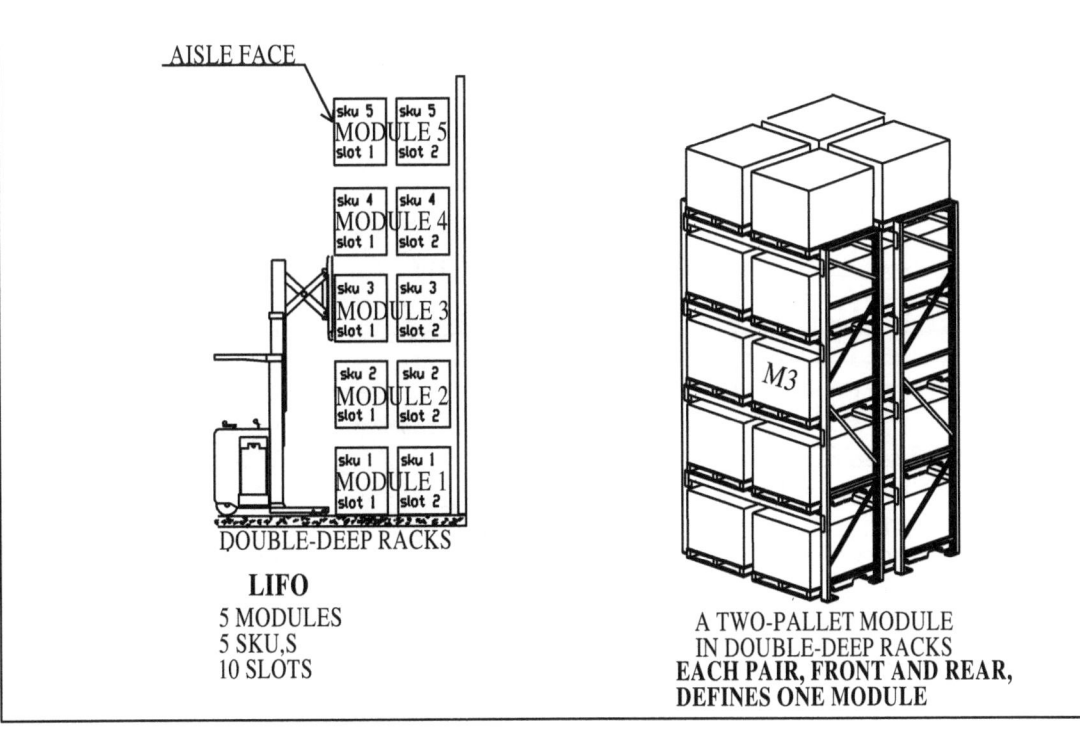

ONE-PALLET MODULES IN SELECTIVE RACKS

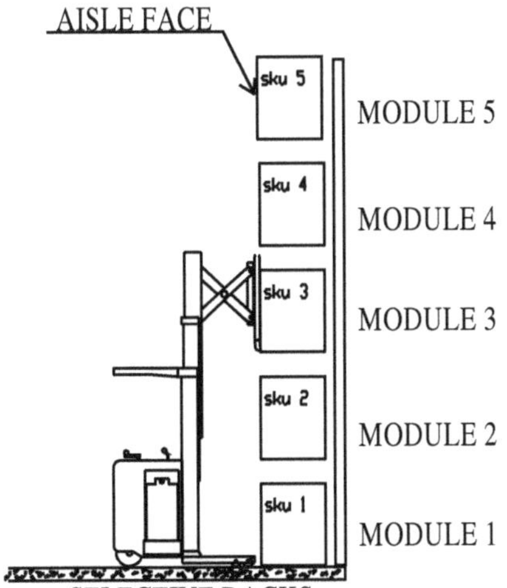

AISLE FACE

MODULE 5
MODULE 4
MODULE 3
MODULE 2
MODULE 1

SELECTIVE RACKS

FIFO OR LIFO
(YOUR CHOICE)

5 MODULES
5 SKU,S
5 SLOTS

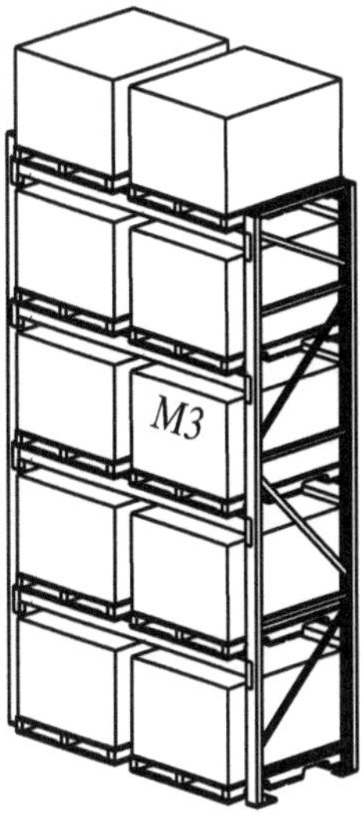

A ONE-PALLET MODULE
IN SELECTIVE RACKS

TWO-PALLET MODULES IN DOUBLE-DEEP RACKS

AISLE FACE

LIFO
5 MODULES
5 SKU,S
10 SLOTS

A TWO-PALLET MODULE
IN DOUBLE-DEEP RACKS
**EACH PAIR, FRONT AND REAR,
DEFINES ONE MODULE**

1 *A BUILDING BLOCK METHOD*

TWO-PALLET MODULES IN PUSH-BACK RACKS

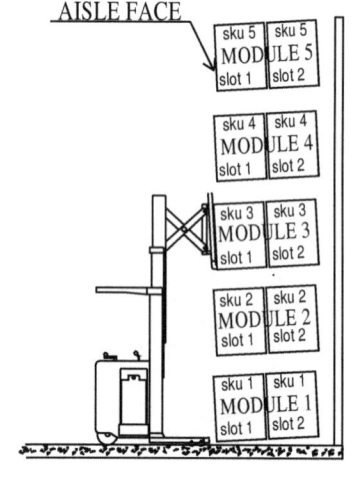

PUSH-BACK RACKS
LIFO
5 MODULES
5 SKU,S
10 SLOTS

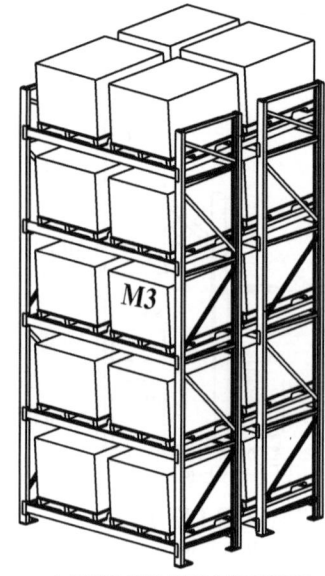

A TWO-PALLET MODULE
IN PUSH-BACK RACKS
EACH PAIR, FRONT AND REAR, DEFINES ONE MODULE

THREE-PALLET MODULES IN PUSH-BACK RACKS

PUSH-BACK RACKS
LIFO
5 MODULES
5 SKU,S
15 SLOTS

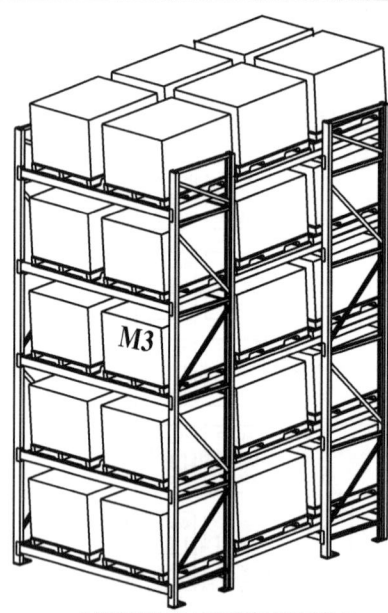

A THREE-PALLET MODULE
IN PUSH-BACK RACKS
EACH ROW OF THREE, FRONT TO REAR, DEFINES ONE MODULE

HOW TO CONFIGURE AND EQUIP YOUR WAREHOUSE

SIX-PALLET MODULES IN FLOW-THROUGH RACKS

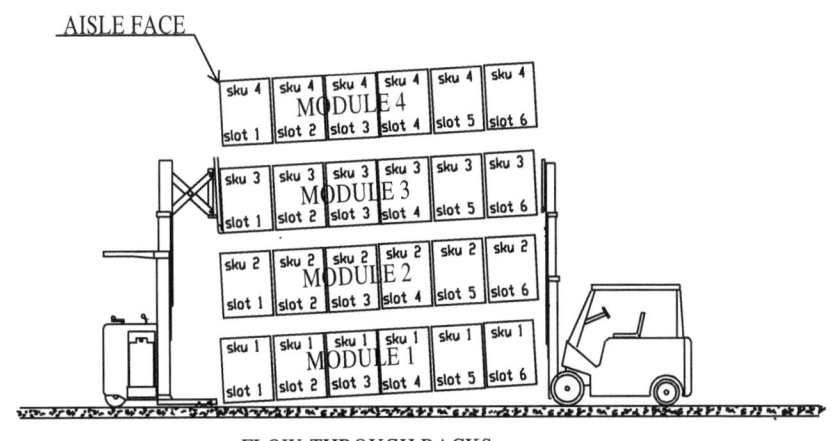

FLOW-THROUGH RACKS
FIFO

4 MODULES
4 SKU,S
24 SLOTS

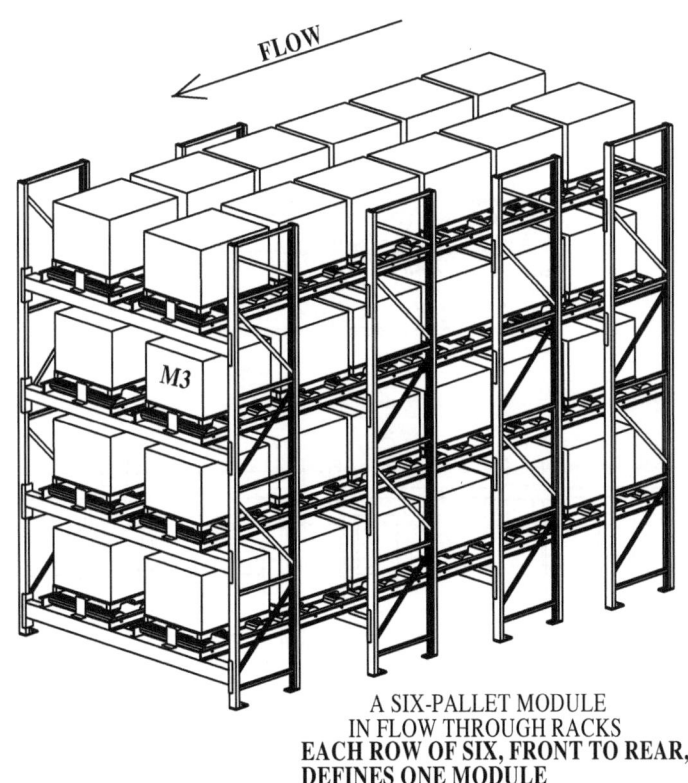

A SIX-PALLET MODULE
IN FLOW THROUGH RACKS
**EACH ROW OF SIX, FRONT TO REAR,
DEFINES ONE MODULE**

1 *A BUILDING BLOCK METHOD*

THIRTEEN-PALLET MODULE IN MOLE-TYPE DEEP RACKS

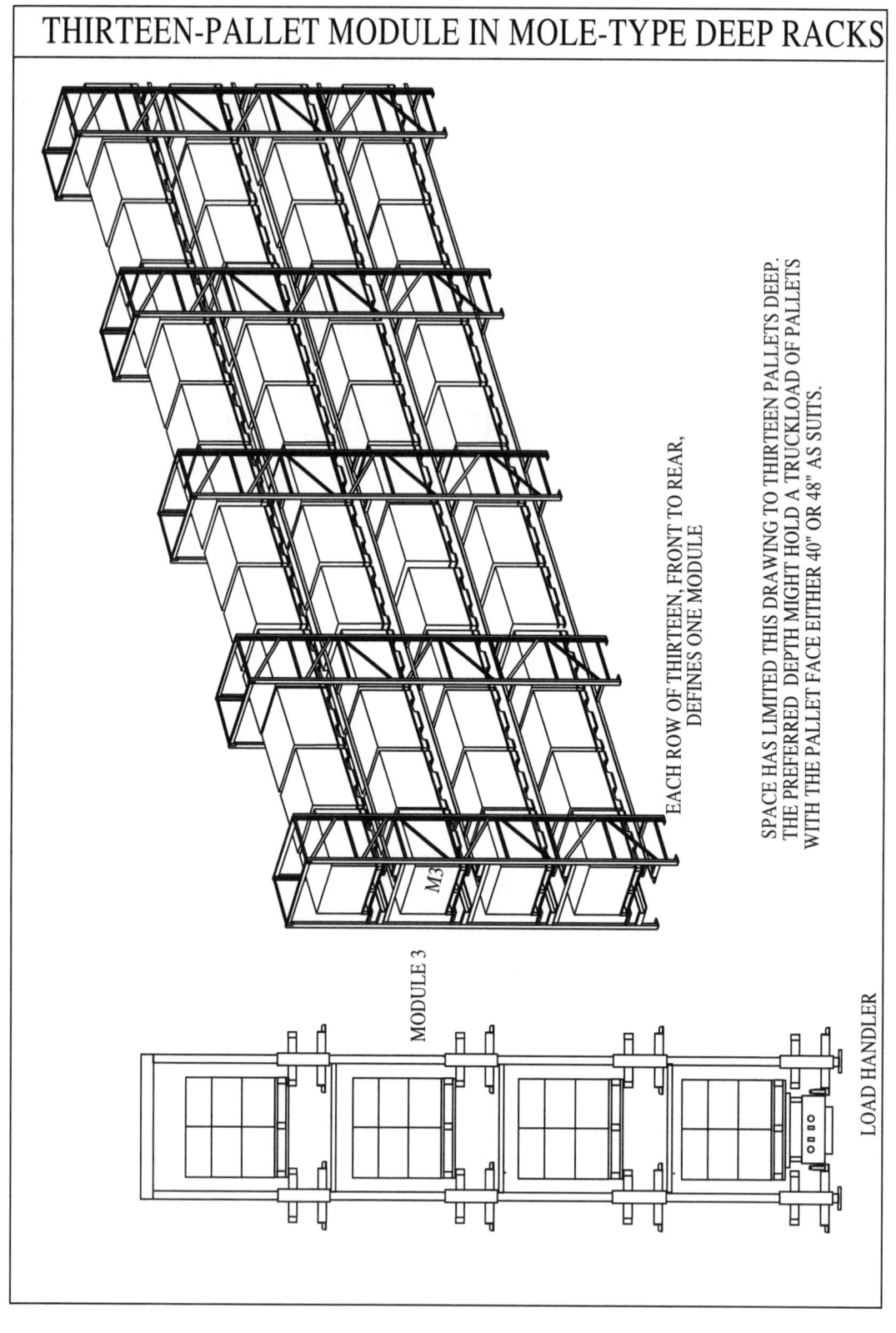

EACH ROW OF THIRTEEN, FRONT TO REAR, DEFINES ONE MODULE

SPACE HAS LIMITED THIS DRAWING TO THIRTEEN PALLETS DEEP. THE PREFERRED DEPTH MIGHT HOLD A TRUCKLOAD OF PALLETS WITH THE PALLET FACE EITHER 40" OR 48" AS SUITS.

MODULE 3

LOAD HANDLER

HOW TO CONFIGURE AND EQUIP YOUR WAREHOUSE

TWENTY-PALLET MODULE IN DRIVE-IN RACKS

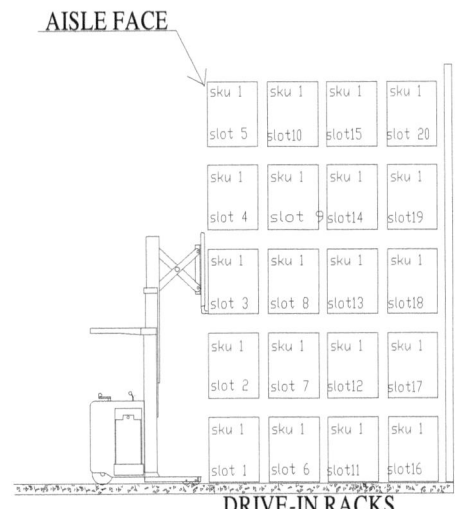

LIFO
1 MODULE
1 SKU
20 SLOTS

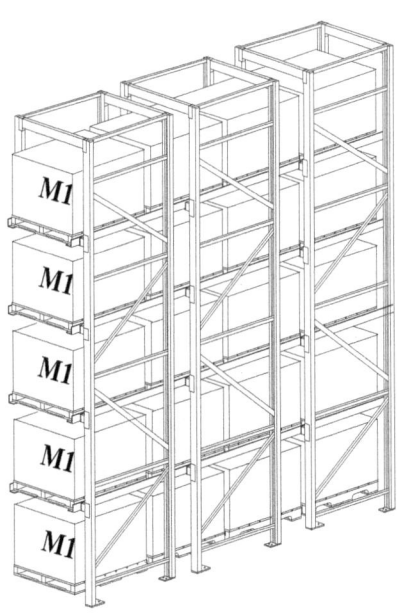

A SINGLE 20-PALLET MODULE IN DRIVE-IN RACKS.
ALL LOADS ARE THE SAME SKU.

1 *A BUILDING BLOCK METHOD*

VARIOUS MODULES IN DRIVE-THROUGH RACKS

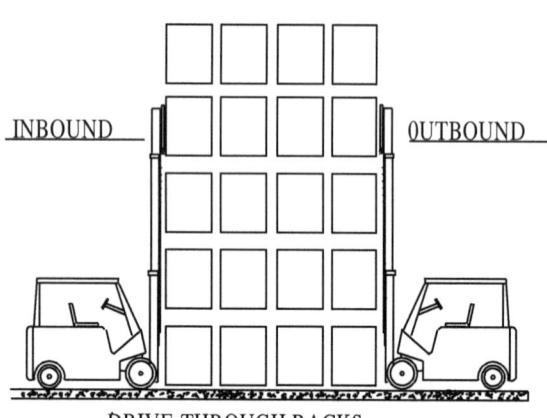

DRIVE-THROUGH RACKS
FIFO
ONE OR MULTIPLE MODULES
ONE OR MULTIPLE SKU,S
20 SLOTS

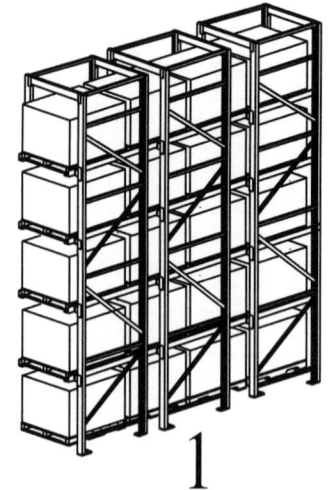

1

A 20-PALLET MODULE IN DRIVE-THROUGH RACKS. LOADS MAY BE ALL ONE SKU OR ALL DIFFERENT WHEN TEMPORARILY STORING PICKED ORDERS.

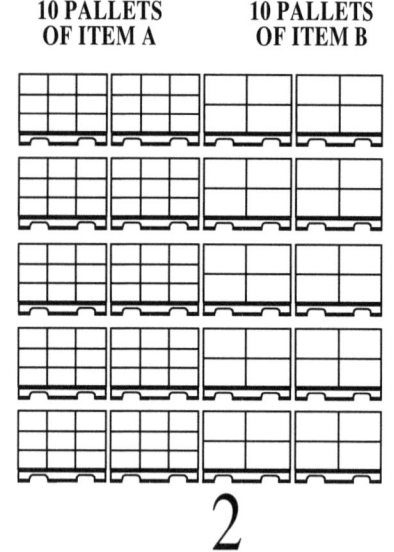

10 PALLETS OF ITEM A   10 PALLETS OF ITEM B

2

USED HERE AS TWO TEN-PALLET DRIVE-IN MODULES BACK-TO-BACK.
NOW LIFO

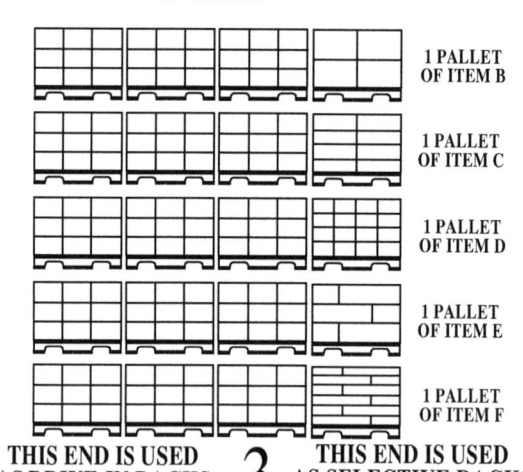

15 PALLETS OF ITEM A

1 PALLET OF ITEM B
1 PALLET OF ITEM C
1 PALLET OF ITEM D
1 PALLET OF ITEM E
1 PALLET OF ITEM F

THIS END IS USED AS DRIVE-IN RACKS   **3**   THIS END IS USED AS SELECTIVE RACKS

USED HERE AS ONE FIFTEEN-PALLET
DRIVE-IN MODULE   **(LIFO)**
BACK-TO-BACK
WITH FIVE SELECTIVE MODULES
(FIFO)

HOW TO CONFIGURE AND EQUIP YOUR WAREHOUSE

VARIOUS MODULES IN FLOOR STACKS

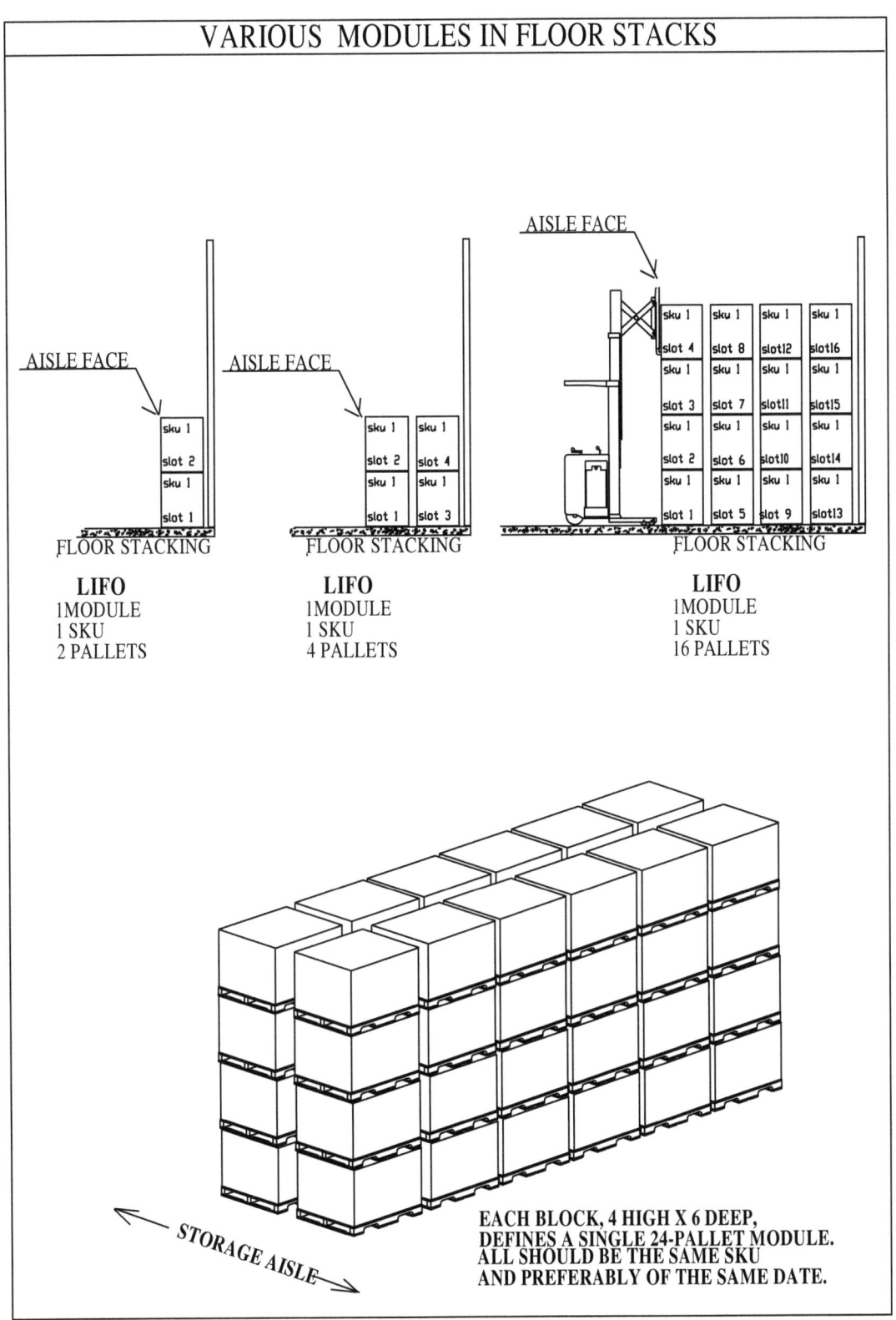

1 *A BUILDING BLOCK METHOD*

DECIDING MODULE TYPES AND SIZES

Now, with an understanding of FIFO, LIFO and STORAGE MODULES we can return to the list of questions listed earlier in this section.

OUR GOAL IS TO FIRST SELECT THE PREFERRED STORAGE MODULES AND THE FORKLIFT TYPES. THEN SOURCE STORAGE AND HANDLING EQUIPMENT TO SUIT. THEN MODIFY AND DIMENSION EACH OF THESE COMPONENTS (I.E. RACKS, FORKLIFT AND AISLE WIDTH) AS MAY BE NECESSARY TO ENABLE THEM TO WORK TOGETHER AS AN EFFICIENT SYSTEM. YOU WILL THEN HAVE A WAREHOUSE SEGMENT WITH KNOWN DIMENSIONS AND AREA, AS WELL AS THE NUMBER OF PALLETS IT CAN CONTAIN. THEN USE THESE FIGURES TO ASSESS ANY BUILDING BEING CONSIDERED OR TO CONFIGURE A NEW BUILDING.

STORAGE RACKS AND FORKLIFTS ARE EXPLAINED ELSEWHERE, AS IS DIMENSIONING THEM TO BE COMPATIBLE AS A SYSTEM.

Modules and rack types are decided upon by a combination of the number of sku's, load quantities per sku, rotation requirements, sales volumes, aisle and pick faces needed and perhaps some special considerations for your particular operations.

NUMBER OF SKUs?
The number of different stock-keeping units - sku's - is important in determining the number of aisle faces and pick faces. These are often needed in different quantities because every aisle face is not necessarily a pick face.

PALLET QUANTITIES OF EACH SKU? PLANNED MAXIMUMS AND MINIMUMS?
This the basic start of deciding on rack types and module depths.

ROTATION REQUIREMENTS?
Rotation control is another key consideration in deciding rack types and depths. Some items may need a FIFO system while others can use LIFO.

DAILY THROUGHPUT?
The number of loads throughput daily is an important factor. Six per day is far different than one per day or long term storage and will require a different system.

NUMBER OF PICK FACES NEEDED?
A pick face is needed for each sku picked and shipped by cases. For the type of system being discussed (pallets and cases) the pick faces may be at the lower levels, within reach of a picker working from floor level. Reserve is stored above. However, sometimes it is necessary or desirable to pick from higher levels.

NUMBER OF AISLE FACES NEEDED?
This is the combined total of case picking and full pallet faces. Multiple faces for the same sku are commonly used. For example, at least two aisle faces are needed for each sku where full loads of reserve are stored at the higher levels to replenish a lower level case picking line.

TOTAL NUMBER OF LOADS TO BE IN STORAGE? STORAGE SLOTS NEEDED?
The total quantity of loads to be in storage may not be needed to decide module types. However it is obviously a crucial figure which will be the basis for the number of storage slots needed. But pallet quantity is only a starting point; to this figure must be added allowances for honeycombing and future growth. Extra slots are needed.

With this data available (*at your discretion the initial data may be estimated from experience and made more precise later as necessary*) **we can now consider and compare the effects of rack types, depths and heights. These comparisons are also linked to selecting a case pick method, desired aisle width and forklift types. In other words the progression will lead from storage modules to storage segments.**

WHAT TYPE OF RACKS?
To decide this question the best starting points are rotation requirements of sku's when grouped by their differing storage quantities.

FIFO OR LIFO?

FIFO
If strict fifo is needed, **when loads are removed irregularly in various quantities,** then your choices are limited to selective, flow-through or drive-through racks. Flow-throughs will always result in fifo regardless of retrieval patterns. Selective racks will need closer attention to be sure of fifo. Drive-throughs are inefficient for this rotation.

However, *if loads are stored and removed in batches*, you could use any of the other racks, providing the storage module is sized to fit the batch. A drive-in rack holding twenty loads will, in effect, provide fifo if all twenty loads are stored and retrieved at the same time, as a batch. Double-deep would hold batches of two loads and push-backs could be sized to suit.

LIFO

A lifo system may be acceptable for a number of situations. Possibly for storage of batches as mentioned above. Or, if the products are not overly time sensitive, active stock could be rotated in the front portion of the racks while some loads remain in the rear until it is necessary to remove them. In a freezer, for instance, this may be an important way to increase storage, although some extra handling will usually result. Or perhaps the lifo potential for honeycombing is just not a problem, with empty slots acceptable until growth uses up the planned expansion space. Then extra handling or expansion will be needed.

Once the module type (lifo, fifo, flow through, etc) has been decided the question of depth becomes prominent. Too deep will leave empty storage slots and quite possibly extra handling to control this honeycombing and fifo. Not deep enough will require a good control system but may be space efficient by allowing small lots to be placed anywhere open.

IDEAL STORAGE DEPTH?

Storage and retrieval patterns are very important in selecting rack type and module size, especially depth. The following are comparisons which do not take into account any re-handling to clear old stock out of the way of newer arrivals. The cost of re-handling may exceed the cost of providing a more efficient system.

TWO RETRIEVAL PATTERNS FROM FOUR-DEEP DRIVE-IN RACKS

"A", on the next page, shows a drive-in rack with sixteen slots loaded on day 1. These loads are held in storage through day six, and then removed as a batch on day seven. Assume the racks remain empty through day seven. They have been occupied for six of the seven days; 86% utilization. If they had been re-stocked soon after being unloaded the utilization would be as close to 100% as is likely to happen. However, for this and the next drawings it is assumed there will be a day when they are empty. A final comment is that if the rack remained full for thirteen days, with the fourteenth day empty, the utilization would be 93%, and so on.

"B" shows the same rack when emptied on an irregular basis over the same week. On day 1 it is loaded with sixteen pallets. On day 2, four are removed; three are removed on day 3, two on day 4, none on day 5, four on day 6 and the last three on day 7, leaving the rack empty most of day 7. In this scenario the average number of loads in this rack is about nine; a 55% utilization for the week. Perhaps another system would do better.

Utilization percentages on pages 34 and 35 are approximate. The main point is to compare storage depth with product flow patterns.

Page 35 shows a different storage method for this situation.

1 *A BUILDING BLOCK METHOD*

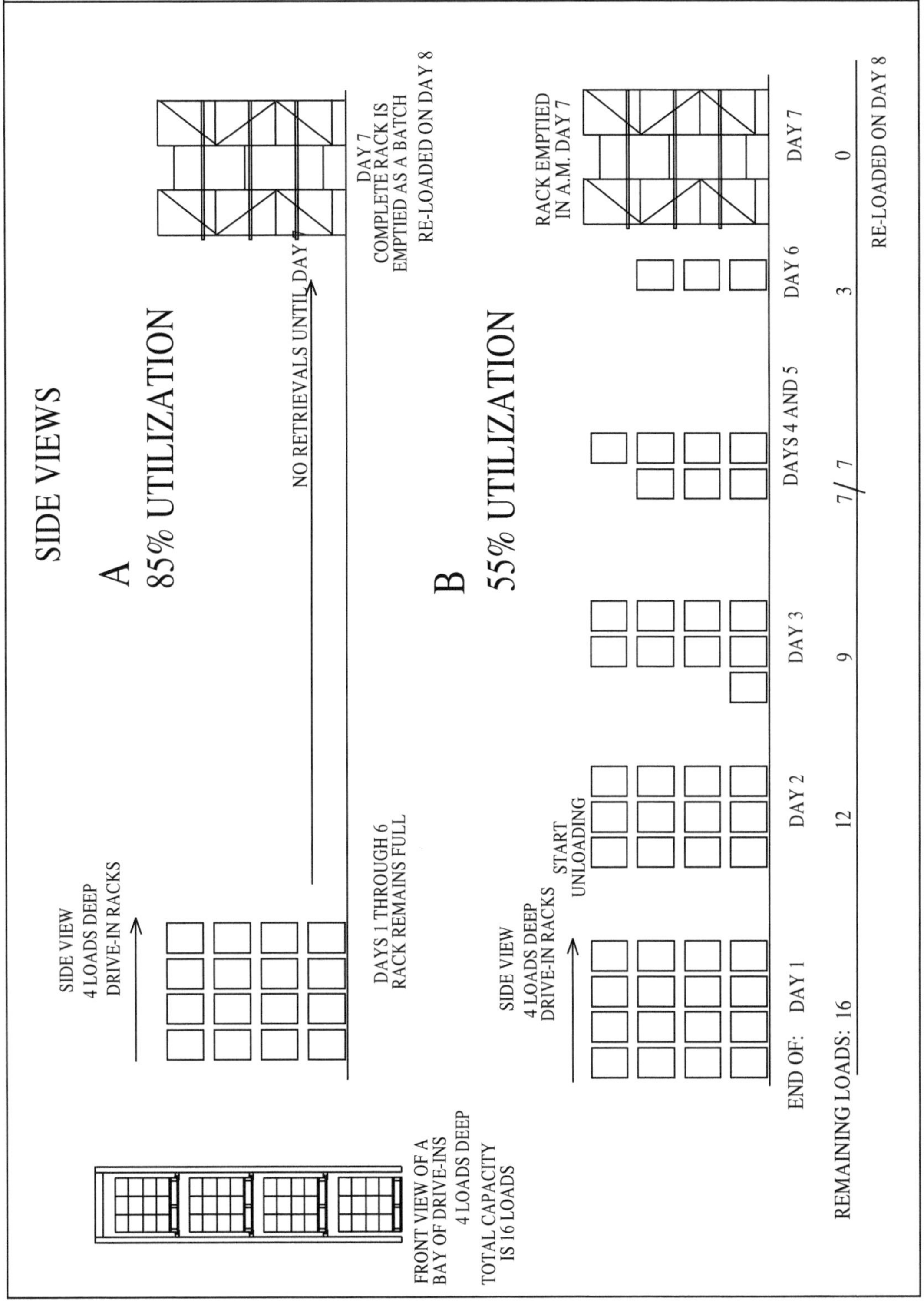

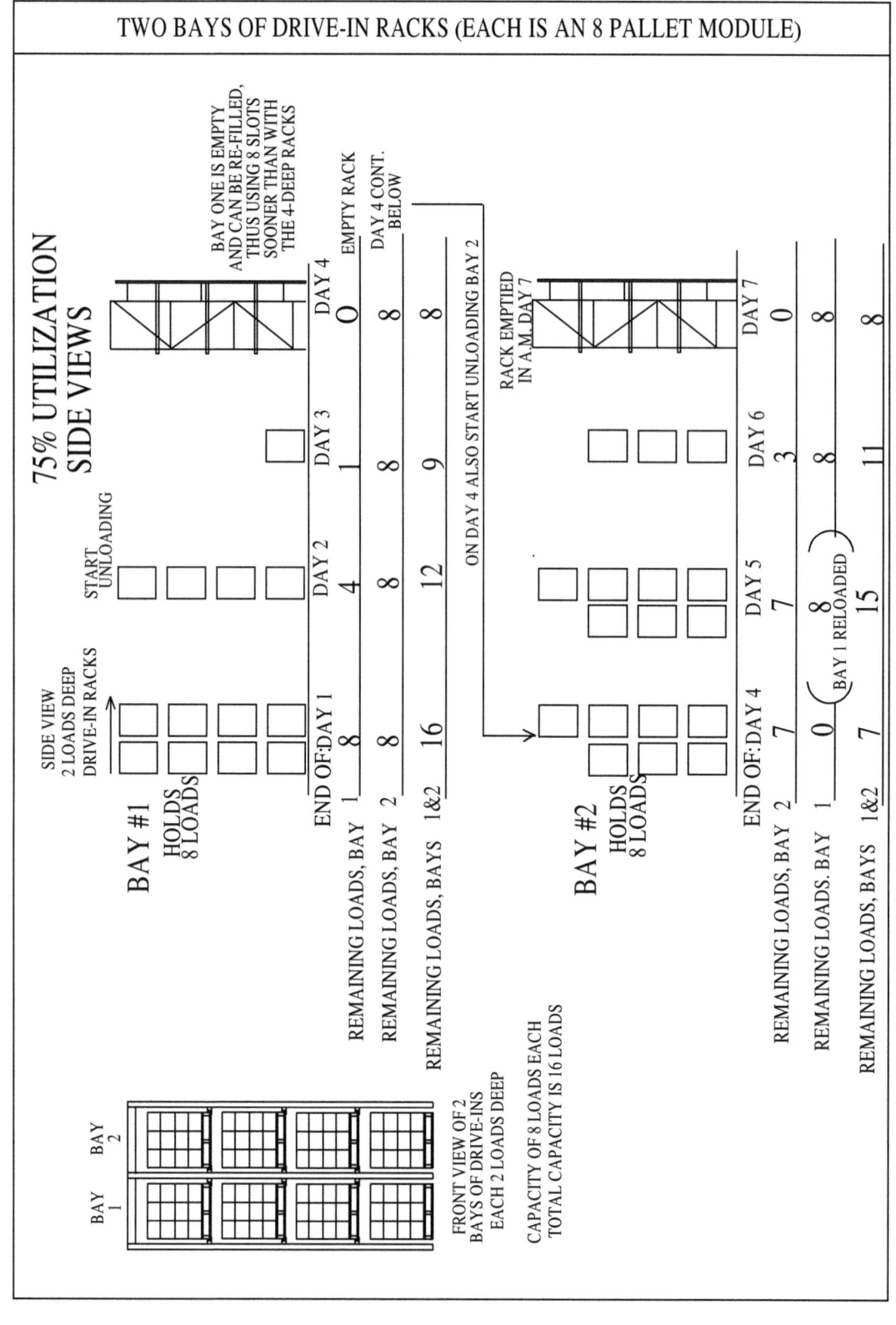

HOW TO CONFIGURE AND EQUIP YOUR WAREHOUSE

Shown here are two bays of drive-in racks, two pallets deep, eight loads each, used instead of the deeper (16 pallet) racks shown on the previous drawing.

This shows the efficiency rate when the batch of sixteen loads is stored in two batches of eight and then removed in the exact same irregular pattern as "B" on Page 34

Bay one is emptied first while bay two remains full. On day four bay one is empty and can now be reloaded with newer product, (a different sku if desired).* Then retrieval begins from bay two.

This flexibility yields an average of twelve loads in storage, a gain of three. Rack utilization is increased from 55% to 75%.

* In real life if, on day 3, the lone remaining pallet is removed, the rack can be re-loaded sooner. But this early re-handling advantage is not included here.

The previous two examples, using drive-in racks, pertain to **percentages** of space utilization within the racks. The next page shows plan views of these same racks; now with a storage aisle. The single 4-deep rack uses less area than the two 2-deep sections. However, using the same withdrawal patterns as used for the 55% and 75% usage examples, shows that the shallower sections are more efficient and are a better choice. They also provide more flexibility for rotation and open storage slots for incoming product. These results apply only to this example. Different inputs will yield different results; which is exactly why comparisons should be done.

Now consider, instead of drive-in racks, using two bays of another type of rack; 2-deep pushbacks; (see page 38). **Here each level is a separate module of only two pallets and so the rack can be almost continuously re-filled.** Utilization will be very high, possibly 85% or more, with little honeycombing. Smaller quantities of each sku are conveniently accepted by the system with these 2-pallet modules.

Selective racks will provide almost 100% use if promptly re-filled but a look at alternates may be justified. Consider the following example where data is shown for single-deep (fifo) with 95% full, and two-deep (lifo) with 85% full. What would be better for *your* situation? These are arbitrary percentages, ignoring flues, columns and access aisles but you can make any comparison with the best data available.

So the storage efficiency of modules and flexibility for varying quantities improve when modules are well keyed to storage quantities and throughput patterns.

1 A BUILDING BLOCK METHOD

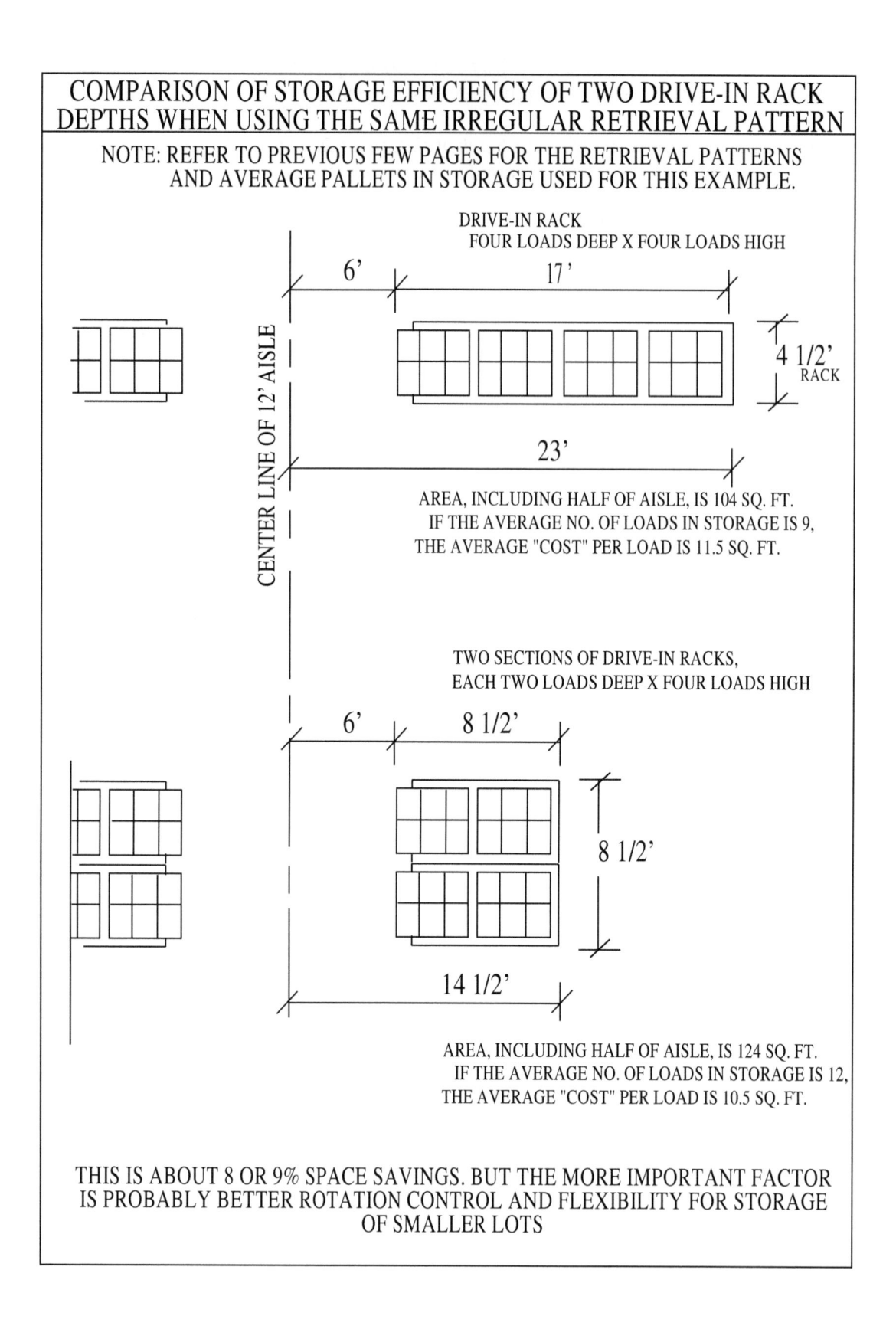

COMPARISON OF STORAGE EFFICIENCY OF TWO DRIVE-IN RACK DEPTHS WHEN USING THE SAME IRREGULAR RETRIEVAL PATTERN

NOTE: REFER TO PREVIOUS FEW PAGES FOR THE RETRIEVAL PATTERNS AND AVERAGE PALLETS IN STORAGE USED FOR THIS EXAMPLE.

DRIVE-IN RACK
FOUR LOADS DEEP X FOUR LOADS HIGH

6'   17'

4 1/2' RACK

CENTER LINE OF 12' AISLE

23'

AREA, INCLUDING HALF OF AISLE, IS 104 SQ. FT.
IF THE AVERAGE NO. OF LOADS IN STORAGE IS 9,
THE AVERAGE "COST" PER LOAD IS 11.5 SQ. FT.

TWO SECTIONS OF DRIVE-IN RACKS,
EACH TWO LOADS DEEP X FOUR LOADS HIGH

6'   8 1/2'

8 1/2'

14 1/2'

AREA, INCLUDING HALF OF AISLE, IS 124 SQ. FT.
IF THE AVERAGE NO. OF LOADS IN STORAGE IS 12,
THE AVERAGE "COST" PER LOAD IS 10.5 SQ. FT.

THIS IS ABOUT 8 OR 9% SPACE SAVINGS. BUT THE MORE IMPORTANT FACTOR IS PROBABLY BETTER ROTATION CONTROL AND FLEXIBILITY FOR STORAGE OF SMALLER LOTS

A COMPARISON OF SYSTEMS TO HOLD 1000 LOADS WHEN TOTALLY FULL

SEGMENT OF SINGLE-DEEP RACKS

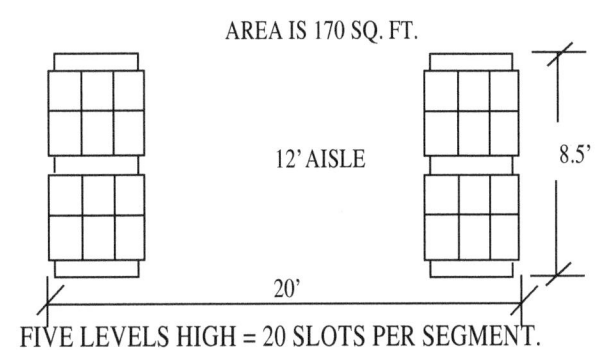

AREA IS 170 SQ. FT.

12' AISLE   8.5'

20'

FIVE LEVELS HIGH = 20 SLOTS PER SEGMENT.
50 SEGMENTS ARE NEEDED FOR 1000 SLOTS. 50 X 170 = 8500 SQ.FT.
AT 95% UTILIZATION THE AVERAGE
AREA "COST" PER LOAD STORED IS
(8500 ÷ 950) = 9 SQ. FT. PER LOAD

SEGMENT OF TWO-DEEP RACKS

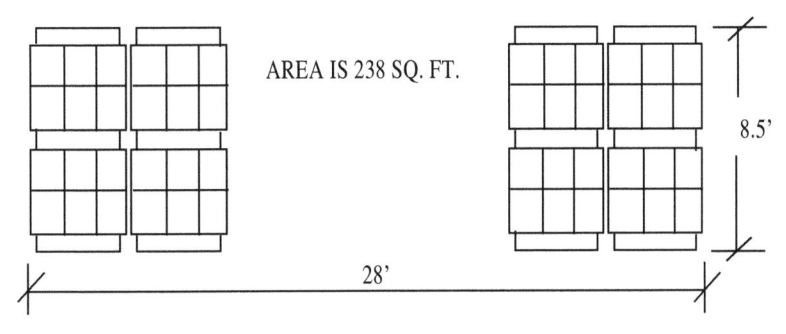

AREA IS 238 SQ. FT.

8.5'

28'

FIVE LEVELS HIGH = 40 SLOTS PER SEGMENT.
25 SEGMENTS ARE NEEDED FOR 1000 SLOTS. 25 X 238 = 6000 SQ.FT.
AT 85% UTILIZATION THE AVERAGE
AREA "COST" PER LOAD STORED IS
(6000 ÷ 850) = 7 SQ. FT. PER LOAD

1 *A BUILDING BLOCK METHOD*

IDEAL STORAGE HEIGHT?

Using overhead space results in cheaper storage by using less area for the same amount of product and may be an important method of allowing for growth. Consider a situation where there is a case picking line in the lower two levels of selective racks, with reserve loads stored above the pick line. Here a four level system will suffice but leave little ability to respond to growth.

A five or six level system may initially leave empty slots at the higher levels but, as volume and the number of sku's increases, the flexibility will exist to accommodate the expansion. The case pick line can be changed from two levels to three or more levels by using a high level orderpicker. Three levels could become pick levels with reserve above. Or all levels may become pick levels, with reserve behind them or stored elsewhere.

Look for a high building, possibly at little or no extra cost, for maximum growth flexibility.

CASE PICK METHOD?

Case picking has been left to the last because many of the answers to previous questions are likely to have an effect on your choice. Picking system options for full loads, cases or pieces and equipment to suit are discussed in sections 8 & 10. The variety ranges from push carts with the picker walking along the aisle to very high lift equipment, either guided or non-guided.

Although you may have decided on a high storage system for full pallets it does not mean the case picking must also be high level. The number of case pick faces will be important because they tend to spread over a large area when they are numerous and are only one or two levels high. But the advantage is that the reserves are above the pick line and replenishment is easy, with a well controlled FIFO system.

With pick faces at all levels and reserve elsewhere FIFO is still easy but re-filling the pick slot may take longer, and may cause more delays or pick errors.

With reserves behind the pick faces replenishment is fast, and is actually automatic in flow racks. However, there is still a bit more potential for honeycombing than exists with selective racks. Try to have rack depth sufficient for a full shift of picking.

If the height of a pick slot in racks is sufficient it becomes possible to remove a near-empty pallet and put the remaining cases on top of the replacement load. In this way a slot need not become empty, with a rush replenishment needed to satisfy picking needs.

Consider each zone as a separate identity. The first questions then become:

Should the full pallet reserves for the pick line be A) above a low or mid-level pick line, B) behind the pick faces or C) remote from the pick line?

SOME CASE PICKING AND RESERVE ALTERNATES

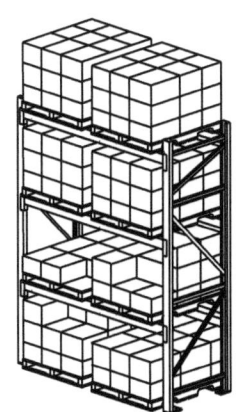

TWO PICK LEVELS WITH
RESERVE ABOVE
8 PALLET SLOTS
8 AISLE FACES
4 PICK FACES
4 RESERVES

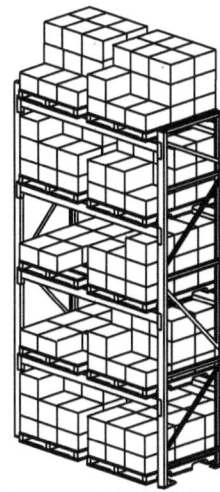

FIVE PICK LEVELS WITH
RESERVE ELSEWHERE
10 PALLET SLOTS
10 AISLE FACES
10 PICK FACES
NO RESERVES

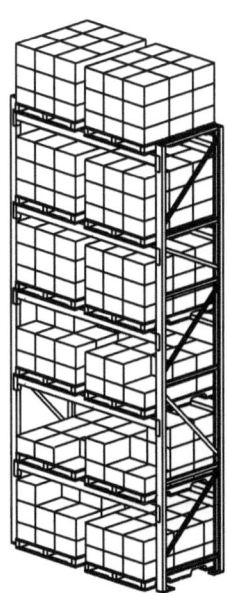

THREE PICK LEVELS WITH
RESERVE ABOVE
12 PALLET SLOTS
12 AISLE FACES
6 PICK FACES
6 RESERVES

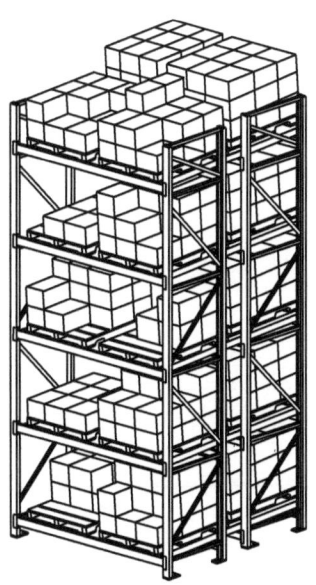

FIVE PICK LEVELS WITH
RESERVE BEHIND
IN PUSH-BACK RACKS
20 PALLET SLOTS
10 AISLE FACES
10 PICK FACES
10 RESERVES

1 *A BUILDING BLOCK METHOD*

SECTION TWO
USES OF STORAGE SEGMENTS AND A DATA FORM 2

CONFIGURE ZONES AND FINAL LAYOUT OF THE STORAGE AREA

AID IN ASSESSING THE SUITABILITY OF ANY BUILDING

AID IN CONFIGURING A NEW BUILDING

BUILDING BLOCKS #'S 3 & 4
STORAGE SEGMENTS AND ZONES

A STORAGE SEGMENT PROVIDES THE DIMENSIONS
AND AREA OF A BASIC BUILDING BLOCK

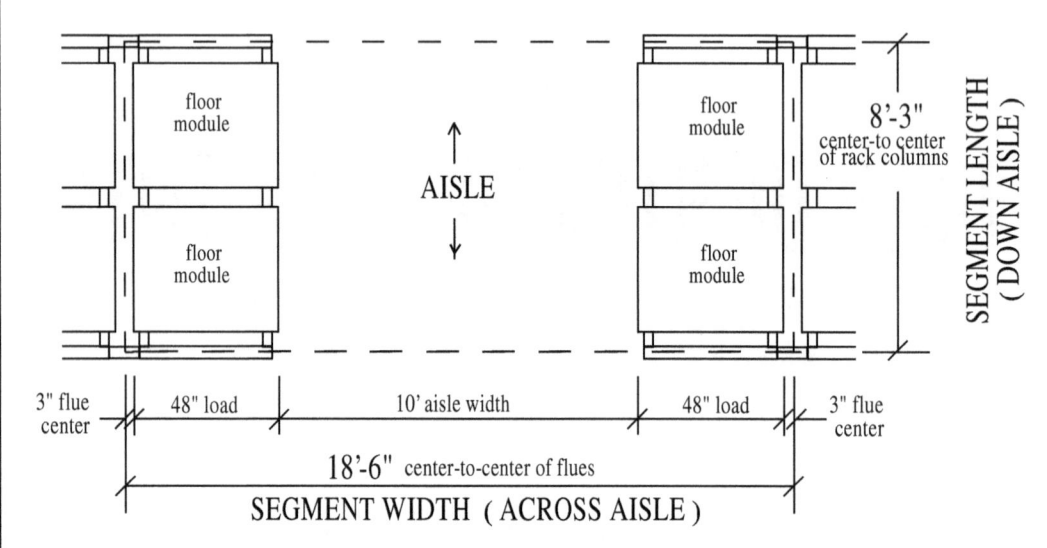

floor module		floor module	8'-3" center-to center of rack columns
floor module	↑ AISLE ↓	floor module	SEGMENT LENGTH (DOWN AISLE)

| 3" flue center | 48" load | 10' aisle width | 48" load | 3" flue center |

18'-6" center-to-center of flues

SEGMENT WIDTH (ACROSS AISLE)

DIMENSIONS WILL VARY ACCORDING TO YOUR ACTUAL CHOICES

SIMPLIFIED FOR SPACE ESTIMATING AND LAYOUT USE

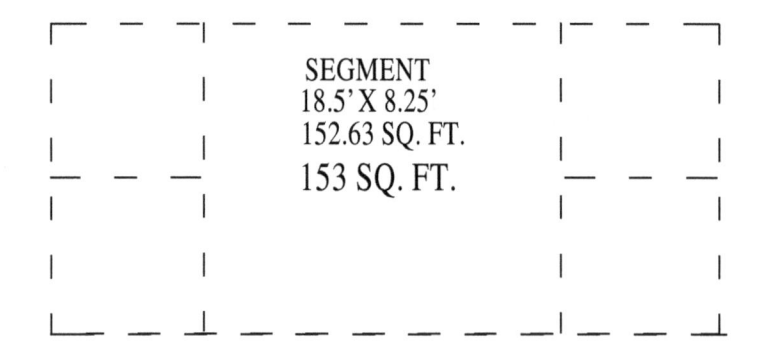

SEGMENT
18.5' X 8.25'
152.63 SQ. FT.
153 SQ. FT.

HOW TO CONFIGURE AND EQUIP YOUR WAREHOUSE

3) SEGMENTS & 4) ZONES

AISLES

Modules have just been explained in some detail and now, **because a segment is comprised of modules and a *storage* aisle,** it is time to discuss types of aisles and their varying widths.

Aisle widths may be exactly as preferred or may be compromised by activities such as the need for passing machines or building restrictions such as columns. When you are able to select an aisle width along with your module selection the result is a segment; a basic building block.

TYPES OF AISLES

There are two types of aisles which concern us at this time; **Access Aisles** and **Storage Aisles.** These are shown in the drawing below.

ACCESS AISLES provide paths to storage aisles. They are sometimes called main aisles. The most important consideration is to make them wide enough for passing traffic, such as two forklifts carrying pallets, or to allow an orderpicker or very narrow aisle truck to swing into a storage aisle. Traffic in access aisles may be heavier and faster than in storage aisles, so ample clearances are recommended.

STORAGE AISLES are where goods are stored, on one or both sides of the aisle. A major consideration is to have sufficient width for passing traffic. Some types of narrow aisle forklifts can operate in aisles too narrow for passing vehicles, so a decision is necessary as to the importance of passing traffic versus the narrowest possible aisle. Very Narrow Aisle forklifts allow no room for passing.

Storage aisles are the subject of the next drawings.

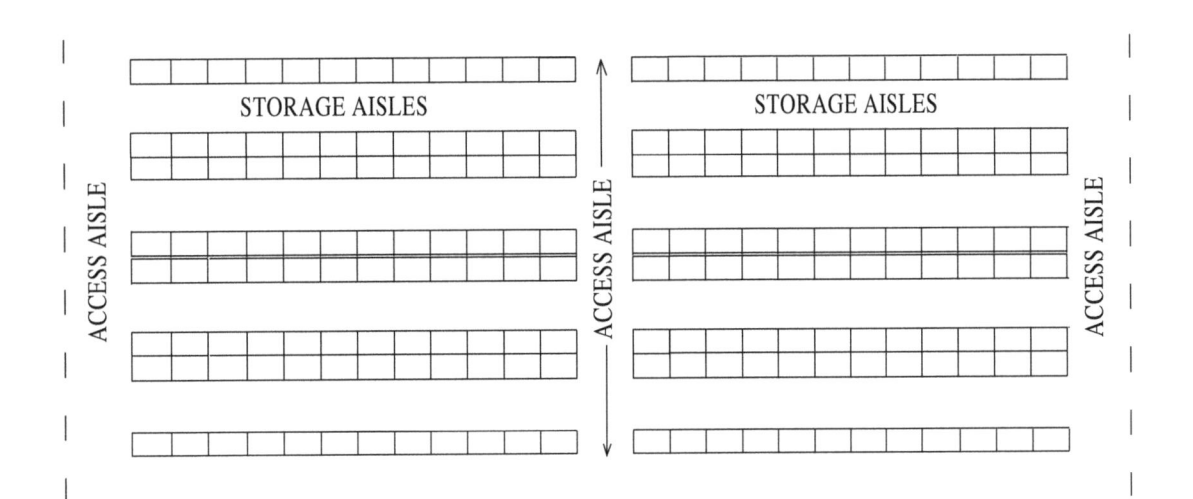

2 *USES OF STORAGE SEGMENTS AND A DATA FORM*

WHAT *IS* STORAGE AISLE WIDTH ?

There has always been a considerable amount of confusion as to the dimension which constitutes a *practical* aisle width, including operating clearance. *Miscalculation of aisle widths has caused many problems over the years and continues to do so. For instance, if building dimensions and column spacing are based on an aisle width which unexpectedly becomes too narrow for efficient forklift operations, the problems are not easily resolved.*

The next drawing is meant to clear up this question; showing the actual width as the narrowest width available, and not necessarily the distance between storage racks or pallets. Following this there are more drawings pertaining to aisle widths, with explanations in the text.

In condition "A" the aisle width is from rack to rack because that is the narrowest width that will occur, with nothing overhanging the front of the racks.

In "B" the width is from pallet to pallet, because the pallets overhang the racks. If the aisle had been mistakenly assumed as rack to rack the actual operating width would be 6" narrower than expected. **This is such a serious and common error that it is worth noting with special emphasis.**

In "C" the goods are overhanging the pallet and protrude still further out from the front of the racks. *Aisle width is goods to goods.*

Note how the aisle narrows with each added overhang.

If only a small percentage of loads are oversize it might not be necessary to plan for them, depending on other clearances allowed. The forklift operator may be able to handle them, using a bit of care. However, if these loads are quite common in the system they should be included in your planning.

When planning aisle width remember to allow sufficient operating clearance. Most manufacturers include on their literature a chart showing the narrowest possible aisle, which is the *theoretical aisle* only. Operating clearance must be added to these minimums. In this way the amount of clearance can be decided according to your preference or to fit within building restrictions. Many aisle charts will advise an addition of six to eighteen inches as an operating clearance. **Don't overlook this very important factor.**

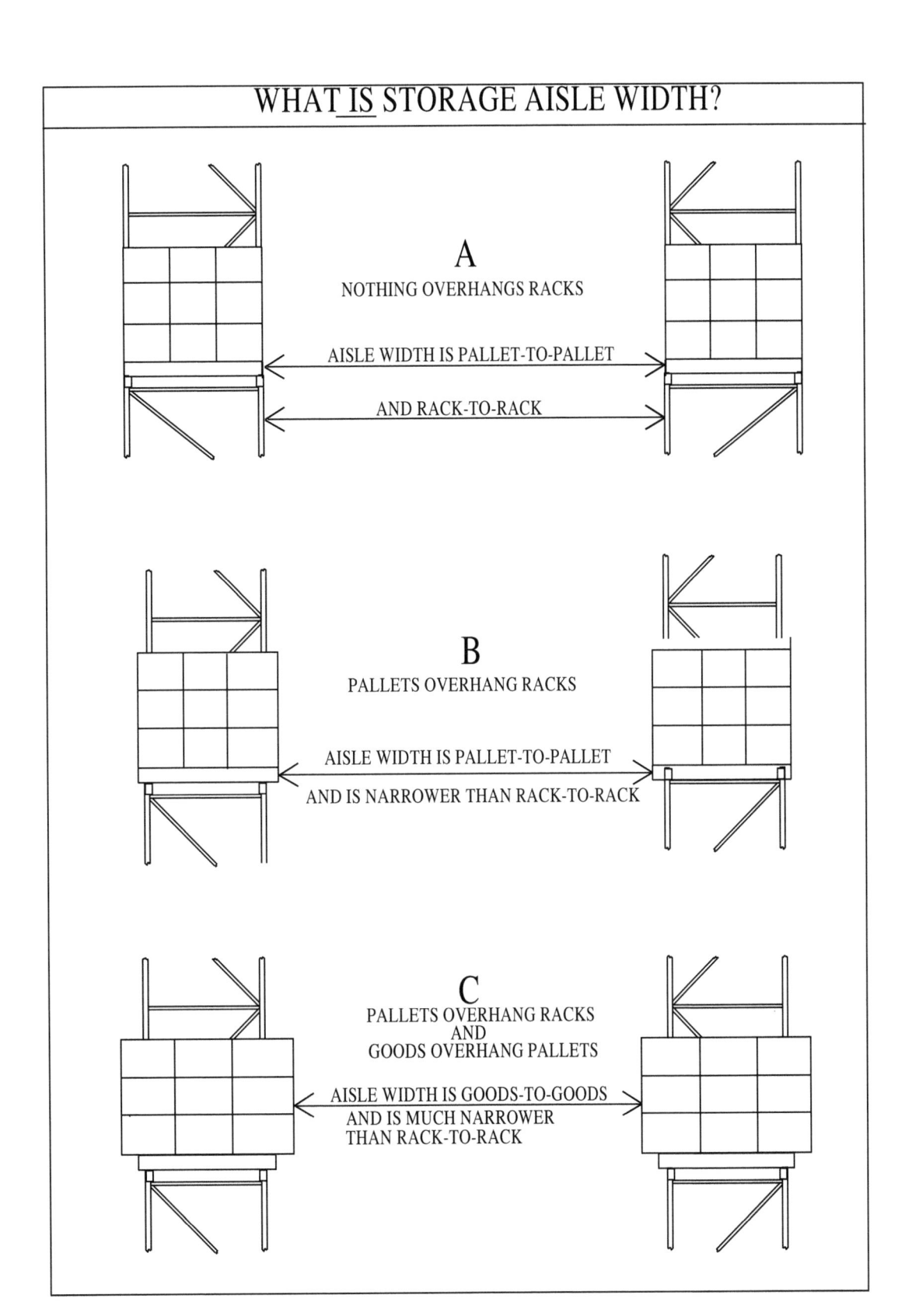

WHAT IS STORAGE AISLE WIDTH?

A
NOTHING OVERHANGS RACKS

AISLE WIDTH IS PALLET-TO-PALLET
AND RACK-TO-RACK

B
PALLETS OVERHANG RACKS

AISLE WIDTH IS PALLET-TO-PALLET
AND IS NARROWER THAN RACK-TO-RACK

C
PALLETS OVERHANG RACKS
AND
GOODS OVERHANG PALLETS

AISLE WIDTH IS GOODS-TO-GOODS
AND IS MUCH NARROWER
THAN RACK-TO-RACK

TYPICAL STORAGE AISLES

The typical aisles shown on the next page are intended as a guide to the width ranges by forklift types, including some allowance for operating clearance. The aisles shown are approximate and may be a bit narrower or wider than needed in some cases. In recent years many manufacturers have introduced models capable of higher lift heights, and these often require wider aisles. The actual aisle should be based on a forklift capable of handling the heaviest loads to the maximum height needed and lighter loads to any height you want. The amount of operating clearance, affecting the total aisle width, is somewhat optional.

Sit-on counterbalanced truck aisles probably vary the most, taking into account electric and engine powered models. There are also some three-wheeled units, usually with limited lift height. Electric powered forklifts can have different sizes of battery compartments, thus affecting the truck length.

Very narrow aisle trucks also have differences; and whether or not the load is to be rotated within the aisle must also be considered.

Deep-reach trucks are generally limited to 3000# capacity, although that could change at any time.

There are other factors in determining aisle width. The effects of side clearances between loads and operating through the notches of a 4-way pallet are explained on the next pages.

Floor conditions can also affect aisle width, especially when high lifts are involved. Any floor deviation from flat and level can cause the forklift to tilt and high lifts will contribute to mast deflection.

With all of these variables it is best to decide what type of forklift is wanted and get an aisle size, including operating clearance, for the exact forklift.

SOME TYPICAL AISLE WIDTHS FOR 48"D X 40"W PALLETS

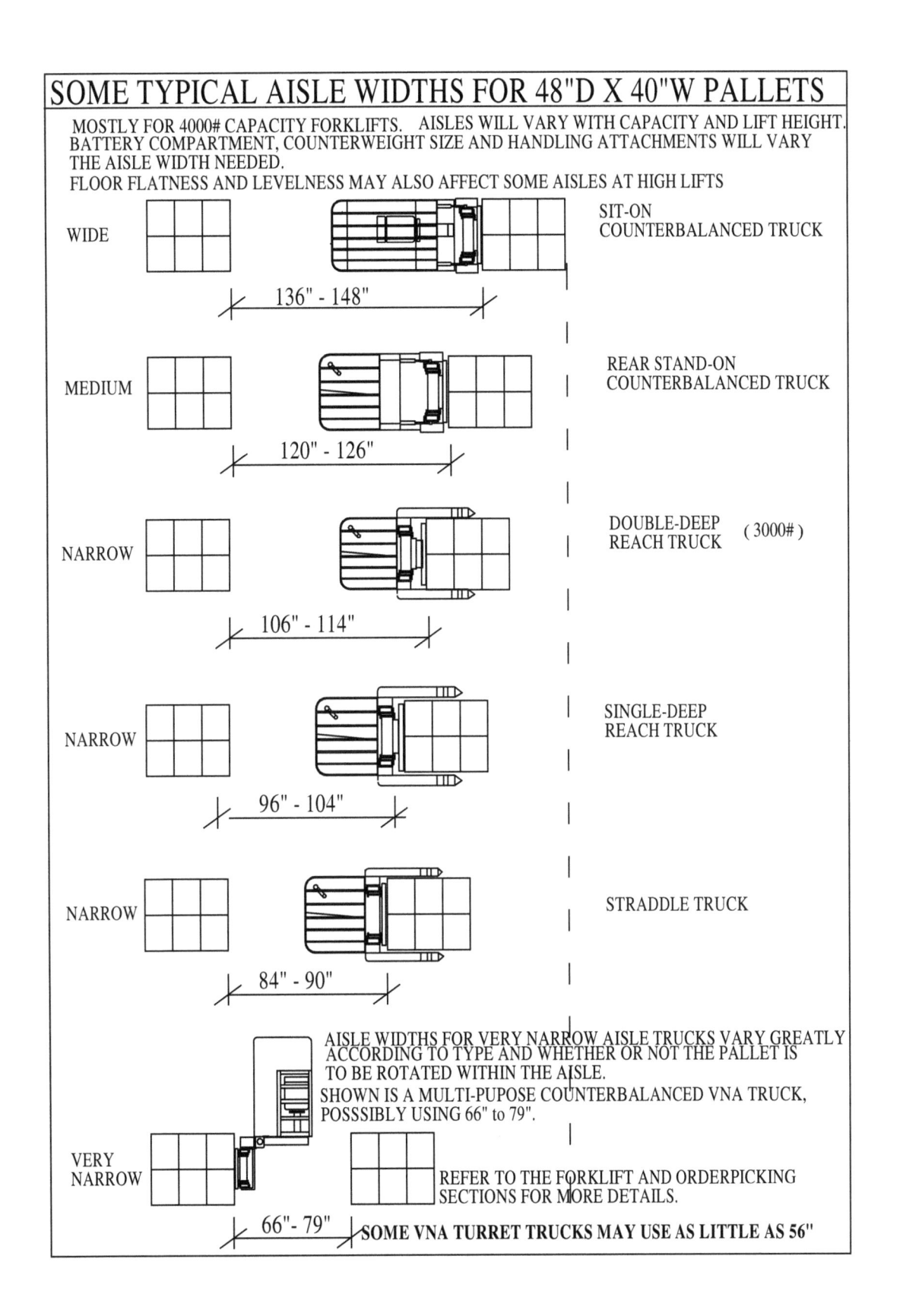

MOSTLY FOR 4000# CAPACITY FORKLIFTS.   AISLES WILL VARY WITH CAPACITY AND LIFT HEIGHT.
BATTERY COMPARTMENT, COUNTERWEIGHT SIZE AND HANDLING ATTACHMENTS WILL VARY
THE AISLE WIDTH NEEDED.
FLOOR FLATNESS AND LEVELNESS MAY ALSO AFFECT SOME AISLES AT HIGH LIFTS

WIDE — 136" - 148" — SIT-ON COUNTERBALANCED TRUCK

MEDIUM — 120" - 126" — REAR STAND-ON COUNTERBALANCED TRUCK

NARROW — 106" - 114" — DOUBLE-DEEP REACH TRUCK (3000#)

NARROW — 96" - 104" — SINGLE-DEEP REACH TRUCK

NARROW — 84" - 90" — STRADDLE TRUCK

AISLE WIDTHS FOR VERY NARROW AISLE TRUCKS VARY GREATLY
ACCORDING TO TYPE AND WHETHER OR NOT THE PALLET IS
TO BE ROTATED WITHIN THE AISLE.
SHOWN IS A MULTI-PUPOSE COUNTERBALANCED VNA TRUCK,
POSSSIBLY USING 66" to 79".

VERY NARROW — 66"- 79" — REFER TO THE FORKLIFT AND ORDERPICKING SECTIONS FOR MORE DETAILS.

SOME VNA TURRET TRUCKS MAY USE AS LITTLE AS 56"

2   USES OF STORAGE SEGMENTS AND A DATA FORM

SIDE CLEARANCE

Side clearances between loads affect the aisle width. Aisle charts are often based on 4" between loads, but may be based on 5" to 8" for straddle or deep-reach trucks. Also, if product overhangs the pallet width, be sure to plan on actual load width, and not just pallet width.

Increasing side clearances as on the next page results in a slightly narrower aisle by providing more side tolerance when swinging the load into position. A very rough rule of thumb is that increasing each side clearance by an inch will reduce the operating aisle by two inches. This obviously can work only to a limited narrowing and should be confirmed by trial with the load and forklift which will be used.

Reducing side clearances will, on the other hand, increase the minimum aisle and may increase product damage because the forklift must make a wider swing for a straight in approach and the operator must take great care in positioning the load.

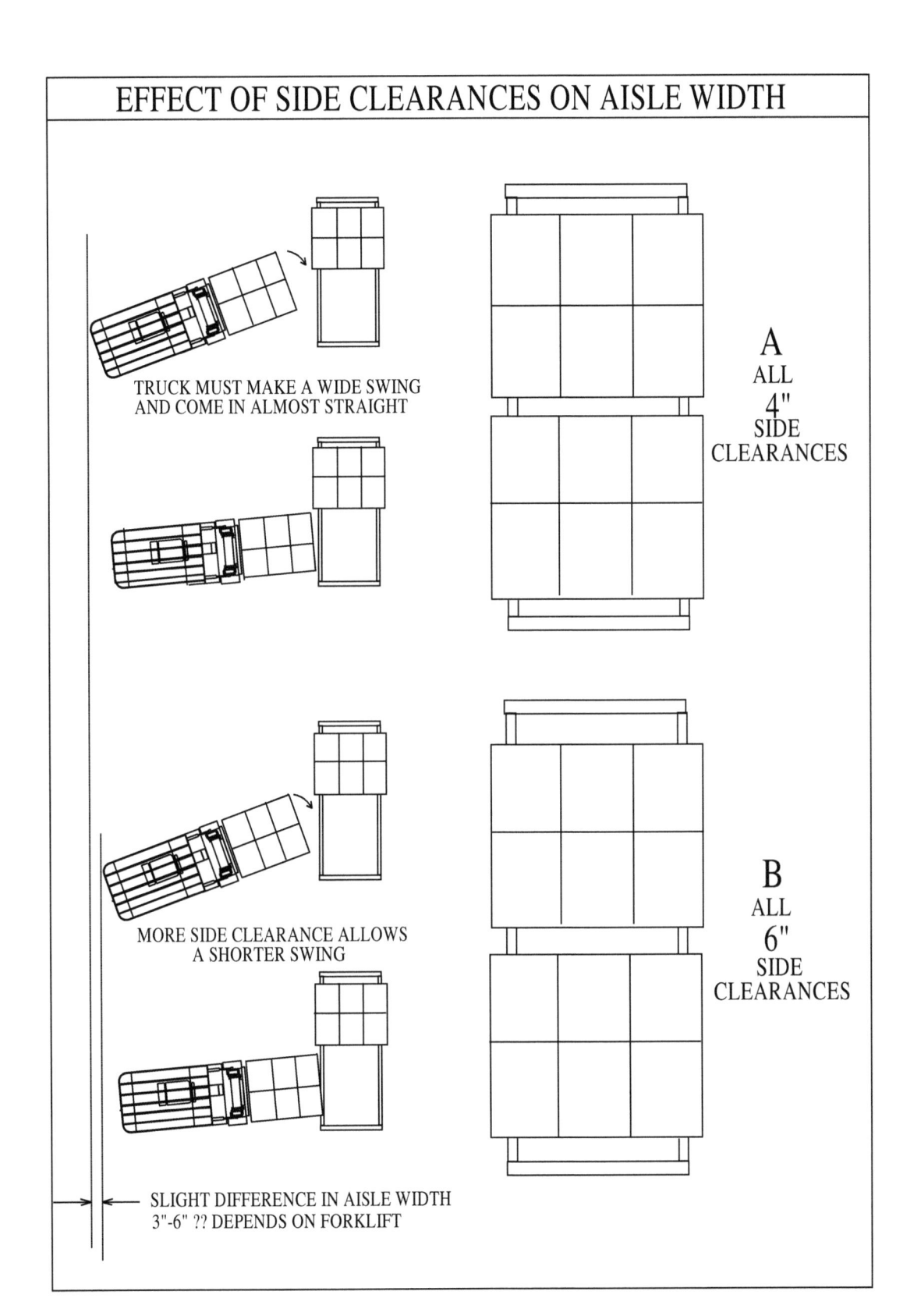

EFFECT OF SIDE CLEARANCES ON AISLE WIDTH

TRUCK MUST MAKE A WIDE SWING AND COME IN ALMOST STRAIGHT

A ALL 4" SIDE CLEARANCES

MORE SIDE CLEARANCE ALLOWS A SHORTER SWING

B ALL 6" SIDE CLEARANCES

SLIGHT DIFFERENCE IN AISLE WIDTH 3"-6" ?? DEPENDS ON FORKLIFT

2 USES OF STORAGE SEGMENTS AND A DATA FORM

EFFECT OF NOTCHED PALLETS ON AISLE WIDTH

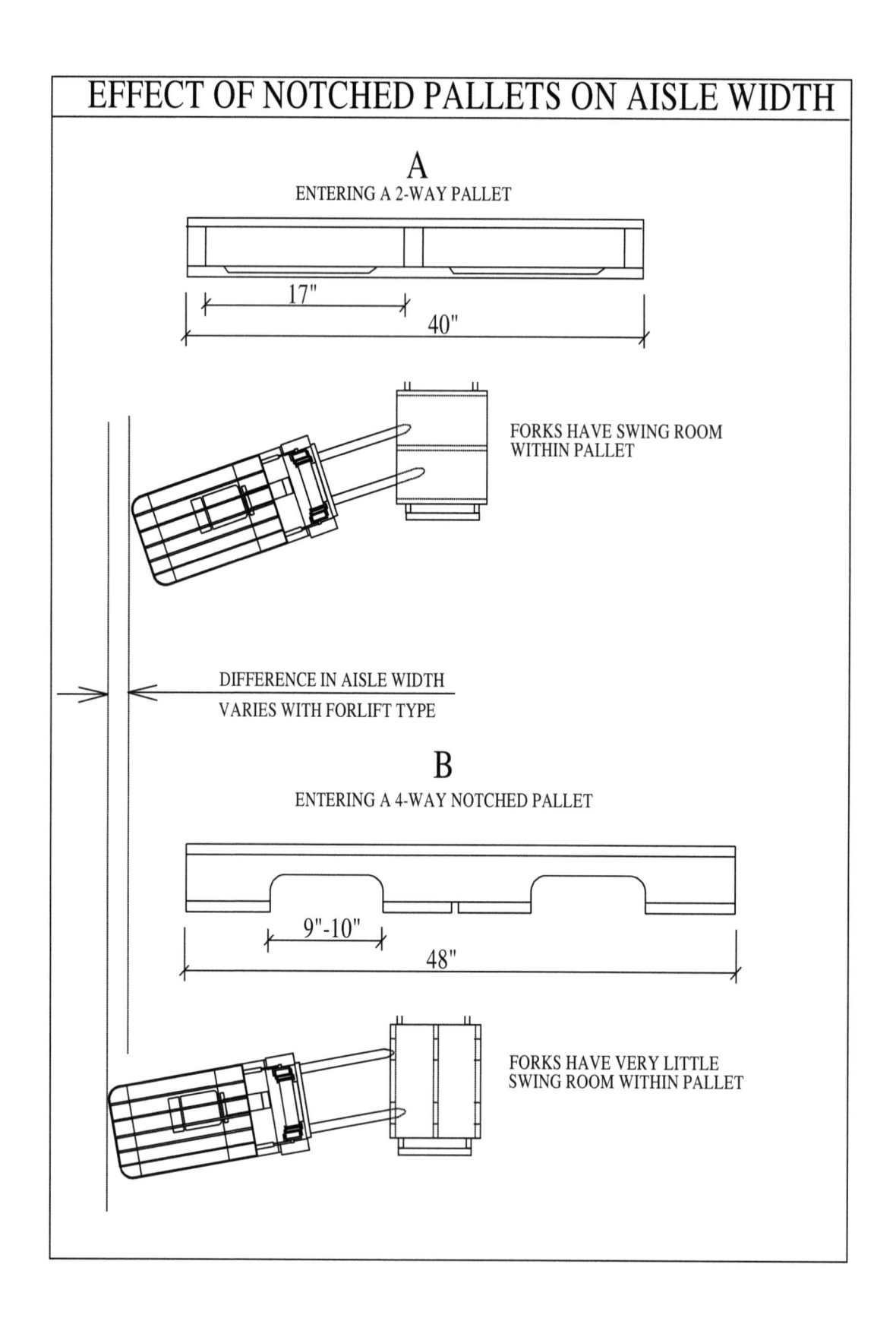

A
ENTERING A 2-WAY PALLET

17"
40"

FORKS HAVE SWING ROOM WITHIN PALLET

DIFFERENCE IN AISLE WIDTH VARIES WITH FORLIFT TYPE

B
ENTERING A 4-WAY NOTCHED PALLET

9"-10"
48"

FORKS HAVE VERY LITTLE SWING ROOM WITHIN PALLET

When operating through the notches of a 4-way pallet it is very important to check the aisle width, either by trial or careful discussion with your forklift supplier. Don't assume the information on literature is correct for this type of pallet.

Refer to the previous page. The top set of sketches show a forklift withdrawing from a 2-way pallet, 40"D x 48"W. Because of the wide space available between pallet stringers the truck can begin it's swing while the forks are still a considerable distance *within* the pallet. This, along with 36" forks, allows the aisle to be kept to a minimum.

The lower set of sketches shows that this swing leeway is not available when working through pallet notches. The forks must be withdrawn almost completely before the truck can begin to swing. This results in a wider aisle. Additionally, fork length must be increased to at least 40", and preferably 42", in order to reach under the rear stringer of the pallet. If the rear stringer is not supported the pallet may rock on the center stringer and become unstable. These two situations are shown below.

When combined, the three factors of reduced side clearances, notched 4-way pallets and longer forks may increase the aisle requirement enough to use up all of the planned operating clearance

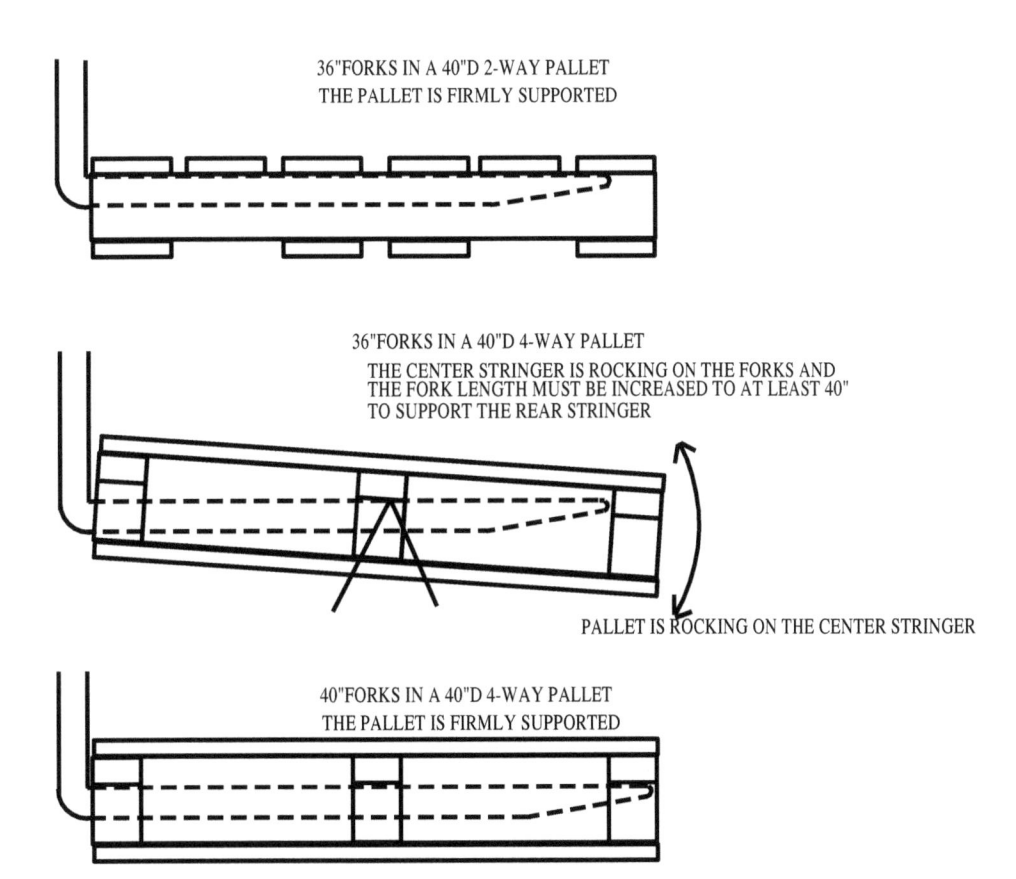

36"FORKS IN A 40"D 2-WAY PALLET
THE PALLET IS FIRMLY SUPPORTED

36"FORKS IN A 40"D 4-WAY PALLET
THE CENTER STRINGER IS ROCKING ON THE FORKS AND
THE FORK LENGTH MUST BE INCREASED TO AT LEAST 40"
TO SUPPORT THE REAR STRINGER

PALLET IS ROCKING ON THE CENTER STRINGER

40"FORKS IN A 40"D 4-WAY PALLET
THE PALLET IS FIRMLY SUPPORTED

SO WHAT AISLE WIDTH DO YOU WANT?

With the considerable selection of forklift types and their varying aisle widths your choice might not be easy. Narrower aisles use less space and many of the highest lifts are available only with machines which operate in very narrow aisles (VNA). However some other types of forklifts, from narrow aisle up to wide aisle, have a lesser initial cost and, in addition, are more appropriate for many situations.

Aisle widths must be watched carefully in relation to your order picking methods. A narrow aisle straddle truck may be able to operate in a seven foot aisle with a 48"D x 40" W pallet but, if you want two order pickers to be able to pass, an appropriate aisle width must be used. So the aisle width is then based on picking requirements and not the narrowest aisle possible for the forklift.

Another example is with high lift reach trucks. This model of truck uses outriggers for stability and they are spread wider as lift height and load weight increase. Overall width of these outriggers could be four feet or more. Do they have to pass in the aisles or can each truck be assigned to a different zone?

Will a reach truck with wide outriggers have to pass orderpickers on a regular basis? Or is the activity very low so one could wait for the other to move out of the way? Could stocking of full pallets take place on one shift and order picking on another, allowing very narrow aisles with no contention between the two differing activities?

These types of questions must be answered to achieve an ideal aisle width and, as you will see, beginning on the next page, **area segments** are an excellent method to quickly compare the effects of aisle widths to help decide where the most efficient trade-off is between space utilization and other activities necessary in the same zone.

USES OF SEGMENTS

Now, utilizing the information provided in the previous explanations of modules and aisles, it is possible to assemble as many different segments as you think might apply to your situation and quickly compare them for results.

Here again, for your convenience, is a list of important segment uses.

- **A** A segment is an easy step toward determining square feet per storage slot at the lowest level, with various aisle widths and storage rack types. This figure can be very useful for comparisons. *Does not include allowance for access aisles; add about 20%*.*

- **B** To provide a tool for a quick estimate of the total storage area needed. *Does not include an allowance for access aisles; add about 20%.*

- **C** To easily try alternate combinations of lengths and widths (configurations) for the storage area needed. This can be especially helpful when searching for a lease building or planning a new one. *Includes allowance for access aisles.*

- **D** To estimate optimum spacing of building columns.

- **E** To experiment with possible layouts *within existing column centers*; quickly showing any problem locations.

- **F** To closely estimate the rack components needed for a selected layout.

A and B are quick area estimates which will yield approximate figures. They do not include an allowance for access aisles so add about 20% for a closer estimate at this stage.

It is important to note that the dimensions include an allowance for a flue space between segments. This will be a factor when determining the preferred spacing between segments to allow for building columns.

* The lowest level slot will be called a floor slot, even though the pallet may actually be sitting on rack load beams.

USING SEGMENTS
A): TO ESTIMATE AREA PER FLOOR SLOT

The drawing on the next page simply uses segment areas to determine square feet per floor slot; a figure which can vary dramatically with different aisle widths and storage depths.

Square feet per floor storage slot is a very basic figure from which much useful information can flow.

Once again, note that segment uses A and B do not include an allowance for access aisles and an addition of about 20% is recommended when using this rough estimate. Shortly, a method to incorporate allowances for access aisles will be introduced.

USING SEGMENTS

A): TO CALCULATE SQUARE FEET PER FLOOR SLOT
(DOES NOT INCLUDE ACCESS AISLES)

SELECTIVE RACKS

10' AISLE
153 SQ. FT.

SEGMENT AREA	NO. OF FLOOR SLOTS	SQ.FT. PER FLOOR SLOT
153	4	38.3

TWO-DEEP RACKS
PUSH-BACK OR DOUBLE DEEP

9 1/2' AISLE
220 SQ. FT.

SEGMENT AREA	NO. OF FLOOR SLOTS	SQ.FT. PER FLOOR SLOT
220	8	27.5

THREE-DEEP RACKS
PUSH-BACK

8 1/2' AISLE
278 SQ. FT.

SEGMENT AREA	NO. OF FLOOR SLOTS	SQ.FT. PER FLOOR SLOT
278	12	23.2

FOUR-DEEP RACKS
PUSH-BACK OR DRIVE-IN

12' AISLE
205 SQ. FT.

SEGMENT AREA	NO. OF FLOOR SLOTS	SQ.FT. PER FLOOR SLOT
205	8	25.8

WITH ANY RACK, USE ANY AISLE WIDTH YOU PREFER
FLOW-THROUGH AND DRIVE-THROUGH RACKS (NOT SHOWN) REQUIRE AISLES FRONT AND REAR
MAKE A SKETCH OF YOUR MODULE TO GET THE SQ. FT. PER FLOOR SLOT.

CONSIDER ADDING ABOUT 20%-25% TO ALLOW FOR ACCESS AISLES IN AN AREA ESTIMATE

USING SEGMENTS
B):   TO ESTIMATE THE TOTAL STORAGE AREA NEEDED

The segment below shows how the segment footprint on page 43 would look when using storage Racks with 5 levels.

The following is for a quick estimate of space. Accuracy is covered a bit later.

Using the area of 153 sq. ft. we get a figure of 7.65 sq. ft. per pallet slot. Thus for 2000 slots you can estimate a need of 15,300 sq. ft. (100 segments). Depending on the number, length and width of access aisles (which are unknown at this time) an additional 20 to 25% can be added to bring this initial rough estimate into the ballpark. Loss of space at building columns may also occur. So 18,500 to 19000 sq. ft. might be used.

Be sure the selected number of segments allows for a percentage of unused slots. The term for these empty slots is Honeycombing. To store 2000 pallets may require 110 segments, 2200 slots, or more, depending greatly on your particular operations.

It cannot be overemphasized that a careful estimate of the usual percentage of empty slots be used. If you are considering a type of system (forklifts, racks and methods) with which you are unfamiliar it would be best to seek out an experienced source.

This is a quick estimate only; actual access aisle area will vary with the layout used. Page 59 begins a method of comparing various length and width configurations of segments. Then a DATAFORM is introduced. This form will allow you to try different zone lengths and widths without any detailed drawings. It will also yield much other useful data for layout comparisons.

A STORAGE SEGMENT

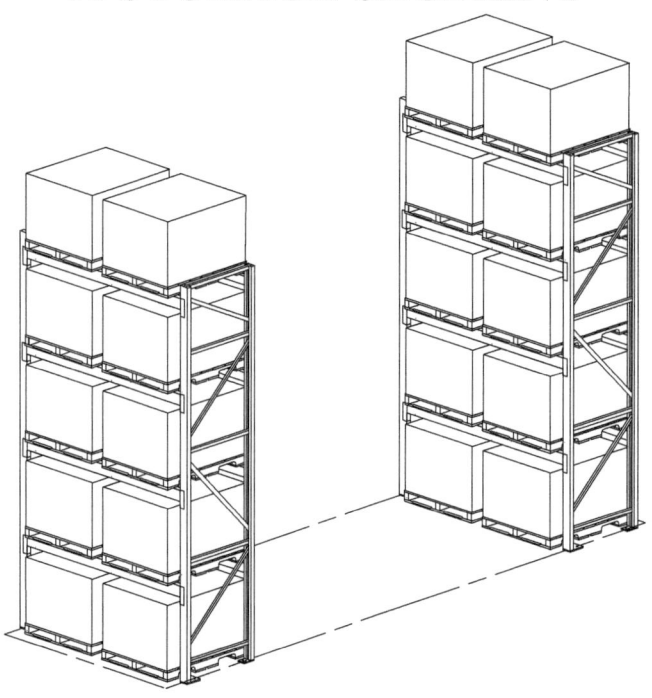

THIS PAGE IS INTENTIONALLY BLANK IN ORDER TO KEEP RELAVENT TEXT AND DRAWINGS TOGETHER ON FOLLOWING PAGES.

2 *USES OF STORAGE SEGMENTS AND A DATA FORM*

USING SEGMENTS
C): TO TRY ALTERNATE CONFIGURATIONS OF ZONE LENGTHS AND WIDTHS

The next page shows two layout configurations from the sample segment. Each of these drawings will later be used with a DATAFORM which will yield additional information. Then the data form is used with simple hand-drawn sketches for additional acceptable alternates.

Trial #1 is for a long and narrow layout 25 segments long by 4 segments wide. Access aisles, 12' wide, are included. Because of the row length three access aisles are used, and the area is shown as 18000 sq. ft.; 242' long by 74' wide.

For this first estimate it might be prudent to add a bit, perhaps 2%–4%, for space losses; such as at building columns. Greater accuracy will come later.

The second trial, of a 10 x 10 layout, shows the need for about 1800 additional sq.ft. This is because although only two access aisles are used, they get longer as the layout width increases.

Alternates are needed when considering an existing building because there may be a desirable building with dimensions and column spacings not compatible with your preferred layout. **When looking for an existing building always be prepared with your preferred system and acceptable layouts to assess the initial suitability of any building.**

More information pertaining to column spacing is the next subject.

C): USING SEGMENTS FOR ZONE CONFIGURATION

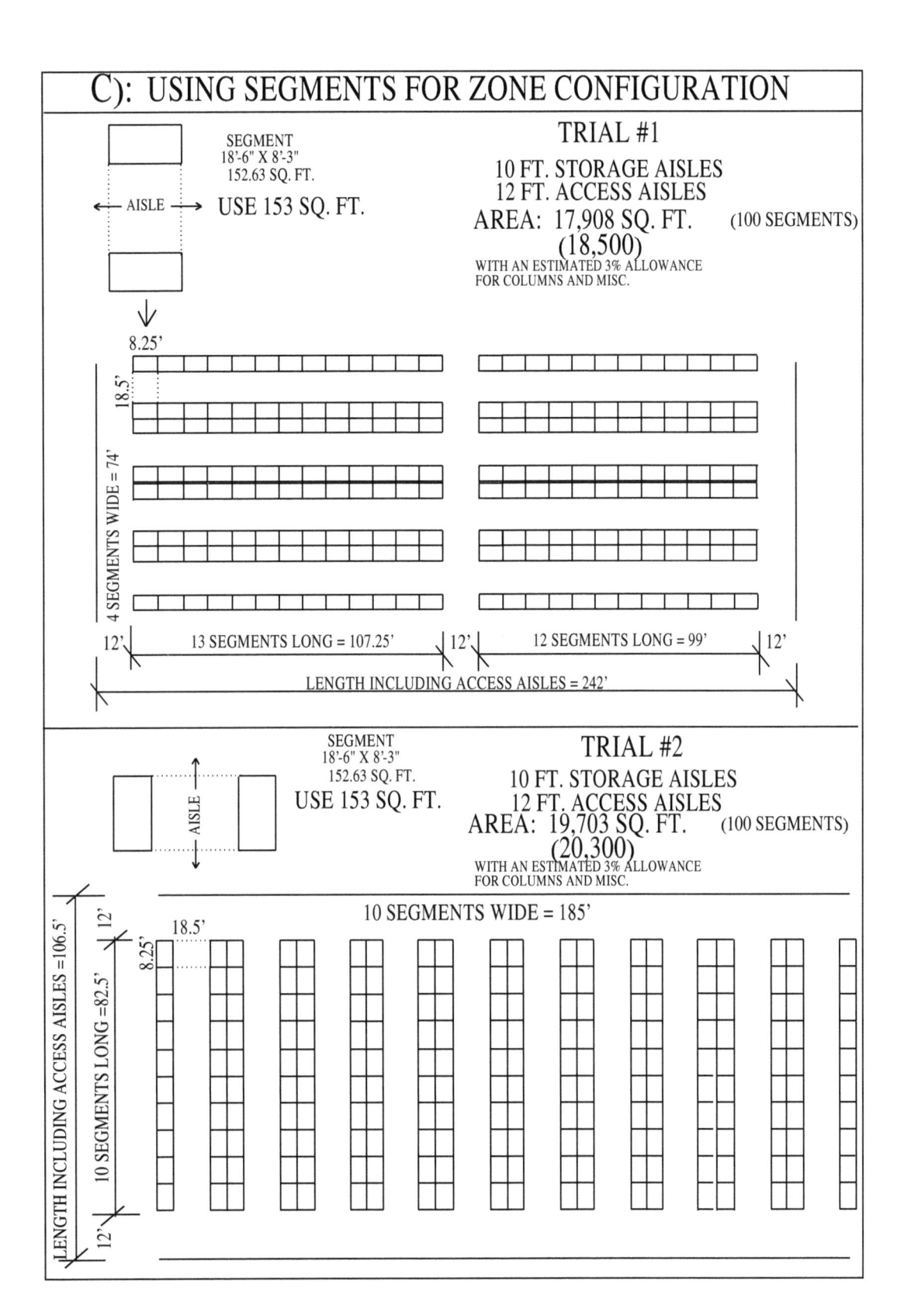

TRIAL #1

SEGMENT
18'-6" X 8'-3"
152.63 SQ. FT.
USE 153 SQ. FT.

10 FT. STORAGE AISLES
12 FT. ACCESS AISLES
AREA: 17,908 SQ. FT. (100 SEGMENTS)
(18,500)
WITH AN ESTIMATED 3% ALLOWANCE
FOR COLUMNS AND MISC.

8.25'
18.5'
4 SEGMENTS WIDE = 74'
12' | 13 SEGMENTS LONG = 107.25' | 12' | 12 SEGMENTS LONG = 99' | 12'
LENGTH INCLUDING ACCESS AISLES = 242'

TRIAL #2

SEGMENT
18'-6" X 8'-3"
152.63 SQ. FT.
USE 153 SQ. FT.

10 FT. STORAGE AISLES
12 FT. ACCESS AISLES
AREA: 19,703 SQ. FT. (100 SEGMENTS)
(20,300)
WITH AN ESTIMATED 3% ALLOWANCE
FOR COLUMNS AND MISC.

10 SEGMENTS WIDE = 185'
12'
8.25' 18.5'
LENGTH INCLUDING ACCESS AISLES =106.5'
10 SEGMENTS LONG =82.5'
12'

USING SEGMENTS
D): TO DETERMINE OPTIMUM COLUMN CENTERS

The next page shows that the most efficient building column centers are determined by segment width.

Sketch #1, starting beside a column, combines two segments. Each is 18'-6" wide, for a total of 37'. If this is considered a good location for the next column (three segments wide is a possible alternate) extra space must be added to the 6" flue provided for in the segment dimensions.

Be aware that the actual column centers may be affected by varying regulations for flue width, sprinklers and sprinkler piping, architectural considerations and even load overhang. Always be sure of these variables before determining exact centers.

In this example 37'-8", center-to-center, is used, but rounding it to as much as 38' may be desirable. That would allow for a large column, load overhang and other unexpected losses.

All of the other examples use different segments. Sketch #2 has the storage aisle reduced to 8' from 10'. Two segments now use 33' of width; with liberal 34' column centers.

In sketch #3 a trial is made of three segments identical to those in #2. The width becomes 49'-6", with column centers of 50'-6" or 51'.

Sketch #4 changes from selective racks to 2-deep, with 9'-6" aisles and the column centers increase to about 54'.

Knowing the segment dimensions and preferred layout and column spacings can be very useful in assessing an existing building or planning a new one. In part E some methods of adjustments to fit troublesome column spacings are explored.

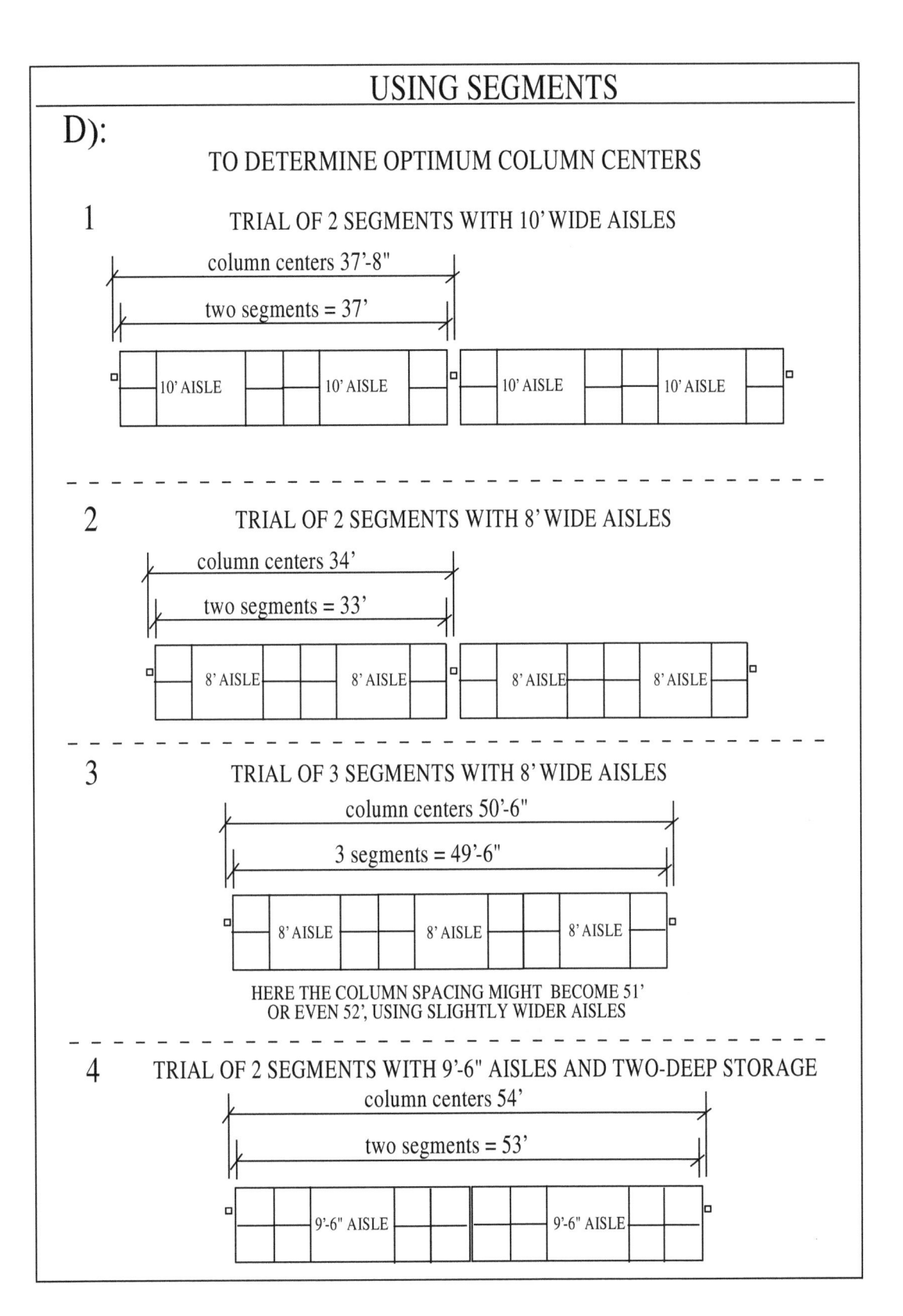

USING SEGMENTS

D):

TO DETERMINE OPTIMUM COLUMN CENTERS

1 TRIAL OF 2 SEGMENTS WITH 10' WIDE AISLES

column centers 37'-8"

two segments = 37'

| 10' AISLE | 10' AISLE | 10' AISLE | 10' AISLE |

---

2 TRIAL OF 2 SEGMENTS WITH 8' WIDE AISLES

column centers 34'

two segments = 33'

| 8' AISLE | 8' AISLE | 8' AISLE | 8' AISLE |

---

3 TRIAL OF 3 SEGMENTS WITH 8' WIDE AISLES

column centers 50'-6"

3 segments = 49'-6"

| 8' AISLE | 8' AISLE | 8' AISLE |

HERE THE COLUMN SPACING MIGHT BECOME 51'
OR EVEN 52', USING SLIGHTLY WIDER AISLES

---

4 TRIAL OF 2 SEGMENTS WITH 9'-6" AISLES AND TWO-DEEP STORAGE

column centers 54'

two segments = 53'

| 9'-6" AISLE | 9'-6" AISLE |

2 USES OF STORAGE SEGMENTS AND A DATA FORM

USING SEGMENTS
E): LAYOUT TRIALS WITHIN EXISTING COLUMN CENTERS

Where an existing building has less than ideal column spacings there are a number of options which can be used to fit a satisfactory layout.

Use of a line of segments is a simple method to quickly determine where there are problems with the proposed layout and for experimenting with fixes. This can be done with a computer CAD program and it is also easy (but time consuming) to use graph paper at this stage, to determine if a satisfactory layout seems possible. If the answer is yes, a computer or manual drawing is then used to establish exact dimensioning. If the answer is no, you have saved considerable time and money by avoiding detailed drawings, or leasing an inappropriate building.

What constitutes a satisfactory layout is your decision. Some companies will not allow building columns to be in an aisle, considering them a danger. Some will accept them, providing they are very close in to the racks. Also, with poor column spacing there will surely be some loss of storage slots.

Page 65 shows a series of trials to fit a number of dimensioned segments across an area with column spacings which are problematic. The following pages show these trials converted into layouts with rack rows 14 bays long. (Trials # 1 and 2 are omitted from layouts as they are impractical).

Trial 1 shows a line of segments, each 17'-6" wide, placed across four storage bays. This provides 10 aisles with 20 rows of racks. Three problems show up immediately. Aisle C has a column a bit into the aisle. This may be acceptable, maybe not. But aisle E has a column directly on the rack line and the column in aisle J is unacceptable.

Trial 2 simply shifts the line of segments to the right a bit and puts the columns in aisles C and E closer to the racks. In this case aisle A has been widened. However, aisle J is in worse shape than before.

Trial 3 alters some aisle widths to position a column in a widened flue between two rows of racks. The column in aisle J is now close in to the racks and the layout is a little wider than the original. A layout of this trial, using 14 segments to form rows of storage, is on page 66. It shows a loss of 9 floor slot positions because of column interference; a loss of 45 if storage is 5 high.

The circled rack bays near the bottom of aisles E and F show a location where storage could be two pallets deep off of aisle F. This could be done at all nine places where columns are causing a loss. However, unless the space is greatly needed it may prove to be too expensive for the gain. Some other alterations are shown in trial 6.

The layout for trial 4 adds a system of two-deep storage at the far right, eliminating aisle J. Rack rows are reduced from 20 to 19 but the layout is repeatable across more bays of the building. The two-deep storage could be block stacking, drive-in racks, push-back racks or double-deep racks with the proper forklift. This dimensional alteration is only valid if you are inserting a change for which you have a reasonable use.

In fact, you can insert other systems such as deeper racks, a high-level picking system, or a shelving area on a mezzanine floor. Whatever fits and is satisfactory in the location selected.

Trial 5 uses two rows of two-deep storage and shortens the layout while also eliminating aisle J.

Trial 6 uses a single row of racks to get the columns in close to the racks. This layout also reduces the racks to 19 rows, in a little less space than the original trial #1.

This drawing also shows some rack beams lengthened to reduce losses at columns. However, this offsets the rack bays so they are not aligned with the bays across the aisle. If this is not acceptable then all beams at columns can be lengthened, so they will align. But another option is to add a single rack bay at the end of the shorter rows, as shown by dotted lines.

Also consider the use of a different forklift with a narrower aisle and/or turning the pallets to use their 40″ dimension as the depth and 48″ as the face. In fact, many prefer doing this, especially where case picking is taking place.

Then trials 7 & 8 have been added. Trial 7 uses a VNA with 48″ D x 40″ W pallets. Trial 8 uses a narrow aisle with 40″ D x 48″ W pallets. Each of these must be adjusted to eliminate the obvious problems.

In any case if all building columns must be placed within the racks, and not in the aisles, then the changes needed will be great; possibly to the extent of making this building unacceptable.

There may be other ways to change and fit, depending on each individual instance. Here is a summary of the most common methods, to be used separately or as a group:

Change the minimum aisle width, with a different forklift if necessary.

Store pallets with a different depth than the layout trials shown, which are based on a 48″ depth,

If practical, use an "in-house" pallet with dimensions to suit only your operations, not to be shipped to other companies.

Widen aisles from their minimum where it helps, especially if building columns can be positioned in the flue between two rows of racks. This will usually need a wider flue than the minimum allowed.

Lengthen rack load beams where this will avoid loss of storage slots.

Use deeper storage from some aisles, in a system which suits your activities.

Insert a system or activity other than pallet storage, located where the layout problem is severe.

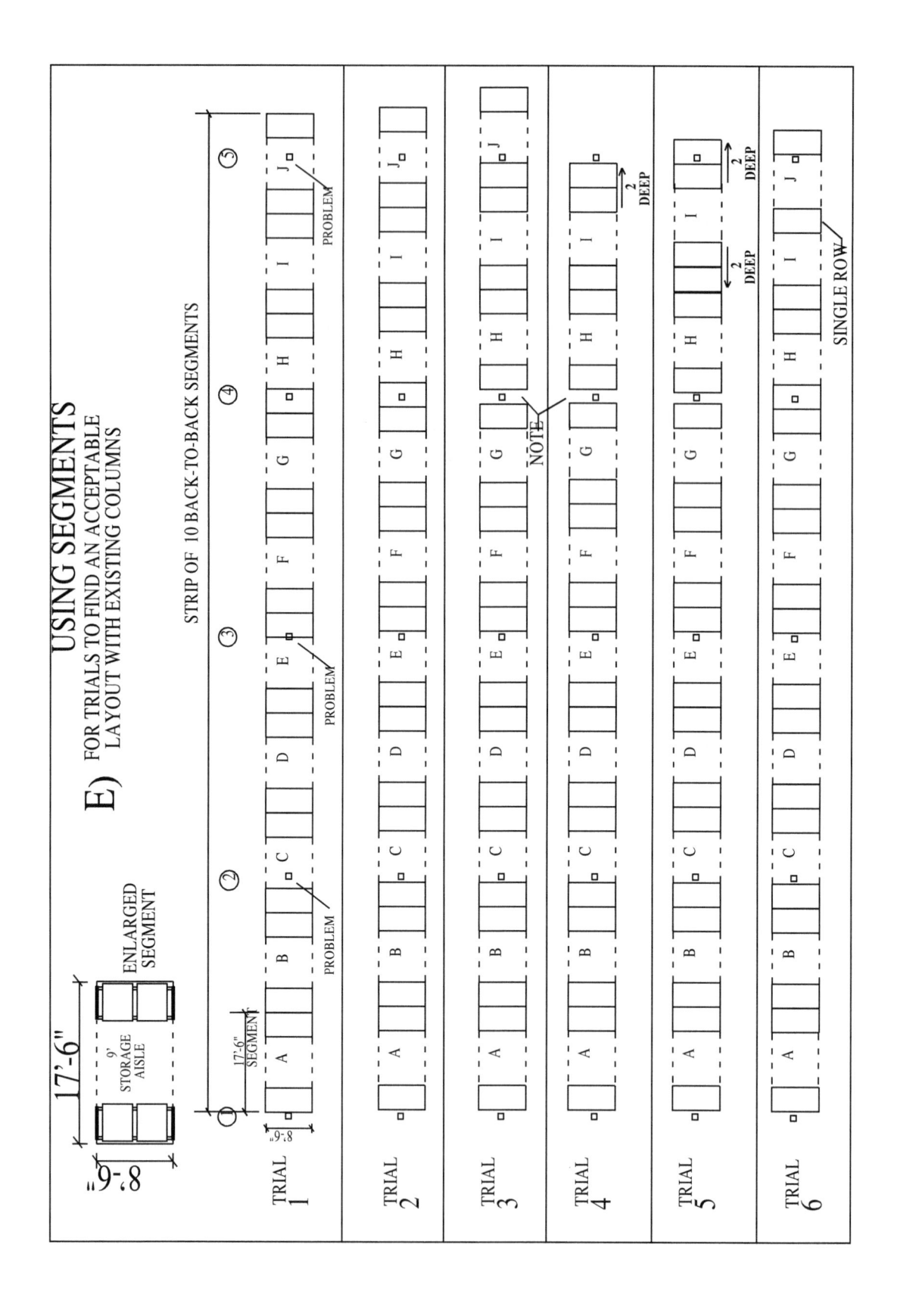

USING SEGMENTS

E) FOR TRIALS TO FIND AN ACCEPTABLE LAYOUT WITH EXISTING COLUMNS

HOW TO CONFIGURE AND EQUIP YOUR WAREHOUSE

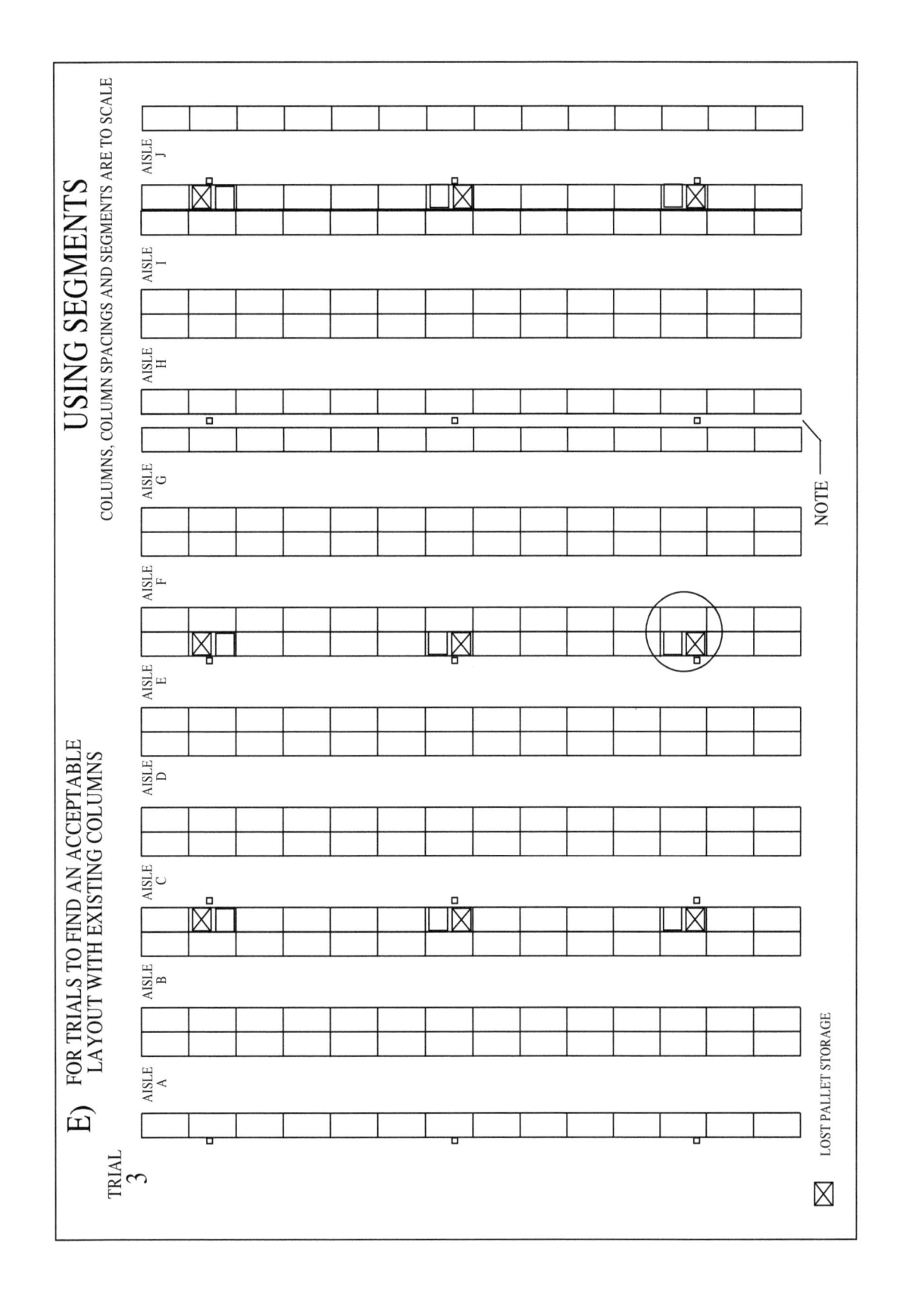

USING SEGMENTS
COLUMNS, COLUMN SPACINGS AND SEGMENTS ARE TO SCALE

E) FOR TRIALS TO FIND AN ACCEPTABLE LAYOUT WITH EXISTING COLUMNS

TRIAL 3

⊠ LOST PALLET STORAGE

2 *USES OF STORAGE SEGMENTS AND A DATA FORM*

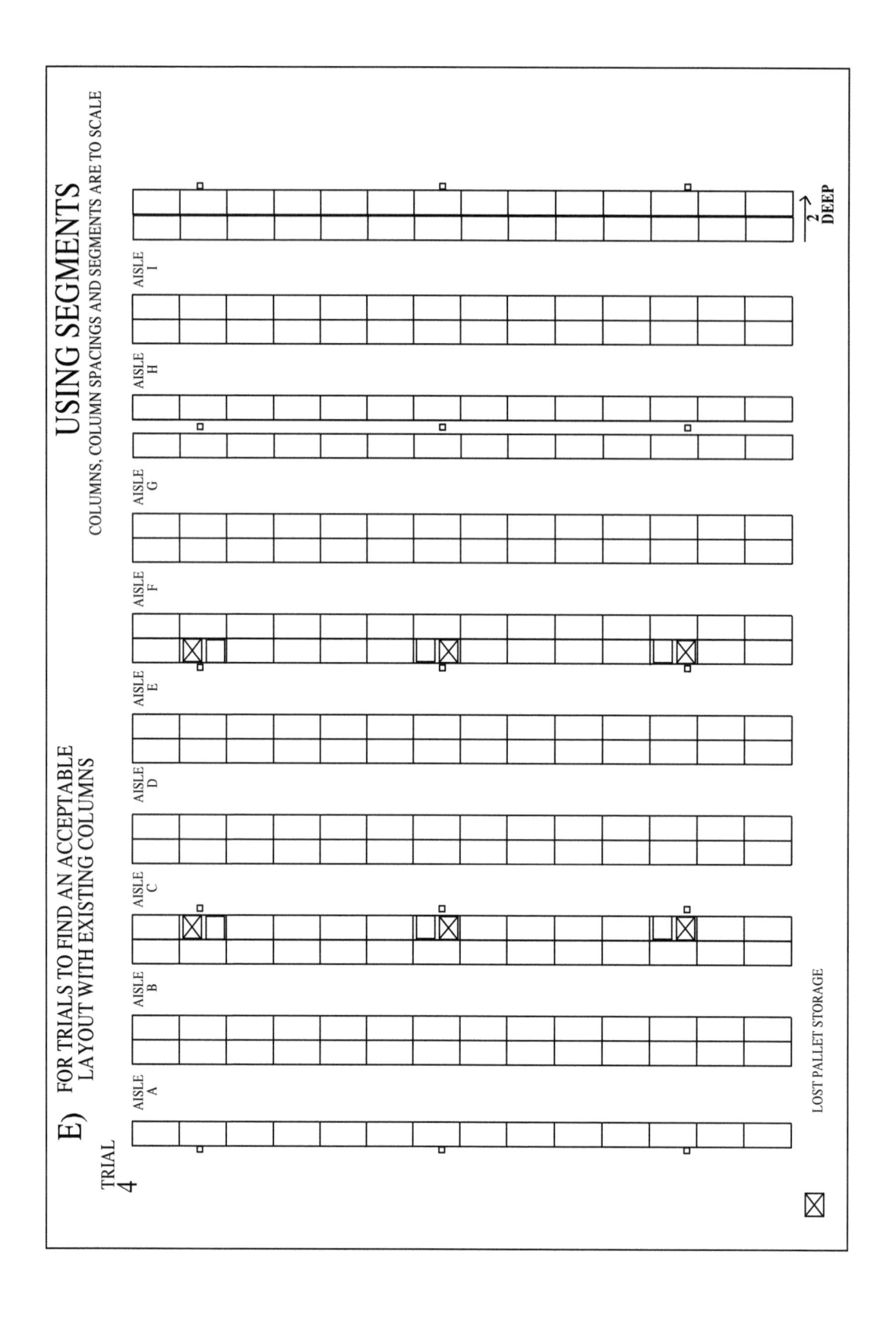

USING SEGMENTS
COLUMNS, COLUMN SPACINGS AND SEGMENTS ARE TO SCALE

E) FOR TRIALS TO FIND AN ACCEPTABLE LAYOUT WITH EXISTING COLUMNS

TRIAL 4

AISLE A
AISLE B
AISLE C
AISLE D
AISLE E
AISLE F
AISLE G
AISLE H
AISLE I

2 DEEP

LOST PALLET STORAGE

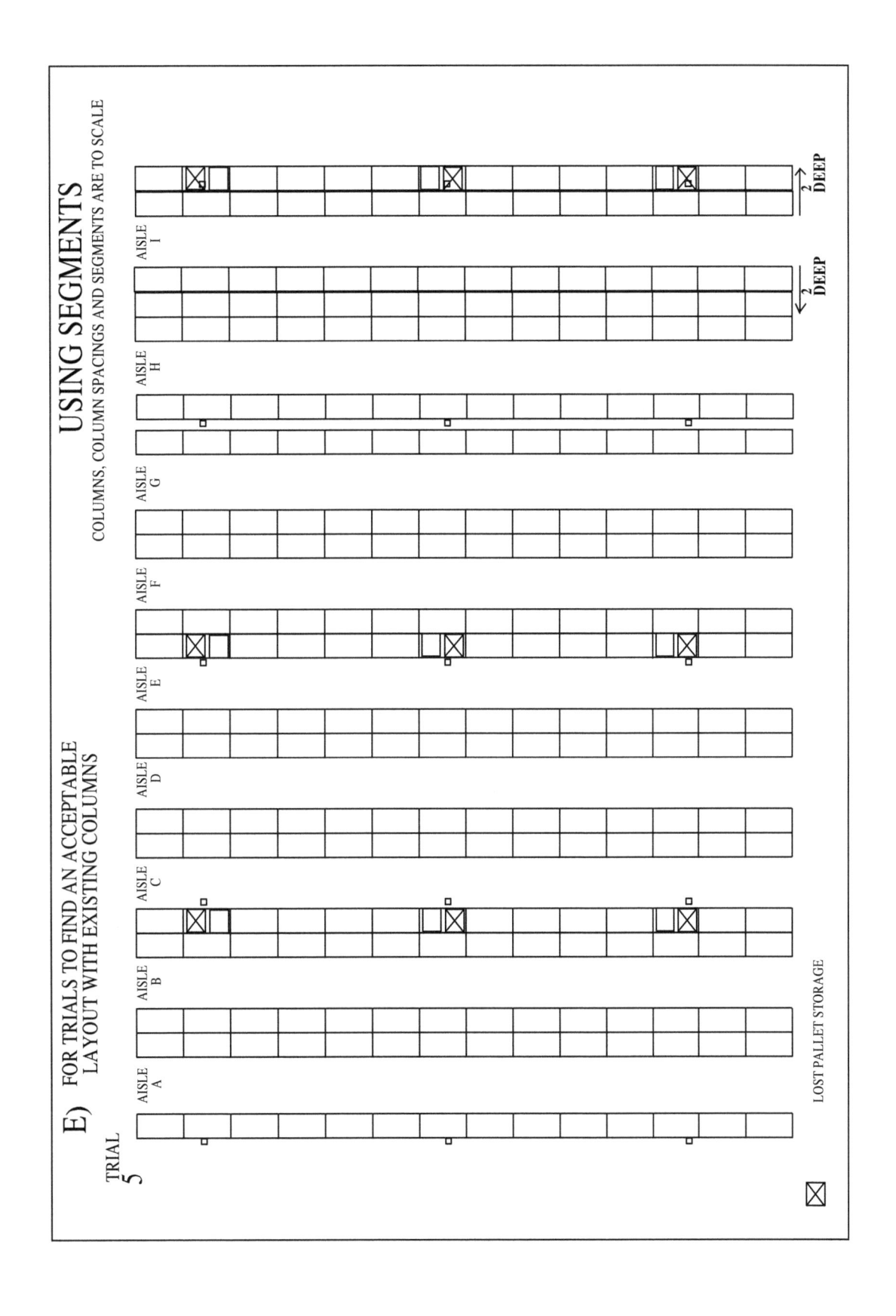

USING SEGMENTS
COLUMNS, COLUMN SPACINGS AND SEGMENTS ARE TO SCALE

E) FOR TRIALS TO FIND AN ACCEPTABLE LAYOUT WITH EXISTING COLUMNS

TRIAL 5

AISLE A
AISLE B
AISLE C
AISLE D
AISLE E
AISLE F
AISLE G
AISLE H
AISLE I

2 DEEP

LOST PALLET STORAGE ⊠

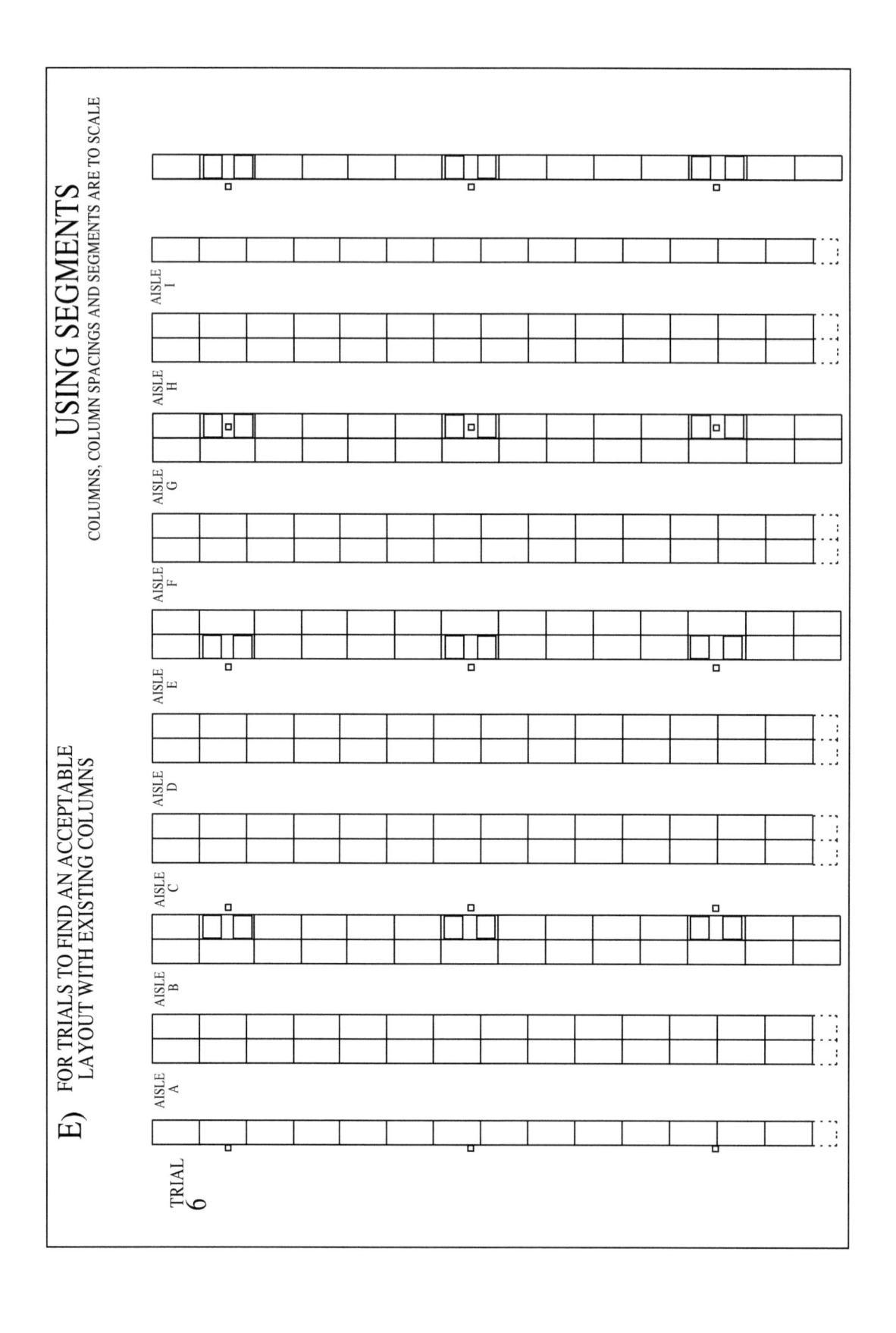

USING SEGMENTS
COLUMNS, COLUMN SPACINGS AND SEGMENTS ARE TO SCALE

E) FOR TRIALS TO FIND AN ACCEPTABLE LAYOUT WITH EXISTING COLUMNS

TRIAL 6

AISLE A

AISLE B

AISLE C

AISLE D

AISLE E

AISLE F

AISLE G

AISLE H

AISLE I

HOW TO CONFIGURE AND EQUIP YOUR WAREHOUSE

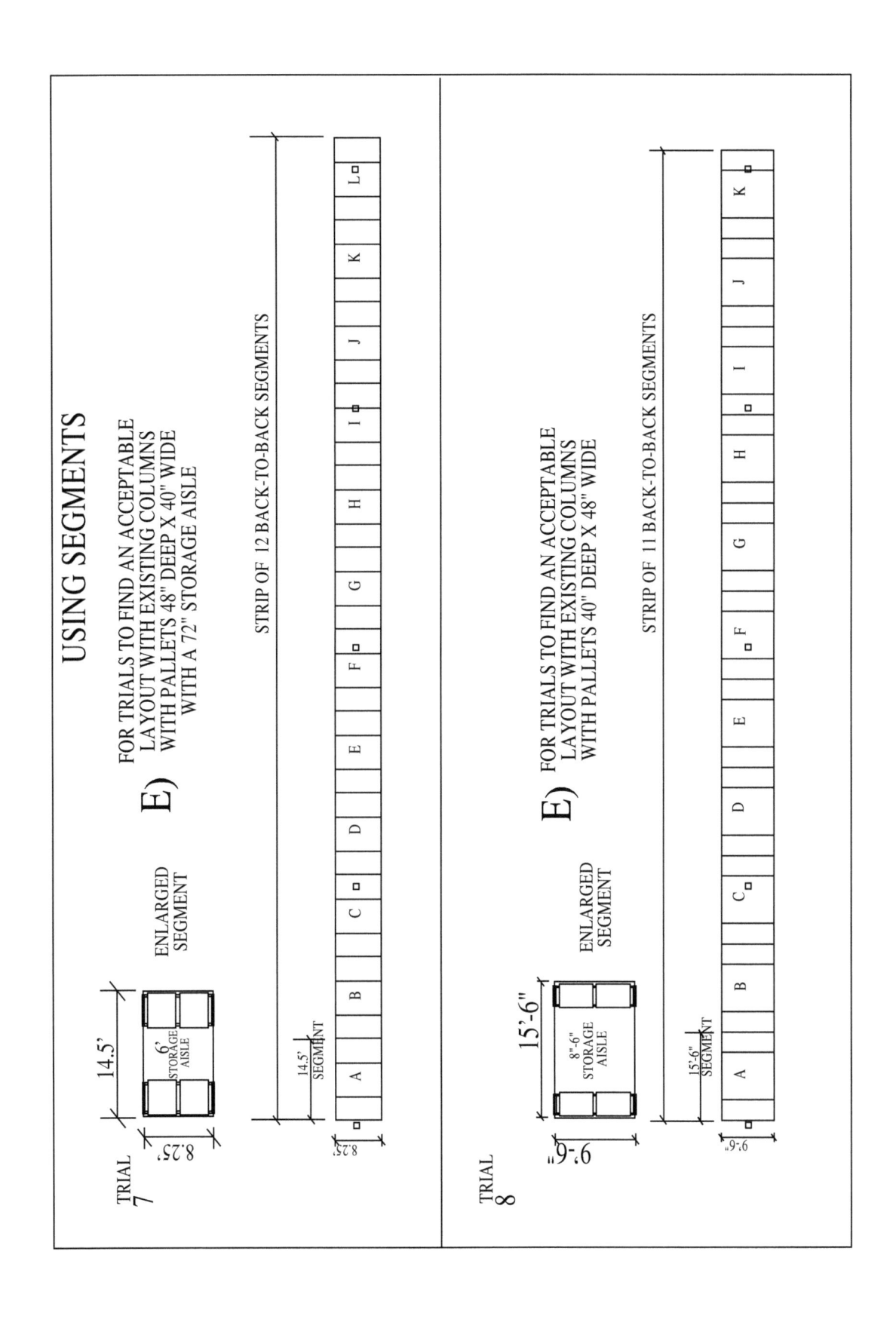

USING SEGMENTS

TRIAL 7

E) FOR TRIALS TO FIND AN ACCEPTABLE LAYOUT WITH EXISTING COLUMNS WITH PALLETS 48" DEEP X 40" WIDE WITH A 72" STORAGE AISLE

ENLARGED SEGMENT — 6' STORAGE AISLE, 8.25', 14.5'

STRIP OF 12 BACK-TO-BACK SEGMENTS

14.5' SEGMENT — 8.25'

A B C D E F G H I J K L

TRIAL 8

E) FOR TRIALS TO FIND AN ACCEPTABLE LAYOUT WITH EXISTING COLUMNS WITH PALLETS 40" DEEP X 48" WIDE

ENLARGED SEGMENT — 8"-6" STORAGE AISLE, 9'-6", 15'-6"

STRIP OF 11 BACK-TO-BACK SEGMENTS

15'-6" SEGMENT — 9'-6"

A B C D E F G H I J K

2 USES OF STORAGE SEGMENTS AND A DATA FORM

USING SEGMENTS
F): STORAGE RACK COMPONENTS

A reasonably close estimate of the required rack components is easily established once the number of segments is known. For each segment, in the example on the next page, two bays of selective racks are needed; one on each side of the aisle. Using five loads high, with the bottom load sitting directly on the floor, means four load beam levels are needed with eight beams per rack bay. Also, one end frame per bay. Then estimate how many rows of racks are needed and add another frame for the end of each row.

So 100 segments will hold 200 rack bays. Load beams: (200 x 8) 1600. For this example assume 16 rows as per the next page. End frames: (200 + 16) = 216.

You will now have rough estimates for area and rack components. With rack prices (including other components needed for stability and safety), plus installation charges, some early decisions are possible, without making any layout drawings.

Most other types of racks can be estimated in the same way. A few, such as drive-in racks, may require help from a supplier.

5) SECTIONS

For a drawing of Zones combined into Sections (or a completed warehouse layout) refer to page 20.

USING SEGMENTS

F): TO DETERMINE RACK COMPONENT COUNT

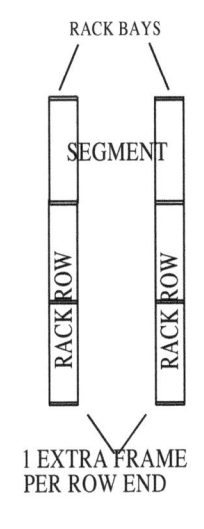

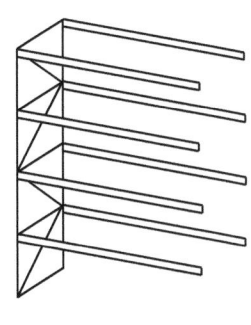

RACK BAYS

SEGMENT

RACK ROW | RACK ROW

1 EXTRA FRAME PER ROW END

RACK COMPONENTS ON EACH SIDE OF THE AISLE
ONE END FRAME
EIGHT LOAD BEAMS

TOTALS PER SEGMENT
END FRAMES   2
LOAD BEAMS   16

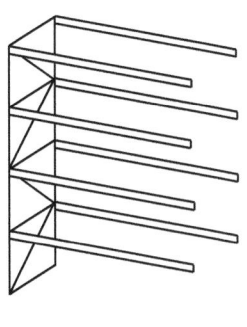

ADD ONE FRAME FOR EACH ROW END

RACK COMPONENTS

NO. OF SEGMENTS	100
RACK BAYS PER SEGMENT	2
NO. OF RACK BAYS AND END FRAMES	200
EST. NO. OF ROWS 16 ADD ONE END FRAME PER ROW	16
TOTAL END FRAMES:	216
LOAD BEAMS PER BAY	8
TOTAL LOAD BEAMS (8 X 200)	1600

ADD FOR BACK-TO-BACK ROW CONNECTORS, FLOOR LAGS
AND ANY OTHER ACCESSORIES BEING CONSIDERED.

2 *USES OF STORAGE SEGMENTS AND A DATA FORM*

The DataForm

The DataForm is used in combination with Storage Segments. This combination allows you to quickly compare the area and storage capabilities of any number of storage and handling systems. It will yield data based on initial input for various situations discussed in the next pages. The results of any trial are not meant to be used for a final drawing, but as a guide to a decision of the systems, areas and layouts to be seriously considered.

It is a two page form which will yield initial system data with only a minimal hand sketch as a starter.

For each trial the basic data output may, depending on input, include:

1) Area required, including access aisles.
2) Results of alternate configurations (length and width) of any area.
3) Percentage of area used by access aisles.
4) Area per floor level storage slot.
5) Area allocation per slot with increasing storage levels.
6) Number of aisle faces with increasing storage levels.
7) Number of pick faces with increasing pick levels.
8) Number of reserves above the pick faces.
9) Number of reserves behind the aisle faces.

The form, while possibly seeming difficult at first look, is actually quite straightforward and, with the following explanations, can be completed in a short time. Repeated use becomes easy.

USING THE DATAFORM IN THE EARLY PLANNING STAGES

The following pages explain the DataForm, using a considerable number of examples.

Prior to the form two pages are first entered here for clarity of terms and to reduce any need to leaf back in the book. Then three pages of tables referring to the effects of stack height are added. These can be used for input on DataForm #2.

The first of these pages is a chart showing the effects on your system and layout choices with different building situations.

At least four different building situations may apply when considering a layout for a storage area. They range from unlimited choices of area, layout and equipment to no choice of the area size or shape and, possibly, limited equipment choices. Comments about each situation are included on the chart.

With building situations #1 and #2 the building columns can be as you choose.

However it is important to be aware that #'s 3 and 4 may be adversely affected by existing building columns, and perhaps other obstructions. These may cause considerable changes to the ideal layout. Refer to the previous explanations of some alternate methods to fit into the area allotted and/or try as many suitable segment types and layouts as practical.

Also included is a drawing of racks with descriptions of the terminology for different uses of storage slots; because the DataForm will show quantity options for each type.

The DataForm actually consists of two forms; of which you can use either or both, according to the depth of data wanted.

SOME DIFFERENT BUILDING SITUATIONS TO CONSIDER

Y = YOUR CHOICE   N = NO CHOICE   P = PERHAPS A CHOICE

	LAYOUT LOCATION	TOTAL AREA	AREA CONFIGURATION LENGTH	WIDTH	HEIGHT	LOCATION OF DOCK	DIRECTION OF AISLES *	SPACING OF BUILDING COLUMNS	AISLE WIDTH	STORAGE DEPTH
1	NEW BUILDING WITH NO LIMITATIONS	Y	Y	Y	Y	Y	Y	Y	Y	Y
2	NEW BUILDING ON A SPECIFIC EXISTING LOT	P	P	P	Y	P	Y	Y	Y	Y
3	AREA WITHIN AN EXISTING BUILDING TO BE CHOSEN	Y	Y	Y	Y	P	Y	Y BUT LIMITED	Y	Y
4	AN AREA WITHIN A SPECIFIC EXISTING BUILDING	N	N	N	N	N	P	N	Y	Y

* With no choice of dock location the choice of direction for access and storage aisles can be more difficult.

1 In this case all options are open to consider many types of equipment and layouts; in a minimum of time

2 Here you may or may not have a choice as to dock location; which has a great effect on aisle directions. But, with the dock location decided, the DataForm can be used for system and layout comparisons.

3 For this situation, where the intent is to select an existing building, alternate acceptable systems and layouts should be developed before the building is selected, as if you were going to build to suit.
In this way you will be able to assess any potential building, with dimensions and data for each of the acceptable layout alternates that will fit. Use of the DataForm. Part E) "USING SEGMENTS" might help if building columns become a problem.

4 This might be the whole building or an area within a building. In either case the height and spacing of building columns are pre-determined and there may be no choices regarding dock equipment or location.

This can be a difficult situation. The easiest layout is by simply locating the columns between back-to-back rows of racks and accepting the results. However this may not result in the optimum efficiency. Alternate ways of dealing with columns are shown in part E) of "USING SEGMENTS"; with aisle widths and storage depths as the main alternates.

WHAT TYPE AND HEIGHT OF RACKS?

(SELECTIVE, DOUBLE-DEEP, PUSH-BACK, FLOW-THROUGH, DRIVE-IN, DRIVE-THROUGH, MOLE-TYPE)

HOW MUCH RESERVE BEHIND AISLE FACES?

HOW MANY AISLE FACES?

RACK HEIGHT?

HOW MANY PICK LEVELS?

HOW MANY STORAGE LEVELS?

AISLE WIDTH?   RACK DEPTH?

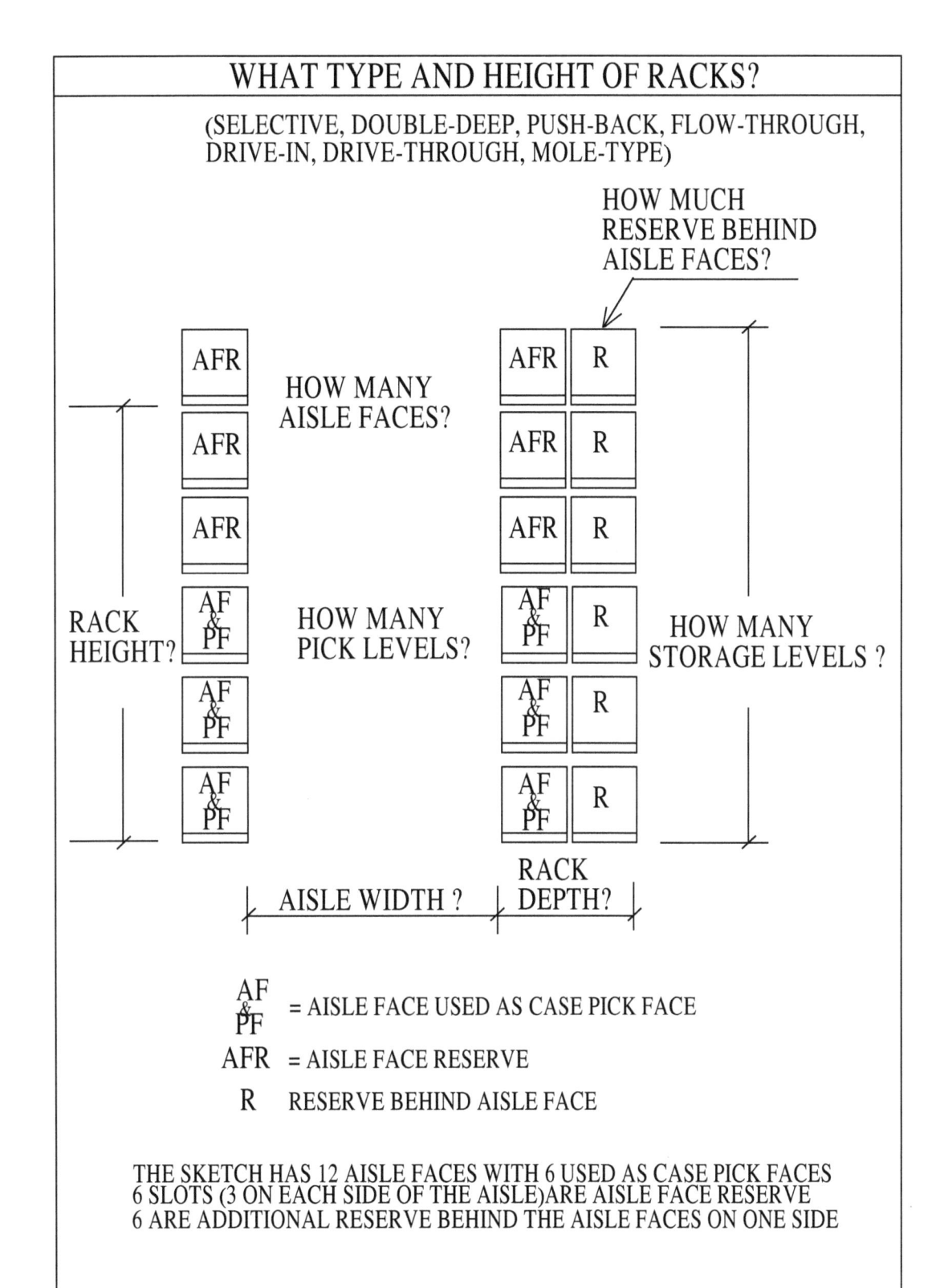

$\dfrac{AF}{\&\ PF}$ = AISLE FACE USED AS CASE PICK FACE

AFR = AISLE FACE RESERVE

R   RESERVE BEHIND AISLE FACE

THE SKETCH HAS 12 AISLE FACES WITH 6 USED AS CASE PICK FACES
6 SLOTS (3 ON EACH SIDE OF THE AISLE) ARE AISLE FACE RESERVE
6 ARE ADDITIONAL RESERVE BEHIND THE AISLE FACES ON ONE SIDE

2 *USES OF STORAGE SEGMENTS AND A DATA FORM*

SQUARE FEET PER SLOT BASED ON STACK HEIGHT

STACK HEIGHT

SQ. FT. Per FLOOR STORAGE SLOT	2	3	4	5	6	7	8
11	5.5	3.67	2.75	2.20	1.83	1.57	1.38
11.5	5.75	3.83	2.88	2.30	1.92	1.67	1.44
12	6	4.00	3.00	2.40	2.00	1.71	1.50
12.5	6.25	4.17	3.13	2.50	2.08	1.79	1.56
13	6.5	4.33	3.25	2.60	2.17	1.86	1.63
13.5	6.75	4.50	3.28	2.70	3.25	1.93	1.69
14	7	4.67	3.50	2.80	2.33	2.00	1.75
14.5	7.25	4.83	3.63	2.90	2.42	2.07	1.81
15	7.5	5.00	3.75	3.00	2.50	2.14	1.88
15.5	7.75	5.17	3.88	3.10	3.58	2.21	1.94
16	8	5.33	4.00	3.20	2.67	2.29	2.00
16.5	8.25	5.50	4.13	3.30	2.75	2.36	2.06
17	8.5	5.67	4.25	3.40	2.83	2.43	2.13
17.5	8.75	5.83	4.38	3.50	2.92	2.50	2.19
18	9	6.00	4.50	3.60	3.00	2.57	2.25
18.5	9.25	6.17	4.63	3.70	3.08	2.64	2.31
19	9.5	6.33	4.75	3.80	3.17	2.71	2.38
19.5	9.75	6.50	4.88	3.90	3.25	2.79	2.44
20	10	6.67	5.00	4.00	3.33	2.86	2.50
20.5	10.25	6.83	5.13	4.10	3.42	2.93	2.56
21	10.5	7.00	5.25	4.20	3.50	3.00	2.63
21.5	10.75	7.17	5.38	4.30	3.58	3.07	2.69
22	11	7.33	5.50	4.40	3.67	3.14	2.75
22.5	11.25	7.50	5.63	4.50	3.75	3.21	2.81
23	11.5	7.67	5.75	4.60	3.83	3.29	2.88
23.5	11.75	7.83	5.88	4.70	3.92	3.36	2.94
24	12	8.00	6.00	4.80	4.00	3.43	3.00
24.5	12.25	8.17	6.13	4.90	4.08	3.50	3.06
25	12.5	8.33	6.25	5.00	4.17	3.57	3.13
25.5	12.75	8.50	6.38	5.10	4.25	3.64	3.19
26	13	8.67	6.50	5.20	4.33	3.71	3.25
26.5	13.25	8.83	6.63	5.30	4.42	3.79	3.31
27	13.5	9.00	6.75	5.40	4.50	3.86	3.38
27.5	13.75	9.17	6.88	5.50	4.58	3.93	4.44
28	14	9.33	7.00	5.60	4.67	4.00	3.50

SQUARE FEET PER SLOT BASED ON STACK HEIGHT

STACK HEIGHT

SQ. FT. Per FLOOR STORAGE SLOT	2	3	4	5	6	7	8
28.5	14.25	9.50	7.13	5.70	4.75	4.07	3.56
29	14.50	9.67	7.25	5.80	4.83	4.14	3.63
29.5	14.75	9.83	7.38	5.90	4.92	4.21	3.69
30	15.00	10.00	7.50	6.00	5.00	4.29	3.75
30.5	15.25	10.17	7.63	6.10	5.08	4.36	3.81
31	15.50	10.33	7.75	6.20	5.17	4.43	3.88
31.5	15.75	10.50	7.88	6.30	5.25	4.50	3.94
32	16.00	10.67	8.00	6.40	5.33	4.57	4.00
32.5	16.25	10.83	8.13	6.50	5.42	4.64	4.06
33	16.50	11.00	8.25	6.60	5.50	4.71	4.13
33.5	16.75	11.17	8.38	6.70	5.58	4.79	4.19
34	17.00	11.33	8.50	6.80	5.67	4.86	4.25
34.5	17.25	11.50	8.63	6.90	5.75	4.93	4.31
35	17.50	11.67	8.75	7.00	5.83	5.00	4.38
35.5	17.75	11.83	8.88	7.10	5.92	5.07	4.44
36	18.00	12.00	9.00	7.20	6.00	5.14	4.50
36.5	18.25	12.17	9.13	7.30	6.08	5.21	4.56
37	18.50	12.33	9.25	7.40	6.17	5.29	4.63
37.5	18.75	12.50	9.38	7.50	6.25	5.36	4.69
38	19.00	12.67	9.50	7.60	6.33	5.43	4.75
38.5	19.25	12.83	9.63	7.70	6.42	5.50	4.81
39	19.50	13.00	9.75	7.80	6.50	5.57	4.88
39.5	19.75	13.17	9.88	7.90	6.58	5.64	4.94
40	20.00	13.33	10.00	8.00	6.67	5.71	5.00
40.5	20.25	13.50	10.13	8.10	6.75	5.79	5.06
41	20.50	13.67	10.25	8.20	6.83	5.86	5.13
41.5	20.75	13.83	10.38	8.30	6.92	5.93	5.19
42	21.00	14.00	10.50	8.40	7.00	6.00	5.25
42.5	21.25	14.17	10.63	8.50	7.08	6.07	5.31
43	21.50	14.33	10.75	8.60	7.17	6.14	5.38
43.5	21.75	14.50	10.88	8.70	7.25	6.21	5.44
44	22.00	14.67	11.00	8.80	7.33	6.29	5.50
44.5	22.25	14.83	11.13	8.90	7.42	6.36	5.56
45	22.50	15.00	11.25	9.00	7.50	6.43	5.63
45.5	22.75	15.17	11.38	9.10	7.58	6.50	5.69
46	23.00	15.33	11.50	9.20	7.67	6.57	5.75
46.5	23.25	15.50	11.63	9.30	7.75	6.64	5.81

SQUARE FEET PER SLOT BASED ON STACK HEIGHT

STACK HEIGHT

SQ. FT. Per FLOOR STORAGE SLOT	2	3	4	5	6	7	8
47	23.5	15.67	11.75	9.40	7.83	6.71	5.88
47.5	23.75	15.83	11.88	9.50	7.92	6.79	5.94
48	24	16.00	12.00	9.60	8.00	6.86	6.00
48.5	24.25	16.17	12.13	9.70	8.08	6.93	6.06
49	24.5	16.33	12.25	9.80	8.17	7.00	6.13
49.5	24.75	16.50	12.38	9.90	8.25	7.07	6.19
50	25	16.67	12.50	10.00	8.33	7.14	6.25
50.5	25.25	16.83	12.63	10.10	8.42	7.21	6.31
51	25.5	17.00	12.57	10.20	8.50	7.29	6.38
51.5	25.75	17.17	12.88	10.30	8.58	7.36	6.44
52	26	17.33	13.00	10.40	8.67	7.43	6.50
52.5	26.25	17.50	13.13	10.50	8.75	7.50	6.56
53	26.5	17.67	13.25	10.60	8.83	7.57	6.63
53.5	26.75	17.83	13.38	10.70	8.92	7.64	6.69
54	27	18.00	13.50	10.80	9.00	7.71	6.75
54.5	27.25	18.17	13.63	10.90	9.08	7.79	6.81
55	27.5	18.33	13.75	11.00	9.17	7.86	6.88
55.5	27.75	18.50	13.88	11.10	9.25	7.93	6.94
56	28	18.67	14.00	11.20	9.33	8.00	7.00
56.5	28.25	18.83	14.13	11.30	9.42	8.07	7.06
57	28.5	19.00	14.25	11.40	9.50	8.14	7.13
57.5	28.75	19.17	14.38	11.50	9.58	8.21	7.19
58	29	19.33	14.50	11.60	9.67	8.29	7.25
58.5	29.25	19.50	14.63	11.70	9.75	8.36	7.31
59	29.50	19.67	14.75	11.80	9.83	8.43	7.38
59.5	29.75	19.83	14.88	11.90	9.92	8.50	7.44
60	30	20.00	15.00	12.00	10.00	8.57	7.50
60.5	30.25	20.17	15.13	12.10	10.08	8.64	7.56
61	30.5	20.33	15.25	12.20	10.17	8.71	7.63
61.5	30.75	20.50	15.38	12.30	10.25	8.79	7.69
62	31	20.67	15.50	12.40	10.33	8.86	7.75
62.5	31.25	20.83	15.63	12.50	10.42	8.93	7.81
63	31.5	21.00	15.75	12.60	10.50	9.00	7.88
63.5	31.75	21.17	15.88	12.70	10.58	9.07	7.94
64	32	21.33	16.00	12.80	10.67	9.14	8.00
64.5	32.25	21.50	16.13	12.90	10.75	9.21	8.06
65	32.5	21.67	16.25	13.00	10.83	9.29	8.13

REGARDING THE EXAMPLES TO FOLLOW FOR DATAFORMS #1 AND #2

There are two basic starting points when considering a new system layout. These are:

1) **A specified number of storage slots.**
   To determine the area needed to provide a specified number of storage slots; first with a selected segment and number of storage levels. Then, based on data produced, potential changes, including completely different segments, can be considered. T**he storage quantity stays within a small range while the area changes to suit.**

2) **A specified area.**
   To determine the number of storage slots which will fit into a given area using acceptable segments. **The area stays within a small range while the storage quantity fluctuates to suit.**

But in any case a specific need for aisle faces, pick faces, reserve above pick faces or rear reserve, may influence the type of storage and handling system selected.

Additionally you may have an interest in comparing, on DataForm #2, alternate layout widths and lengths. These can reveal some surprising data.

Note that row length before a breakthrough (access aisle) is best based on your storage and retrieval patterns. Sometimes, especially with a very narrow aisle system, long rows are wanted, at other times they can be counter-productive.

In many instances it will pay off to prepare a range of acceptable alternates before committing to any choices you may have; including the selection of an existing building.

Before considering any storage system you may want to note or estimate some, or all, of the following as being needed or acceptable.

Number of SKUs
Area
Number of storage slots
Number of storage levels
Number of aisle faces*
Number and height of pick faces
Number of aisle face reserves above pick faces*
Storage depth
Number of SKUs which can be stored in depth

* Aisle face reserves over the pick faces can be converted to pick faces if needed for growth; with reserves moved elsewhere.

Following are some sets of examples; each concentrating on one of the two basics described above.

EXAMPLES OF THE USE OF DATAFORMS #1 AND #2

EXAMPLE SET ONE

In this first set of examples more drawings are shown than in later examples. This is to demonstrate a starting point and input data for the DataForms. Subsequent example sets are simplified.

First a segment is again shown; this time with detailed dimensions, including an allowance at each side for flue and column needs. Two very different building column spacing's are shown for the segment used. The next page, bottom half, then shows a simplified version with overall dimensions, which are all that is needed to use the DataForms.

Then a detailed drawing is shown, having a layout of 5 segments wide x 25 segments long. These 125 segments will yield 2000 storage slots if four storage levels are used. This is our starting point. Directly below it is a hand drawn sketch, with no scale, which provides the same information; slightly rounded because exactness will come in a final drawing.

The next page shows a different layout with 14 segments wide x 9 segments long; 126 segments.

On DataForm #1 the choice has been made to seek information about the 5 x 25 layout and known data entered in panel one. Other possible needs, such as the number of pick faces, reserves, etc. have been left to flow from the form to assess them.

The request for 2000 slots and other obvious numbers are entered into panel two. Filling in panel three will reveal a series of slot data as storage levels and/or pick face levels are increased.

In panel four enter as many different potential layouts as you think might apply; with varying heights, widths, lengths and segment quantities.

Upon trying each layout on DataForm #2 a range of area information will result. These include segment area and total area with access aisles included. Access aisle percentages and area are also noted. For the sq. ft. per storage slot with increasing storage levels, the previously provided **stack height tables**, or simple math, can be used.

On DataForm #2 the 5 x 25 and 14 x 9 layouts have been tried first. Then, having shown the simplicity of hand drawings, we return to computer drawings for clarity and neatness.

The 12 x 7 trial with 84 segments, provides a very different set of area data. In particular, note under the heading "Area Per Each Slot", the results for storage 4 and 5 high have been crossed out. Although they may be of interest they will not hold the 2000 slots requested. A minimum of 6 storage levels are required. Storage levels of 4 to 7 have been used here, but use any range which may seem to apply.

Storage levels, with differing numbers of pick and reserve faces, are shown on DataForm #1.

EXAMPLE SET ONE — A STORAGE SEGMENT

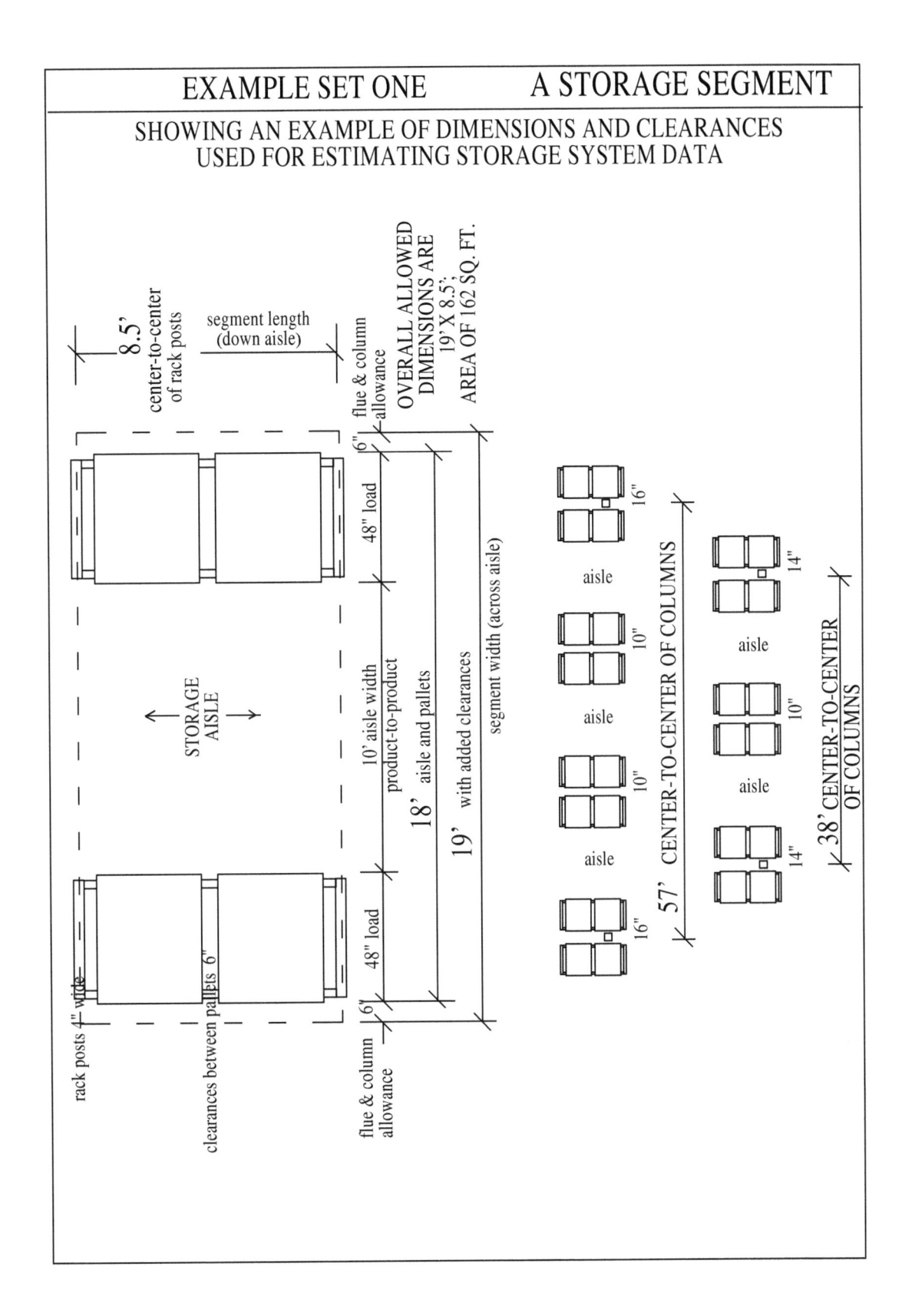

SHOWING AN EXAMPLE OF DIMENSIONS AND CLEARANCES USED FOR ESTIMATING STORAGE SYSTEM DATA

- 8.5' center-to-center of rack posts
- segment length (down aisle)
- flue & column allowance 6"
- 48" load
- STORAGE AISLE
- 10' aisle width product-to-product
- 18' aisle and pallets
- 19' with added clearances
- segment width (across aisle)
- 48" load
- clearances between pallets 6"
- rack posts 4" wide
- flue & column allowance 6"

OVERALL ALLOWED DIMENSIONS ARE 19' X 8.5'; AREA OF 162 SQ. FT.

- 16" / aisle / 10" / aisle / 10" / aisle / 16"
- 57' CENTER-TO-CENTER OF COLUMNS
- 14" / aisle / 10" / aisle / 14"
- 38' CENTER-TO-CENTER OF COLUMNS

82

2 *USES OF STORAGE SEGMENTS AND A DATA FORM*

EXAMPLE SET ONE — SIMPLIFIED SEGMENT

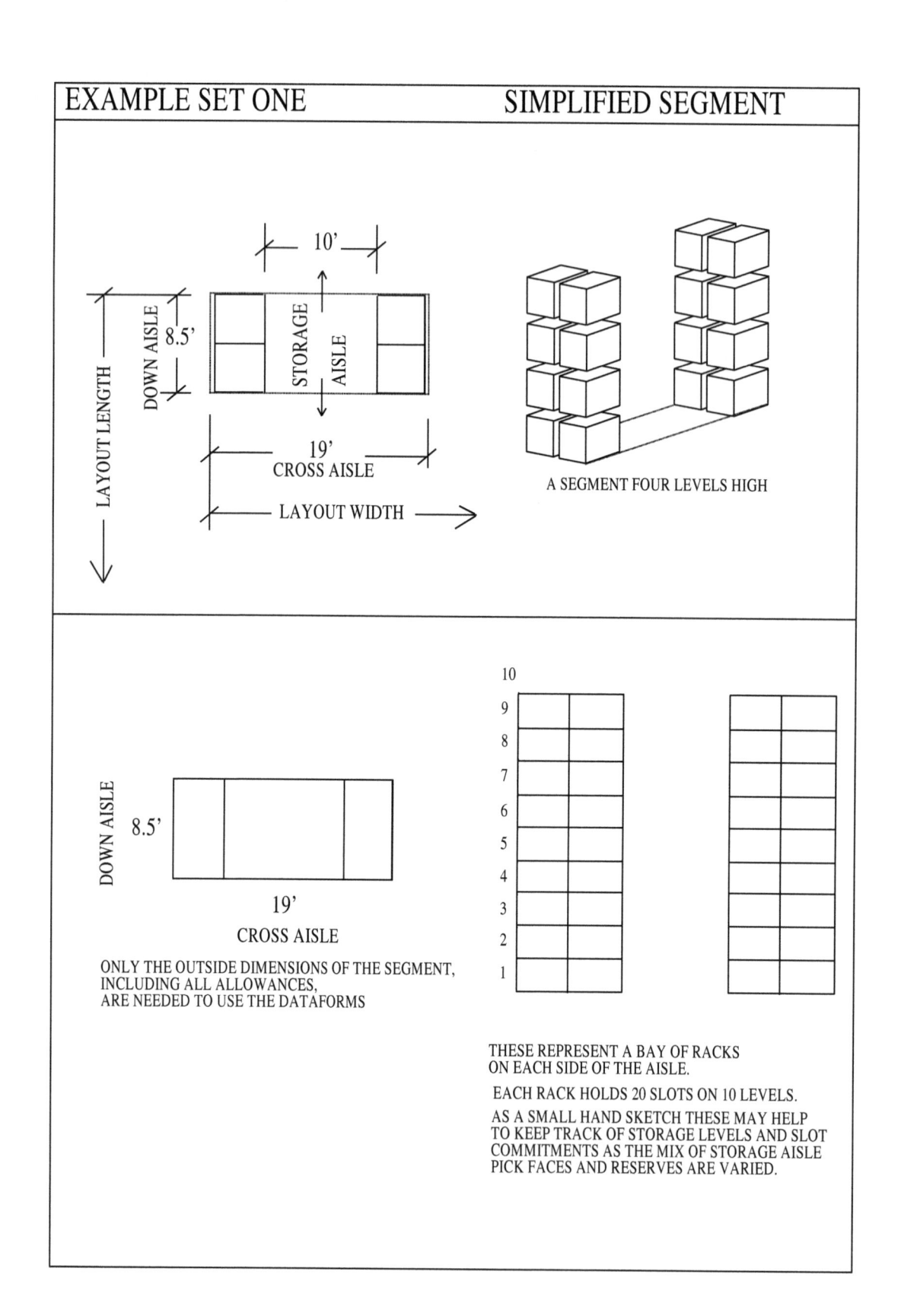

A SEGMENT FOUR LEVELS HIGH

ONLY THE OUTSIDE DIMENSIONS OF THE SEGMENT, INCLUDING ALL ALLOWANCES, ARE NEEDED TO USE THE DATAFORMS

THESE REPRESENT A BAY OF RACKS ON EACH SIDE OF THE AISLE.

EACH RACK HOLDS 20 SLOTS ON 10 LEVELS.

AS A SMALL HAND SKETCH THESE MAY HELP TO KEEP TRACK OF STORAGE LEVELS AND SLOT COMMITMENTS AS THE MIX OF STORAGE AISLE PICK FACES AND RESERVES ARE VARIED.

HOW TO CONFIGURE AND EQUIP YOUR WAREHOUSE

EXAMPLE SET ONE

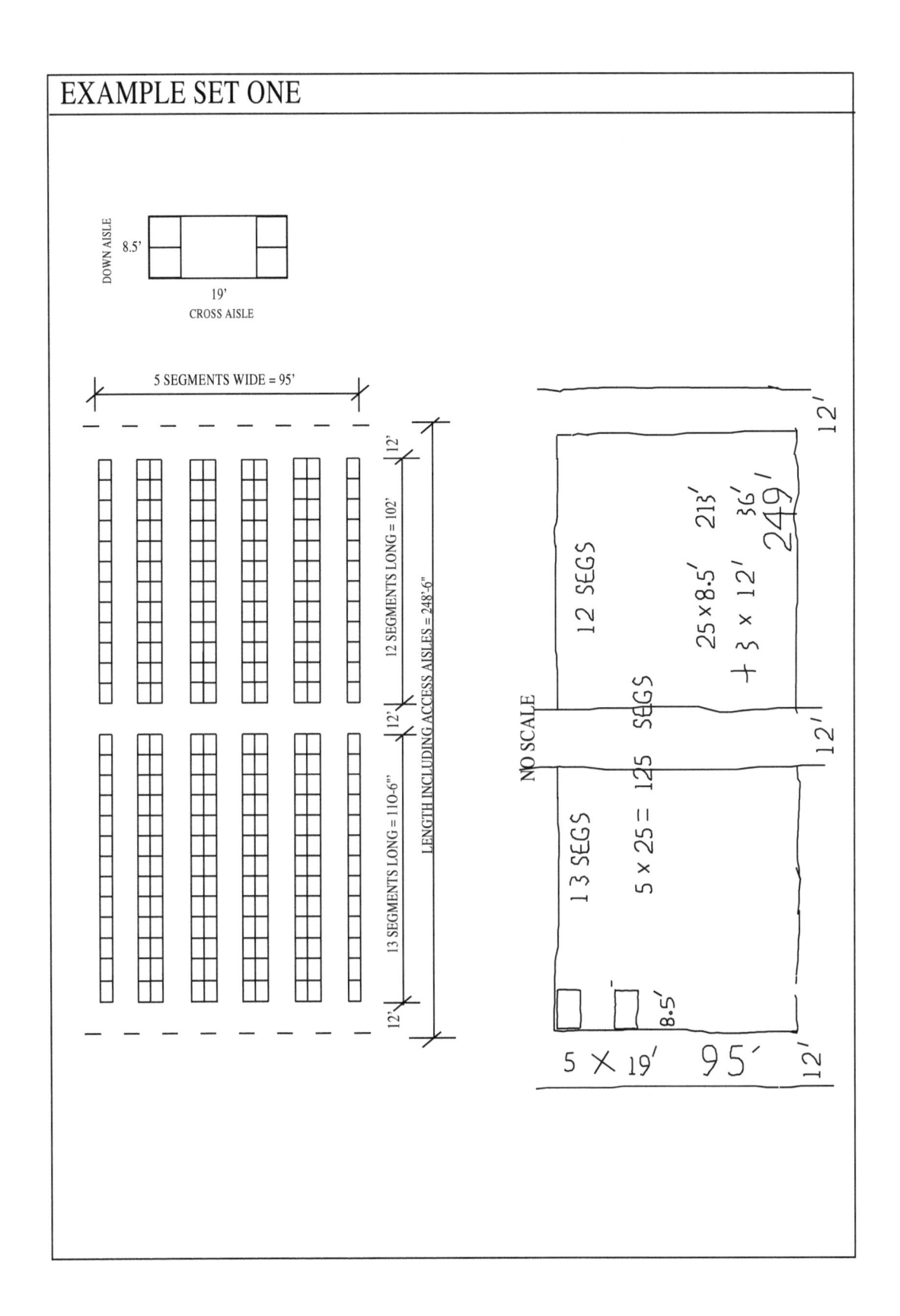

DOWN AISLE 8.5'
19'
CROSS AISLE

5 SEGMENTS WIDE = 95'

12'
12 SEGMENTS LONG = 102'
12'
LENGTH INCLUDING ACCESS AISLES = 248'-6"
13 SEGMENTS LONG = 110'-6"
12'

NO SCALE

12'
12 SEGS
25 × 8.5' 213'
+ 3 × 12' 36'
249'
12'
SEGS
13 SEGS
5 × 25 = 125 SEGS
8.5'
5 × 19' 95'
12'

2 *USES OF STORAGE SEGMENTS AND A DATA FORM*

EXAMPLE SET ONE

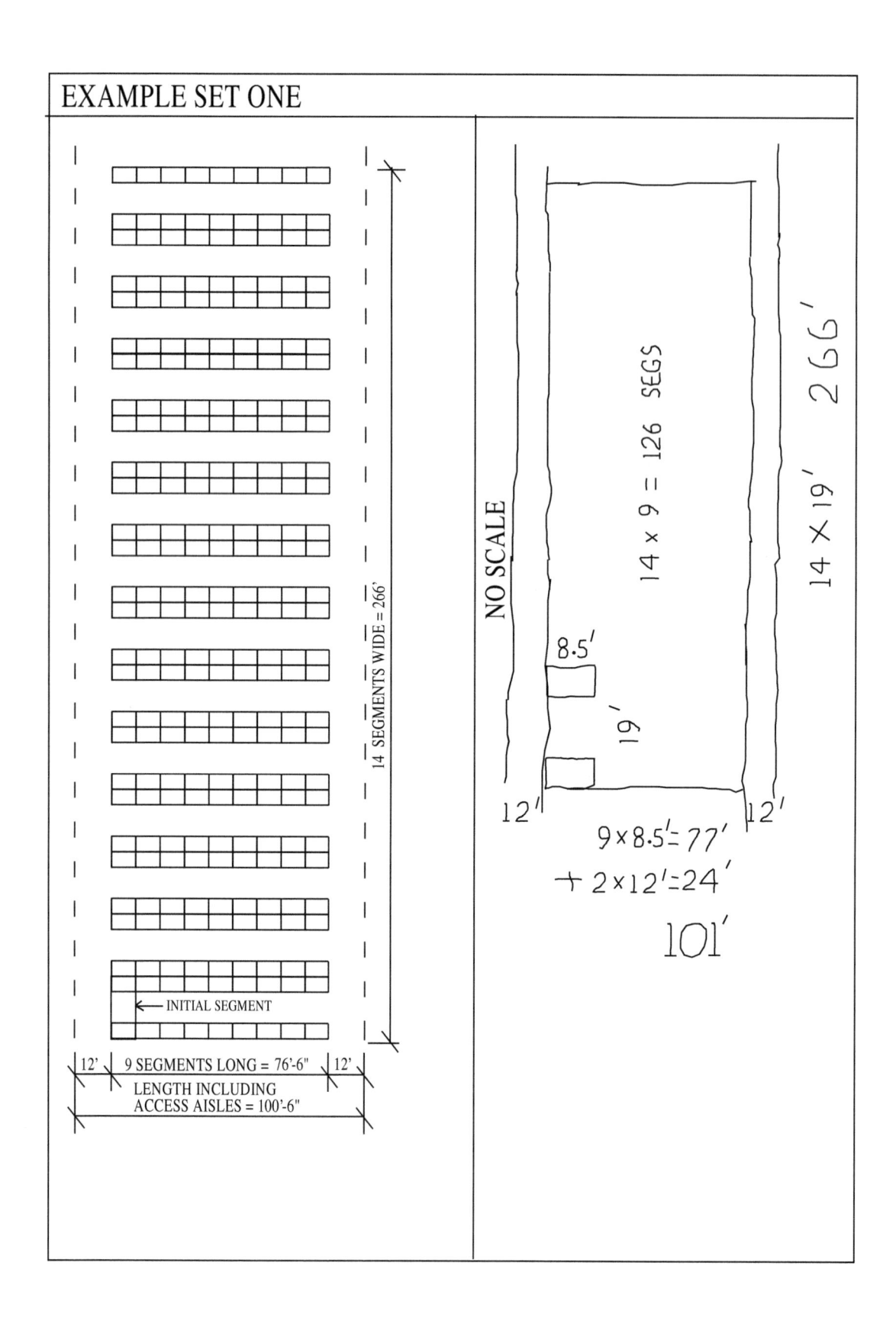

14 SEGMENTS WIDE = 266'

←— INITIAL SEGMENT

12' | 9 SEGMENTS LONG = 76'-6" | 12'
LENGTH INCLUDING
ACCESS AISLES = 100'-6"

NO SCALE

14 × 9 = 126 SEGS

14 × 19' 266'

8.5'
19'
12'   12'

9 × 8.5' = 77'
+ 2 × 12' = 24'
101'

HOW TO CONFIGURE AND EQUIP YOUR WAREHOUSE

DATAFORM EXAMPLE: SET #1

DATAFORM #1

THIS FORM IS PROVIDED FOR, AND LIMITED TO, THE SOLE USE OF THE PURCHASER OF THE MANUAL
"HOW TO CONFIGURE AND EQUIP YOUR WAREHOUSE"

DF128

PANEL ONE — INITIAL INPUT

- AREA: TBD
- FLOOR SLOTS / SEGMENT: 4
- PICK FACES WANTED: TBD
- SLOTS WANTED: 2000
- TOTAL SLOTS / SEGMENT: 16
- AISLE FACES WANTED: TBD
- # OF STORAGE LEVELS: 4
- SEGMENTS NEEDED: 125
- RESERVE SLOTS WANTED: TBD

AREA ÷ SQ. FT. PER SEG. = SEGMENTS

PANEL TWO — ALTERNATE STORAGE LEVELS ("STACK HEIGHTS")

# OF STORAGE LEVELS	4	5	6	
# OF FLOOR SLOTS	4	4	4	
SLOTS PER SEGMENT	16	20	24	
SEGS. FOR 2000 SLOTS	125	100	84	
REVISED TOTAL SLOTS	2000	2000	2016	

PANEL THREE

	PER SEG.	TOTAL	PER SEG.	TOTAL	PER SEG.	TOTAL	PER SEG.	TOTAL
AISLE FACES	16	2000	20	2000	24	2016		
PICK FACES @ 2 HIGH	8	1000	8	800	8	672		
AISLE FACE RESERVES	8	1000	12	1200	16	1344		
REAR RESERVES	0	0	0	0	0	0		
TOTAL RESERVES		1000		1200		1344		
PICK FACES @ 3 HIGH	12	1500	12	1200	12	1008		
AISLE FACE RESERVES	4	500	8	800	12	1008		
REAR RESERVES	0	0	0	0	0	0		
TOTAL RESERVES		500		800		1008		
PICK FACES @ 4 HIGH	16	2000	16	1600	16	1344		
AISLE FACE RESERVES	0	0	4	400	8	672		
REAR RESERVES	0	0	0	0	0	0		
TOTAL RESERVES		0		400		672		

PANEL FOUR — ALTERNATE CONFIGURATIONS OF LAYOUT WIDTHS AND LENGTHS

TRIAL LAYOUTS	INITIAL # OF SEGS.	A (W X L)	ACTUAL SEGS. #	B (W X L)	ACTUAL SEGS. #	C (W X L)	ACTUAL SEGS. #
#1	125	5 x 25	125	14 x 9	126	8 x 16	128
#2	100	10 x 10	100	6 x 17	102	x	
#3	84	12 x 7	84	6 x 14	84	x	
#4		x		x		x	

2 USES OF STORAGE SEGMENTS AND A DATA FORM

AREA DATA FOR DIFFERENT CONFIGURATIONS — DATAFORM #2

THIS FORM IS PROVIDED FOR, AND LIMITED TO, THE SOLE USE OF THE PURCHASER OF THE MANUAL "HOW TO CONFIGURE AND EQUIP YOUR WAREHOUSE"

SET #1 DF129

ALTERNATE CONFIGURATIONS OF LAYOUT WIDTHS AND LENGTHS.

NOTE: SKETCHES WILL HELP DETERMINE THE NUMBER OF ACCCESS AISLES WANTED.

TRIALS FROM FORM #1	INITIAL # OF SEGS.	A: W X L	ACTUAL SEGS. #	B: W X L	ACTUAL SEGS. #	C: W X L	ACTUAL SEGS. #
#1	125	5 x 25	125	14 x 9	126	X	
#2		X		X		X	
#3		X		X		X	
#4		X		X		X	

REF. TRIAL # 1A

* TOTAL AREA ÷ ACTUAL # OF SEGMENTS

SEGMENTS CROSS AISLE WIDTH	DOWN AISLE LENGTH	AREA DIMENSIONS	AREA (SQ.FT.)	ACTUAL # OF SEGS.	SEGMENT AREA INCL. ACCESS AISLES. SQ. FT.	FLOOR SLOTS PER SEG.	AREA PER FLOOR SLOT SQ. FT.	AREA PER EACH SLOT @4 LEVELS	AREA PER EACH SLOT @5 LEVELS	AREA PER EACH SLOT @6 LEVELS	AREA PER EACH SLOT @7 LEVELS
5	X	x 19 = 95 FT	20,235	125	190	4	48	12	9.6	8	6.9
X	25	x 8.5 = 213 FT									

ACCESS AISLE AREA FROM SKETCH: 3 x 12 x 95 = 3420

TOTAL AREA IS: 23,655 SQ. FT.

ACCESS AISLES ARE: 17 % ADD-ON AND 14 % OF TOTAL AREA

REVISED LENGTH: 213 + 36 (ACCESS AISLES 3x12) = 249'

OVERALL DIMENSIONS: WIDTH: 95' LENGTH: 249'

REF. TRIAL # 1B

* TOTAL AREA ÷ ACTUAL # OF SEGMENTS

SEGMENTS CROSS AISLE WIDTH	DOWN AISLE LENGTH	AREA DIMENSIONS	AREA (SQ.FT.)	ACTUAL # OF SEGS.	SEGMENT AREA INCL. ACCESS AISLES. SQ. FT.	FLOOR SLOTS PER SEG.	AREA PER FLOOR SLOT SQ. FT.	AREA PER EACH SLOT @4 LEVELS	AREA PER EACH SLOT @5 LEVELS	AREA PER EACH SLOT @6 LEVELS	AREA PER EACH SLOT @7 LEVELS
14	X	x 19 = 266 FT	20,482	126	214	4	54	13.5	10.8	9	7.7
X	9	x 8.5 = 77 FT									

ACCESS AISLE AREA FROM SKETCH: 2 x 12 x 266 = 6384

TOTAL AREA IS: 26,866 SQ. FT.

ACCESS AISLES ARE: 31 % ADD-ON AND 24 % OF TOTAL AREA

REVISED LENGTH: 77 + 24 (ACCESS AISLES 2x12) = 101'

OVERALL DIMENSIONS: WIDTH: 266' LENGTH: 101'

EXAMPLE SET ONE

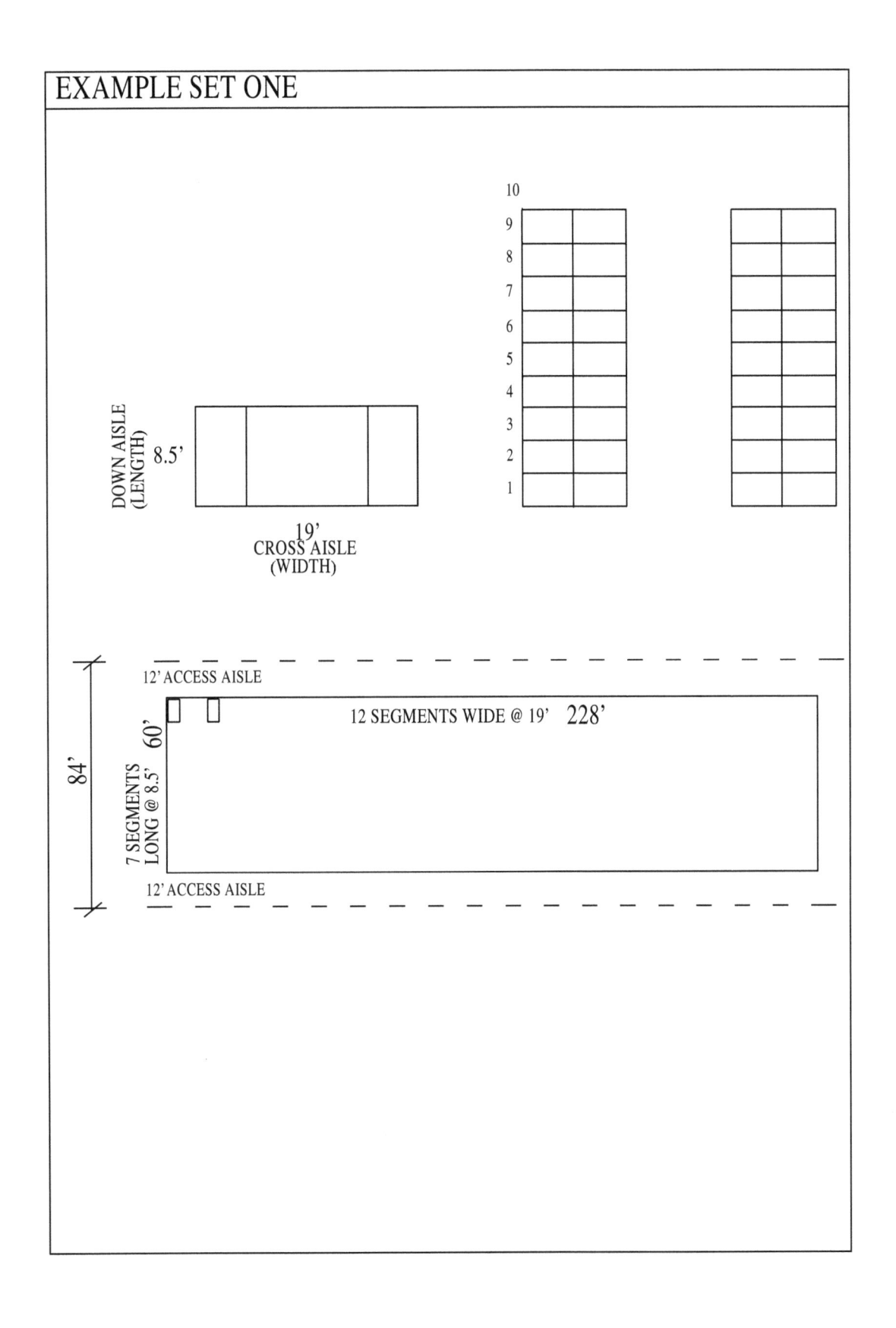

88

DOWN AISLE (LENGTH) 8.5'

19' CROSS AISLE (WIDTH)

10
9
8
7
6
5
4
3
2
1

12' ACCESS AISLE

84'

7 SEGMENTS LONG @ 8.5' 60'

12 SEGMENTS WIDE @ 19' 228'

12' ACCESS AISLE

2 *USES OF STORAGE SEGMENTS AND A DATA FORM*

AREA DATA FOR DIFFERENT CONFIGURATIONS — DATAFORM #2

THIS FORM IS PROVIDED FOR, AND LIMITED TO, THE SOLE USE OF THE PURCHASER OF THE MANUAL "HOW TO CONFIGURE AND EQUIP YOUR WAREHOUSE"

SET #1 DF129

ALTERNATE CONFIGURATIONS OF LAYOUT WIDTHS AND LENGTHS.

NOTE: SKETCHES WILL HELP DETERMINE THE NUMBER OF ACCCESS AISLES WANTED.

TRIALS FROM FORM #1	INITIAL # OF SEGS.	A: W X L	ACTUAL SEGS. #	B: W X L	ACTUAL SEGS. #	C: W X L	ACTUAL SEGS. #
#1		X		X		X	
#2		X		X		X	
#3	84	12 X 9	84	X		X	
#4		X		X		X	

SEGMENTS — REF. TRIAL # **3A**

CROSS AISLE WIDTH	DOWN AISLE LENGTH	AREA DIMENSIONS	AREA (SQ.FT.)
12		X 19 = 228 FT	13,680
	7	X 8.5 = 60 FT	

ACTUAL # OF SEGS.	SEGMENT AREA INCL. ACCESS AISLES. SQ. FT.	FLOOR SLOTS PER SEG.	AREA PER FLOOR SLOT SQ. FT.	AREA PER EACH SLOT @ 4 LEVELS	AREA PER EACH SLOT @ 5 LEVELS	AREA PER EACH SLOT @ 6 LEVELS	AREA PER EACH SLOT @ 7 LEVELS
84	228	4	57	14.3	11.4	9.5	8.1

ACCESS AISLE AREA FROM SKETCH: **2 x 12 x 228 = 5472**

TOTAL AREA IS: **19,152** SQ. FT.

ACCESS AISLES ARE: **40** % ADD-ON
AND **29** % OF TOTAL AREA

REVISED LENGTH: **60** + **24** (2 x 12) = **84'**

OVERALL DIMENSIONS: WIDTH: **228'** LENGTH: **84'**

SEGMENTS — REF. TRIAL # ___

CROSS AISLE WIDTH	DOWN AISLE LENGTH	AREA DIMENSIONS	AREA (SQ.FT.)
		X ___ = ___ FT	
		X ___ = ___ FT	

ACCESS AISLE AREA FROM SKETCH: ___ X ___ X ___

TOTAL AREA IS: ___ SQ. FT.

ACCESS AISLES ARE: ___ % ADD-ON
AND ___ % OF TOTAL AREA

REVISED LENGTH: ___ + ___ = ___

OVERALL DIMENSIONS: WIDTH: ___ LENGTH: ___

EXAMPLES OF THE USE OF DATAFORMS #1 AND #2

EXAMPLE SET TWO

In example #2, the segment has been changed to have 2-deep storage on one side of each aisle. This will provide a greater percentage of reserves but, with the same goal of approximately 2000 slots, the number of segments and the number of aisle faces will be reduced.

Here, with 6 floor slots per segment, only 84 segments are needed for 2016 slots, with four storage levels. Increasing the storage levels to 5 would result in 68 segments with 2040 slots.

This time the first options tried are layouts with segments 11 wide x 8 long and then reversed to 8 long x 11 wide. Each has 88 segments. The figures for each are shown on DataForm #2.

These two layouts are also shown again on page 92, showing what the layouts would look like with all segments drawn.

A layout of 4 wide x 17 long has also been noted on DataForm #1 and a sketch of this narrow but long layout is also included. It is based on 5 storage levels and only 68 segments. A third access aisle has been added due to the storage aisle length. See DataForm #2 for area results.

Examples #3 and #4 will try a smaller segment, showing the results for a given area and the alternate areas for a given number of slots.

DATAFORM EXAMPLE: SET #2   DATAFORM #1

THIS FORM IS PROVIDED FOR, AND LIMITED TO, THE SOLE USE OF THE PURCHASER OF THE MANUAL
" HOW TO CONFIGURE AND EQUIP YOUR WAREHOUSE"

DF128

PANEL ONE — INITIAL INPUT

- AREA: TBD
- FLOOR SLOTS / SEGMENT: 6
- PICK FACES WANTED: TBD
- SLOTS WANTED: 2000
- TOTAL SLOTS / SEGMENT: 24
- AISLE FACES WANTED: TBD
- # OF STORAGE LEVELS: 4
- SEGMENTS NEEDED: TBD
- RESERVE SLOTS WANTED: TBD

AREA ÷ SQ. FT. PER SEG. = SEGMENTS

PANEL TWO — ALTERNATE STORAGE LEVELS ("STACK HEIGHTS")

# OF STORAGE LEVELS	4	5			
# OF FLOOR SLOTS	6	6			
SLOTS PER SEGMENT	24	30			
SEGS. FOR 2000 SLOTS	84	(67) 68			
REVISED TOTAL SLOTS	2016	2040			

PANEL THREE

	PER SEG.	TOTAL	PER SEG.	TOTAL	PER SEG.	TOTAL	PER SEG.	TOTAL
AISLE FACES	16	1344	20	1360				
PICK FACES @ 2 HIGH	8	672	8	544				
AISLE FACE RESERVES	8	672	12	816				
REAR RESERVES	8	672	10	680				
TOTAL RESERVES		1344		1496				
PICK FACES @ 3 HIGH	12	1008	12	816				
AISLE FACE RESERVES	4	336	8	544				
REAR RESERVES	8	672	10	680				
TOTAL RESERVES		1008		1224				
PICK FACES @ 4 HIGH	16	1344	16	1088				
AISLE FACE RESERVES	0	0	4	272				
REAR RESERVES	8	672	10	680				
TOTAL RESERVES		672		952				

PANEL FOUR — ALTERNATE CONFIGURATIONS OF LAYOUT WIDTHS AND LENGTHS.

TRIAL LAYOUTS	INITIAL # OF SEGS.	A (W x L)	ACTUAL SEGS. #	B (W x L)	ACTUAL SEGS. #	C (W x L)	ACTUAL SEGS. #
#1	84	11 x 8	88	8 x 11	88	4 x 21	84
#2	68	4 x 17	68	x		x	
#3		x		x		x	
#4		x		x		x	

HOW TO CONFIGURE AND EQUIP YOUR WAREHOUSE

EXAMPLE SET TWO

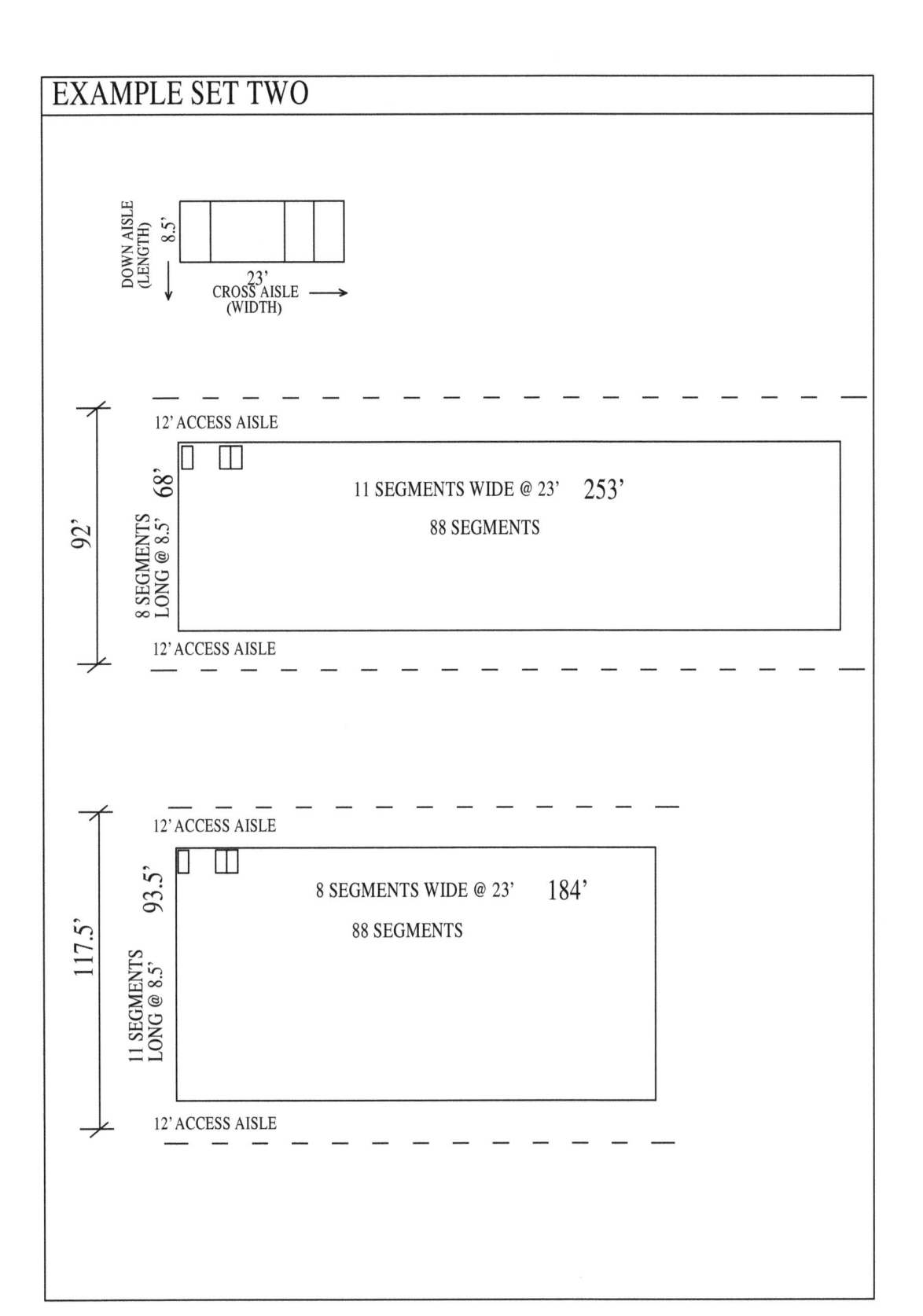

DOWN AISLE (LENGTH) 8.5'
23' CROSS AISLE (WIDTH)

12' ACCESS AISLE

92'
68'
8 SEGMENTS LONG @ 8.5'

11 SEGMENTS WIDE @ 23'   253'

88 SEGMENTS

12' ACCESS AISLE

12' ACCESS AISLE

117.5'
93.5'
11 SEGMENTS LONG @ 8.5'

8 SEGMENTS WIDE @ 23'   184'

88 SEGMENTS

12' ACCESS AISLE

2 *USES OF STORAGE SEGMENTS AND A DATA FORM*

EXAMPLE SET TWO

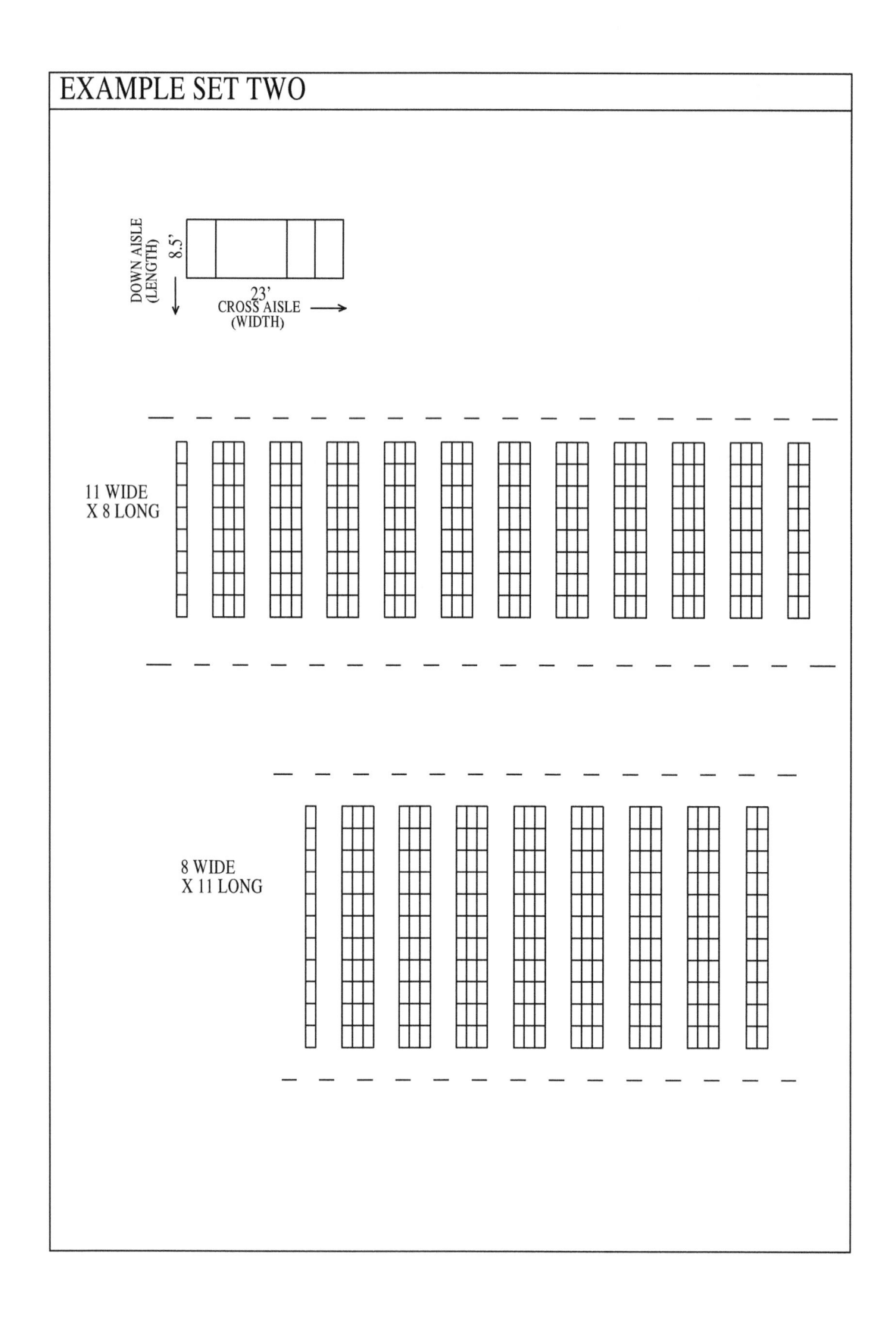

DOWN AISLE (LENGTH) 8.5'
23' CROSS AISLE (WIDTH)

11 WIDE X 8 LONG

8 WIDE X 11 LONG

AREA DATA FOR DIFFERENT CONFIGURATIONS — DATAFORM #2

THIS FORM IS PROVIDED FOR, AND LIMITED TO, THE SOLE USE OF THE PURCHASER OF THE MANUAL "HOW TO CONFIGURE AND EQUIP YOUR WAREHOUSE"

SET # 2 DF129

ALTERNATE CONFIGURATIONS OF LAYOUT WIDTHS AND LENGTHS.

NOTE: SKETCHES WILL HELP DETERMINE THE NUMBER OF ACCCESS AISLES WANTED.

TRIALS FROM FORM #1	INITIAL # OF SEGS.	A (W X L)	ACTUAL SEGS. #	B (W X L)	ACTUAL SEGS. #	C (W X L)	ACTUAL SEGS. #
#1	84	11 x 8	88	8 x 11	88	4 x 21	84
#2		X		X		X	
#3		X		X		X	
#4		X		X		X	

* TOTAL AREA ÷ ACTUAL # OF SEGMENTS

REF. TRIAL # 1 A

SEGMENTS								USE "STACK HEIGHT" CHARTS
CROSS AISLE WIDTH	DOWN AISLE LENGTH	AREA DIMENSIONS	AREA (SQ.FT.)	ACTUAL # OF SEGS.	SEGMENT AREA INCL. ACCESS AISLES. SQ.FT.	FLOOR SLOTS PER SEG.	AREA PER FLOOR SLOT SQ.FT.	AREA PER EACH SLOT @4 LEVELS / @5 / @6 / @7

- 11 x 23 = 253 FT
- 8 x 8.5 = 68 FT
- Area: 17,204
- 88 | 265 | 6 | 44 | 11 | 8.8 | 7.4 | 6.3

ACCESS AISLE AREA FROM SKETCH: 2 x 12 x 253 = 6072

ACCESS AISLES ARE: 35 % ADD-ON

TOTAL AREA IS: 23,276 SQ.FT.

AND 26 % OF TOTAL AREA

REVISED LENGTH: 68 + 24 (ACCESS AISLES, 2x12) = 92'

OVERALL DIMENSIONS: WIDTH: 253' LENGTH: 92'

REF. TRIAL

SEGMENTS								USE "STACK HEIGHT" CHARTS
CROSS AISLE WIDTH	DOWN AISLE LENGTH	AREA DIMENSIONS	AREA (SQ.FT.)	ACTUAL # OF SEGS.	SEGMENT AREA INCL. ACCESS AISLES SQ.FT.	FLOOR SLOTS PER SEG.	AREA PER FLOOR SLOT SQ.FT.	@4 / @5 / @6 / @7 LEVELS

- 8 x 23 = 184 FT
- 11 x 8.5 = 94 FT
- Area: 17,296
- 88 | 247 | 6 | 42 | 10.5 | 8.4 | 7 | 6

ACCESS AISLE AREA FROM SKETCH: 2 x 12 x 184 = 4416

ACCESS AISLES ARE: 26 % ADD-ON

TOTAL AREA IS: 21,712 SQ.FT.

AND 20 % OF TOTAL AREA

REVISED LENGTH: 94 + 24 (ACCESS AISLES, 2x12) = 118'

OVERALL DIMENSIONS: WIDTH: 184' LENGTH: 118'

2 USES OF STORAGE SEGMENTS AND A DATA FORM

EXAMPLE SET TWO

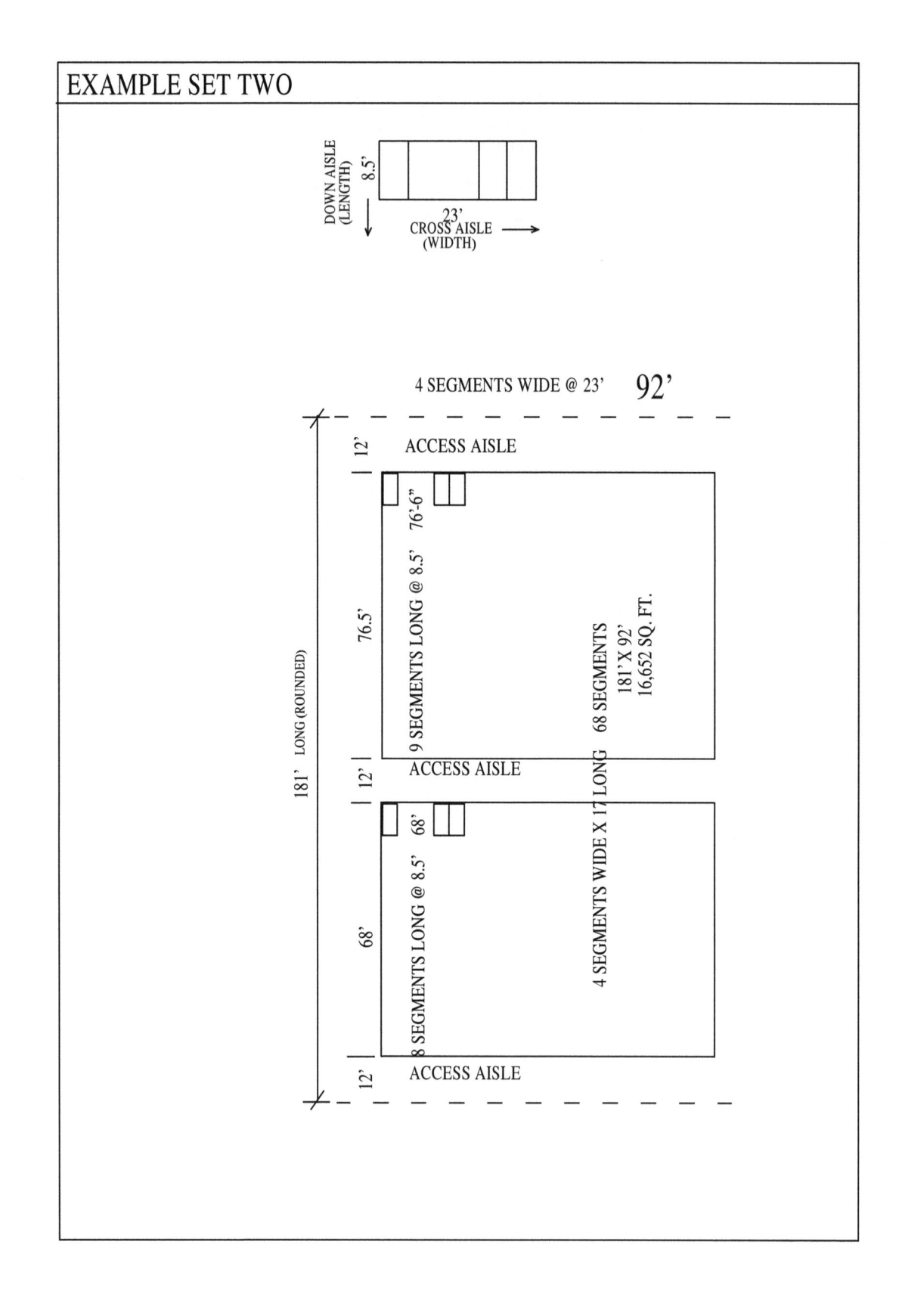

DOWN AISLE (LENGTH) 8.5'
CROSS AISLE (WIDTH) 23'

4 SEGMENTS WIDE @ 23'   **92'**

ACCESS AISLE — 12'

76'-6"

9 SEGMENTS LONG @ 8.5'   76.5'

4 SEGMENTS WIDE X 17 LONG   68 SEGMENTS
181' X 92'
16,652 SQ. FT.

ACCESS AISLE — 12'

68'

8 SEGMENTS LONG @ 8.5'   68'

4 SEGMENTS WIDE X 17 LONG

ACCESS AISLE — 12'

181' LONG (ROUNDED)

HOW TO CONFIGURE AND EQUIP YOUR WAREHOUSE

AREA DATA FOR DIFFERENT CONFIGURATIONS — DATAFORM #2

THIS FORM IS PROVIDED FOR, AND LIMITED TO, THE SOLE USE OF THE PURCHASER OF THE MANUAL "HOW TO CONFIGURE AND EQUIP YOUR WAREHOUSE"

SET # 2 DF129

ALTERNATE CONFIGURATIONS OF LAYOUT WIDTHS AND LENGTHS.

NOTE: SKETCHES WILL HELP DETERMINE THE NUMBER OF ACCCESS AISLES WANTED.

TRIALS FROM FORM #1	INITIAL # OF SEGS.	A: W X L	ACTUAL SEGS. #	B: W X L	ACTUAL SEGS. #	C: W X L	ACTUAL SEGS. #
#1		X		X		X	
#2	68	4 x 17	68	X		X	
#3		X		X		X	
#4		X		X		X	

* TOTAL AREA ÷ ACTUAL # OF SEGMENTS

SEGMENTS — REF. TRIAL # **2 A**

CROSS AISLE WIDTH	DOWN AISLE LENGTH	AREA DIMENSIONS	AREA (SQ.FT.)	ACTUAL # OF SEGS.	SEGMENT AREA INCL. ACCESS AISLES. SQ. FT.	FLOOR SLOTS PER SEG.	AREA PER FLOOR SLOT SQ.FT.	AREA PER EACH SLOT @ 4 LEVELS	AREA PER EACH SLOT @ 5 LEVELS	AREA PER EACH SLOT @ 6 LEVELS	AREA PER EACH SLOT @ 7 LEVELS
4		X 23 = 92 FT	13,340	68	245	6	41	10.3	8.2	6.8	5.9
	17	X 8.5 = 145 FT									

ACCESS AISLE AREA FROM SKETCH: 3 x 12 x 92 = 3312

TOTAL AREA IS: 16,652 SQ. FT.

ACCESS AISLES ARE: 25 % ADD-ON AND 20 % OF TOTAL AREA

REVISED LENGTH: 145 + 36 = 181' (ACCESS AISLES, 3x12)

OVERALL DIMENSIONS: WIDTH: 92' LENGTH: 181'

---

* TOTAL AREA ÷ ACTUAL # OF SEGMENTS

SEGMENTS — REF. TRIAL #

CROSS AISLE WIDTH	DOWN AISLE LENGTH	AREA DIMENSIONS	AREA (SQ.FT.)	ACTUAL # OF SEGS.	SEGMENT AREA INCL. ACCESS AISLES. SQ. FT.	FLOOR SLOTS PER SEG.	AREA PER FLOOR SLOT SQ.FT.	AREA PER EACH SLOT @ LEVELS	AREA PER EACH SLOT @ LEVELS	AREA PER EACH SLOT @ LEVELS	AREA PER EACH SLOT @ LEVELS
		X ___ = ___ FT									
		X ___ = ___ FT									

ACCESS AISLE AREA FROM SKETCH: ___ X ___ X ___

TOTAL AREA IS: ___ SQ. FT.

ACCESS AISLES ARE: ___ % ADD-ON AND ___ % OF TOTAL AREA

REVISED LENGTH: ___ + ___ = ___ (___)

OVERALL DIMENSIONS: WIDTH: ___ LENGTH: ___

2 USES OF STORAGE SEGMENTS AND A DATA FORM

EXAMPLES OF THE USE OF DATAFORMS #1 AND #2

EXAMPLE SET THREE

In example set three the segment has been changed to have the pallets stored with a 40" depth and a 48" width, with a 66" aisle. This narrower aisle assumes the use of a very narrow aisle forklift and, probably, a high level order picking truck. Using a pallet depth of 40" is very common with this type of system, allowing the picker easier, safer and faster picking.

The starting point remains as a need for 2000 slots, with four levels of storage and the configuration of 5 segments wide x 25 segments long, with 125 segments, as used in example 1A. This will allow some comparisons with that previous layout.

The area needed is considerably reduced while most other data is identical. However, as a reminder that this equipment may need wider access aisles they have been arbitrarily increased to 13'. Also note that each row of racks is longer because the segment length has increased from 8.5' to 9.9'.

This new segment is shown with detailed dimensions and then with only the needed outside dimensions.

The first drawing is narrow and long and has a third access aisle inserted for the use of picking equipment. Very Narrow Aisle systems may not require or want this extra aisle; especially if only full unit loads are in the system, without case picking.

However two more sketches are added, each wide and short. These may apply for smaller VNA equipment and the necessity of short rows. They will again show, on DataForm #2, space comparisons for differing layout configurations and heights.

DATAFORM EXAMPLE: SET #3

DATAFORM #1

THIS FORM IS PROVIDED FOR, AND LIMITED TO, THE SOLE USE OF THE PURCHASER OF THE MANUAL
"HOW TO CONFIGURE AND EQUIP YOUR WAREHOUSE"

DF128

PANEL ONE — INITIAL INPUT

- AREA: TBD
- FLOOR SLOTS / SEGMENT: 4
- PICK FACES WANTED: TBD
- SLOTS WANTED: 2000
- TOTAL SLOTS / SEGMENT: 16
- AISLE FACES WANTED: TBD
- # OF STORAGE LEVELS: 4
- SEGMENTS NEEDED: TBD
- RESERVE SLOTS WANTED: TBD

AREA ÷ SQ. FT. PER SEG. = SEGMENTS

PANEL TWO — ALTERNATE STORAGE LEVELS ("STACK HEIGHTS")

# OF STORAGE LEVELS	4	5	6	
# OF FLOOR SLOTS	4	4	4	
SLOTS PER SEGMENT	16	20	24	
SEGS. FOR 2000 SLOTS	125	100	84	
REVISED TOTAL SLOTS	2000	2000	2016	

PANEL THREE

	PER SEG.	TOTAL	PER SEG.	TOTAL	PER SEG.	TOTAL	PER SEG.	TOTAL
AISLE FACES	16	2000	20	2000	24	2016		
PICK FACES @ 2 HIGH	8	1000	8	800	8	672		
AISLE FACE RESERVES	8	1000	12	1200	16	1344		
REAR RESERVES	0	0	0	0	0	0		
TOTAL RESERVES		1000		1200		1344		
PICK FACES @ 3 HIGH	12	1500	12	1200	12	1008		
AISLE FACE RESERVES	4	500	8	800	12	1008		
REAR RESERVES	0	0	0	0	0	0		
TOTAL RESERVES		500		800		1008		
PICK FACES @ 4 HIGH	16	2000	16	1600	16	1344		
AISLE FACE RESERVES	0	0	4	400	8	672		
REAR RESERVES	0	0	0	0	0	0		
TOTAL RESERVES		0		400		672		

PANEL FOUR — ALTERNATE CONFIGURATIONS OF LAYOUT WIDTHS AND LENGTHS.

TRIAL LAYOUTS	INITIAL # OF SEGS.	A: W X L	A ACTUAL SEGS. #	B: W X L	B ACTUAL SEGS. #	C: W X L	C ACTUAL SEGS. #
#1	125	5 x 25	125	14 x 9	126	8 x 16	128
#2	100	10 x 10	100	6 x 17	102	X	
#3	84	12 x 7	84	6 x 14	84	7 x 12	84
#4		X		X		X	

2 USES OF STORAGE SEGMENTS AND A DATA FORM

EXAMPLE SET THREE

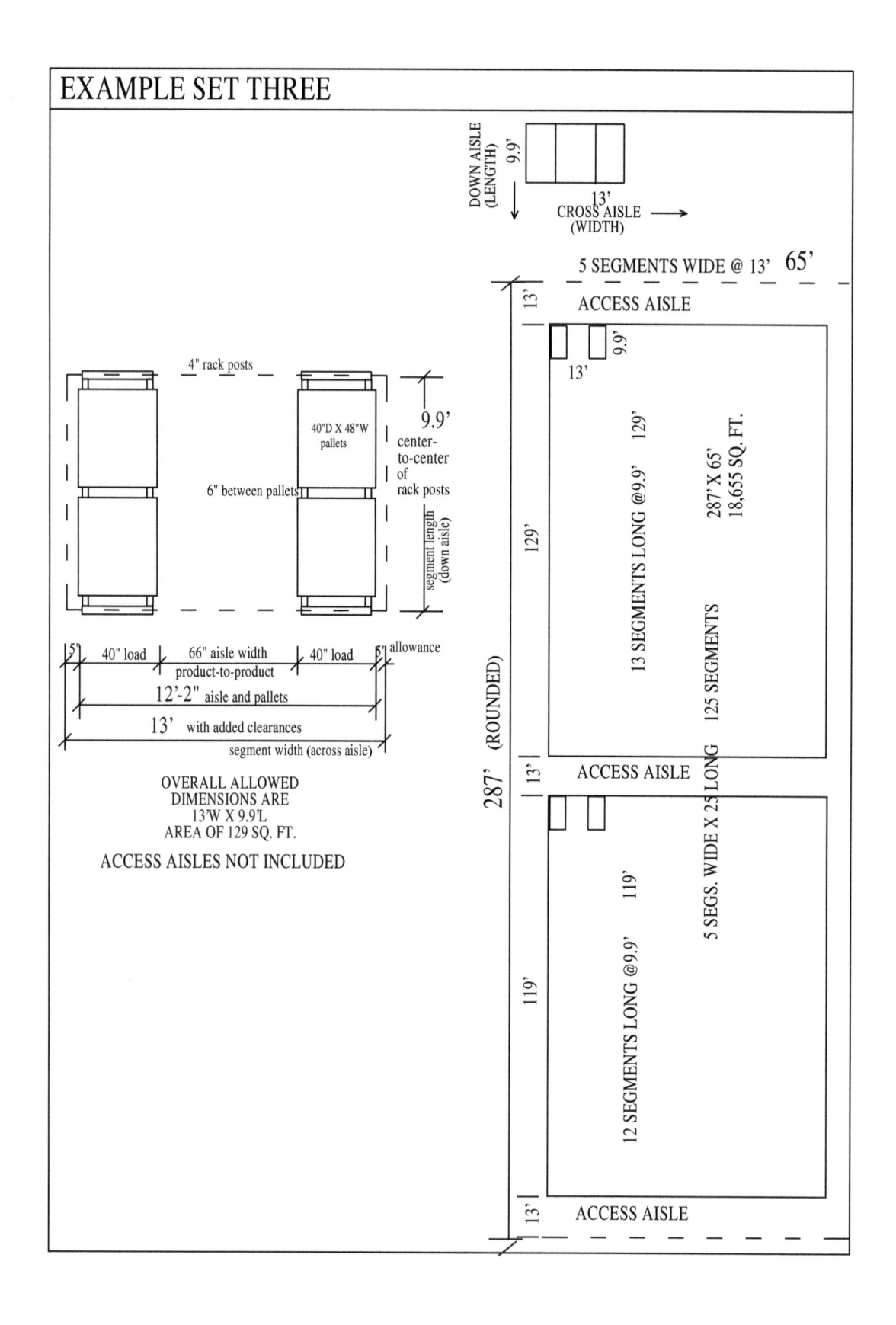

DOWN AISLE (LENGTH) 9.9'
CROSS AISLE (WIDTH) 13'

4" rack posts

40"D X 48"W pallets

6" between pallets

9.9' center-to-center of rack posts

segment length (down aisle)

5' | 40" load | 66" aisle width product-to-product | 40" load | 5" allowance

12'-2" aisle and pallets

13' with added clearances

segment width (across aisle)

OVERALL ALLOWED DIMENSIONS ARE 13'W X 9.9'L AREA OF 129 SQ. FT.

ACCESS AISLES NOT INCLUDED

5 SEGMENTS WIDE @ 13' — 65'

13' ACCESS AISLE

9.9'

13'

129'

13 SEGMENTS LONG @ 9.9' — 129'

287' X 65'
18,655 SQ. FT.

125 SEGMENTS

287' (ROUNDED)

13' ACCESS AISLE

119'

12 SEGMENTS LONG @ 9.9' — 119'

5 SEGS. WIDE X 25 LONG

13' ACCESS AISLE

HOW TO CONFIGURE AND EQUIP YOUR WAREHOUSE

AREA DATA FOR DIFFERENT CONFIGURATIONS — DATAFORM #2

THIS FORM IS PROVIDED FOR, AND LIMITED TO, THE SOLE USE OF THE PURCHASER OF THE MANUAL "HOW TO CONFIGURE AND EQUIP YOUR WAREHOUSE"

SET #3 DF129

ALTERNATE CONFIGURATIONS OF LAYOUT WIDTHS AND LENGTHS.

NOTE: SKETCHES WILL HELP DETERMINE THE NUMBER OF ACCCESS AISLES WANTED.

TRIALS FROM FORM #1	INITIAL # OF SEGS.	A (W x L)	ACTUAL SEGS. #	B (W x L)	ACTUAL SEGS. #	C (W x L)	ACTUAL SEGS. #
#1	125	5 x 25	125	14 x 9	126	X	
#2		X		X		X	
#3		X		X		X	
#4		X		X		X	

---

* TOTAL AREA ÷ ACTUAL # OF SEGMENTS

REF. TRIAL # 1 A

USE "STACK HEIGHT" CHARTS

SEGMENTS (CROSS AISLE WIDTH / DOWN AISLE LENGTH)	AREA DIMENSIONS	AREA (SQ.FT.)	ACTUAL # OF SEGS.	SEGMENT AREA INCL. ACCESS AISLES. SQ.FT.	FLOOR SLOTS PER SEG.	AREA PER FLOOR SLOT SQ.FT.	AREA PER EACH SLOT @ 4 LEVELS	AREA PER EACH SLOT @ 5 LEVELS	AREA PER EACH SLOT @ 6 LEVELS	AREA PER EACH SLOT @ 7 LEVELS
5 / —	x 13 = 65 FT	16,120	125	150	4	38	9.5	7.6	6.4	5.4
— / 25	x 9.9 = 248 FT									

ACCESS AISLE AREA FROM SKETCH
3 x 13 x 65 = 2535

TOTAL AREA IS: 18,655 SQ.FT.

ACCESS AISLES ARE: 16 % ADD-ON
AND 14 % OF TOTAL AREA

REVISED LENGTH: 248 + 39 (ACCESS AISLES) = 287'
(3 x 13)

OVERALL DIMENSIONS:
WIDTH: 65'   LENGTH: 287'

---

* TOTAL AREA ÷ ACTUAL # OF SEGMENTS

REF. TRIAL # 1 B

USE "STACK HEIGHT" CHARTS

SEGMENTS (CROSS AISLE WIDTH / DOWN AISLE LENGTH)	AREA DIMENSIONS	AREA (SQ.FT.)	ACTUAL # OF SEGS.	SEGMENT AREA INCL. ACCESS AISLES. SQ.FT.	FLOOR SLOTS PER SEG.	AREA PER FLOOR SLOT SQ.FT.	AREA PER EACH SLOT @ 4 LEVELS	AREA PER EACH SLOT @ 5 LEVELS	AREA PER EACH SLOT @ 6 LEVELS	AREA PER EACH SLOT @ 7 LEVELS
14 / —	x 13 = 182 FT	16,198	126	166	4	42	10.5	8.4	7	6
— / 9	x 9.9 = 89 FT									

ACCESS AISLE AREA FROM SKETCH
2 x 13 x 182 = 4732

TOTAL AREA IS: 20,930 SQ.FT.

ACCESS AISLES ARE: 29 % ADD-ON
AND 23 % OF TOTAL AREA

REVISED LENGTH: 89 + 26 (ACCESS AISLES) = 115'
(2 x 13)

OVERALL DIMENSIONS:
WIDTH: 182'   LENGTH: 115'

EXAMPLE SET THREE

Legend:
- 13' CROSS AISLE (WIDTH)
- 9.9' DOWN AISLE (LENGTH)

Left Layout

115' OAL
13' | 9 SEGMENTS LONG @ 9.9' = 89' | 13'

13' cross aisle
9.9' down aisle

14 SEGS. WIDE X 9 LONG   126 SEGMENTS
14 SEGS. @ 13'   182' WIDE
115' X 182'
20,930 SQ. FT.

ACCESS AISLE (both sides)

Right Layout

96' OAL
13' | 7 SEGMENTS LONG @ 9.9' = 70' | 13'

13' cross aisle
9.9' down aisle

12 SEGS. WIDE X 7 LONG   84 SEGMENTS
12 SEGS. @ 13'   156' WIDE
96' X 156'
14,976 SQ. FT.

ACCESS AISLE (both sides)

HOW TO CONFIGURE AND EQUIP YOUR WAREHOUSE

AREA DATA FOR DIFFERENT CONFIGURATIONS — DATAFORM #2

THIS FORM IS PROVIDED FOR, AND LIMITED TO, THE SOLE USE OF THE PURCHASER OF THE MANUAL
"HOW TO CONFIGURE AND EQUIP YOUR WAREHOUSE"

SET #3 DF129

ALTERNATE CONFIGURATIONS OF LAYOUT WIDTHS AND LENGTHS.

NOTE: SKETCHES WILL HELP DETERMINE THE NUMBER OF ACCCESS AISLES WANTED.

TRIALS FROM FORM #1	INITIAL # OF SEGS.	A — W X L	ACTUAL SEGS. #	B — W X L	ACTUAL SEGS. #	C — W X L	ACTUAL SEGS. #
#1		X		X		X	
#2		X		X		X	
#3	84	12 X 7	84	6 X 14	84	X	
#4		X		X		X	

REF. TRIAL # 3 A

* TOTAL AREA ÷ ACTUAL # OF SEGMENTS

USE "STACK HEIGHT" CHARTS

SEGMENTS		AREA DIMENSIONS	AREA (SQ.FT.)	ACTUAL # OF SEGS.	SEGMENT AREA INCL. ACCESS AISLES. SQ. FT.	FLOOR SLOTS PER SEG.	AREA PER FLOOR SLOT SQ. FT.	AREA PER EACH SLOT @ 4 LEVELS	AREA PER EACH SLOT @ 5 LEVELS	AREA PER EACH SLOT @ 6 LEVELS	AREA PER EACH SLOT @ 7 LEVELS
CROSS AISLE WIDTH	DOWN AISLE LENGTH										
12	X	X 13 = 156 FT	10,920								
X	7	7 X 9.9 = 70 FT		84	179	4	45	11.3	9	7.5	6.5

ACCESS AISLE AREA FROM SKETCH
2 X 13 X 156 = 4056

ACCESS AISLES ARE: 37 % ADD-ON

TOTAL AREA IS: 14,976 SQ. FT.

AND 27 % OF TOTAL AREA

REVISED LENGTH: 70 + 26 (ACCESS AISLES) = 96'
(2 X 13)

OVERALL DIMENSIONS:
WIDTH: 156' LENGTH: 96'

NO DRAWING!

REF. TRIAL # 3 B

* TOTAL AREA ÷ ACTUAL # OF SEGMENTS

USE "STACK HEIGHT" CHARTS

SEGMENTS		AREA DIMENSIONS	AREA (SQ.FT.)	ACTUAL # OF SEGS.	SEGMENT AREA INCL. ACCESS AISLES. SQ. FT.	FLOOR SLOTS PER SEG.	AREA PER FLOOR SLOT SQ. FT.	@ 4 LEVELS	@ 5 LEVELS	@ 6 LEVELS	@ 7 LEVELS
CROSS AISLE WIDTH	DOWN AISLE LENGTH										
6	X	X 13 = 78 FT	10,842								
X	14	14 X 9.9 = 139 FT		84	153	4	38	9.5	7.6	6.3	5.4

ACCESS AISLE AREA FROM SKETCH
2 X 13 X 78 = 2028

ACCESS AISLES ARE: 19 % ADD-ON

TOTAL AREA IS: 12,870 SQ. FT.

AND 16 % OF TOTAL AREA

REVISED LENGTH: 139 + 26 (ACCESS AISLES) = 165
(2 X 13)

OVERALL DIMENSIONS:
WIDTH: 78' LENGTH: 165'

---

2 *USES OF STORAGE SEGMENTS AND A DATA FORM*

EXAMPLES OF THE USE OF DATAFORMS #1 and #2

EXAMPLE SET FOUR

In example set four, the same segment as in set 3 has been used. However, a major change is that an area has been specified rather than the previous examples with a specified number of storage slots. The area of approximately 23,700 sq. ft., as developed in the first example set has been chosen; again for ease of comparisons.

The first thing needed under the method about to be described is the area used per segment, including an allowance for access aisles.*

This trial is started by using the segment area (129 sq. ft.) and adding a **guestimated** add-on percentage for access aisles. The 25% add-on brings the segment area from 129 to 161 sq. ft. Dividing 23,700 by 161 gives an estimated 148 segments.

Trying a 10 wide x 15 long layout results in 150 segments in 22,750 sq. ft. This could be accepted or another try could be 10 x 16; 160 segments in 24,050 sq. ft.

An 8 wide x 20 long layout has also been added.

Try any other layouts acceptable and use the DataForms as wanted.

*The guestimate for access aisles merely provided a starting point. If the actual length and width dimensions of the layout without access aisles are known they can be used to get access aisle area.

EXAMPLE SET FOUR

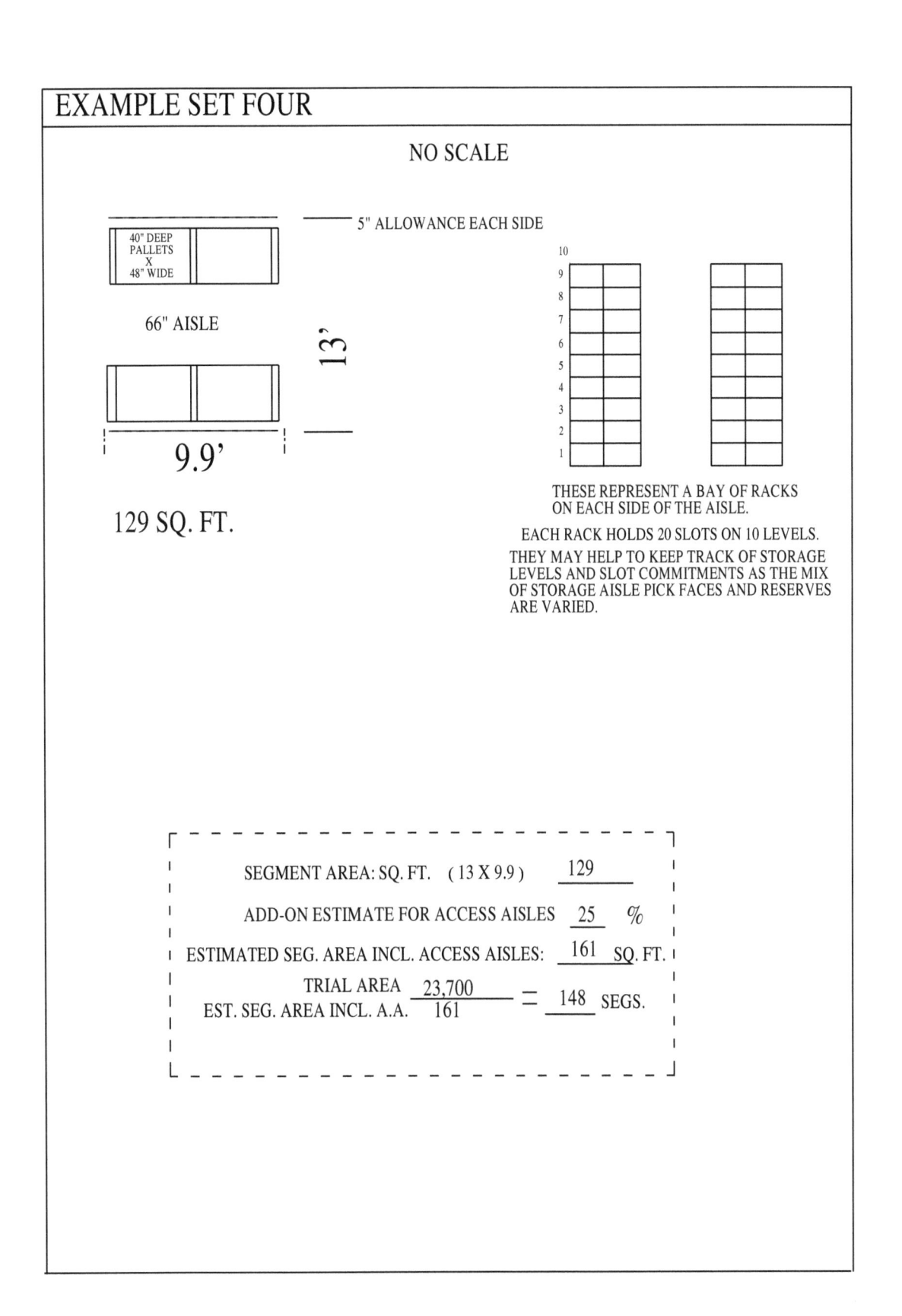

NO SCALE

40" DEEP PALLETS X 48" WIDE

5" ALLOWANCE EACH SIDE

66" AISLE

13'

9.9'

129 SQ. FT.

THESE REPRESENT A BAY OF RACKS ON EACH SIDE OF THE AISLE.

EACH RACK HOLDS 20 SLOTS ON 10 LEVELS. THEY MAY HELP TO KEEP TRACK OF STORAGE LEVELS AND SLOT COMMITMENTS AS THE MIX OF STORAGE AISLE PICK FACES AND RESERVES ARE VARIED.

104

SEGMENT AREA: SQ. FT. (13 X 9.9)   129

ADD-ON ESTIMATE FOR ACCESS AISLES   25 %

ESTIMATED SEG. AREA INCL. ACCESS AISLES: 161 SQ. FT.

$$\frac{\text{TRIAL AREA}}{\text{EST. SEG. AREA INCL. A.A.}} \frac{23{,}700}{161} = 148 \text{ SEGS.}$$

2 *USES OF STORAGE SEGMENTS AND A DATA FORM*

DATAFORM EXAMPLE: SET #4

DATAFORM #1

THIS FORM IS PROVIDED FOR, AND LIMITED TO, THE SOLE USE OF THE PURCHASER OF THE MANUAL
" HOW TO CONFIGURE AND EQUIP YOUR WAREHOUSE"

DF128

PANEL ONE — INITIAL INPUT

- AREA: _____
- FLOOR SLOTS / SEGMENT: 4
- PICK FACES WANTED: _____
- SLOTS WANTED: TBD
- TOTAL SLOTS / SEGMENT: 16
- AISLE FACES WANTED: _____
- # OF STORAGE LEVELS: 4
- SEGMENTS NEEDED: 7
- RESERVE SLOTS WANTED: _____

23,700 ÷ 161 = 148
AREA ÷ SQ. FT. PER SEG. = SEGMENTS

PANEL TWO — ALTERNATE STORAGE LEVELS ("STACK HEIGHTS")

# OF STORAGE LEVELS	4	4		
# OF FLOOR SLOTS	4	4		
SLOTS PER SEGMENT	16	16		
SEGS. FOR ___ SLOTS	148 × 16	150 × 16		
REVISED TOTAL SLOTS	2368	2400		

PANEL THREE

	PER SEG.	TOTAL	PER SEG.	TOTAL	PER SEG.	TOTAL	PER SEG.	TOTAL
AISLE FACES	16	2368	16	2400				
PICK FACES @ 2 HIGH	8	1184	8	1200				
AISLE FACE RESERVES	8	1184	8	1200				
REAR RESERVES	0	0	0	0				
TOTAL RESERVES		1184		1200				
PICK FACES @ 3 HIGH	12	1776	12	1800				
AISLE FACE RESERVES	4	592	4	600				
REAR RESERVES	0	0	0	0				
TOTAL RESERVES		592		600				
PICK FACES @ 4 HIGH	16	2368	16	2400				
AISLE FACE RESERVES	0	0	0	0				
REAR RESERVES	0	0	0	0				
TOTAL RESERVES		0		0				

PANEL FOUR — ALTERNATE CONFIGURATIONS OF LAYOUT WIDTHS AND LENGTHS

TRIAL LAYOUTS	INITIAL # OF SEGS.	A W × L	ACTUAL SEGS. #	B W × L	ACTUAL SEGS. #	C W × L	ACTUAL SEGS. #
#1	148	10 × 15	150	10 × 16	160	8 × 20	160
#2		×		×		×	
#3		×		×		×	
#4		×		×		×	

EXAMPLE SET FOUR

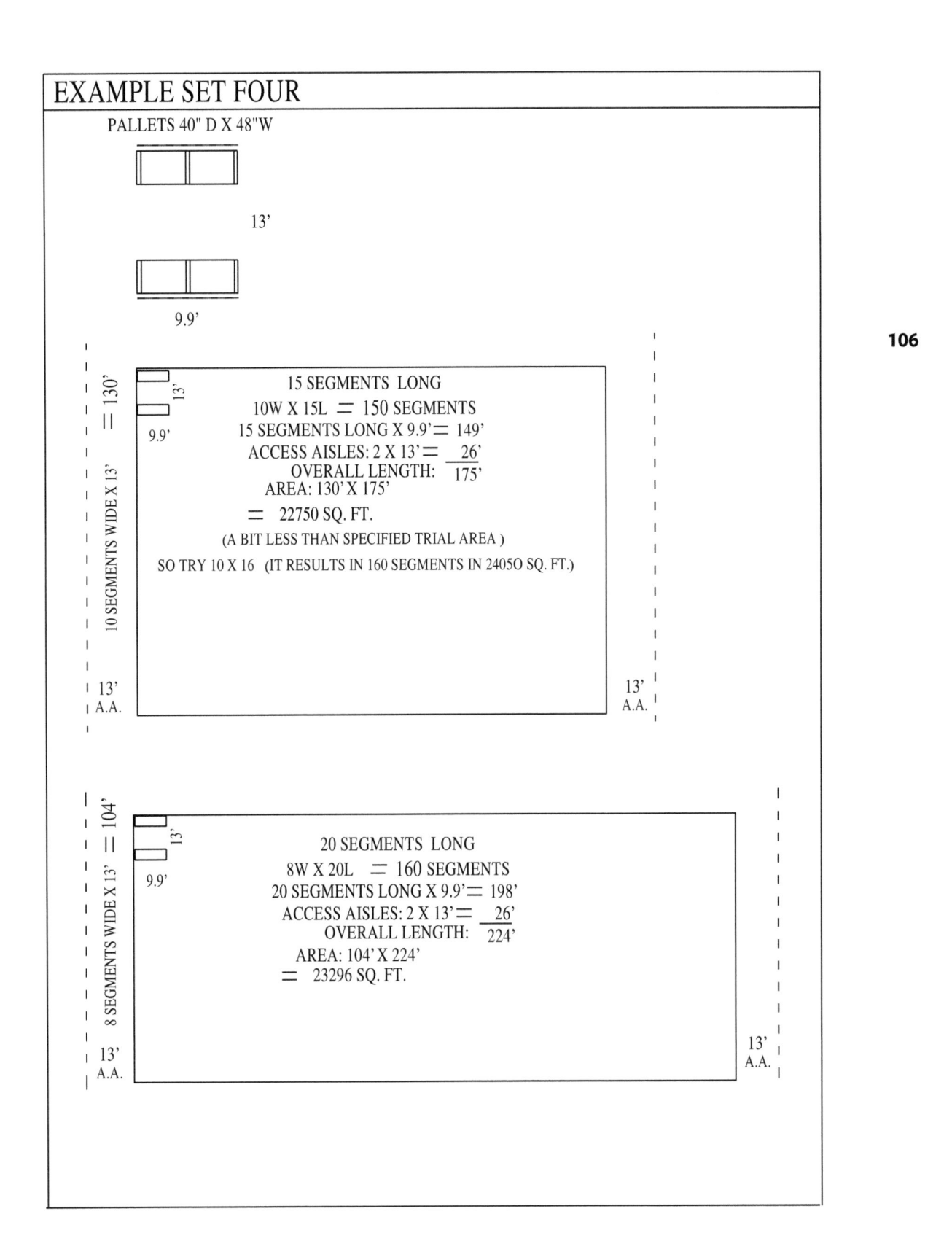

PALLETS 40" D X 48"W

13'

9.9'

First layout (10W x 15L):

10 SEGMENTS WIDE X 13' = 130'

13'
9.9'

15 SEGMENTS LONG
10W X 15L = 150 SEGMENTS
15 SEGMENTS LONG X 9.9' = 149'
ACCESS AISLES: 2 X 13' = 26'
OVERALL LENGTH: 175'
AREA: 130' X 175'
= 22750 SQ. FT.
(A BIT LESS THAN SPECIFIED TRIAL AREA)
SO TRY 10 X 16 (IT RESULTS IN 160 SEGMENTS IN 24050 SQ. FT.)

13' A.A.   13' A.A.

Second layout (8W x 20L):

8 SEGMENTS WIDE X 13' = 104'

13'
9.9'

20 SEGMENTS LONG
8W X 20L = 160 SEGMENTS
20 SEGMENTS LONG X 9.9' = 198'
ACCESS AISLES: 2 X 13' = 26'
OVERALL LENGTH: 224'
AREA: 104' X 224'
= 23296 SQ. FT.

13' A.A.   13' A.A.

2 *USES OF STORAGE SEGMENTS AND A DATA FORM*

AREA DATA FOR DIFFERENT CONFIGURATIONS — DATAFORM #2

THIS FORM IS PROVIDED FOR, AND LIMITED TO, THE SOLE USE OF THE PURCHASER OF THE MANUAL "HOW TO CONFIGURE AND EQUIP YOUR WAREHOUSE"

SET 4 DF129

ALTERNATE CONFIGURATIONS OF LAYOUT WIDTHS AND LENGTHS.

NOTE: SKETCHES WILL HELP DETERMINE THE NUMBER OF ACCCESS AISLES WANTED.

TRIALS FROM FORM #1	INITIAL # OF SEGS.	A — W X L	ACTUAL SEGS. #	B — W X L	ACTUAL SEGS. #	C — W X L	ACTUAL SEGS. #
#1	148	10 x 15	150	10 x 16	160	8 x 20	160
#2		X		X		X	
#3		X		X		X	
#4		X		X		X	

---

* TOTAL AREA ÷ ACTUAL # OF SEGMENTS

REF. TRIAL # 1 A

SEGMENTS — CROSS AISLE WIDTH: 10 ; DOWN AISLE LENGTH: 15

AREA DIMENSIONS:
- 10 x 13 = 130 FT
- 15 x 9.9 = 149 FT

AREA (SQ.FT.): 19,370

ACTUAL # OF SEGS.: 150
SEGMENT AREA INCL. ACCESS AISLES SQ. FT.: 152
FLOOR SLOTS PER SEG.: 4
AREA PER FLOOR SLOT SQ. FT.: 38

USE "STACK HEIGHT" CHARTS
- AREA PER EACH SLOT @ 4 LEVELS: 9.5
- @ 5 LEVELS: 7.6
- @ 6 LEVELS: 6.4
- @ 7 LEVELS: 5.5

ACCESS AISLE AREA FROM SKETCH: 2 x 13 x 130 = 3380

ACCESS AISLES ARE: 18 % ADD-ON

TOTAL AREA IS: 22,750 SQ. FT. AND 15 % OF TOTAL AREA

REVISED LENGTH: 149 + 26 = 175' (2 x 13)

OVERALL DIMENSIONS: WIDTH: 130' LENGTH: 175'

---

* TOTAL AREA ÷ ACTUAL # OF SEGMENTS

REF. TRIAL # 1 B

SEGMENTS — CROSS AISLE WIDTH: 10 ; DOWN AISLE LENGTH: 16

AREA DIMENSIONS:
- 10 x 13 = 130 FT
- 16 x 9.9 = 159 FT

AREA (SQ.FT.): 20,670

ACTUAL # OF SEGS.: 160
SEGMENT AREA INCL. ACCESS AISLES SQ. FT.: 151
FLOOR SLOTS PER SEG.: 4
AREA PER FLOOR SLOT SQ. FT.: 38

USE "STACK HEIGHT" CHARTS
- @ 4 LEVELS: 9.5
- @ 5 LEVELS: 7.6
- @ 6 LEVELS: 6.4
- @ 7 LEVELS: 5.5

ACCESS AISLE AREA FROM SKETCH: 2 x 13 x 130 = 3380

ACCESS AISLES ARE: 17 % ADD-ON

TOTAL AREA IS: 24,050 SQ. FT. AND 14 % OF TOTAL AREA

REVISED LENGTH: 159 + 26 = 185' (2 x 13)

OVERALL DIMENSIONS: WIDTH: 130' LENGTH: 185'

DATAFORM EXAMPLE: SET #4

DATAFORM #1

THIS FORM IS PROVIDED FOR, AND LIMITED TO, THE SOLE USE OF THE PURCHASER OF THE MANUAL
" HOW TO CONFIGURE AND EQUIP YOUR WAREHOUSE"

DF128

PANEL ONE — INITIAL INPUT

- AREA: 23,700
- FLOOR SLOTS / SEGMENT: 4
- PICK FACES WANTED: TBD
- SLOTS WANTED: TBD
- TOTAL SLOTS / SEGMENT: 16
- AISLE FACES WANTED: TBD
- # OF STORAGE LEVELS: 4
- SEGMENTS NEEDED: 160
- RESERVE SLOTS WANTED: TBD

AREA ÷ SQ. FT. PER SEG. = SEGMENTS

PANEL TWO — ALTERNATE STORAGE LEVELS ("STACK HEIGHTS")

# OF STORAGE LEVELS	4	5	6	7
# OF FLOOR SLOTS	4	4	4	4
SLOTS PER SEGMENT	16	20	24	28
SEGS. FOR SLOTS	160 X 16	160 X 20	160 X 24	160 X 28
REVISED TOTAL SLOTS	2560	3200	3840	4480

PANEL THREE

	PER SEG.	TOTAL	PER SEG.	TOTAL	PER SEG.	TOTAL	PER SEG.	TOTAL
AISLE FACES	16	2560	20	3200	24	3840	28	4480
PICK FACES @ 2 HIGH	8	1280	8	1280	8	1280	8	1280
AISLE FACE RESERVES	8	1280	12	1920	16	2560	20	3200
REAR RESERVES	0	0	0	0	0	0	0	0
TOTAL RESERVES		1280		1920		2560		3200
PICK FACES @ 3 HIGH	12	1920	12	1920	12	1920	12	1920
AISLE FACE RESERVES	4	640	8	1280	12	1920	16	2560
REAR RESERVES	0	0	0	0	0	0	0	0
TOTAL RESERVES		640		1280		1920		2560
PICK FACES @ 4 HIGH	16	2560	16	2560	16	2560	16	2560
AISLE FACE RESERVES	0	0	4	640	8	1280	12	1920
REAR RESERVES	0	0	0	0	0	0	0	0
TOTAL RESERVES		0		640		1280		1920

PANEL FOUR — ALTERNATE CONFIGURATIONS OF LAYOUT WIDTHS AND LENGTHS.

TRIAL LAYOUTS	INITIAL # OF SEGS.	A (W X L)	ACTUAL SEGS. #	B (W X L)	ACTUAL SEGS. #	C (W X L)	ACTUAL SEGS. #
#1	160	8 X 20	160	X		X	
#2		X		X		X	
#3		X		X		X	
#4		X		X		X	

108

2 USES OF STORAGE SEGMENTS AND A DATA FORM

AREA DATA FOR DIFFERENT CONFIGURATIONS
DATAFORM #2

THIS FORM IS PROVIDED FOR, AND LIMITED TO, THE SOLE USE OF THE PURCHASER OF THE MANUAL "HOW TO CONFIGURE AND EQUIP YOUR WAREHOUSE"

SET 4 DF129

ALTERNATE CONFIGURATIONS OF LAYOUT WIDTHS AND LENGTHS.
NOTE: SKETCHES WILL HELP DETERMINE THE NUMBER OF ACCCESS AISLES WANTED.

TRIALS FROM FORM #1	INITIAL # OF SEGS.	A (W X L)	ACTUAL SEGS. #	B (W X L)	ACTUAL SEGS. #	C (W X L)	ACTUAL SEGS. #
#1		X		X		8 X 20	160
#2		X		X		X	
#3		X		X		X	
#4		X		X		X	

REF. TRIAL # 1 C

* TOTAL AREA ÷ ACTUAL # OF SEGMENTS

USE "STACK HEIGHT" CHARTS

SEGMENTS (CROSS AISLE WIDTH / DOWN AISLE LENGTH)	AREA DIMENSIONS	AREA (SQ.FT.)	ACTUAL # OF SEGS.	SEGMENT AREA INCL. ACCESS AISLES. SQ. FT.	FLOOR SLOTS PER SEG.	AREA PER FLOOR SLOT SQ. FT.	AREA PER EACH SLOT @4 LEVELS	AREA PER EACH SLOT @5 LEVELS	AREA PER EACH SLOT @6 LEVELS	AREA PER EACH SLOT @7 LEVELS
8 / 20	X 13 = 104 FT / X 9.9 = 198 FT	20,592	160	146	4	37	9.3	7.4	6.2	5.3

ACCESS AISLE AREA FROM SKETCH: 2 X 13 X 104 = 2704

ACCESS AISLES ARE: 13 % ADD-ON

TOTAL AREA IS: 23,296 SQ. FT.

AND 12 % OF TOTAL AREA

REVISED LENGTH: 198 + 26 = 224' (2×13)

OVERALL DIMENSIONS: WIDTH: 104' LENGTH: 224'

REF. TRIAL # _____

* TOTAL AREA ÷ ACTUAL # OF SEGMENTS

SEGMENTS (CROSS AISLE WIDTH / DOWN AISLE LENGTH)	AREA DIMENSIONS	AREA (SQ.FT.)	ACTUAL # OF SEGS.	SEGMENT AREA INCL. ACCESS AISLES. SQ. FT.	FLOOR SLOTS PER SEG.	AREA PER FLOOR SLOT SQ. FT.	AREA PER EACH SLOT @ LEVELS	AREA PER EACH SLOT @ LEVELS	AREA PER EACH SLOT @ LEVELS	AREA PER EACH SLOT @ LEVELS
	X ___ = ___ FT / X ___ = ___ FT									

ACCESS AISLE AREA FROM SKETCH: ___ X ___ X ___

ACCESS AISLES ARE: ___ % ADD-ON

TOTAL AREA IS: ___ SQ. FT.

AND ___ % OF TOTAL AREA

REVISED LENGTH: ___ + ___ = ___ ( )

OVERALL DIMENSIONS: WIDTH: ___ LENGTH: ___

SECTION THREE
DOCK EQUIPMENT & PALLETS 3

RECEIVING AND SHIPPING DOCKS

For many years docks were given little thought in the overall process of designing and equipping a warehouse or distribution center. Choices of dock equipment, along with considerations of safety, were sparse. This often resulted in dangerous and inefficient locations to work.

However in the last decade or two, perhaps spurred by greater safety awareness and by the many changes in the height and width of carriers, there has been the introduction of a large selection of dock equipment.

Along with the new designs to solve new situations has come a variety of powered actuating methods, such as mechanical, hydraulic, electric and air, and also a range of automation possibilities.

So, as with so many other explanations in this book, a big question to start with is whether the answers sought after are limited by an existing building, or are they unhindered for a new facility.

This section will describe the most common types of dock, equipment with a brief description of their uses. However in many applications, advice should be sought to consider the great many potential combinations involving height differential, capacity, type of actuating mechanism, forklift grade capability, forklift grade clearance, lip design, level of automation and safety considerations.

Beginning with the approach apron in front of the dock, it should be noted if this area is flat and horizontal, or if there is a slope, because this can have an effect on the dock equipment. For instance door seals may be tapered to better match the angle of the truck surface pressing against it.

Dock bumpers, installed on the dock face, will protect the dock and soften impacts from trucks, and a drain will be useful, especially if the surface slants down toward the dock.

The servicing of carriers might be from a dock which is flush with the side of the building or there may be an outside receiving platform. The flush dock requires the carrier to line up with an open door while a receiving platform, often used for railcar activities, allows much more leeway in carrier positioning.

For simplicity each type will be referred to here as a dock.

In deciding on dockplates, dockboards and dock levelers some of the important considerations (in addition to automation potential) are: length and width, capacity, range of height differential up and down, angle of lip bend if it is not adjustable, curbs, safety features and building security.

Forklifts can run into problems if the ramp incline is too steep and the lip bend too severe. Even if they have enough power for the incline they could have insufficient underclearance and "hang up" at the crest of the board. Insufficient fork tilt can also become a problem for pallet handling. Section 7, Forklift Comparative Specifications, can be referred to for guidance in early planning.

The two most basic aids to span from the dock to carrier are the Dockplate and Dockboard.

The Dockplate is typically made of light weight metal and is manually placed where wanted. It has limited capacity and height differential (the height difference between dock and carrier) and has a predetermined bend on the front.

The Dockboard is also usually made of light metal but with a thicker plate and side curbs for greater capacity or longer spans. It may have folding stirrups so it can be handled by forklift. Dockboards can be used for trucks or for rail cars when equipped with the correct span-locking devices. Both ends may have predetermined bends, depending on usage.

Docklevelers, much larger than dockplates or dockboards, are typically fixed in place, either within a pit in the dock or as a fixture placed in front of the dock.

These are offered with a large range of sizes and capabilities, actuated by a choice of mechanical, electro-mechanical, hydraulic and air. They also offer many combinations of automation, safety features and dock accessories.

The trend has definitely been towards larger levelers, both wider and longer. But more than one dock height may be needed if the range of carrier sizes is too great. Ground level receiving may also be required.

A couple of other boards used to span to the carrier include the Edge of Dock and the Vertically Mounted leveler.

The edge of dock can be used to allow doors to be closed securely with a seal to the floor, preventing drafts, and might be used for coolers or freezers. However, being short, it can only be used for a small range of truck heights.

The vertically mounted leveler is often used on a loading platform for servicing rail cars. It can be mounted on a track and moved along the dock face to the location needed.

Many options and other dock equipment, such as door seals, dock shelters, truck restraints and control panels are available.

With all of the above (and more) choices, it seems logical to consider the dock situation very carefully with a knowledgeable source. If practical, the suppliers of the dock equipment, and the forklifts, should confirm their compatibility for the uses intended.

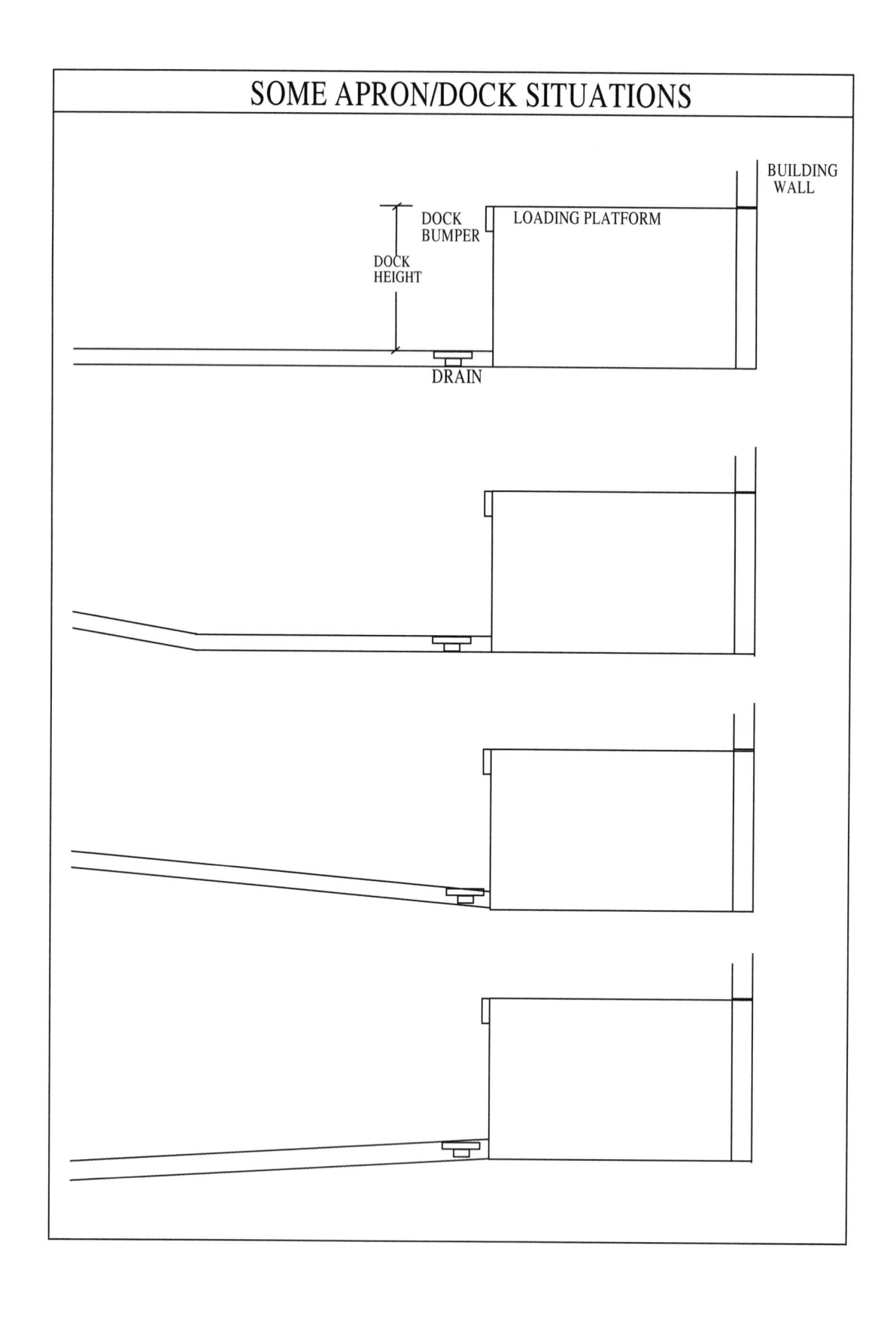

SOME APRON/DOCK SITUATIONS

HOW TO CONFIGURE AND EQUIP YOUR WAREHOUSE

SOME APRON/DOCK SITUATIONS

RAIL ACCESS

LOADING PLATFORM

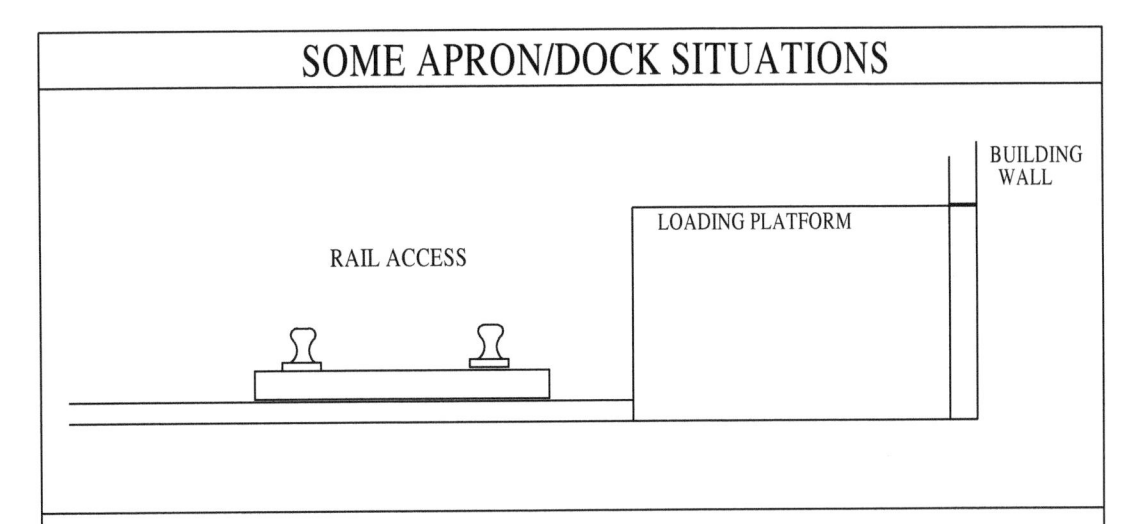

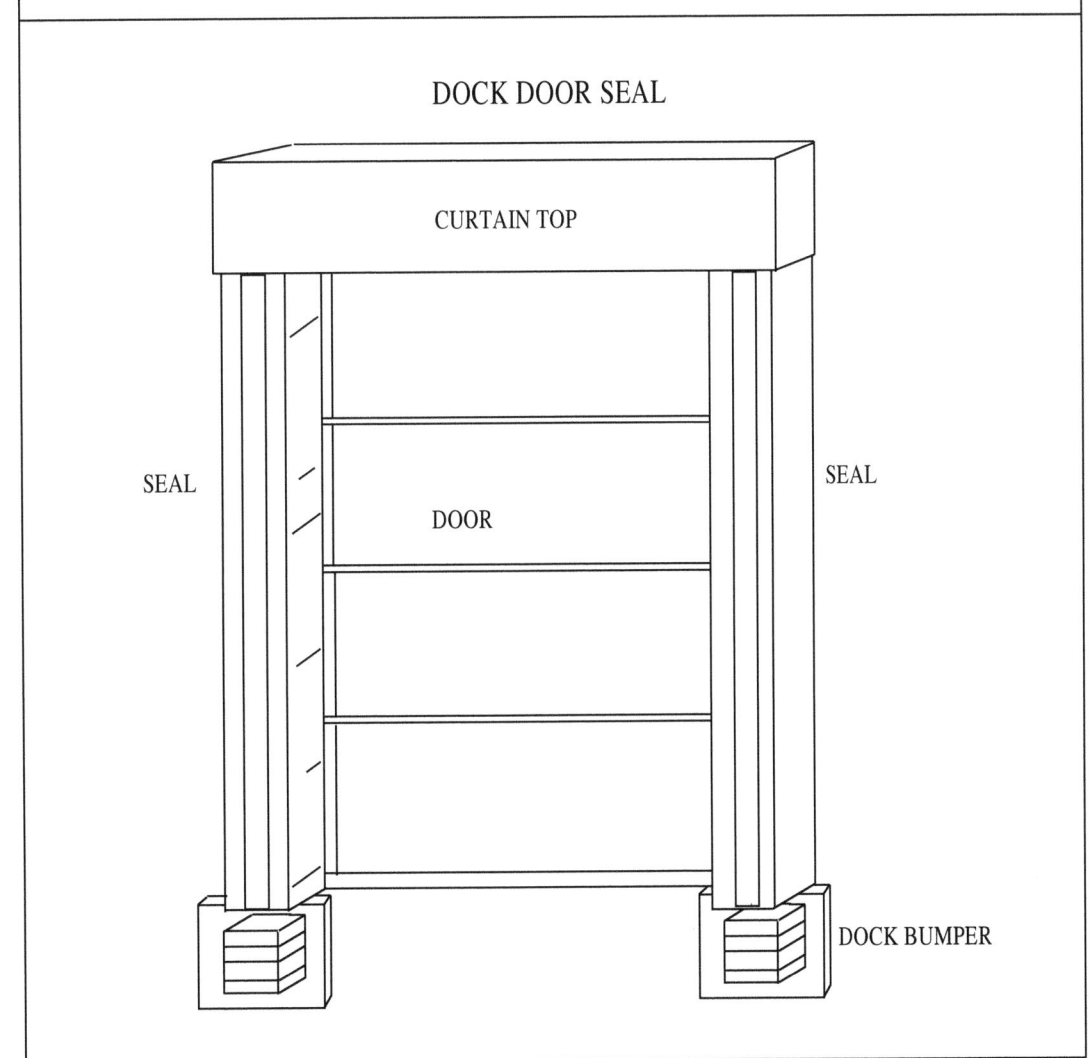

BUILDING WALL

114

DOCK DOOR SEAL

CURTAIN TOP

SEAL

DOOR

SEAL

DOCK BUMPER

3 *DOCK EQUIPMENT & PALLETS*

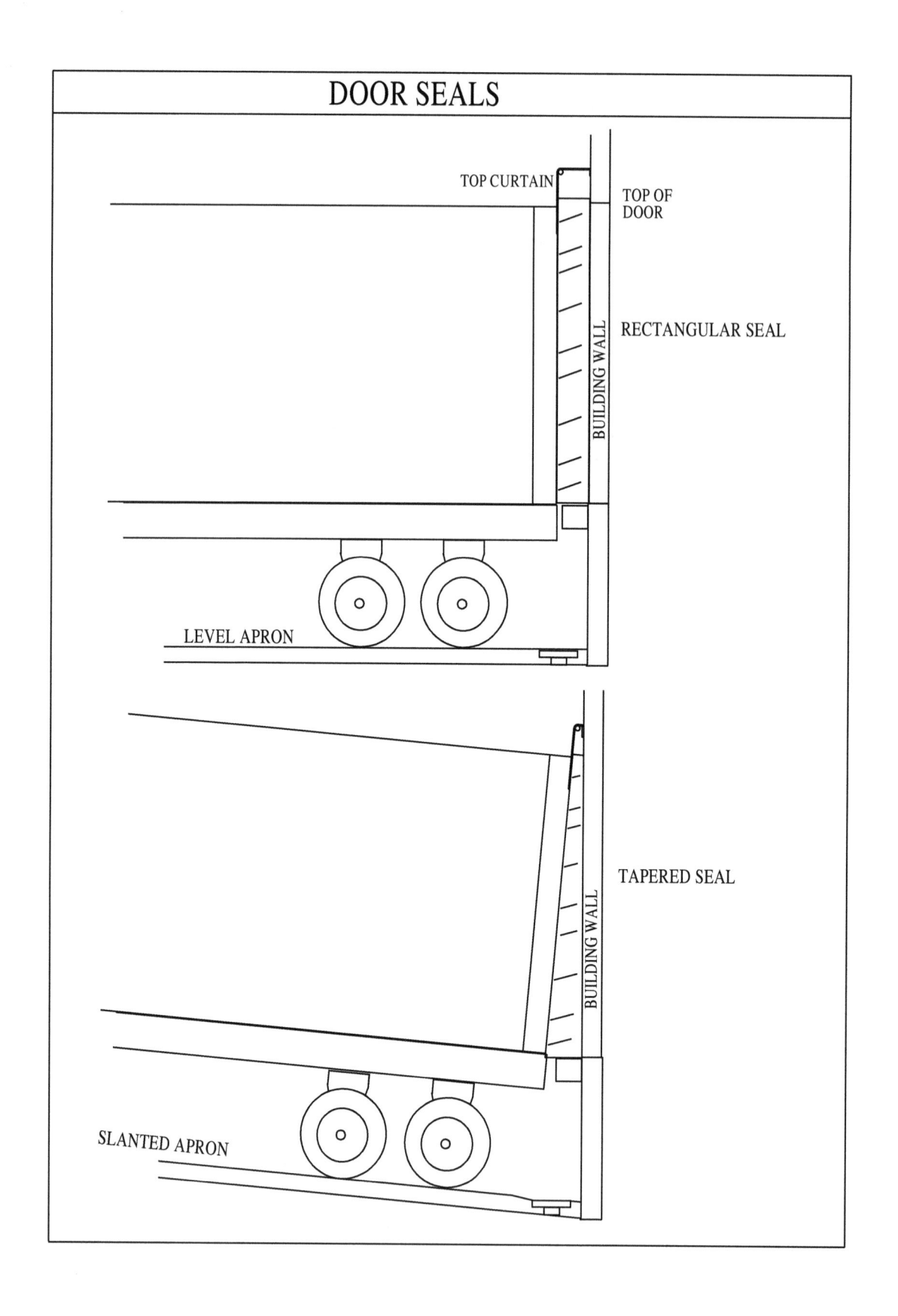

DOOR SEALS

TOP CURTAIN
TOP OF DOOR
RECTANGULAR SEAL
BUILDING WALL
LEVEL APRON

TAPERED SEAL
BUILDING WALL
SLANTED APRON

HOW TO CONFIGURE AND EQUIP YOUR WAREHOUSE

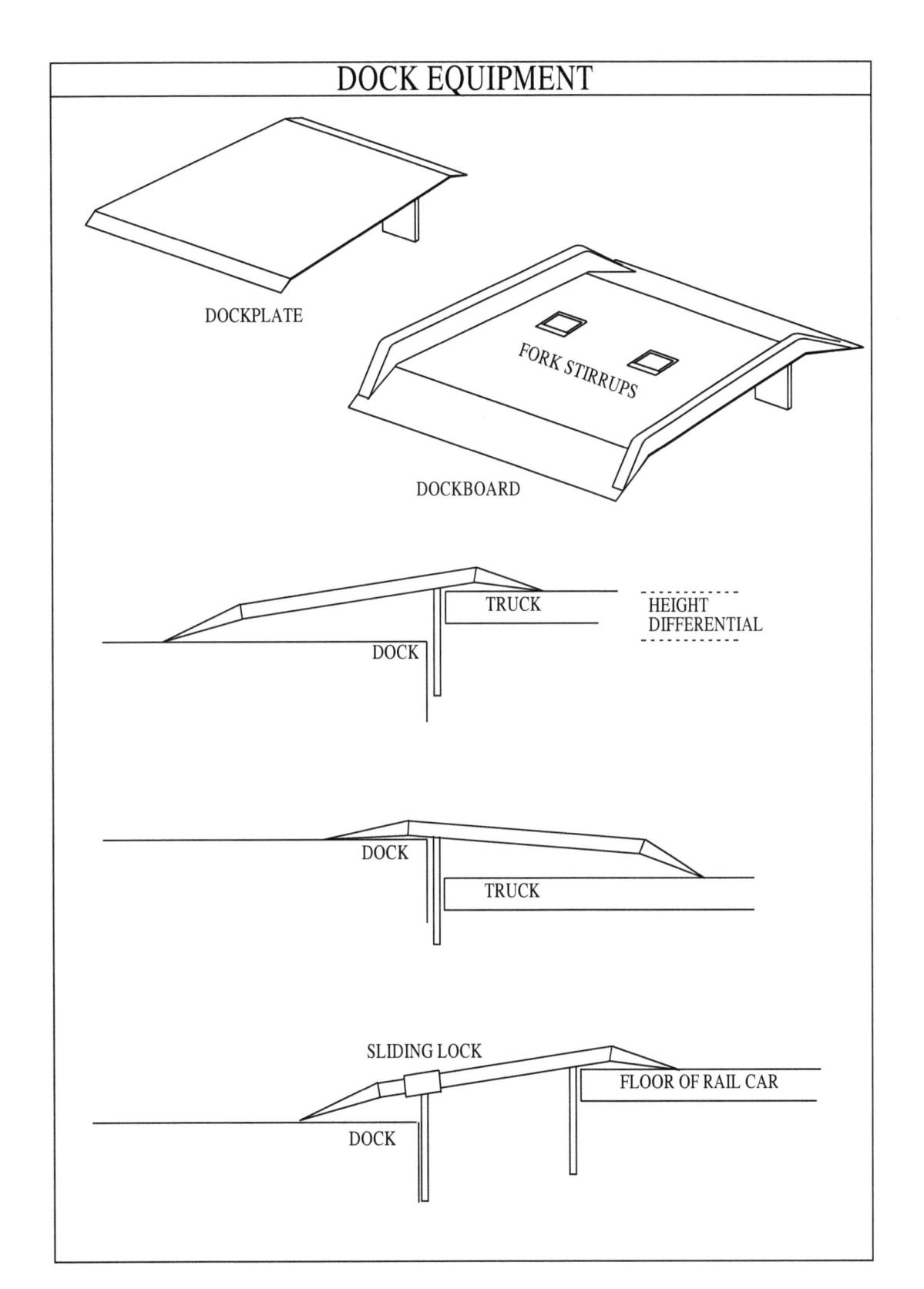

DOCK EQUIPMENT

DOCKPLATE

FORK STIRRUPS

DOCKBOARD

TRUCK

HEIGHT DIFFERENTIAL

DOCK

DOCK

TRUCK

SLIDING LOCK

FLOOR OF RAIL CAR

DOCK

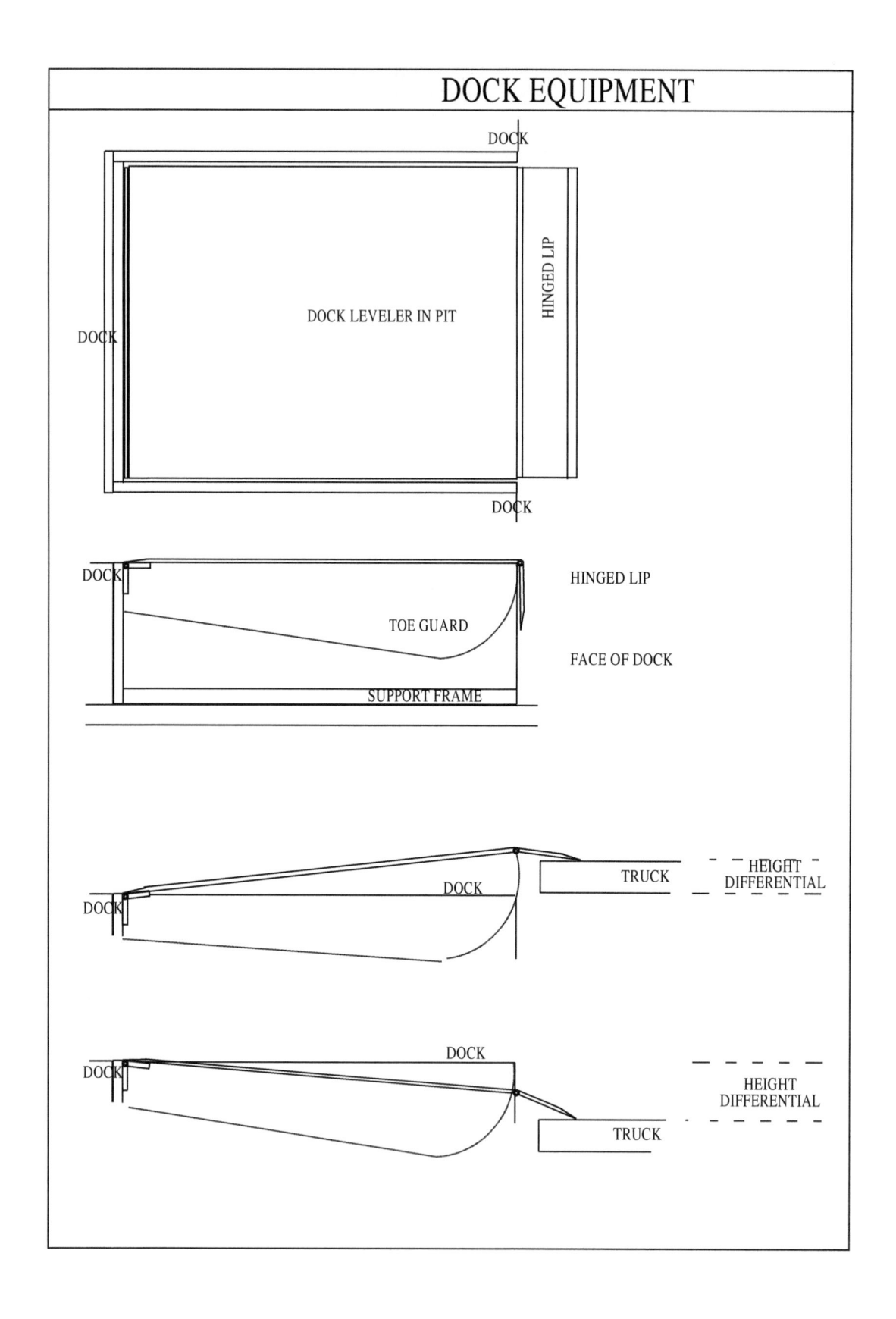

DOCK EQUIPMENT

HOW TO CONFIGURE AND EQUIP YOUR WAREHOUSE

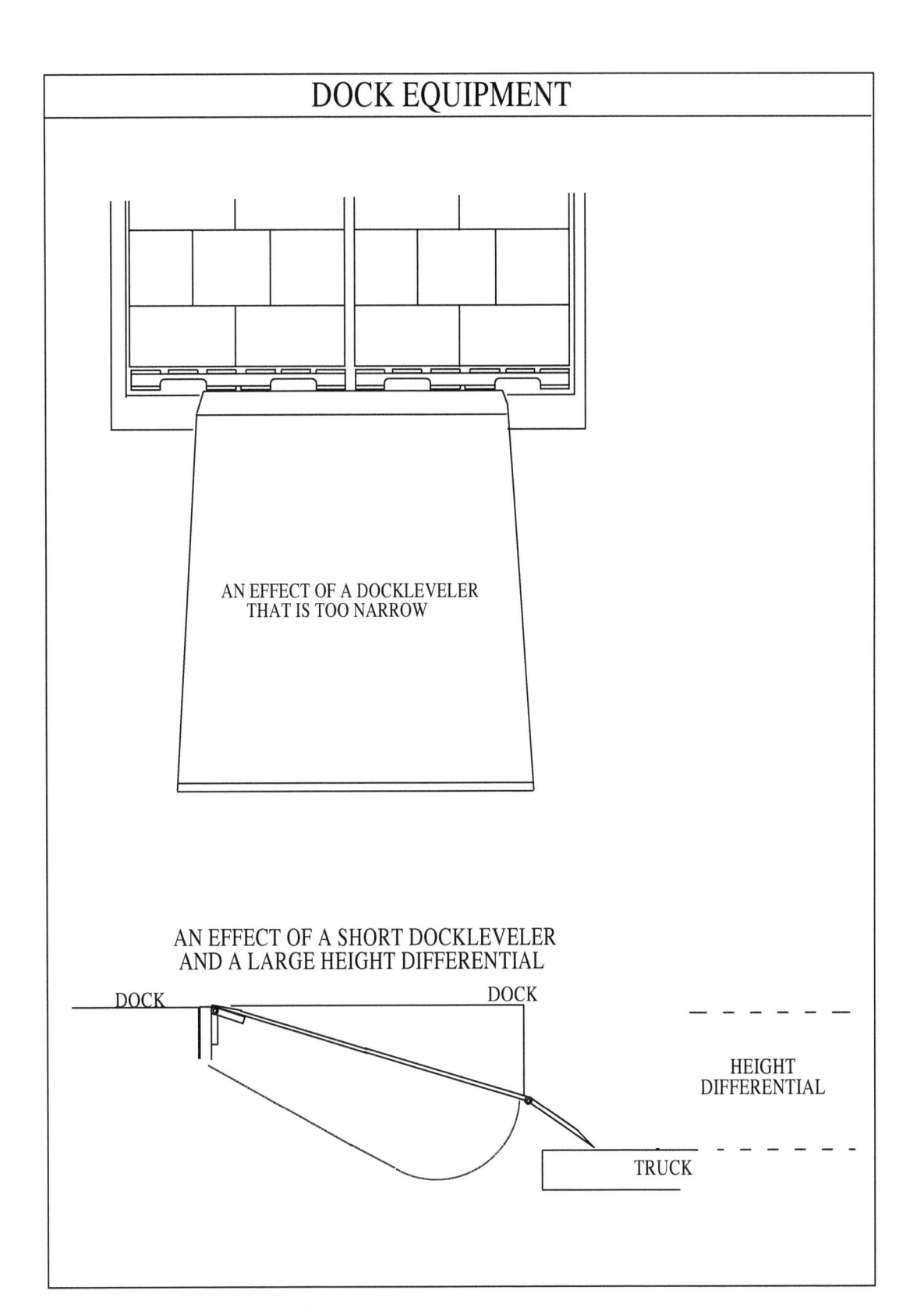

DOCK EQUIPMENT

AN EFFECT OF A DOCKLEVELER
THAT IS TOO NARROW

AN EFFECT OF A SHORT DOCKLEVELER
AND A LARGE HEIGHT DIFFERENTIAL

DOCK   DOCK

HEIGHT
DIFFERENTIAL

TRUCK

DOCK EQUIPMENT

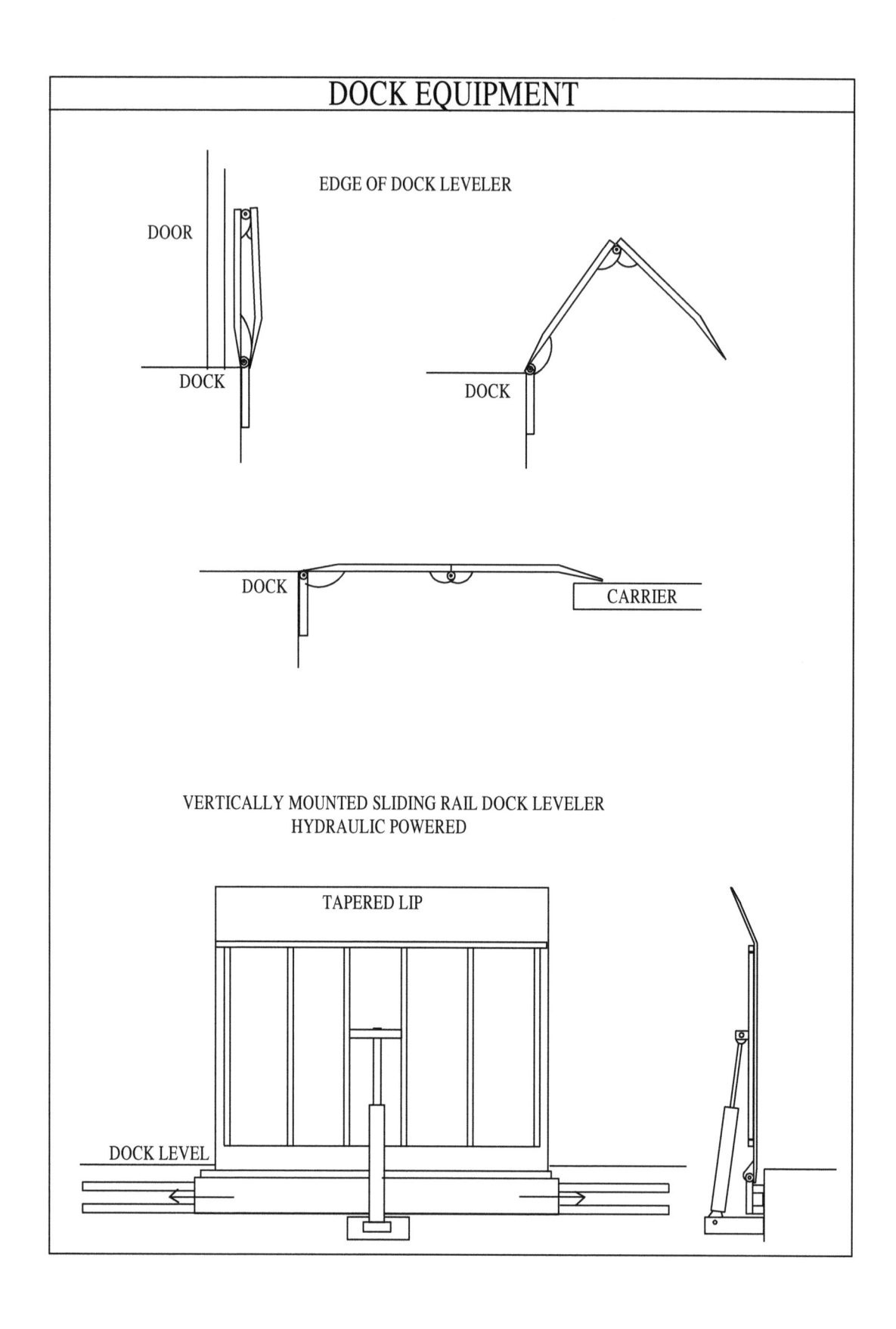

EDGE OF DOCK LEVELER

DOOR

DOCK

DOCK

DOCK

CARRIER

VERTICALLY MOUNTED SLIDING RAIL DOCK LEVELER
HYDRAULIC POWERED

TAPERED LIP

DOCK LEVEL

HOW TO CONFIGURE AND EQUIP YOUR WAREHOUSE

DOCK EQUIPMENT

SIDE RAIL

PANTOGRAPH LIFT PLATFORM
LOCATED IN FRONT OF DOCK

DOCK

SIDE RAIL

SIDE RAILS NOT SHOWN

ELEVATED TO
CARRIER HEIGHT

MOVES UP OR DOWN
TO MATCH TRUCK
AND/ OR DOCK

DOCK

DOCK

LOWERED IN PIT
TO BE FLUSH WITH
APPROACH LEVEL

3 *DOCK EQUIPMENT & PALLETS*

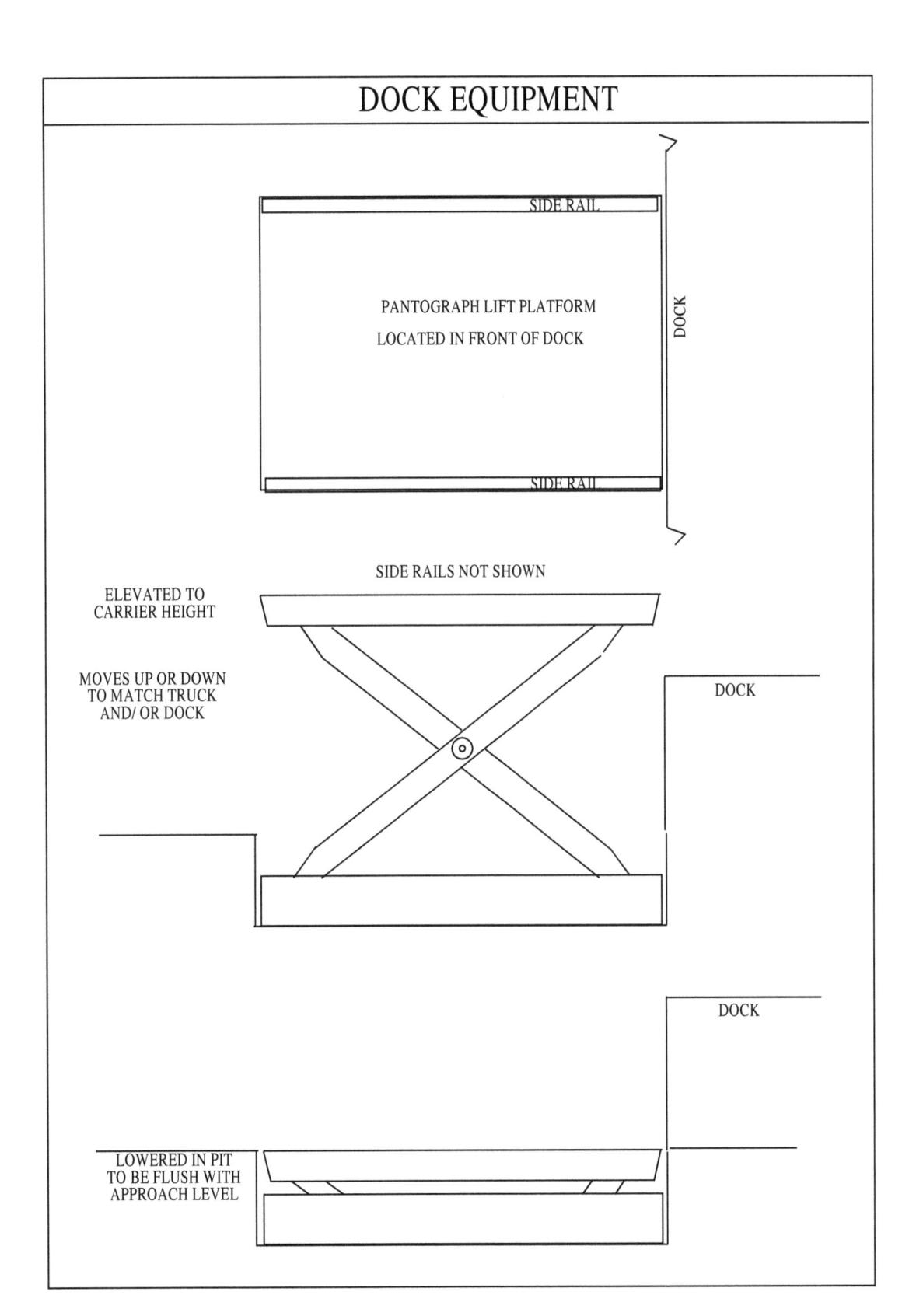

PALLETS

In most instances it is common practice to state the pallet depth - front to rear - first and the width second. So a 48" deep x 40" wide pallet, with stringers running in the depth direction, is referred to as a 48" x 40" pallet. Unfortunately this rule of thumb is not always followed. Be sure in all communications that all parties have the same understanding of the dimensions because an error here, at the very heart of system and building planning, can result in huge problems. Everything from dock equipment, racks and aisle widths to spacing of building columns could be affected. To avoid any misunderstanding in this manual a D will be added for depth and a W for width; thus a 48"D x 40"W pallet.

Be particularly careful in the case of 4-way pallets! These may be shipped, handled, and stored with either dimension as the face or depth. Pallets may be received with the 48" dimension across the truck but handled and stored internally from the 40" face. Or vice versa.

The 48"D x 40"W notched 4-way pallet is probably the most used in distribution centers. But the 4-way block pallet is also very popular. This pallet has various designs; some meant to provide more board surface on the bottom for less crushing when stacked. It may be the most prone to misunderstandings of handling and storing orientations.

Some facilities use other types and sizes for specific reasons within their own companies.

Pallets are still primarily constructed of wood but other materials, such as plastic and aluminum, are available for special needs.

VARIOUS PALLETS AND SKIDS

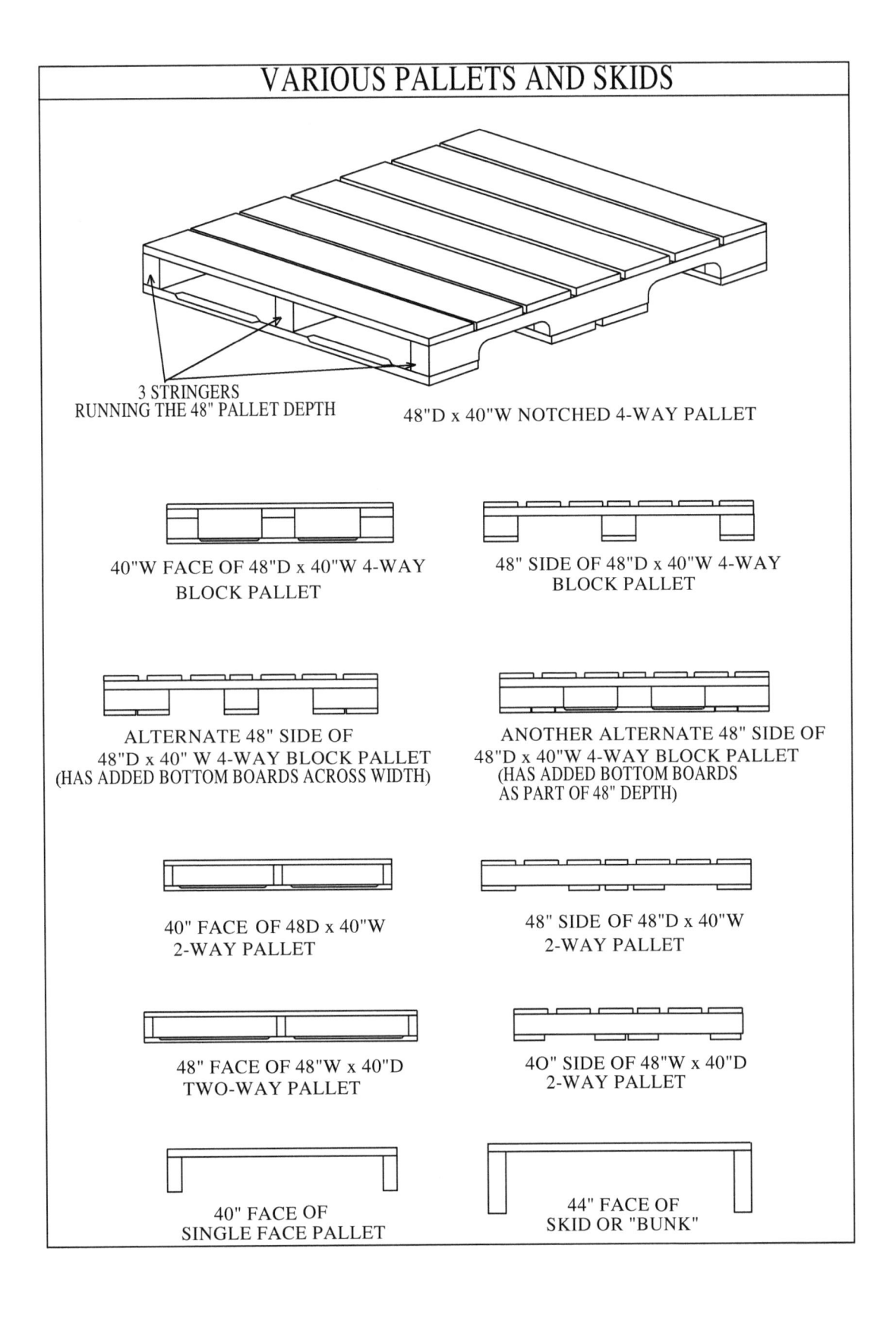

3 STRINGERS
RUNNING THE 48" PALLET DEPTH

48"D x 40"W NOTCHED 4-WAY PALLET

40"W FACE OF 48"D x 40"W 4-WAY
BLOCK PALLET

48" SIDE OF 48"D x 40"W 4-WAY
BLOCK PALLET

ALTERNATE 48" SIDE OF
48"D x 40" W 4-WAY BLOCK PALLET
(HAS ADDED BOTTOM BOARDS ACROSS WIDTH)

ANOTHER ALTERNATE 48" SIDE OF
48"D x 40"W 4-WAY BLOCK PALLET
(HAS ADDED BOTTOM BOARDS
AS PART OF 48" DEPTH)

40" FACE OF 48D x 40"W
2-WAY PALLET

48" SIDE OF 48"D x 40"W
2-WAY PALLET

48" FACE OF 48"W x 40"D
TWO-WAY PALLET

40" SIDE OF 48"W x 40"D
2-WAY PALLET

40" FACE OF
SINGLE FACE PALLET

44" FACE OF
SKID OR "BUNK"

DOCK EQUIPMENT & PALLETS

SECTION FOUR
SHELVING, CAROUSELS & VERTICAL LIFT MODULES

4

SHELVING

This section contains drawings, descriptions and comments pertaining to the most commonly used types of shelving.

First it is necessary to define the difference between shelving and racks; a definition which is sometimes blurred. So the following are offered here for the purpose of making clear the descriptions and comments in this manual.

Shelving is a product designed to store cases, cartons or pieces which are always hand loaded; except in some instances with automated systems. *Shelving is not designed to be loaded by forklift.*

Pallet or unit load storage racks are designed to hold much heavier loads, usually, but not always, on pallets, and also to withstand the shocks involved when the loads are deposited by a forklift. Racks are also sometimes used as heavy-duty shelving, hand loaded, for heavy items and large odd shapes.

There is also a product called wide span. It looks like a light duty pallet rack but it is not meant to be loaded by forklift.

In distribution centers or plant stores the preferred types of shelving are of all metal construction or a metal framework with plywood or other wood-product shelves. The wood-product shelf panels may be unpainted or, preferably, painted or have a specialty coating. Wire mesh shelves may be used to avoid the collection of dust and these may also help in the efficiency of sprinklers.

Metal shelving is most often painted, with a choice of colors. Galvanized components are quite common in cold storage or wet areas, because they resist rust far better than painted shelving.

Three types of shelving will be described.

STATIC SHELVING has no moving parts. This category includes the shelving all of us are aware of, usually three or four feet wide and used in our garages and many stores. It also includes wide span shelving and flow shelving. Although not shelving, the *special category* of storage cabinets is also included here, simply because they are static. **With all of these the picker moves to the pieces to be picked.**

MOBILE SHELVING allows each *row* to be moved laterally, closing one aisle and opening up another so a different row can be accessed **The picker moves to the pieces to be picked**.

DYNAMIC SHELVING. Carousels are examples of this type of shelving. (NOTE: the designation "dynamic shelving" is used here to make you aware that it is different in design and use from the other two shelving types.) **The pieces to be picked are moved to the picker.**

Shelving is available in a wide range of heights, widths and depths. The most commonly used are up to 8′ high, 4′ wide and 24″ deep but all dimensions can be increased to suit; very high shelving can be attained by the use of strengthened posts. Shelf widths wider than 5′ or 6′ are often called **wide span** shelving and these have a heavier design, in order to support greater weights on longer spans. *Safety can become a factor if wide span shelving is mistaken for a pallet storage rack and overloaded or serviced by a forklift.*

In all shelving the ability to vertically adjust shelf spacing is very important; allowing the placement of shelves with the desired spacings and facilitating changes when needed. Most shelving systems allow these adjustments but some are more convenient than others, having a "quick change" design, with few or no bolts. The vertical adjustment increments may vary from 1″ to as much as 3″ and the smaller spacing is preferable.

When seismic compliance is required, do so with the certification of an engineer.

If a second level is contemplated for the future now is the time to construct and install the lower level to support it. And post height should be high enough to meet local regulations, which, in addition to lighting, may require sprinklers below the second level. To retrofit the lower level when expansion is needed can be very disruptive to daily operations and quite costly. Some multi-level concepts are considered later in this section and section 10.

STATIC SHELVING

Static shelving consists of three main components; POSTS, BRACING AND SHELVES. A considerable number of optional components are also offered for safety and efficiency.

POSTS

The type and shape of shelving posts are surprisingly important factors which should not be decided on a casual basis.

Post shape, bracing requirements, vertical shelf adjustment and method of shelf connection are all factors which can affect the initial and long term suitability of shelving. Posts are perforated with holes of different shapes to be used for shelf connections.

The nominal width of a bay may not be the expected width. The type and size of the posts can alter the bay width by as much as 2", thereby changing the overall length of a row. So shelving with a nominal width of 48" may actually *be* 48" or may be as much as 50" or more. The posts may also reduce the **expected clear opening** by as much as 3".

There is not necessarily a right or wrong post design but you should know which is more important for your situation; clear opening or row length. If, for example, the plan is to store 8 containers snugly on a 48" shelf then T posts causing a reduced clear dimension of 45" will mess up your plans, allowing only 7 containers to fit between the posts. If 8 containers are inserted two of them will have corners locked in behind the faces of the T posts. On the other hand if the length of the shelving rows allows no room for error an unexpected extra width of 2" per bay, when using square or rectangular posts, will mean an unacceptable row length.

These alternate possibilities are shown on the next page.

Sketch A shows two very different post designs and their effect on clear opening and center-to-center bay width.

Sketch B shows how a reduced clear opening could make it impractical to store the planned number of containers on a shelf. Two containers may be locked in behind the posts, making it necessary to remove another container to get the one wanted. This is a lesser problem when storing miscellaneous items instead of containers. But the point is to be aware of actual clear shelf width and plan for it.

Sketch C shows the effect of square posts on row length and, in this case, the resulting reduction of access aisle widths. Alternate methods to solve the narrowed access aisle problem would be to shorten row lengths by removing shelving bays or, if possible, take space from the adjoining activity area. In any case it is a preventable problem if the shelving dimensions are understood.

If there is any chance that a height addition may be wanted in the future be sure the post design allows an easy, inexpensive extension and has the ultimate capacity needed for the height addition or a second level with catwalks or a full floor, or purchase the original posts with sufficient height and strength for the future additions.

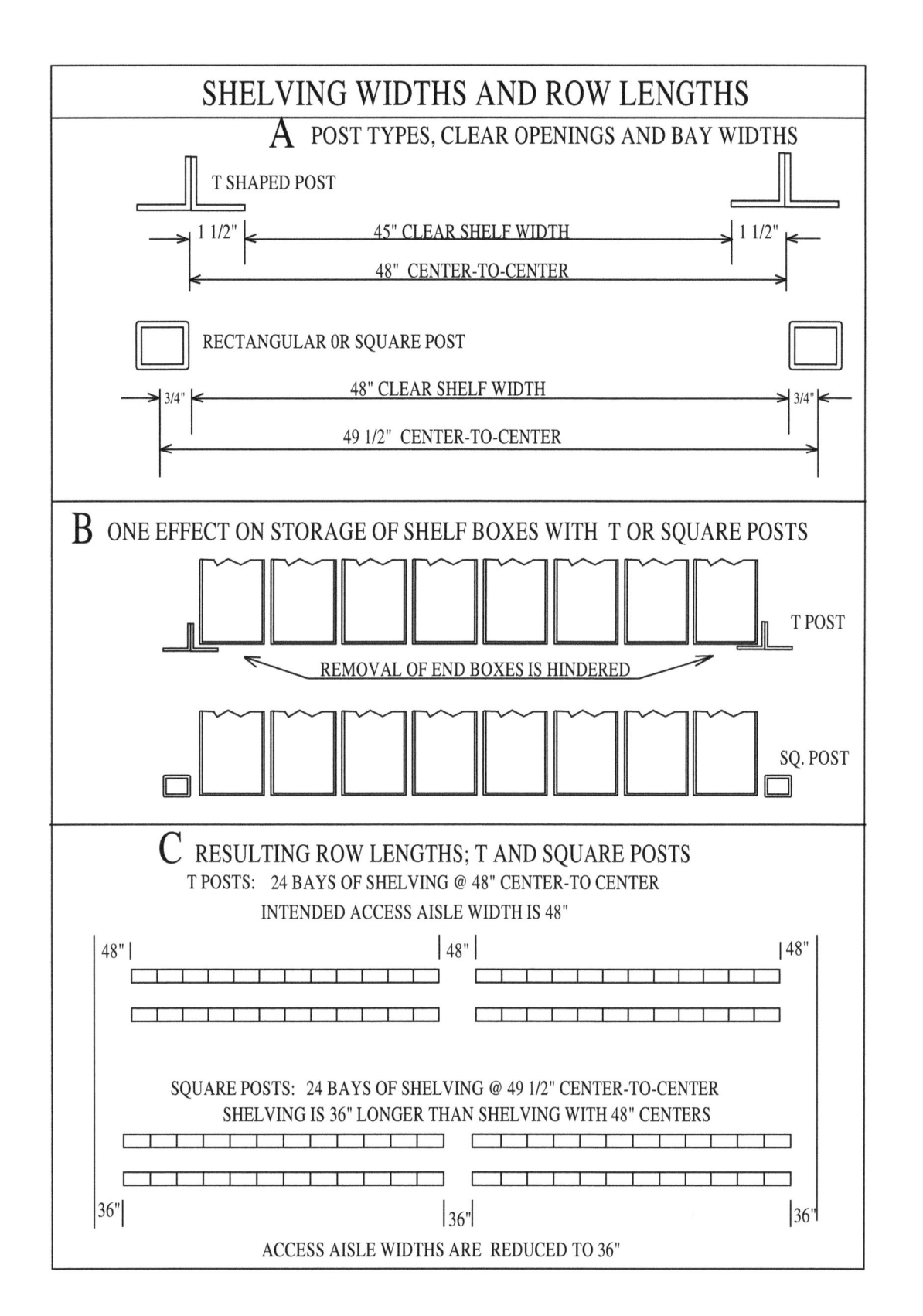

SHELVING WIDTHS AND ROW LENGTHS

A POST TYPES, CLEAR OPENINGS AND BAY WIDTHS

T SHAPED POST
1 1/2" — 45" CLEAR SHELF WIDTH — 1 1/2"
48" CENTER-TO-CENTER

RECTANGULAR OR SQUARE POST
3/4" — 48" CLEAR SHELF WIDTH — 3/4"
49 1/2" CENTER-TO-CENTER

B ONE EFFECT ON STORAGE OF SHELF BOXES WITH T OR SQUARE POSTS

T POST
REMOVAL OF END BOXES IS HINDERED

SQ. POST

C RESULTING ROW LENGTHS; T AND SQUARE POSTS

T POSTS: 24 BAYS OF SHELVING @ 48" CENTER-TO-CENTER
INTENDED ACCESS AISLE WIDTH IS 48"

48"   48"   48"

SQUARE POSTS: 24 BAYS OF SHELVING @ 49 1/2" CENTER-TO-CENTER
SHELVING IS 36" LONGER THAN SHELVING WITH 48" CENTERS

36"   36"   36"

ACCESS AISLE WIDTHS ARE REDUCED TO 36"

4 *SHELVING, CAROUSELS & VERTICAL LIFT MODULES*

SHELVES AND SHELF SUPPORTS

There are four types of shelves commonly used in industrial applications; Metal, plywood, wood-products and wire mesh. Each has a weight capacity, based on uniformly distributed loading, which can be obtained from the supplier. Depending on the shelving design the shelves may be connected to the posts with screws or bolts, shelf clips, or full width metal support bars which hook into the posts. The full width metal support bars may make cross bracing unnecessary. Some designs may use bolted top and bottom shelves, with boltless shelf clips supporting all other levels.

Metal shelves have formed edges for strength. However, beyond 24" deep, or 48" wide, it may be necessary to add re-enforcing to some or all of the edges to obtain a satisfactory capacity.

Plywood and wood-products are used mostly as panels sitting on metal support bars, where they do a satisfactory job in a great many applications, at a lesser cost than metal. They may sometimes be supported only on shelf clips but their capacity is very limited, often resulting in permanent sagging. Check the capacity for the span and weights involved. Full width shelf support bars, usually with clip-in ends, are available in a wide range of capacities. Uncoated wood will result in extra dust.

Wire mesh shelves may be used for neatness (they don't collect dust) and to allow more efficient sprinkler action. When galvanized they are very good in wet and corrosive situations.

SHELVES AND SHELF SUPPORTS

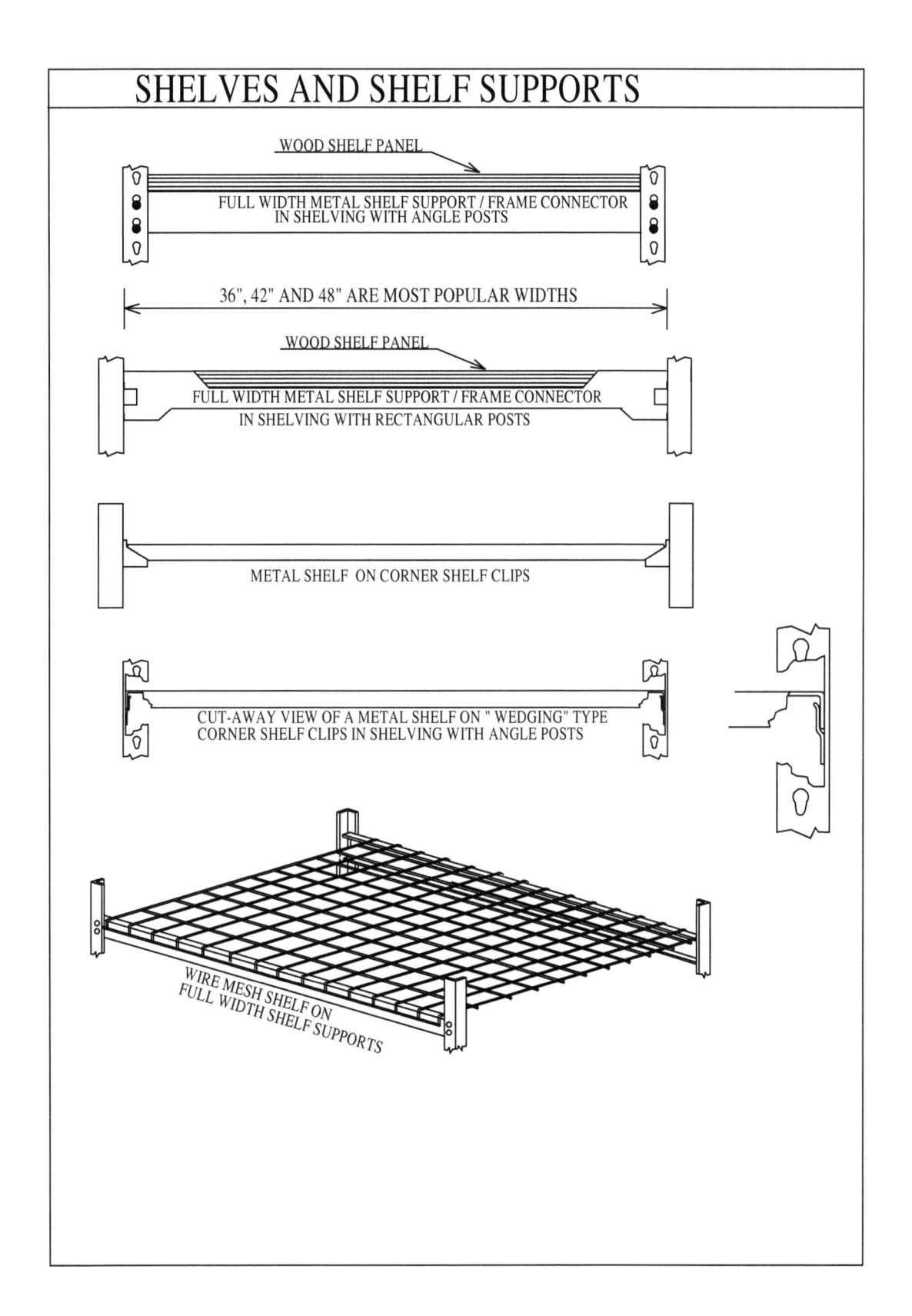

WOOD SHELF PANEL

FULL WIDTH METAL SHELF SUPPORT / FRAME CONNECTOR IN SHELVING WITH ANGLE POSTS

36", 42" AND 48" ARE MOST POPULAR WIDTHS

WOOD SHELF PANEL

FULL WIDTH METAL SHELF SUPPORT / FRAME CONNECTOR IN SHELVING WITH RECTANGULAR POSTS

METAL SHELF ON CORNER SHELF CLIPS

CUT-AWAY VIEW OF A METAL SHELF ON "WEDGING" TYPE CORNER SHELF CLIPS IN SHELVING WITH ANGLE POSTS

WIRE MESH SHELF ON FULL WIDTH SHELF SUPPORTS

4 *SHELVING, CAROUSELS & VERTICAL LIFT MODULES*

BRACING

Bracing is described here only because the amount and type of bracing needed can affect the accessibility and method of use of the shelving, initially and when future changes are wanted.

Bracing is used on shelving to connect the posts, thereby providing the strength and stability needed. Side bracing connects a front and rear post to form a side frame. Rear bracing connects the rear posts of two side frames, forming a bay.

Side bracing may be horizontal or crossed, either of which can allow small items to slip through to a shelf in an adjoining bay, where they don't belong. Or a full metal panel can be used, preventing such misplacement of items.

Designs which use full width shelf supports, connected to the posts, often do not require any additional rear bracing; thus allowing picking access from both sides of the shelving. Some designs with corner gussets will also eliminate rear bracing. The use of large shelves to store and pick from both sides at the same level is less costly than two back-to-back rows, but the flexibility to adjust shelf openings differently on each side is lost.

The next page shows some alternate bracing and two bays of shelving with different shelves and bracing. Bay "A" shows rear bracing as it might be needed when bolting only the top and bottom shelves, with the others on shelf clips. Two back-to-back rows are used and the shelves can be independently adjusted on each side.

"B" shows shelves supported on full width shelf supports which connect to the posts in a bolt-less manner. These connector/supports are bracing in themselves, eliminating the need for rear bracing. The shelves can then be independent on each side, as in A or can be a single large shelf, accessed from both sides, as in B. Use of a single shelf reduces the quantity of posts and side bracing but it loses the ability to separately adjust each side of the row. Also, because of the increased price of longer side braces and larger shelves, the savings may not be as much as expected and will depend somewhat on the weights being stored.

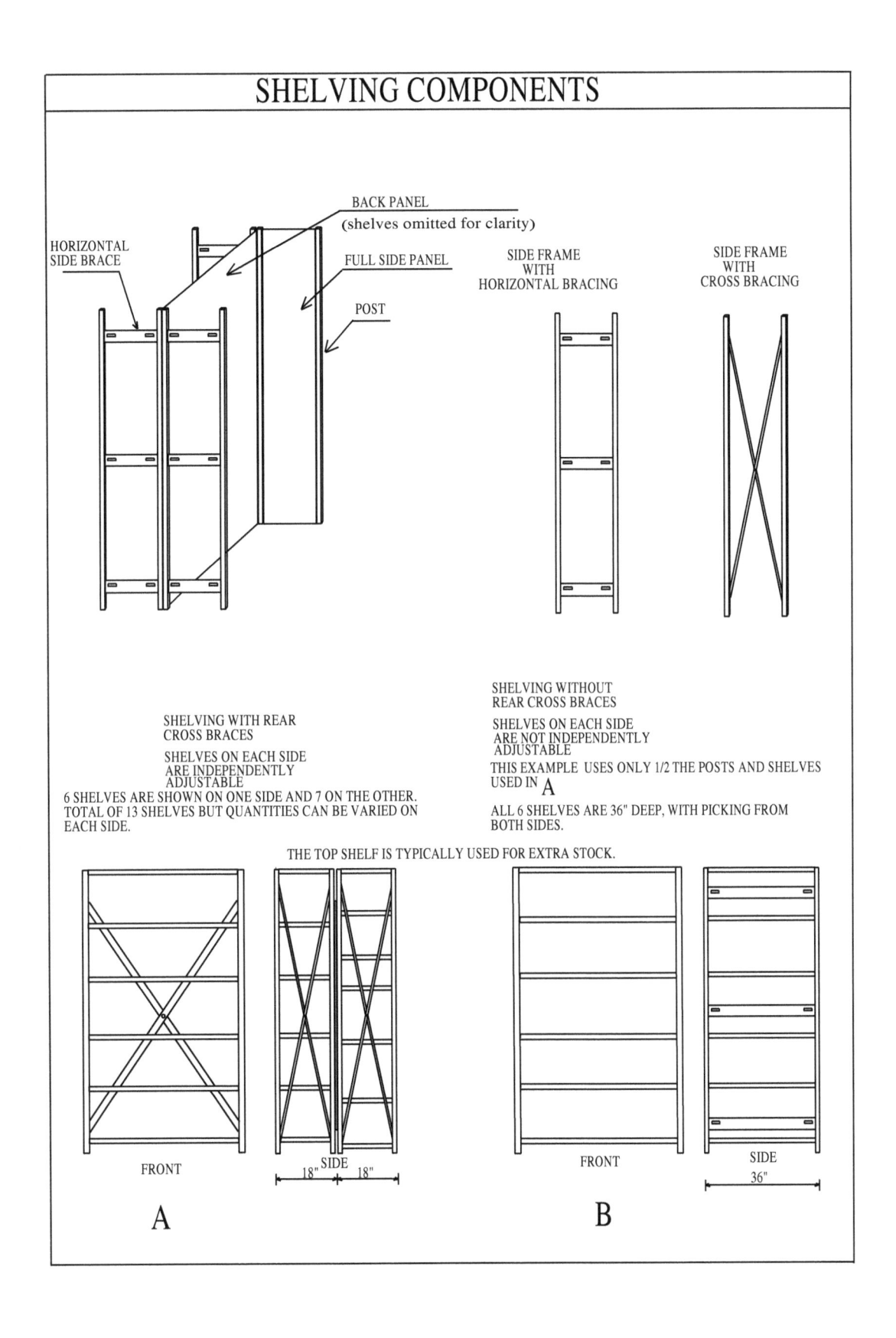

SHELVING COMPONENTS

- HORIZONTAL SIDE BRACE
- BACK PANEL (shelves omitted for clarity)
- FULL SIDE PANEL
- POST

SIDE FRAME WITH HORIZONTAL BRACING

SIDE FRAME WITH CROSS BRACING

SHELVING WITH REAR CROSS BRACES

SHELVES ON EACH SIDE ARE INDEPENDENTLY ADJUSTABLE

6 SHELVES ARE SHOWN ON ONE SIDE AND 7 ON THE OTHER. TOTAL OF 13 SHELVES BUT QUANTITIES CAN BE VARIED ON EACH SIDE.

SHELVING WITHOUT REAR CROSS BRACES

SHELVES ON EACH SIDE ARE NOT INDEPENDENTLY ADJUSTABLE

THIS EXAMPLE USES ONLY 1/2 THE POSTS AND SHELVES USED IN A

ALL 6 SHELVES ARE 36" DEEP, WITH PICKING FROM BOTH SIDES.

THE TOP SHELF IS TYPICALLY USED FOR EXTRA STOCK.

FRONT — SIDE 18" 18"

A

FRONT — SIDE 36"

B

4 *SHELVING, CAROUSELS & VERTICAL LIFT MODULES*

OPTIONAL SHELVING COMPONENTS

In addition to a choice of posts, shelves and bracing there are many optional add-ons available to make shelving more efficient, stronger, safer and better in appearance. In fact there are so many add-ons, some very specific to a company's unique design, that the following list can only be partial. Ask a supplier about the existence of an option to solve a particular problem and if it doesn't already exist, he will probably come up with an answer.

Here are some of the options:

Post sizes are offered with different capacities and are a factor when considering second level storage and seismic requirements.

Corner gussets may be used in lieu of rear bracing under certain conditions.

Label holders, on shelf fronts, are for item identification.

Shelf dividers convert a shelf into a number of bins

Bin fronts prevent items from falling off the shelves.

Shelf re-enforcers add considerably to shelf capacity.

Bin boxes, some with dividers or cups for small parts, are available in metal, plastic, cardboard and other materials in a wide selection of sizes.

Kickplates cover the opening beneath the bottom shelf to prevent items and dirt from entering.

Foot plates provide a means to anchor posts to the floor.

Full metal panel sides and backs improve appearance, keep items separated, act as bracing and may have an effect on fire prevention or containment.

Wrap around end panels are an appearance option for the ends of rows.

Hinged doors convert a bay of shelving into a cabinet, which can also have optional locks.

SOME SHELVING OPTIONS

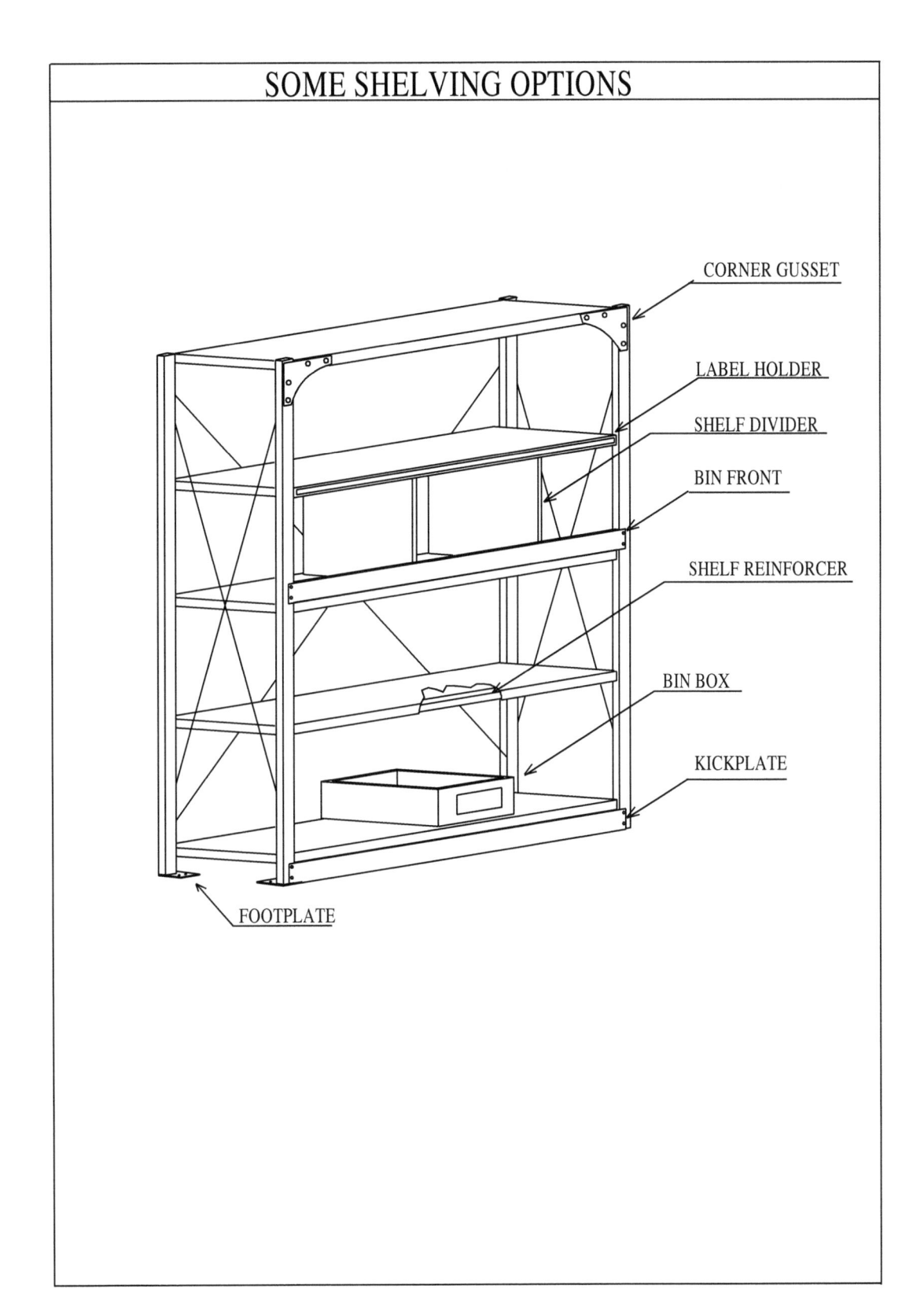

- CORNER GUSSET
- LABEL HOLDER
- SHELF DIVIDER
- BIN FRONT
- SHELF REINFORCER
- BIN BOX
- KICKPLATE
- FOOTPLATE

SHELVING CONFIGURATIONS

There are a number of methods to store and retrieve products in shelving and each can affect the shelf spacings and the number of bays required. Picking efficiencies are also a part of the equation.

Two methods are shown on the next page. Sketch A shows products of a family group stored in numerical sequence without regard to size or velocity of sales. In this instance 26 items are in the bay, on 6 shelves. Some fast moving items occupy two or three positions so there are 35 frontages for the 26 items. This method could be used where it is essential to keep products in family groupings and in numerical sequence. However, it is a poor use of cube and lacks picking efficiency because the fastest movers are not as easily accessed as they might be. Also, any new items in this product line must either be stored elsewhere or cause a location shift of every item in the bay. If this method is used for a very small operation do not fill it as shown here. Leave some expansion room.

Sketch B shows the same items re-arranged so the fastest movers are at the most convenient heights, with the medium and slow movers occupying the other levels in order of their velocity. The mid levels are known as the *Golden Zone* because they are the easiest to access for order picking. This method will yield better pick rates but the order form must be printed in the same sequence as the items are stored or the picker will become confused. Computers will arrange the needed sequence very easily. New items can be inserted into the system anywhere they will fit, in this or an adjoining bay storing the same family group.

Note that this shows **random storage within a family group.** But the items are random only in regard to velocity. The next drawings will show the effect of storing according to size as well as velocity, while still retaining the family grouping.

SHELVING CONFIGURATIONS

A
FAMILY GROUPING STORED IN NUMERICAL SEQUENCE

B
FAMILY GROUPING STORED BY VELOCITY

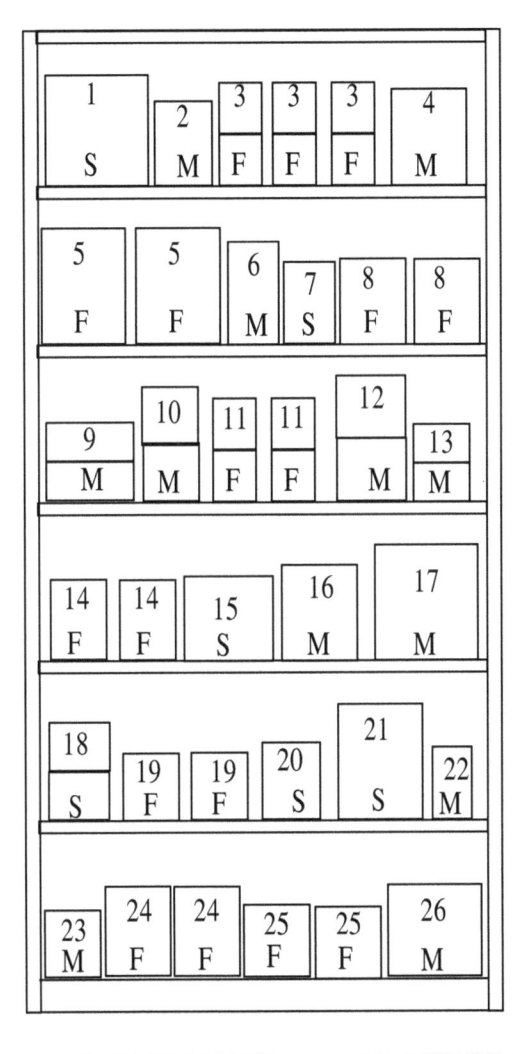

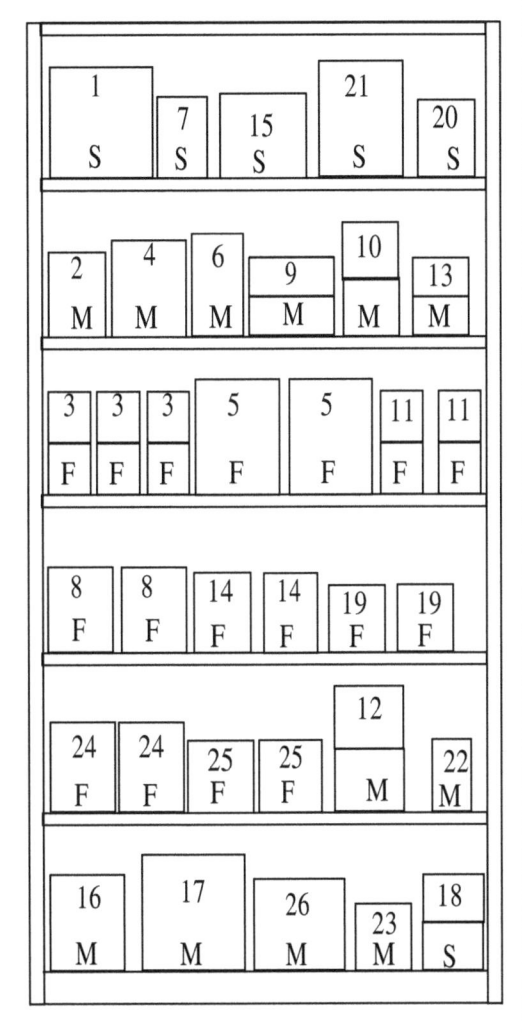

F = FAST MOVER   M = MEDIUM MOVER   S = SLOW MOVER

SHELVING CONFIGURATIONS (CONT.)

On the next page, sketch A from the previous page is retained and is now compared to sketch C. Items are still sorted by fast, medium and slow movement *and are now also sorted by height*. Using various shelf spacings for items of different heights has resulted in the addition of another shelf, leaving extra space for more items in each bay. One bay will be saved from every seven bays originally planned in sketch A. Or the space gained in each bay can be left for product line expansion.

Systems which do not insist on keeping family items together will often be still more space efficient. Storage spaces for groupings by velocity and sizes, without regard to family, can be controlled to a greater degree. This method may have picking advantages or disadvantages, depending on your business. And, of course, higher levels of storage, to be discussed elsewhere, can be used to reduce the area needed and, with some systems, will also increase pick rates.

The storage method and placement of SKUs can be complicated and time consuming. The examples shown here are rudimentary, based on size and sales velocity. There are often additional factors, such as quantities of each SKU, weights, fragility and value which are to be considered. Use of a computer program to do the placement (termed "slotting") is highly recommended unless the system is tiny. Consultants are experienced in this activity and will be able to determine results of comparative trials.

SHELVING CONFIGURATIONS

A
FAMILY GROUPING STORED IN NUMERICAL SEQUENCE

1 S	2 M	3 F	3 F	3 F	4 M
5 F	5 F	6 M	7 S	8 F	8 F
9 M	10 M	11 F	11 F	12 M	13 M
14 F	14 F	15 S	16 M	17 M	
18 S	19 F	19 F	20 S	21 S	22 M
23 M	24 F	24 F	25 F	25 F	26 M

C
STORED ACCORDING TO VELOCITY AND SIZES

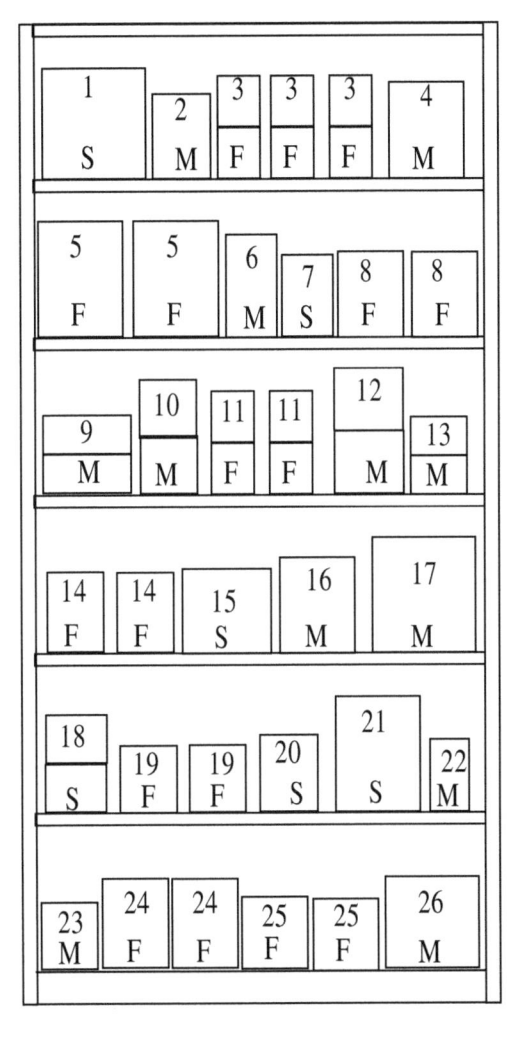

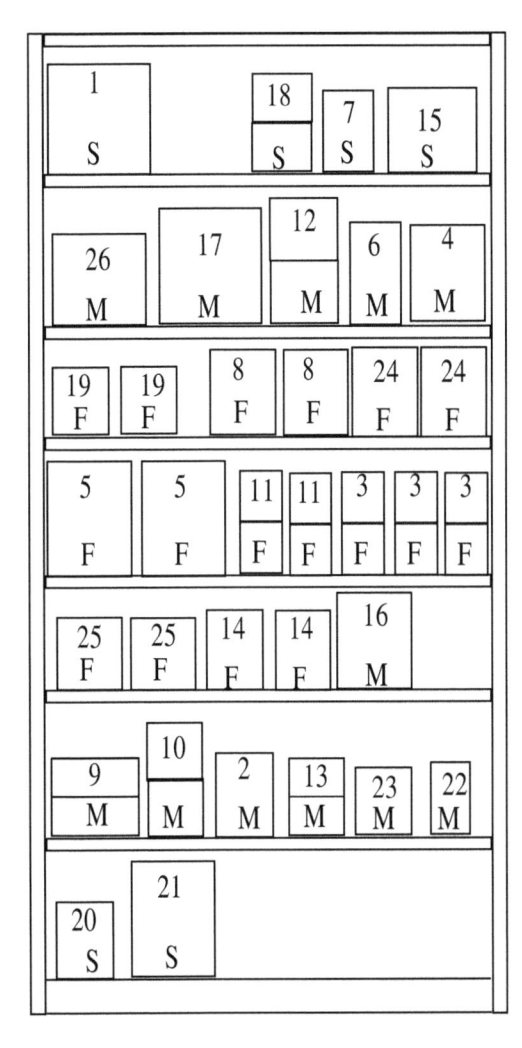

1 S	18 S	7 S	15 S		
26 M	17 M	12 M	6 M	4 M	
19 F	19 F	8 F	8 F	24 F	24 F
5 F	5 F	11 F	11 F	3 F	3 F	3 F
25 F	25 F	14 F	14 F	16 M	
9 M	10 M	2 M	13 M	23 M	22 M
20 S	21 S				

F = FAST MOVER   M = MEDIUM MOVER   S = SLOW MOVER

MULTI-LEVEL SHELVING

Shelving is quite often installed on multiple levels, stacked two or three high. The sketches on the next page show two methods of doing this. For clarity they are shown without stairs, extra bracing or guardrails, which may all be needed.

The top sketch shows very high shelving which also supports walkways for second level access. In this layout the top is a duplicate of the bottom.

The lower sketch shows shelving topped with a full platform, which becomes the floor for the second level. This full floor allows much more flexibility in the use of the second level; perhaps with a different type of shelving or none at all.

Whether lighting and sprinklers for the lower level are a requirement or not they should be considered. The lower level must be high enough to accommodate them, since they will be attached to the underside of the platform or walkways.

Remember that this type of construction may need to conform to local and seismic codes.

TWO-LEVEL SHELVING

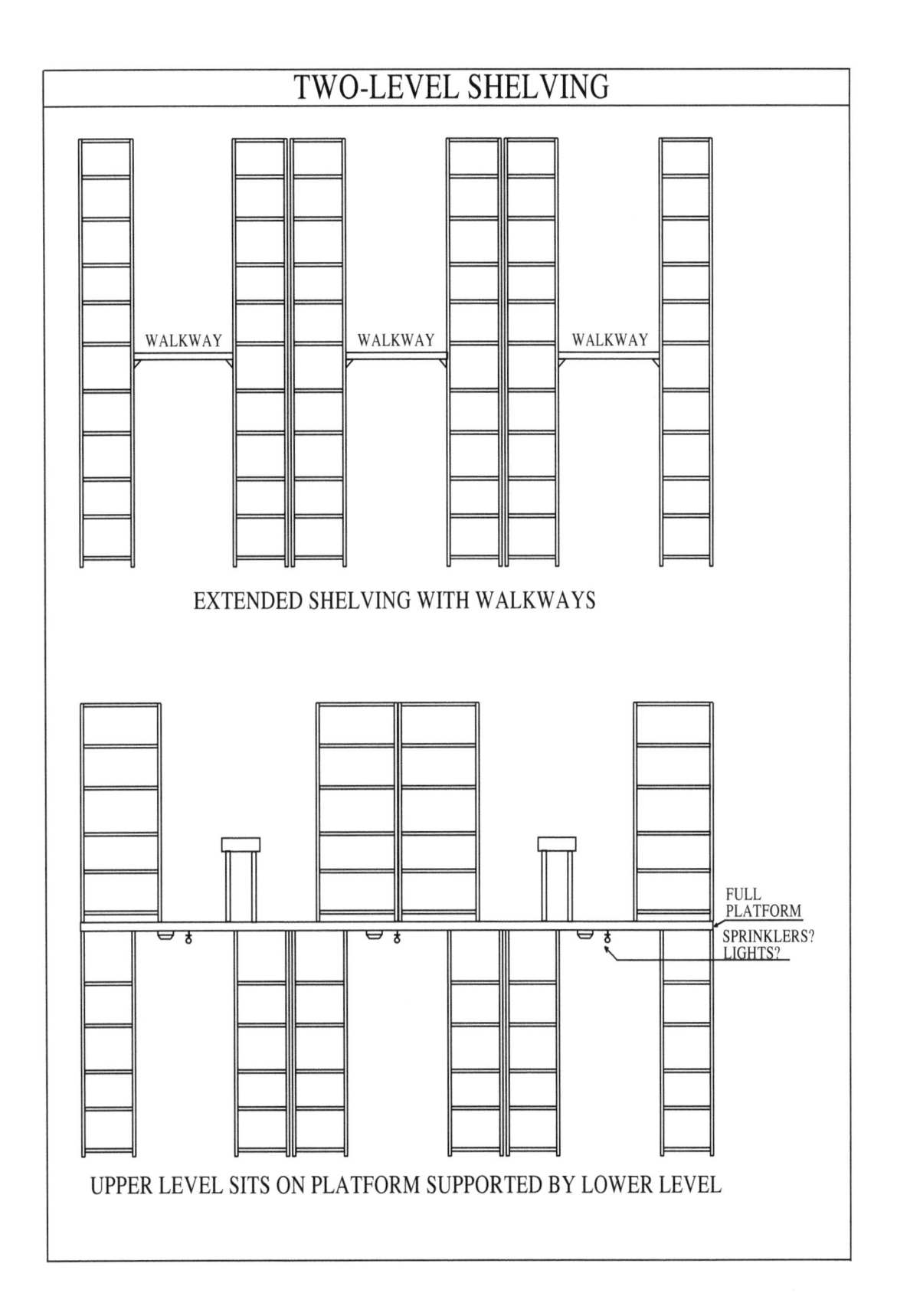

WALKWAY WALKWAY WALKWAY

EXTENDED SHELVING WITH WALKWAYS

FULL PLATFORM
SPRINKLERS?
LIGHTS?

UPPER LEVEL SITS ON PLATFORM SUPPORTED BY LOWER LEVEL

WIDE SPAN SHELVING

This type of shelving is called wide span, or long span, because the shelf width is more than standard shelving. The most common beam length is 8' but longer beams are available for light loads. Available shelf depths also exceed those of standard size shelving.

This is a good shelving for long or bulky loads and is also often used for unpalletized grocery items. A type of this model is sometimes found in super markets.

Some designs look like a small version of pallet racks. These are generally the sturdiest models and may be used in guided high level stockpicking systems. Frames may be welded or bolted and often have posts about 2" wide, with shelf height adjustments on 2" increments. The shelf supports may look like downsized pallet rack load beams and be shaped to support wood or metal panels to make the shelf deck. Wire mesh shelf panels are also commonly used with this product.

Safety may become a problem because some designs resemble pallet racks so closely that they are mistakenly loaded, and often overloaded, with pallets, using a forklift truck. The authors have seen this a number of times and the danger of collapse cannot be overstated.

WIDE SPAN / LONG SPAN SHELVING

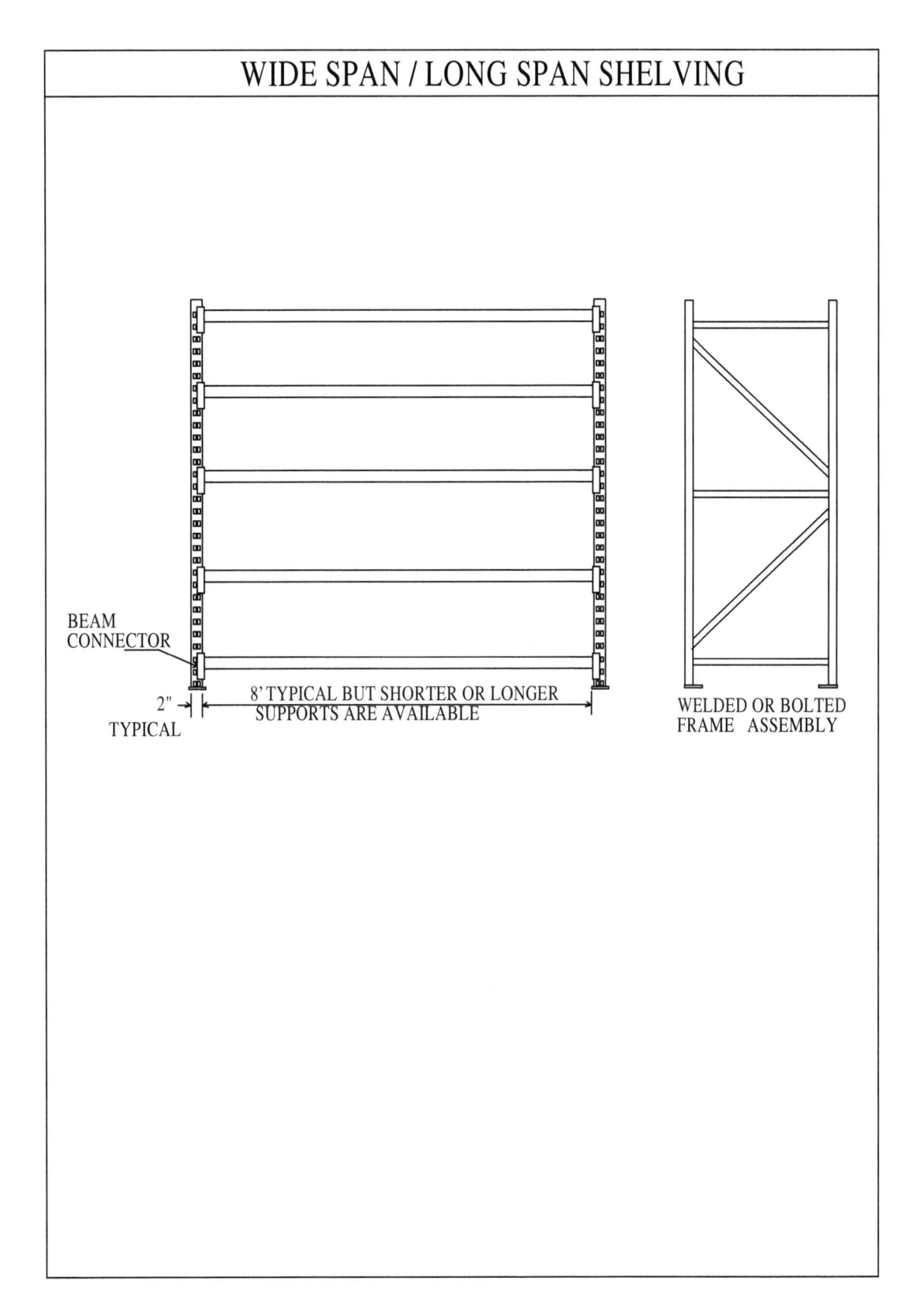

BEAM CONNECTOR

2" TYPICAL

8' TYPICAL BUT SHORTER OR LONGER SUPPORTS ARE AVAILABLE

WELDED OR BOLTED FRAME ASSEMBLY

GRAVITY FLOW SHELVING

Gravity flow shelving is a design which provides storage in depths far deeper than other types of shelving. Items are loaded into each track from the rear and move to the front pick face by gravity. In this manner only one pick face is needed for each product, with more of the same sku stored behind it. Page 136 shows how multiple faces are sometimes needed for fast movers in other types of shelving. This lengthens the aisle frontage and slows the pick rate. Flow shelving, in addition to concentrating a lot of pick faces in a short distance, provides FIFO (first-in, first-out).

The next page shows a number of sketches of this design. There are four basic components and a number of options and accessories to facilitate efficient picking. The basic components are frames, shelves, tracks and guides.

Frames and shelves are offered with a range of standard widths and depths, with a variety of front face options to suit full case picking or smaller piece picking. Other sizes are available when needed. Shelves are vertically adjustable and the width of each track is adjustable to fit the item to be stored in it.

To facilitate product flow to the front of the tracks they are offered with optional designs including a liner of low-friction material, a series of small rollers (as shown in the drawing) or, for heavier items, full width rollers

Guides serve to keep the products separated and flowing straight.

This is still a static type of shelving because the picker moves to the item to be picked; however some versions of the system can be automated to a considerable degree with items such as pick lights etc.

Flow shelving can be interfaced with a computer by using a series of indicator lights attached to the front of each shelf. This is commonly known as pick-to-light. Depending on the system selected the lights may advise the picker what sku's to pick and the quantity of each. Pushing a button will confirm the pick was made, update the inventory, and turn off the indicator. Other systems go further, allowing the picker to signal a shortage in quantity, which also updates the shipping papers and inventory. These are only some examples of possibilities; check with a supplier or advisor for systems to suit your needs.

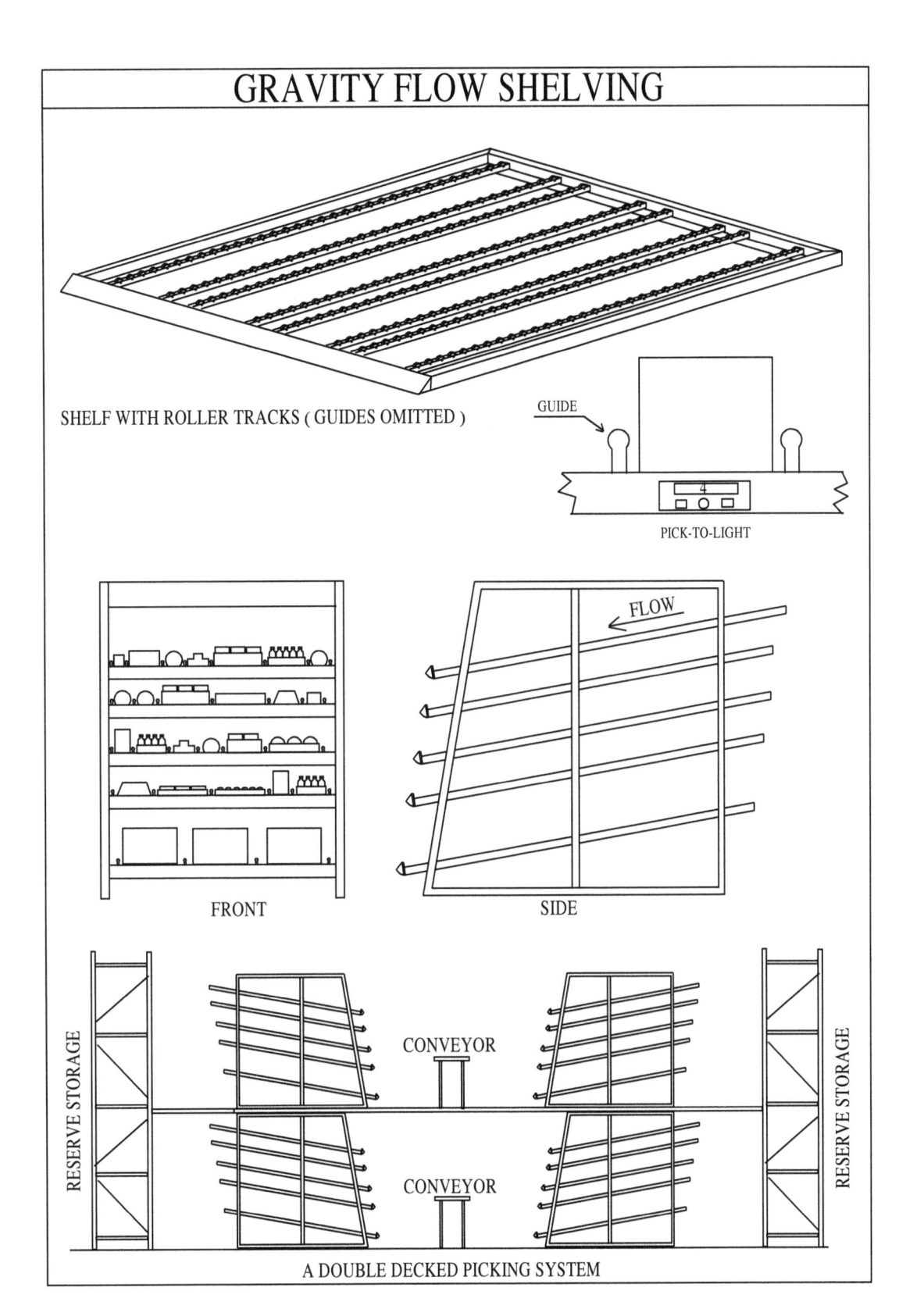

GRAVITY FLOW SHELVING

SHELF WITH ROLLER TRACKS (GUIDES OMITTED)

PICK-TO-LIGHT

GUIDE

FRONT

FLOW

SIDE

RESERVE STORAGE

CONVEYOR

CONVEYOR

RESERVE STORAGE

A DOUBLE DECKED PICKING SYSTEM

4   SHELVING, CAROUSELS & VERTICAL LIFT MODULES

MOBILE SHELVING

Mobile shelving is simply static shelving placed on frames with wheels. The wheeled frames are on tracks running the width of the installation, so they can be moved to open an aisle to access the row wanted. The tracks are imbedded flush in a sub floor which can be installed with the system. All of the bays in each row are joined and the row is moved as a unit. Multiple rows can be shifted as a block. Movement, with help from a mechanical assist, is accomplished by a wheel located on the end of each row. Electric powered movement is a popular option, especially when heavy weights are involved.

This shelving has an important use where space is expensive or limited. Any office is a possible user, along with museums and other facilities, such as golf clubs, where a specific item is wanted each time the shelving is moved for access.

In any location, including plant stores or a warehouse, mobile shelving also offers an increased level of security, with a locking mechanism to prevent movement of the rows.

MOBILE SHELVING

STATIC SHELVING   6 ROWS

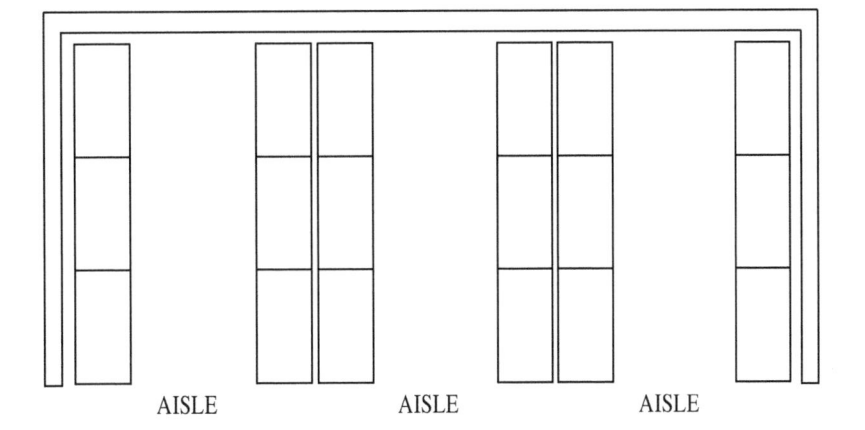

AISLE   AISLE   AISLE

MOBILE SHELVING   10 ROWS
(66% INCREASE)

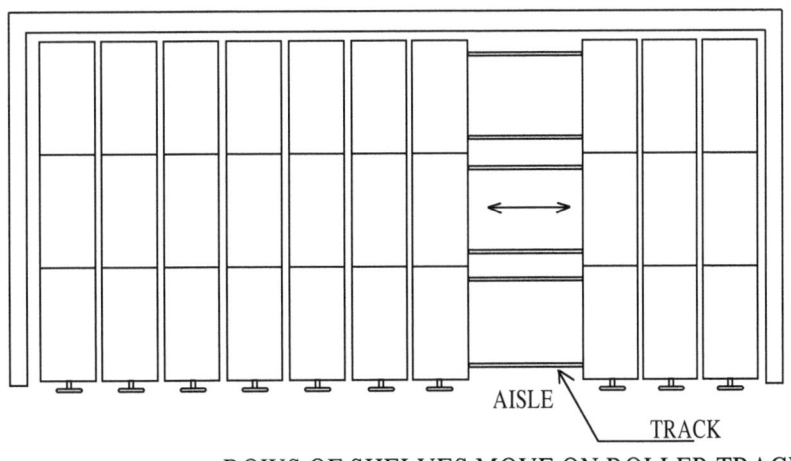

AISLE   TRACK

ROWS OF SHELVES MOVE ON ROLLER TRACKS

SINGLE AISLE OPENS WHERE NEEDED

SHELVING, CAROUSELS & VERTICAL LIFT MODULES

MODULAR STORAGE CABINETS

These are static but are very different from shelving, in fact they are advertised as a product to replace shelving. Every plant stores should consider them because they excel in that application. Many warehouses also could use at least some cabinets along with other shelving types. If you are storing small quantities of small to medium sized items they may also compare well with horizontal carousels, particularly for space savings.

The reasons for using modular cabinets are many, with space savings and security being high on the list, particularly when a great number of small items are being stored. Each drawer, using an arrangement of partitions and dividers, can be configured into a large number of compartments of various shapes and sizes. These compartments, within a drawer of the optimum height, will save much of the cube lost in shelving and may reduce the floor area by half or more.

Cabinets are offered with a number of heights and widths and can be double stacked and used to support a second level of storage. A different combination of drawer heights can be selected for each cabinet. Plastic drawer inserts can be used for tools or other items needing protection, and anti-static designs are also offered for electronics. Security is enhanced by optional locks for the cabinet as a unit or for each drawer separately.

Look for drawers which extend fully from the cabinet, as those that do not may be inconvenient.

Each manufacturer's literature will show many other options for your consideration.

MODULAR STORAGE CABINETS

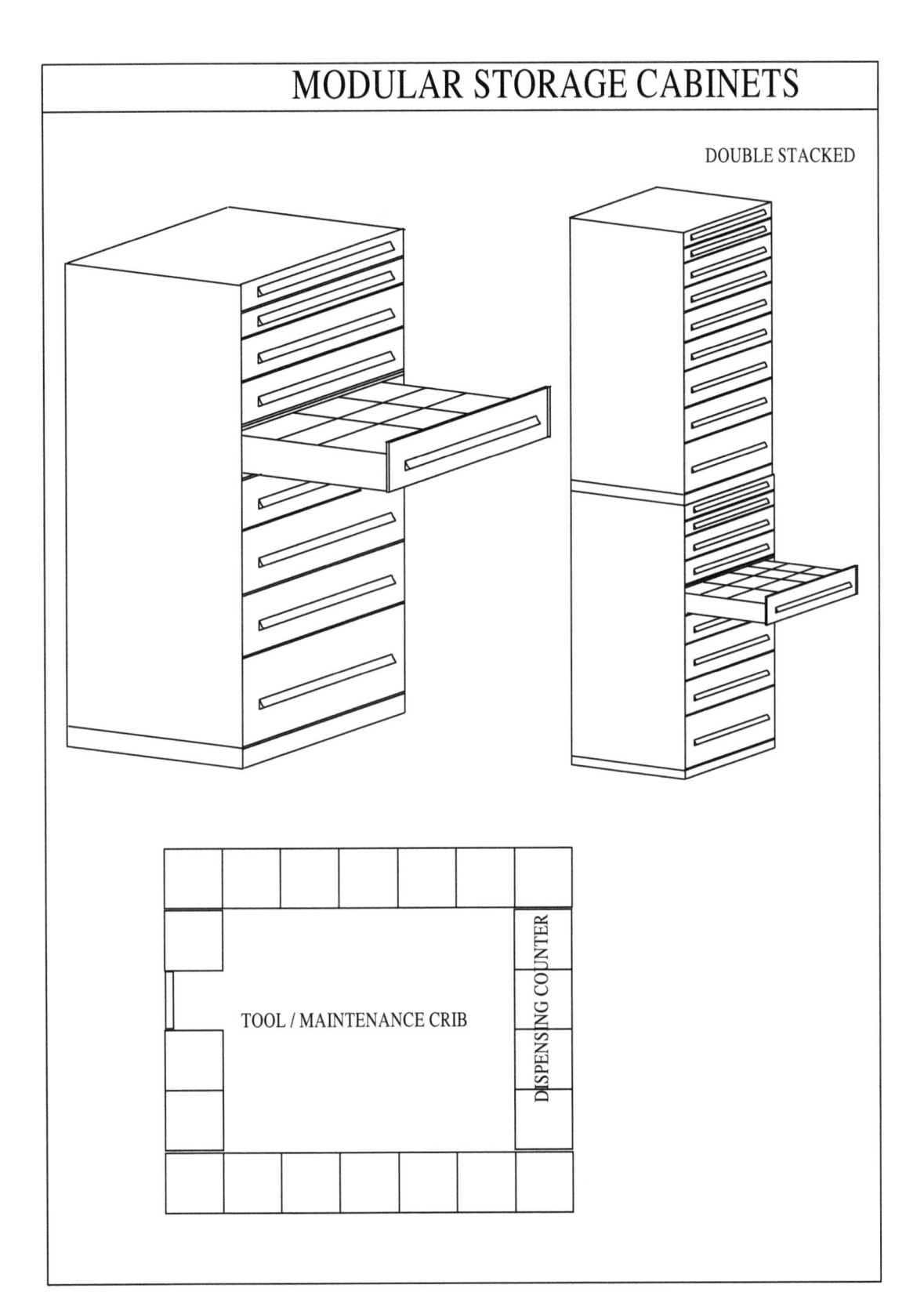

DOUBLE STACKED

TOOL / MAINTENANCE CRIB

DISPENSING COUNTER

HORIZONTAL AND VERTICAL CAROUSELS

Carousels are dynamic shelving because *they move the pieces to the picker.*

Horizontal carousels rotate **carriers** to a pick station, usually considered to be at the front of the system. Each carrier is, in fact, a narrow bay of shelving. Although horizontal carousels are typically constructed of wire mesh, they may occasionally have full metal panels. Carriers are most often only about 18" to 24" wide but can be wider. Each one has shelves, again usually of wire mesh, which can be varied in number and vertical spacing.

The next page shows a horizontal carousel and also a top view of two carousels, each with 26 carriers, servicing a single pick station. In this way the picker can be picking from one carousel while the other is rotating the next carrier with a required pick item into position at the pick station.

Each carousel can be operated by a simple push button or can be very highly automated, even to the point of eliminating the picker when containers are to be stored and retrieved. Between these two extremes there are quite a number of possibilities to increase picking rates. They can also be double stacked to save floor space, and use headroom, if available.

Vertical carousels also have a range of automation possibilities. With this design the carriers are rotated vertically, rather like a fair ground Ferris wheel. The requested carrier stops at a front opening, positioned at a convenient height for easy removal of a single shelf box or a complete tray of parts onto a shelf or a conveyor.

This kind of carousel is excellent for assembling a quantity of different parts into a kit and their minimal use of floor space is also important as they can occupy the full available clear building height; two factors which are of particular benefit in a manufacturing process. Easily closed and locked, the inherent security is yet another consideration.

Vertical carousels also bring all loads to the perfect picking height with no stooping down or use of steps to access items. Ergonomically they offer huge advantages over normal shelving systems, plus picker travel is almost eliminated, as the pick product is brought right to the picker, reducing fatigue and also speeding up the picking process while improving pick and replenishment accuracy; by only bringing one shelf to the picker.

Refer to Order Picking section for additional information.

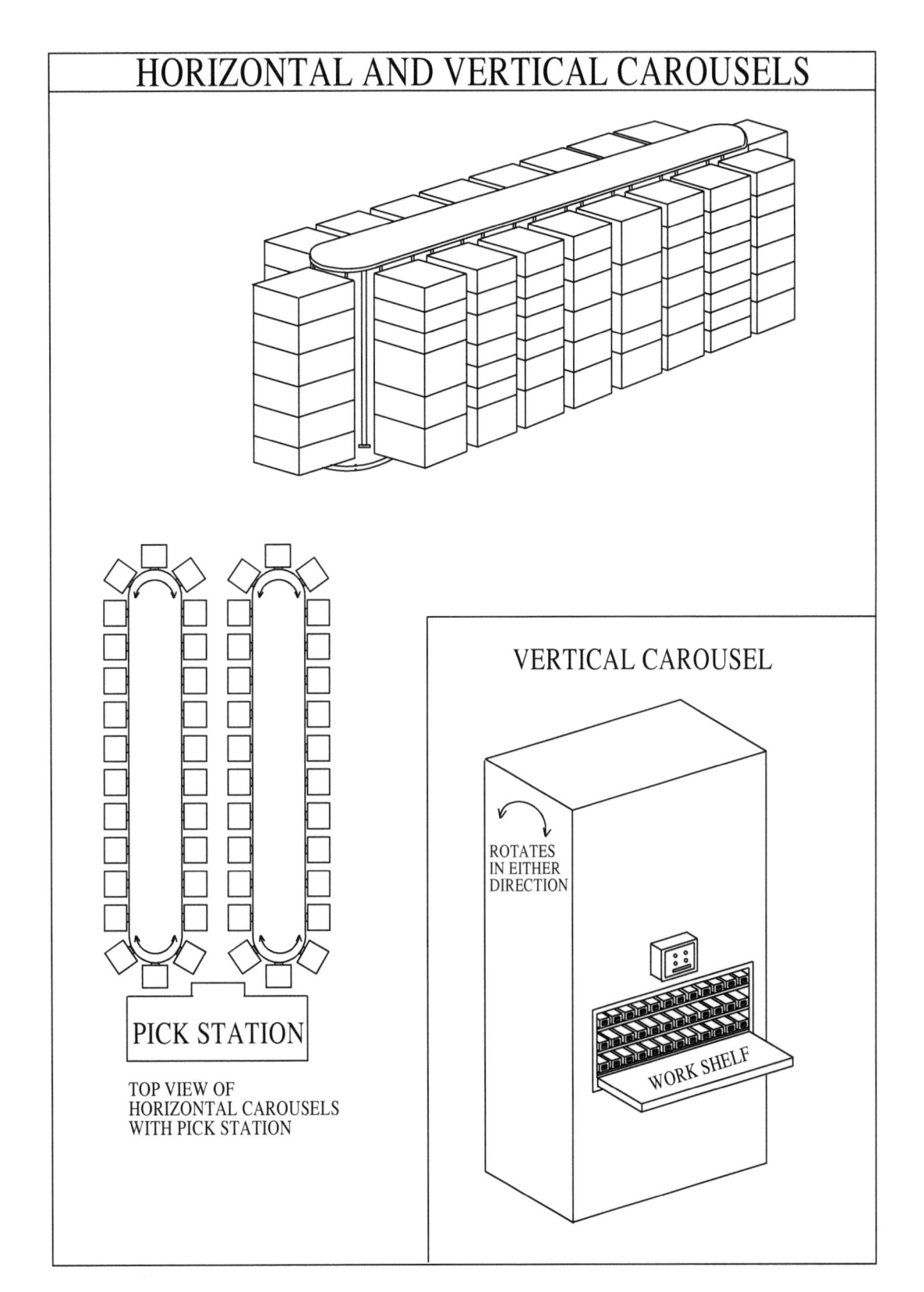

HORIZONTAL AND VERTICAL CAROUSELS

150

VERTICAL CAROUSEL

ROTATES IN EITHER DIRECTION

WORK SHELF

PICK STATION

TOP VIEW OF
HORIZONTAL CAROUSELS
WITH PICK STATION

4 *SHELVING, CAROUSELS & VERTICAL LIFT MODULES*

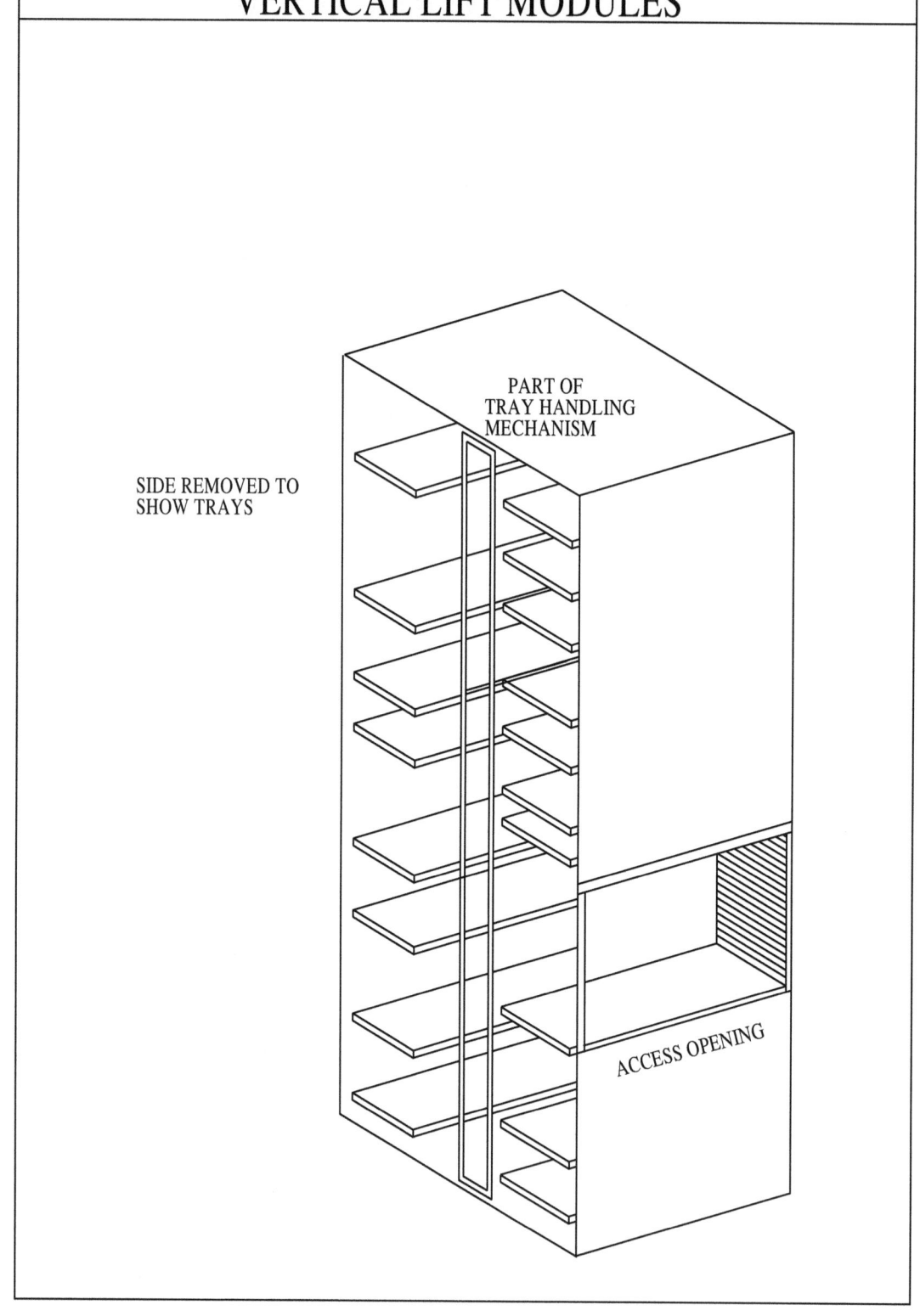

VERTICAL LIFT MODULES

PART OF TRAY HANDLING MECHANISM

SIDE REMOVED TO SHOW TRAYS

ACCESS OPENING

HOW TO CONFIGURE AND EQUIP YOUR WAREHOUSE

VERTICAL LIFT MODULE

The Vertical Lift Module, or VLM is often referred to as a "Shuttle". This term tends to reduce the confusion between Vertical Carousel (as previously described) and the Vertical Lift Module (Shuttle).

The VLM (Shuttle) operates by utilizing steel pans usually in the region of 24" to 34" deep but other sizes are offered, and widths from 48", up to 144" in normally 24" steps, but again, alternates can be built to suit specific requirements. The tray sides are as standard about 3" high .

The center of the VLM (Shuttle) is built with a vertical lifting platform fitted with belt drives to pull trays onto this platform or alternatively index them into a given storage location high up inside the unit.

The trays can be stored in the front of the unit (over the normal operator station) and also into the rear of the unit. Typically the inside edges of the VLM are made of corrugated steel sides or alternatively, steel rails to store the trays onto. The rails or corrugations allow for trays to be stored with the minimum clearance between the top of the tallest load on a tray and the bottom of the stored tray, typically 1" clearance approximately.

The VLM, when storing a new tray, as the shuttle mechanism pulls the tray onto the central platform ready to be lifted. The tray passes through a series of photo eyes shining across the rear of the units operator opening, these eyes are able to determine the maximum height of any product being stored on the tray. The VLM then knows which opening it can utilize to store that tray, maximizing the vertical space utilization, automatically, without any human intervention.

The tray capacities are also flexible and typically can be from 200 # / tray through 1050 # or more. The VLM is able to identify each tray stored by number and was advised at installation time when the tray was initially stored, and what capacity that tray had. If when the tray is pulled back onto the central platform for storage, the system detects that the tray is over capacity (ie 600# is being stored on a 400# capacity tray), then the VLM will reject the tray, back to the pick window and display the fact the tray is overloaded, so the operator can take corrective action.

Typically VLM's are best utilized in pairs at the minimum, to reduce access time waits by the operator, unless of course this is not a high throughput application.

A single VLM could reasonably be able to access and restock say 60 trays within an hour. A pair of units, under computer control with one operator could expect to achieve a throughput of 100 to 120 trays / hour.

VLM's by virtue of their construction can normally be added to in the event a taller area of the building becomes available. Thus allowing maximum use of the available building envelope.

Vertical Carousels and Horizontal Carousels can however not be changed in height once manufactured, so do not offer that potential advantage.

Because of the pick window opening (access opening) being fairly large (usually around 36" overall height internally), this prohibits storage in that area, thus if your headroom available is limited to say 19' or below, you will likely find that a vertical carousel will offer more cubic storage within that limited height. However, above 20' typically the VLM begins to show that it has the cube advantage based on the height available.

Both the vertical carousel and VLM can be enclosed in a refrigerated environment to offer protection from elevated summer temperatures near the roof of higher warehouse, especially for the storage of drugs and pharmaceuticals (or other heat sensitive products), which often demand that temperatures must be kept below 25° C.

SECTION FIVE
STORAGE RACKS

5

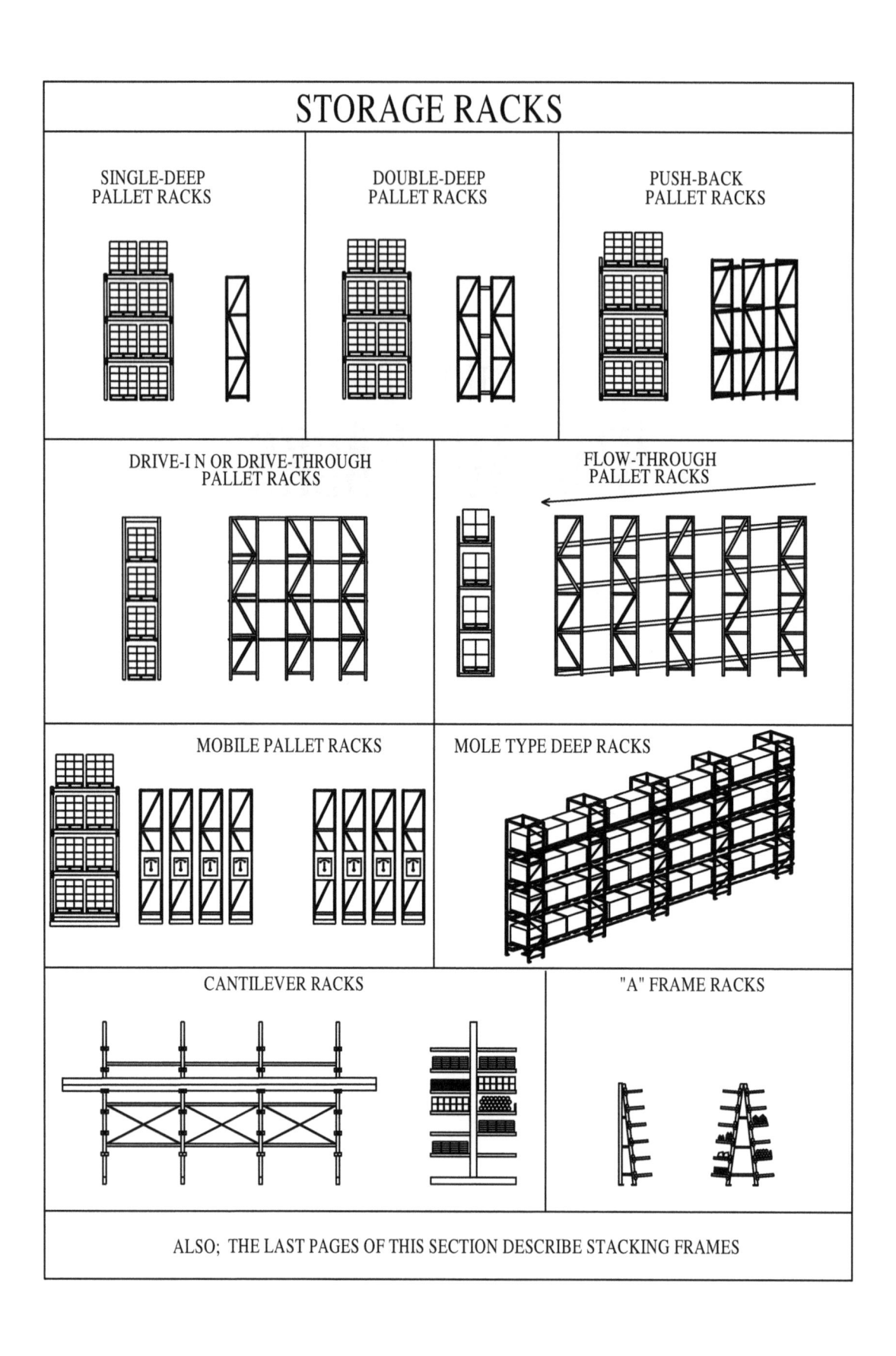

STORAGE RACKS

SINGLE-DEEP PALLET RACKS

DOUBLE-DEEP PALLET RACKS

PUSH-BACK PALLET RACKS

DRIVE-IN OR DRIVE-THROUGH PALLET RACKS

FLOW-THROUGH PALLET RACKS

MOBILE PALLET RACKS

MOLE TYPE DEEP RACKS

CANTILEVER RACKS

"A" FRAME RACKS

ALSO; THE LAST PAGES OF THIS SECTION DESCRIBE STACKING FRAMES

HOW TO CONFIGURE AND EQUIP YOUR WAREHOUSE

STORAGE RACKS

Storage racks are an alternate to stacking directly on the floor because floor stack heights may be quite limited due to crushing or uneven materials. Also, floor stacks allow unhindered access only to the top load and prevent case picking from the lower pallets

THERE ARE SIX TYPES OF UNIT LOAD STORAGE RACKS IN GENERAL USE, AND THEY ARE EXPLAINED IN THIS ORDER.

- SELECTIVE RACKS
- DOUBLE–DEEP RACKS
- PUSH-BACK RACKS
- DRIVE-IN OR DRIVE THROUGH- RACKS
- FLOW-THROUGH RACKS
- MOLE TYPE DEEP RACK SYSTEM

MOST UNIT LOADS ARE ON PALLETS AND FOR EASE OF EXPLANATIONS THESE RACKS WILL OFTEN BE REFERRED TO AS PALLET RACKS.

ADDITIONALLY, THERE ARE OTHER SPECIALIZED RACKS OF WHICH THREE OF THE MOST NOTABLE ARE:

- MOBILE RACKS
- CANTILEVER RACKS
- A-FRAME RACKS

By using racks you may gain some or all of the following benefits:

- Higher Stacks
- Increased Storage
- Reduced Storage Area
- Increased Number Of SKUs
- Increased Number Of Pick Faces
- Increased Access To Specific Loads
- Increased Control Of FIFO
- Reduced Product Damage
- Increased Safety From Falling Stacks

Of these choices selective racks are by far the most widely used. Double-deep and drive-in racks are popular for specific applications and the use of the push-back design is growing. Flow-through, Mole-type and mobile racks can solve certain situations better than other types.

The cantilever design is primarily for the storage of long loads but is also used for some awkward materials. A-frames may be used as another type of cantilever design for long loads stored horizontally or may hold products, such as moldings or tubing, stored vertically.

The general construction and common usages of these nine models will be shown in this section. Section nine will present information to help you decide which type to use and how to determine the best specifications.

STORAGE RACK COMPONENTS

157 The simplest basic racks are named **selective racks** and are assembled from three main components; **upright end frames, load beams** and, to a lesser but still important degree, **back-to-back row connectors.** Other types of racks, such as drive-ins and push-backs require additional components. In addition to the essential components most racks offer a variety of optional accessories for increased efficiency or safety. (see page 161)

END FRAMES

End frames (also called uprights) are constructed of posts joined together with horizontal and diagonal braces. A footplate with holes for anchoring to the floor is welded to the bottom of each post. A series of holes, usually with two to four inch vertical spacing, is punched into each post for load beam connections. Beams are commonly attached to the posts with boltless connectors. Bolts may be needed for very heavy capacities or when a seismic design is needed,

Frames are typically designed with capacities from about 12,000 lbs. to 40,000 lbs. Heavier capacities are available. Both roll formed and structural uprights are available.

Loading end frames to the maximum capacity is attainable only under certain conditions which, perhaps because of complexity, are not stated on most literature. These conditions may vary between manufacturers and may include such things as the number and size of floor anchors, the number and vertical spacing of load beams, etc. So it is very important to have a confirmed capacity from the supplier for the conditions of intended use.

LOAD BEAMS

Load beams have a number of specifications which must be considered. Initially look for the correct *length* and *capacity per pair*, as shown on the manufacturer's literature.

Beam length is usually stated in inches rather than feet and inches. So 136" is shown on most literature instead of 11'- 4".

Rated capacity is stated for a pair of load beams and is based on a load which is uniformly distributed. This is termed UDL, for uniformly distributed loading, and the safety hazard when not adhering to this part of the specification is shown in more detail in section nine.

Other considerations are the ***allowable deflection*** and the ***built-in safety factor*** to avoid collapse. All beams will deflect when loaded and a typical maximum allowable deflection is 1/180 of the beam length. Deflection beyond the stated limit may permanently damage the beam and is dangerous. On long beams the maximum deflection is quite noticeable and may cause safety concerns although the beams are not overloaded. This perception of overloading may be unacceptable in facilities open to the public. Consider using beams with some extra capacity to reduce deflection

The factor of safety should be clearly stated and should meet all applicable design standards. Load beams have three common shapes; rectangular, "C" shape and step shape. Of these the step shape is by far the most poplar because it provides a supporting ledge for easier and less costly use of many accessories, such as safety bars, and is often more adaptable to changing requirements. However there could be a small savings by using one of the other designs. Most rack designs allow the beams to be connected to the frame posts without the use of bolts. This provides for a fast and easy rack installation, and the beams are easily repositioned for changing needs. Some have a locking device at each end of the beam to prevent accidental dislodgement by the forklift. Others use separately installed locking pins.

ROW CONNECTORS

Back-to-back row connectors are also called row spacers because they serve both purposes. They are deceptively simple but important components of many rack installations. Not only do they space back-to-back rack rows at a desired dimension but, if adequately designed and securely fastened to the end frame posts, they can add to frame capacity and stability. This is becoming increasingly more important with the advent of very high lift forklifts and higher rack systems.

ACCESSORIES

There are many standard accessories to enhance the storage and safety capabilities of storage racks. Most are for use in selective or double-deep types, but a few are available for other racks. The most commonly used are as follows:

Post Guards

Row Connectors (These have been discussed above)

Wall Connectors

Safety Bars

Fork Entry Bars

Skid Channels

Drum Cradles

Wire Mesh Decks

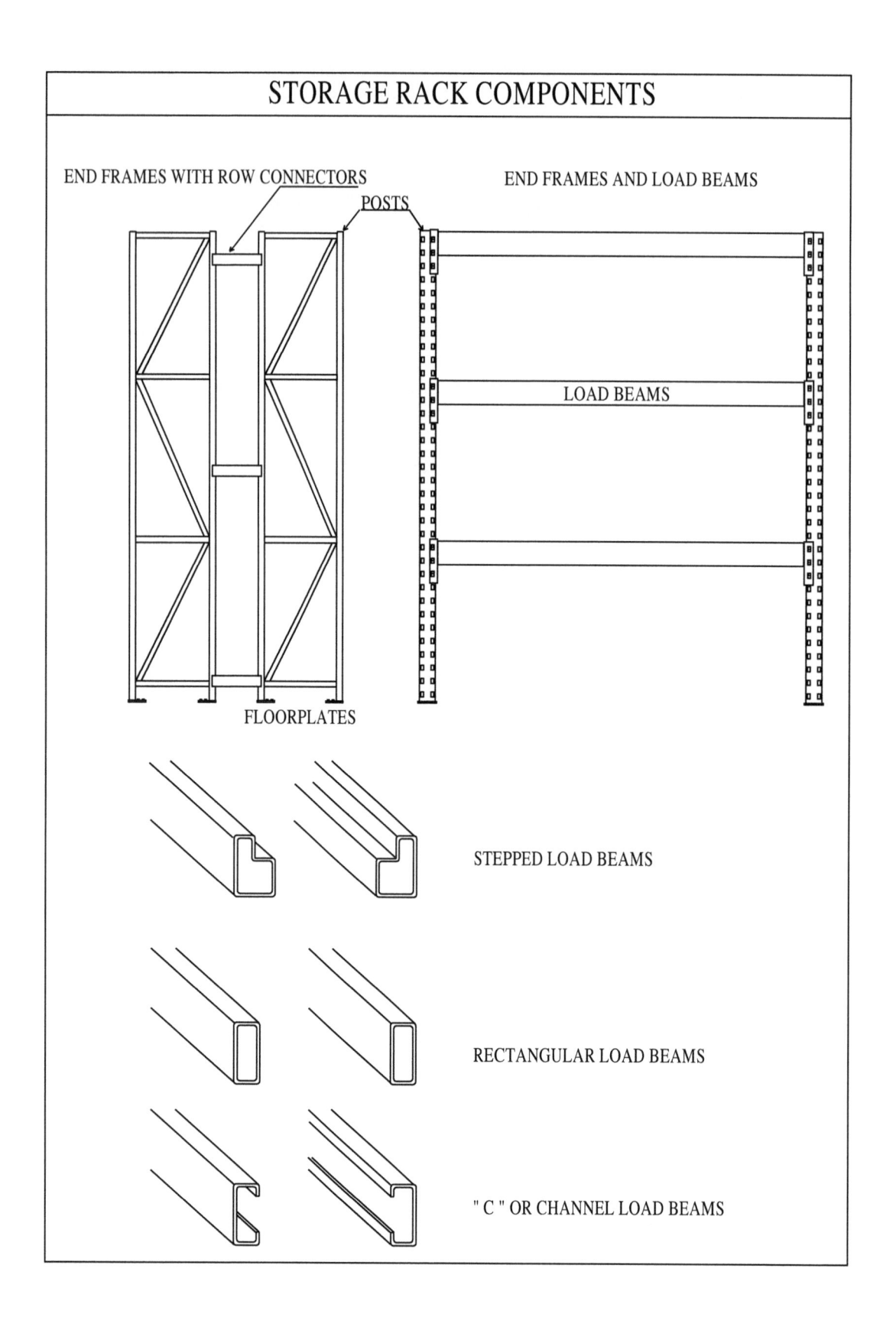

STORAGE RACK COMPONENTS

END FRAMES WITH ROW CONNECTORS

POSTS

END FRAMES AND LOAD BEAMS

LOAD BEAMS

FLOORPLATES

STEPPED LOAD BEAMS

RECTANGULAR LOAD BEAMS

" C " OR CHANNEL LOAD BEAMS

HOW TO CONFIGURE AND EQUIP YOUR WAREHOUSE

STORAGE RACK MISCELLANEOUS

EXTENDED FRAMES WITH OVER-AISLE BRACING

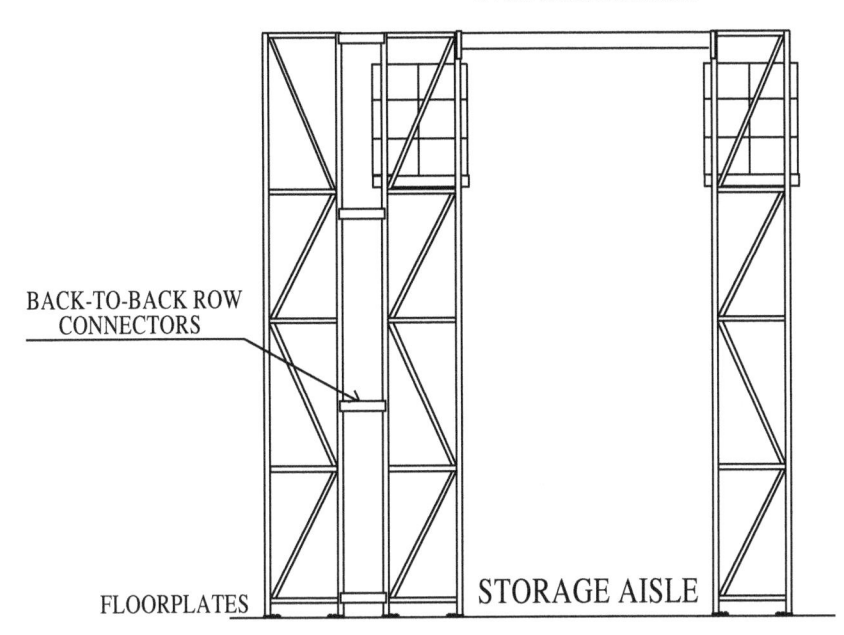

BACK-TO-BACK ROW CONNECTORS

FLOORPLATES

STORAGE AISLE

FRAMES MAY BE EXTENDED AT ROW ENDS ONLY FOR SAFETY FROM FALLING GOODS OR MAY BE USED AS NEEDED ALONG THE RACK ROW WITH OVER-AISLE BRACING

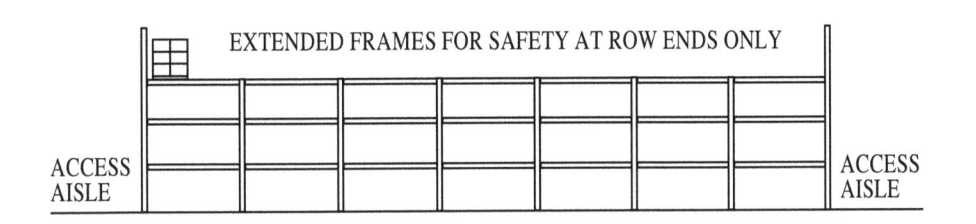

EXTENDED FRAMES FOR SAFETY AT ROW ENDS ONLY

ACCESS AISLE

ACCESS AISLE

FULL DECKS AND EXTENDED FRAMES FOR EXTRA SAFETY WITH STORAGE OVER ACCESS AISLES

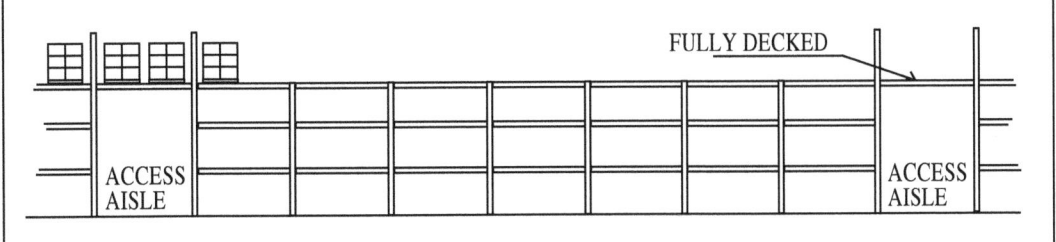

FULLY DECKED

ACCESS AISLE

ACCESS AISLE

5 *STORAGE RACKS*

ACCESSORIES

Post guards prevent most of the damage caused by forklift activities. They not only add to safety but usually save more than their cost. Most damage to end frame posts is caused not by severe impacts but from repetitive small hits by forklifts or the corners of pallets. When a frame must be replaced it is necessary to unload two rack bays and remove all load beams. After the frame is replaced the beams and pallet loads are also replaced. This costly and disruptive procedure can be avoided with post guards.

Row connectors have been explained above. Although they are usually shown as an accessory, they really should be considered as a basic component.

Wall connectors should be used cautiously, with the wall construction considered. In particular they may be a poor selection if the wall is of cement block design or where seismic factors are a consideration.

Safety bars are placed beneath loads - usually two beneath each pallet - as an extra measure of safety against careless placement or pallet breakage. They sit flush with the tops of the beams and can be a factor in deciding what shape of beams you should acquire

Drop-in safety bars, of metal or wood, rest on the steps of stepped beams. They are the least costly type.

Drop-over safety bars, metal only, have brackets which sit on rectangular or "C" shaped load beams. Their extra cost may prompt a decision to use step beams.

Fork entry bars are raised above the beam surface to provide a space for fork entry beneath non-palletized loads which do not have built-in entry space.

Skid channels are to store loads which have feet or other protrusions which prevent them from sitting safely on load beams. These channels have raised sides to prevent the load from slipping off.

Drum cradles are used to store drums on their sides while allowing room for fork entry.

Wire mesh decks are an alternate to full wooden decks and are very good for cleanliness or wet conditions. In some instances they may favorably affect insurance premiums.

Some manufacturers have developed too many accessories to show on their literature. Ask for their solutions for any special storage needs.

STORAGE RACK ACCESSORIES

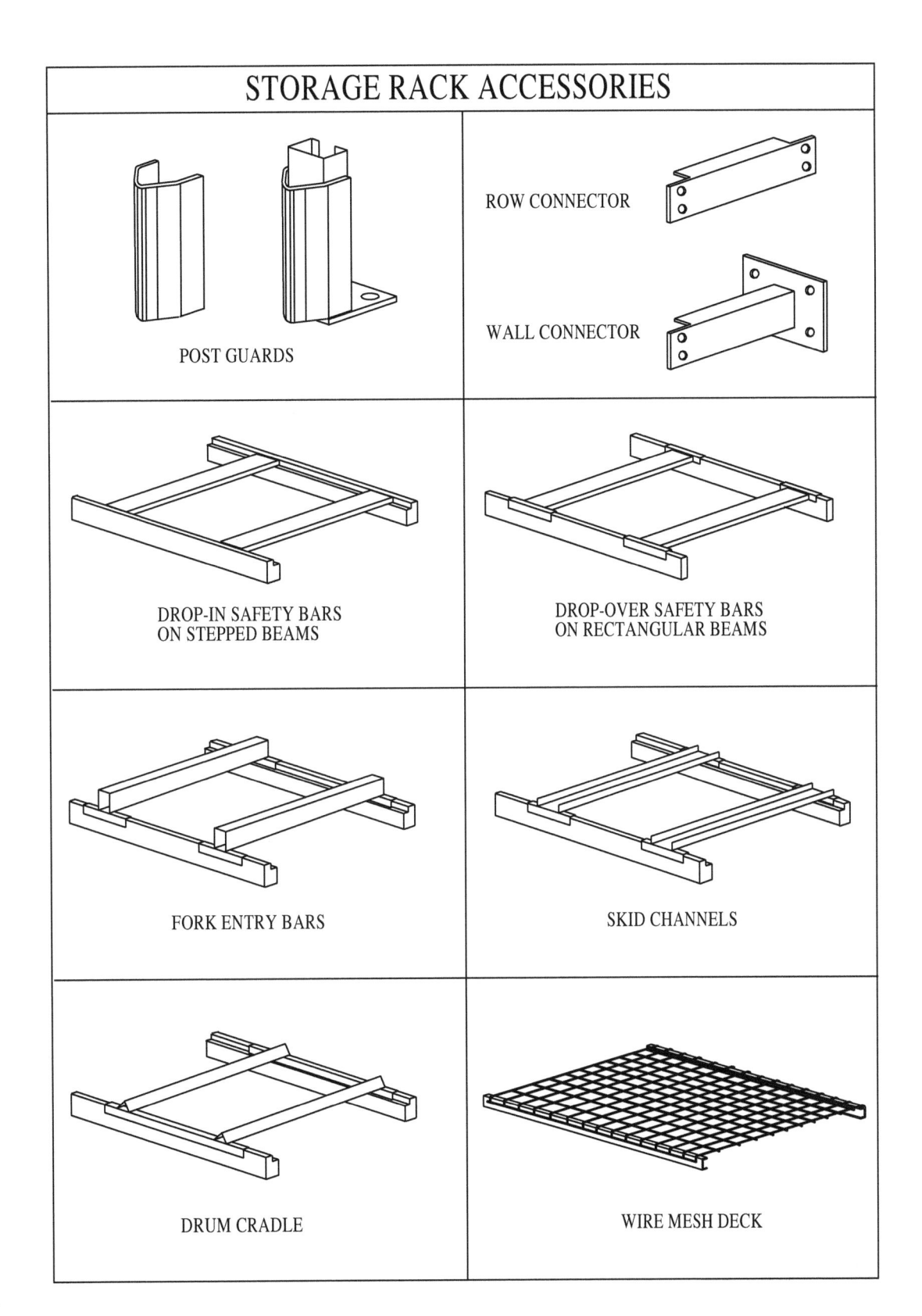

POST GUARDS	ROW CONNECTOR WALL CONNECTOR
DROP-IN SAFETY BARS ON STEPPED BEAMS	DROP-OVER SAFETY BARS ON RECTANGULAR BEAMS
FORK ENTRY BARS	SKID CHANNELS
DRUM CRADLE	WIRE MESH DECK

162

5 *STORAGE RACKS*

BLOCK STACKING

Racks are an alternate to storing directly on the floor so an explanation of floor storage is inserted here before the rack descriptions are begun.

BLOCK STACKING is also known as bulk stacking and is so named because no racks are used and pallets are stored directly on top of each other for as high and as deep as is practical. Each row forms a block; preferably all loads of the same sku with identical dates.

Only the top front pallet of each row is immediately accessible; all others are below or behind it.

This storage configuration is best used not only for multiple loads of the same item but, preferably, batch sizes which will fill a row and be retrieved all at one time.

Cube utilization of the warehouse can be excellent or poor, depending on the batch sizes and retrieval patterns. Half empty rows will result in a lot of unused space. There is more detail on storage and retrieval patterns in the order picking section.

BLOCK STACKING

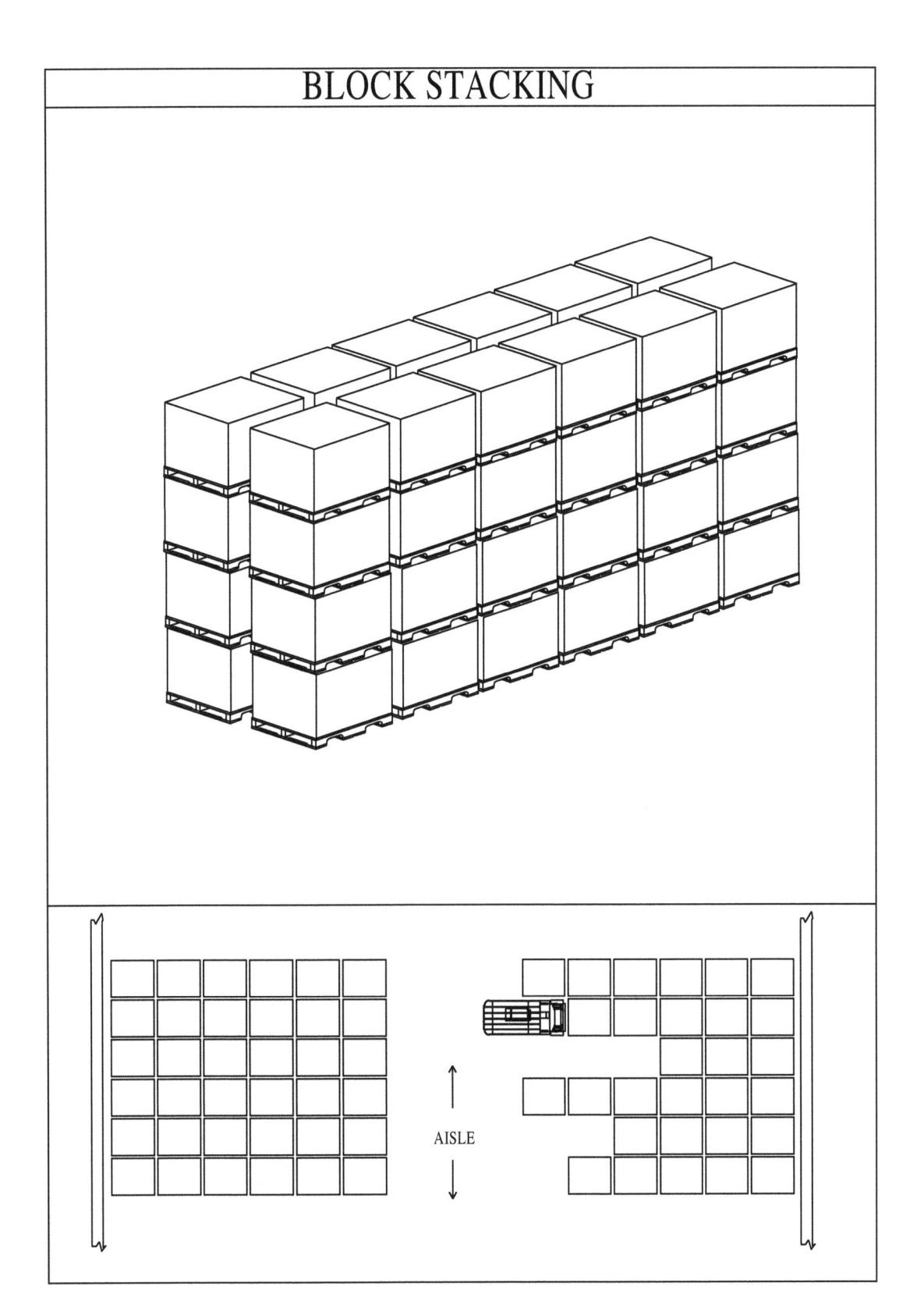

164

5 *STORAGE RACKS*

SELECTIVE STORAGE RACKS

SELECTIVE RACKS are so named because each pallet at each level is clearly accessible along the edge of an aisle and can be retrieved – selected – without moving any other pallet. Pallets are stored only one deep on each side of the aisle.

Cube utilization of the warehouse is low but may be justified by use of very high storage, excellent accessibility, easily attained first-in, first-out rotation, and minimum honeycombing.

This rack type is the most commonly used and is best for low unit load quantities; one to three loads of each sku. A frequent method of use is to place loads for case picking at the lower levels and reserve pallets of the same items at the higher levels. In other systems all levels are accessed for picking, using a high level orderpicker. Sometimes one or more levels are decked and used as heavy duty shelving for hand loaded storage of slow moving items.

If a considerable number of sku's is stored in quantities of two or more unit loads you may want to consider one of the multi-depth types of racks which follow. Turnover rate is a factor when considering a multi-depth rack and is discussed with drive in racks in section one.

SINGLE-DEEP (SELECTIVE) RACKS

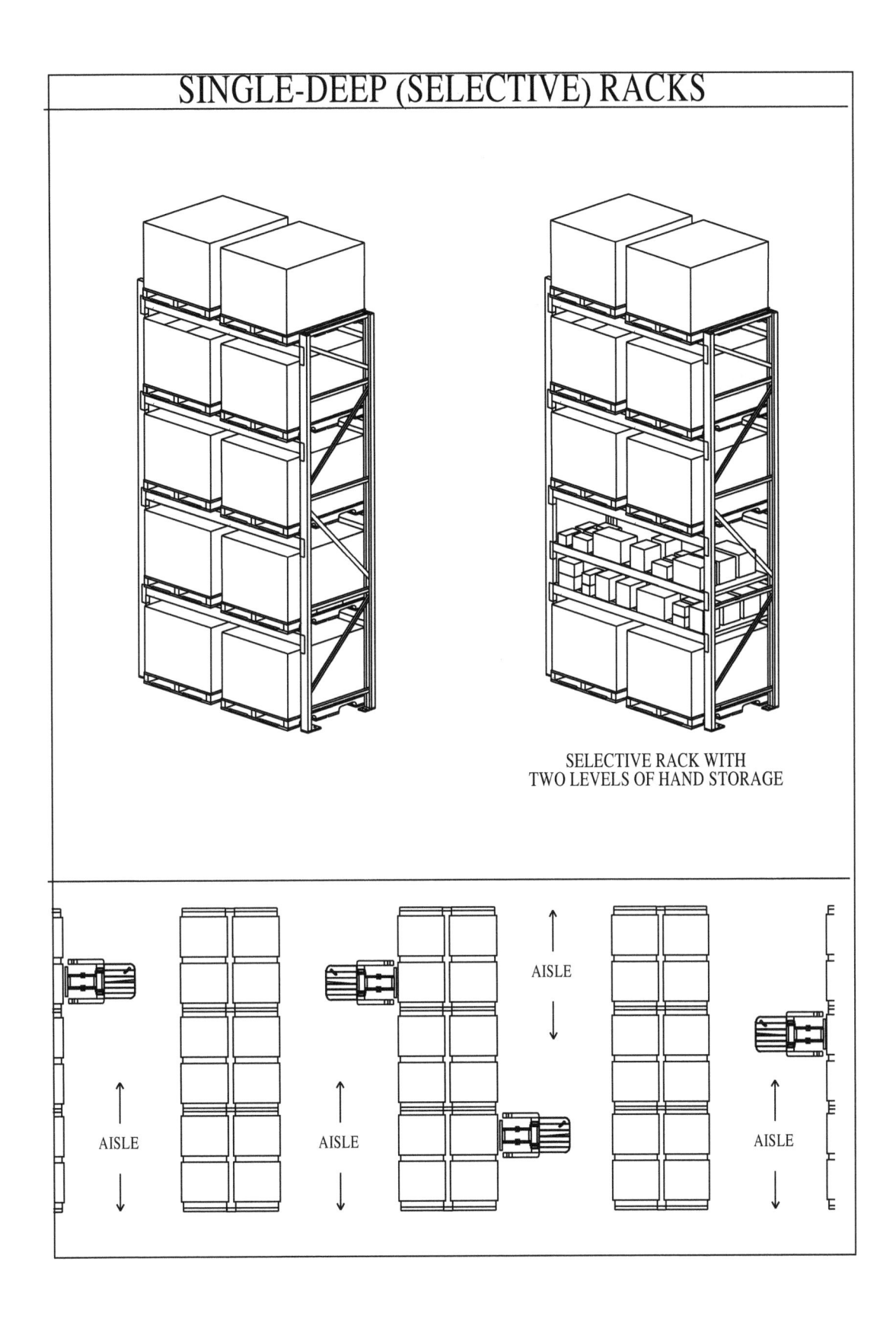

SELECTIVE RACK WITH
TWO LEVELS OF HAND STORAGE

DOUBLE-DEEP RACKS

DOUBLE-DEEP RACKS are so named because two pallets are stored on each side of the aisle by placing one behind the other, using a double-deep reach truck. Both loads should contain the same sku. The front load only is clearly accessible and must be removed to access the second load. These racks are actually two rows of selective racks, with one row placed directly behind the other. The rows are joined with appropriate row connectors to maintain a small space between them and keep them aligned.

Cube utilization is greater than with selective racks but the possibility of honeycombing, double handling or problems with rotation management must be considered when using this LIFO storage method. These potential problems will be minimal with a basic computerized warehouse control system.

Double-deep racks will yield very good results when quantities of each sku are from about two to six loads with turnover and min/max quantities being a large factor in the decision. Also to be considered is the type of storage method; fixed slots or random storage. Random storage is preferable because the flexibility allows much better use of empty pallet locations.

For larger load quantities and faster turnover you may want to consider one of the other multi-depth racks which follow.

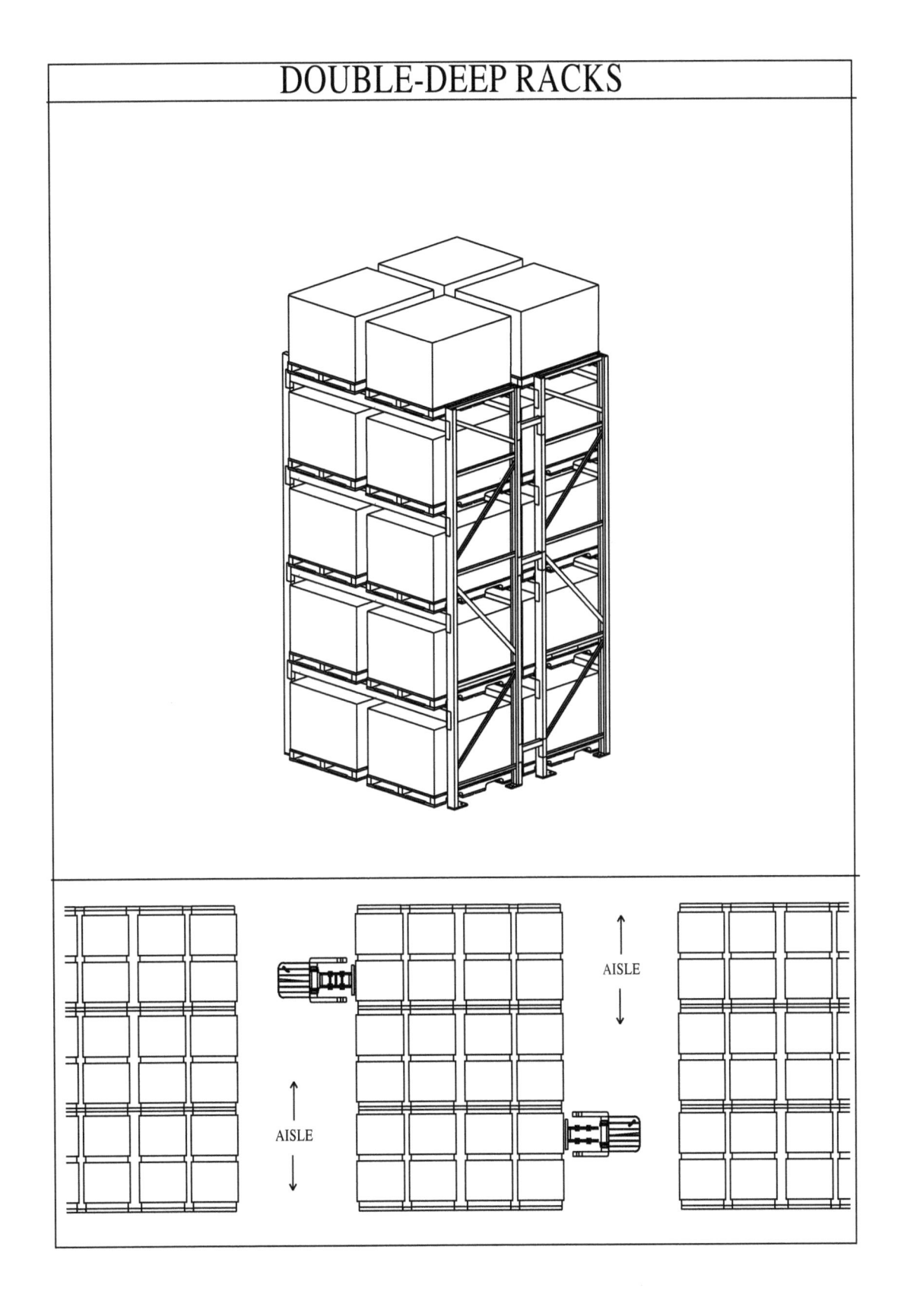

DOUBLE-DEEP RACKS

168

5 *STORAGE RACKS*

PUSH-BACK RACKS

PUSH-BACK RACKS are so named because all loads are inserted from the front, with each load pushed deeper into the racks – on rollers or dollies – by the next load being inserted.

Each lane at each level can be used for a different sku. The front load only is clearly accessible but when it is retrieved all other loads in the lane roll forward.

Cube utilization is increased according to lane depth, which is typically two to six loads deep. This LIFO system combines front selectivity with multi-depth storage but, once again, there is a need to assess potential rotation and honeycombing problems. The trick is to select the most efficient depth for your quantities and turnover. Selection of rack depths is covered in section one.

Push-back racks are increasing in popularity, especially where strict FIFO is not needed. For instance a firm which stores multiple loads of the same sku of packaging materials may find FIFO to be unimportant, at least in the short term, allowing them to insert newer incoming loads in front of older goods, again pushing them to the rear, until the day comes when the lane must be totally emptied.

A comparison of a two-deep system using a double-deep forklift versus push-back racks, serviced by any forklift, might come down to your preference rather than any distinct advantage of one over the other. However, push-backs cost more and there also may be some important dimensional differences.

For large quantities of the same sku you may want to consider other racks which follow.

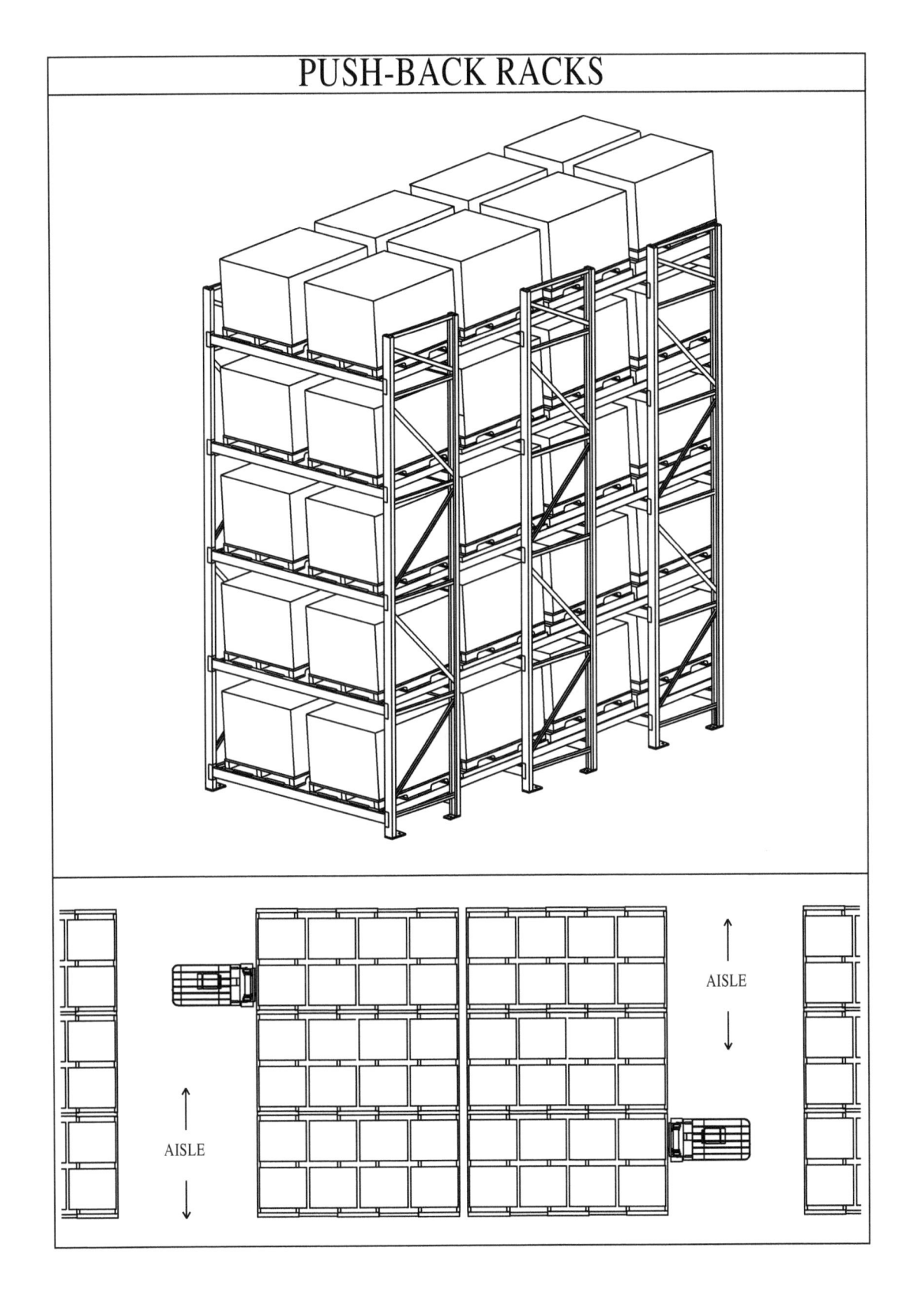

PUSH-BACK RACKS

170

5 *STORAGE RACKS*

DRIVE-IN RACKS

DRIVE-IN RACKS are so named because forklifts can drive into "tunnels" within the racks to deposit loads onto rails placed at suitable heights. Storage may be ten or more pallets deep, although depths of three to six are more common because it can become a slow and damage-prone process to go deeper. Forklifts must be operated with care when in the tunnels. Some deep installations include floor rails and guide wheels on the forklift to increase handling speed and reduce damage.

Each tunnel, including all levels, is best used to contain all loads of the same sku and same batch number.

Cube utilization is high and increases with tunnel depth. This is a LIFO system, with only the front pallets on the aisle face; all others must be stored and retrieved by driving into the tunnels.

Drive-in racks are intended for storage of large quantities of like items. Careful analysis is required to determine optimum height and depth. Used as intended they provide very efficient storage. Used poorly they can be quite inefficient, with multiple handlings needed to overcome problems of rotation control and honeycombing.

Sometimes they can be used to advantage for longer term storage of mixed goods, such as seasonal or frozen items known to be unwanted for some time.

Because of the inability to cross-brace the tunnels in drive-in racking, (except at the very top), great care should be taken to assure acceptability of this style of racking if the runs are over 5 pallets deep or very high, especially in seismic affected areas.

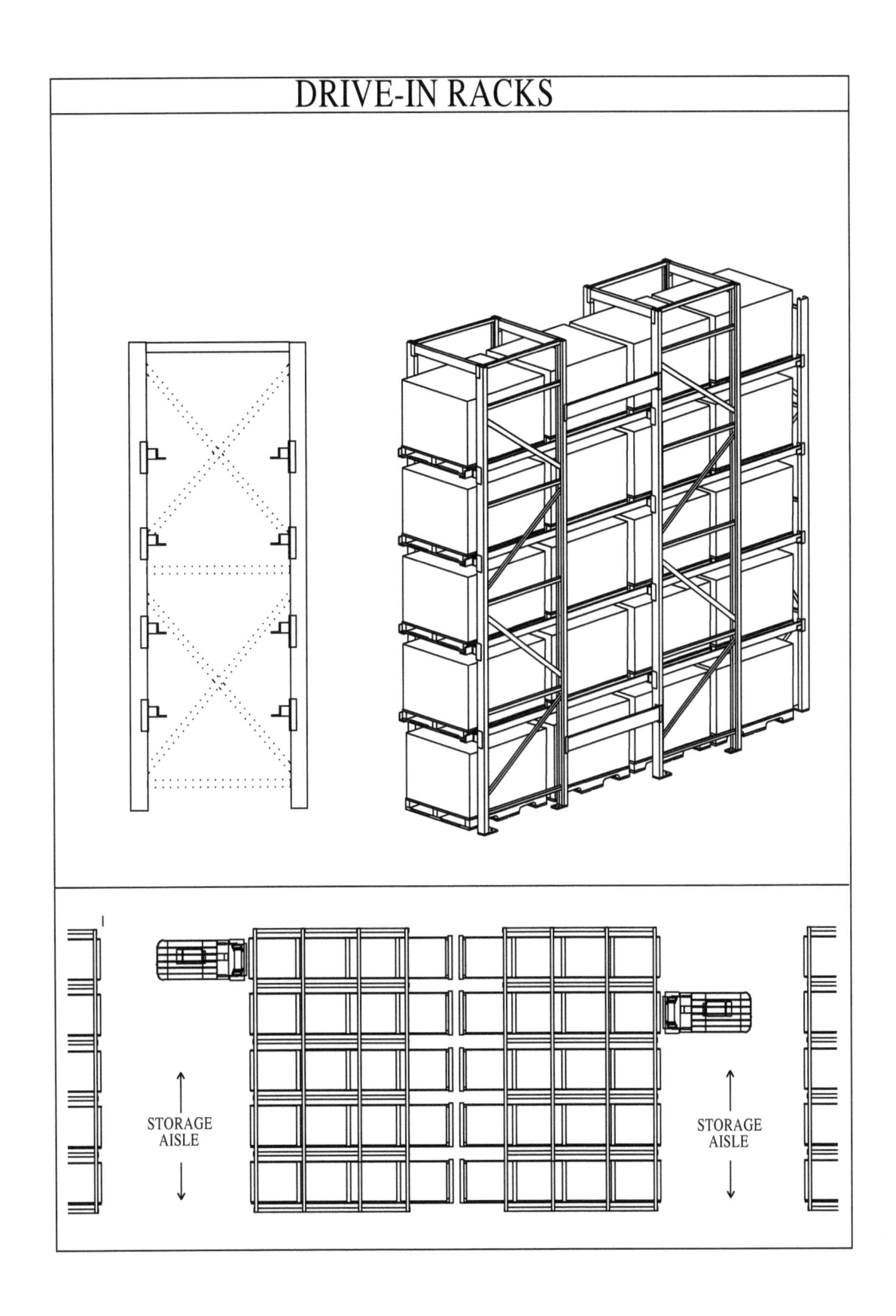

DRIVE-IN RACKS

172

STORAGE AISLE

STORAGE AISLE

5 *STORAGE RACKS*

DRIVE-THROUGH RACKS

DRIVE-THROUGH RACKS are so named because forklifts can drive into "tunnels" within the racks to deposit loads onto rails placed at suitable heights. Unlike drive-in racks they can be entered from either end. In actual use the forklift seldom drives through the tunnels; common usage is to load from one end and retrieve from the other, thus achieving a first-in, first-out situation.

Cube utilization is high and increases with tunnel depth but, because front and rear aisles are necessary, they use more space than drive-ins for the same amount of storage. Drive-through racks are the chameleons of the rack world and can be used as LIFO or FIFO. They can be fully loaded with only one sku or have a variety of sku's, accessed from both ends.

This system is often used to load, from one end, all of the pallets holding picked orders (non-stackable) intended for a truckload and sequenced to suit the delivery route. When retrieved from the other end of the rack, the truck will be loaded correctly for its' delivery route. This is a considerable saving of dock space. Flow-through racks (described next) may also be used for this purpose.

As with all multi-depth racks their height and depth should be chosen carefully. The alternate methods of using drive-through racks is shown in section one.

Because of the inability to cross-brace the tunnels in drive-through racking, (except at the very top), great care should be taken to assure acceptability of this style of racking if the runs are over 5 pallets deep or very high, especially in seismic affected areas.

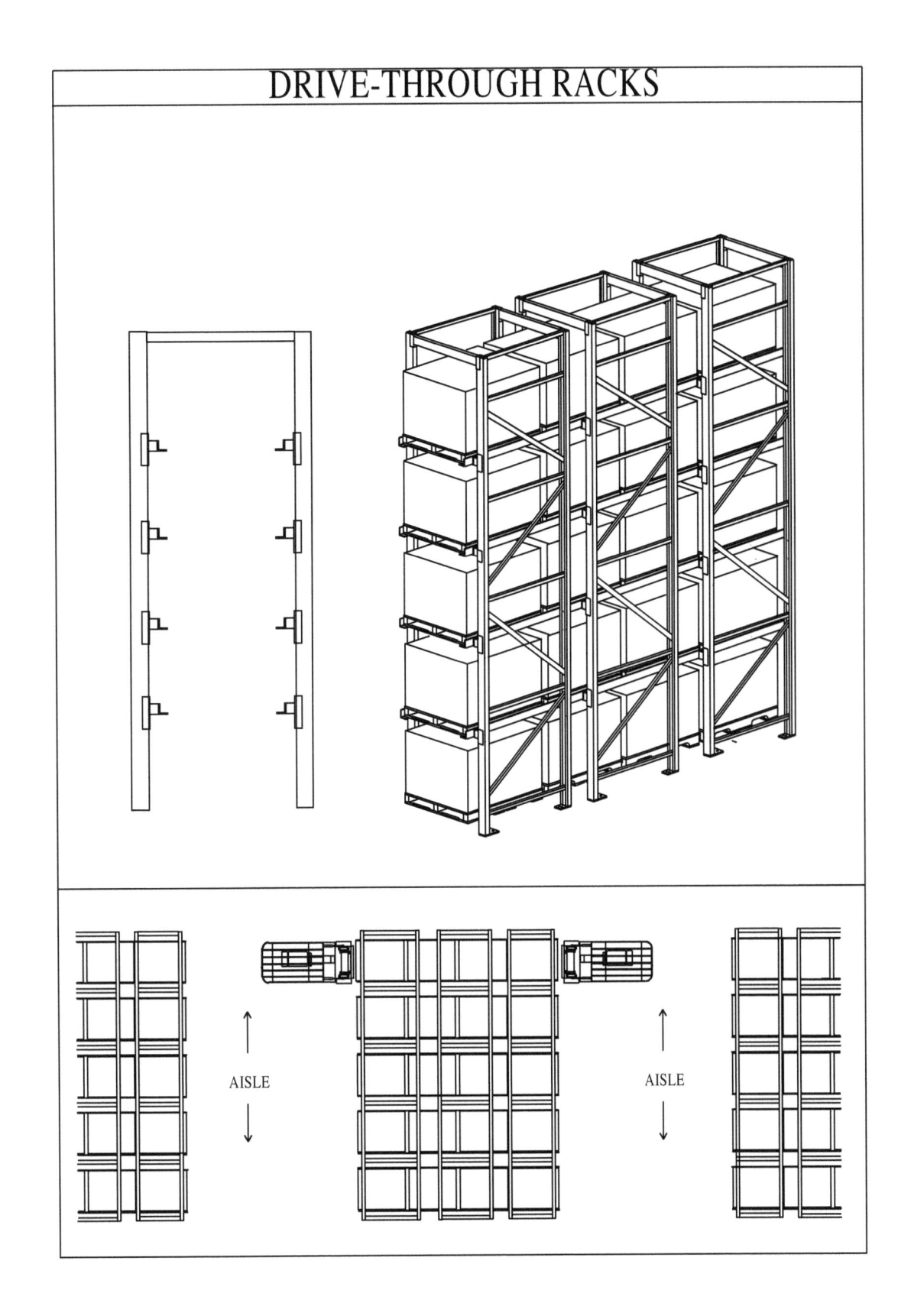

DRIVE-THROUGH RACKS

174

5 *STORAGE RACKS*

FLOW-THROUGH RACKS

FLOW-THROUGH RACKS are so named because pallets are inserted into the lanes from the rear and flow on rollers to the front for retrieval. Front and rear aisles are needed.

Each lane at each level can be used for a different product. All loads are accessible from the front aisle because as each pallet is removed, the one behind it rolls to the front position.

Cube utilization is good and increases with lane depth, which may be limited only by weights or mechanical factors. This is a FIFO system, often used where first-in, first-out is mandatory. It is also commonly used as a buffer between manufacturing processes, manufacture and shipping or picking and shipping.

The design and use of flow-through racks require a very high level of attention to detail. Very troublesome hang-ups in mid lane are not uncommon when poor quality pallets are used. Rail slope and control of acceleration should be adjustable for *each lane* because varying weights will act differently within the system.

Some systems use specially designed pallets and others may use unique designs of wheeled carriers and rails instead of rollers.

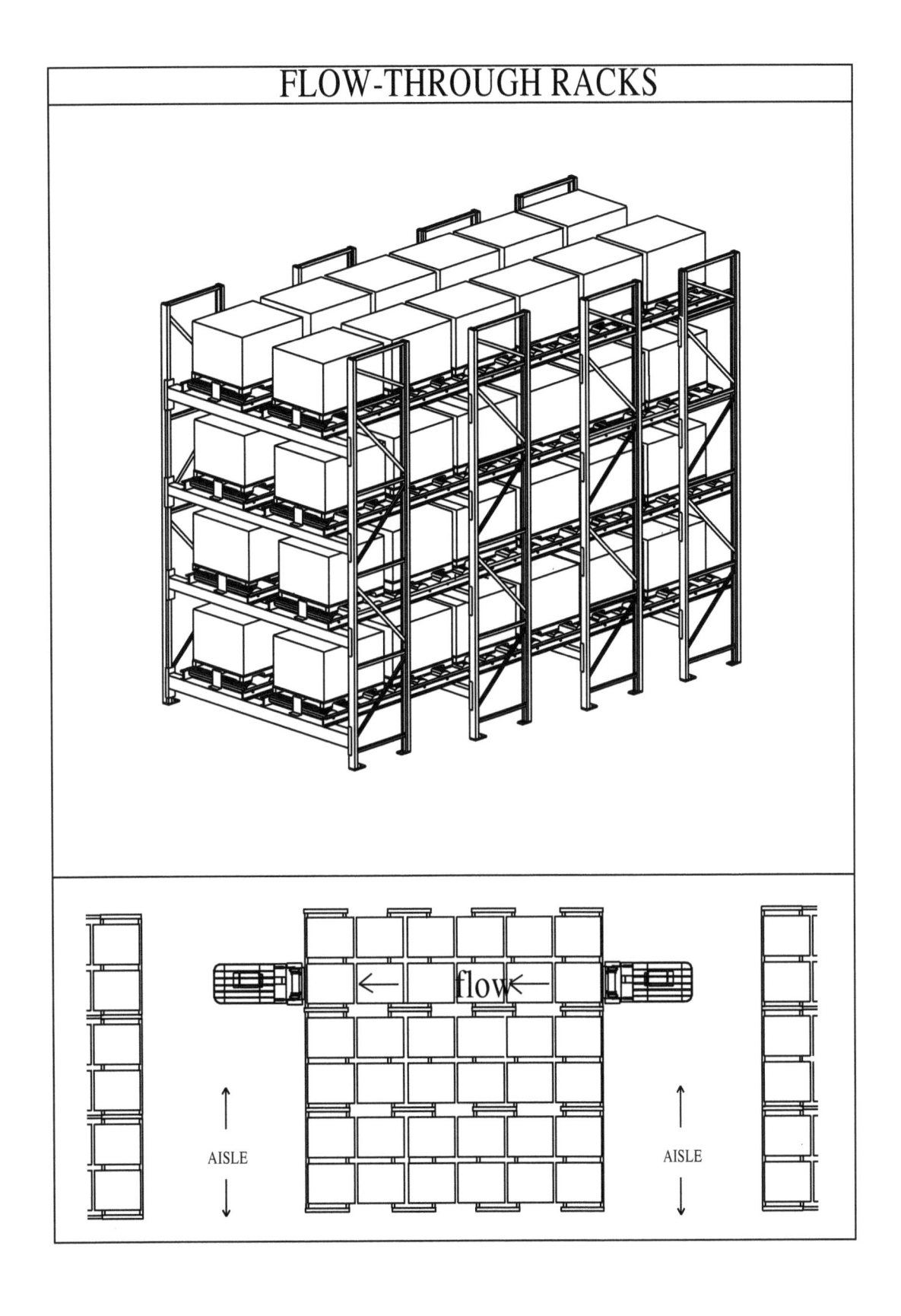

FLOW-THROUGH RACKS

AISLE

flow

AISLE

MOLE-TYPE RACK SYSTEMS

These systems somewhat resemble a drive-in rack system but there are numerous advantages they have to offer.

The structure of drive-in racking has to be wide open and unobstructed throughout the entire length of the drive-in lane. For this reason drive-in racking demands a very heavy rack upright to be used, as when a fully loaded drive-in system has a row gradually emptied, until the oldest product (which was the first one placed in that lane, and is all the way at the back end of the lane.

The products stored on either side is now exerting substantial loads sideways on the frames, which now have no counterbalancing load on the other side. For this reason, many jurisdictions have now placed a maximum depth of drive-in rack, sometime as little as 5 pallets deep maximum, to overcome some of this bending moment on the exposed frames.

The mole type system does not require the forklift to ever enter the system, and as such horizontal cross braces can be placed at each level, at each pallet location, which make the structure extremely stable.

The mole vehicle is a battery powered cart generally driven with servo motors on each wheel, and servo motors for its lifting platen. The mole has four wheels, one on each corner, which are supported on rails attached to the same post brackets as the pallet supports.

At the start of a cycle to load a full tunnel in the system, the "mole" type vehicle is placed by a forklift into the required tunnel. The fork truck operator selects "put away", or "retrieve" for the unit via a simple RF unit.

Once a pallet is placed at the end of the tunnel, the mole will travel under it; raise its lift deck (platen) about 2 inches, lifting the pallet from the side support rails. The mole then travels down the tunnel, constantly checking for other pallets already stored, or the end of the tunnel, whichever the case. On reaching that area, the mole will slow right down, gently touch against the stored pallet, then back up about 2 inches and then slowly lower its load (thus overcoming unevenly stacked pallet loads from sliding past one another in the load lowering process).

Retrieval of loads stored in the tunnel is the same way. The mole will continue its given retrieve or store process until the line is empty, or full, respectively.

There is no actual entry of the forklift into the tunnel, so rack damage is almost completely eliminated, unlike drive-in racks where the forklift needs to tread itself and its load with just a couple of inches leeway down to the full depth of the drive-in system.

Another huge advantage of the mole type system is that each lane is unique. You may have 6 levels of tunnels in what would have been just one drive in lane. Several different SKUs or products can be placed in what would have had to be just one product if in a drive-in system lane. As one "Mole" tunnel is emptied, the tunnel is now 100% open to receive any product for storage.

In drive-in, there is not that flexibility. All pallet loads must be removed from the drive-in lane. As a consequence, average slot utilization in drive-in is 40 – 45%, but with the mole type system, slot utilization can reach over 90%, without creating any significant management intervention.

The mole vehicles are designed to operate in ambient or cold storage conditions, and battery life will generally last at least a full 8 hour shift. The batteries are very light and can easily be changed for a charged set in just a couple of minutes. Recharge time is recommended to be 8 hours.

With multiple shifts in ambient temperatures, it is recommended to have 3 batteries per mole vehicle. One set in use, one on charge and the last set in cool down, so the batteries do not start the next work shift at an elevated temperature.

In any system, where you have very high density storage, sprinkler requirements need to be checked.

With the mole type system, sprinklers required within the system can be installed under the pallet, just under the mole guideway, and alongside the cross aisle bracing previously mentioned.

We recommend retaining a "Fire Code" consultant to confirm requirement in your mole system.

Two drawings follow. Also refer to page 27.

MOLE TYPE DEEP RACK SYSTEMS

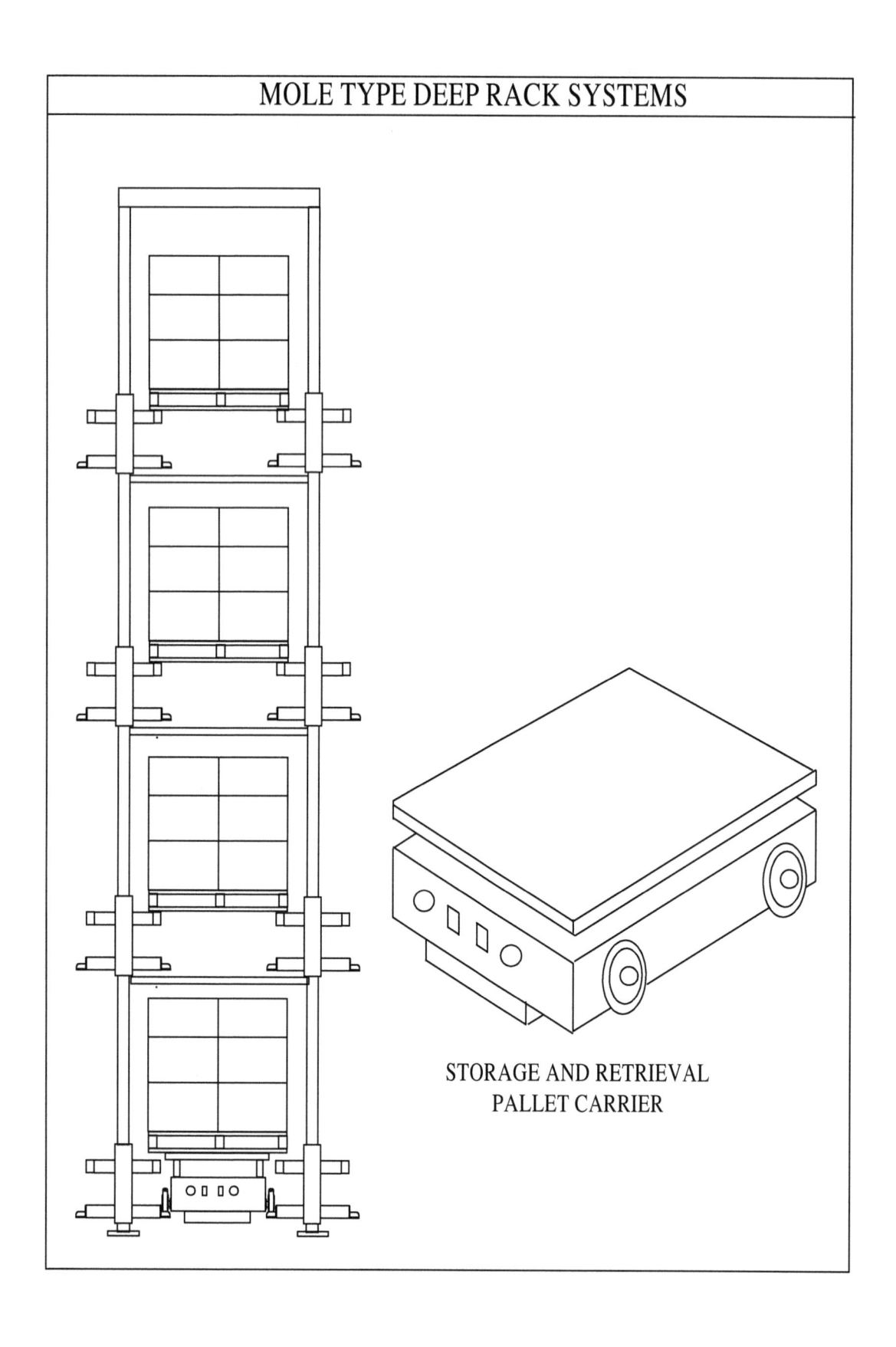

STORAGE AND RETRIEVAL
PALLET CARRIER

HOW TO CONFIGURE AND EQUIP YOUR WAREHOUSE

MOLE TYPE DEEP RACK SYSTEMS

FRONT VIEW OF STORAGE RACK
WITH RAIL SUPPORT ARMS

LIFTING PLATTEN IS LOWERED
PALLET IS IN STORAGE ON RAILS

LIFTING PLATTEN IS RAISED
TO MOVE PALLET FOR
STORAGE OR RETRIEVAL

NOTE: CONCEPT ONLY. MANUFACTURERS MODELS WILL VARY IN APPEARANCE AND ACTUATION

MOBILE RACKS

MOBILE RACKS are so named because they are fitted with wheels running on floor mounted guide rails. These are actually selective racks with only one storage aisle allotted to a multiple of rows. By shifting the racks this lone aisle can be opened between any two rows to allow entry of a forklift.

Movement in small systems may be by large diameter hand wheels, but electric power push button, or remotely controlled, is preferable in many instances.

Cube utilization is very high due to the elimination of most aisles and, additionally, this design has the advantages of selective racks, with FIFO available when wanted.

Mobile racks are typically used in high cost space with low throughput, or as an alternate to moving when no additional space is available for a growing inventory. Security may also be improved.

Ongoing design improvements are opening up a broader range of suitable applications.

MOBILE RACKS

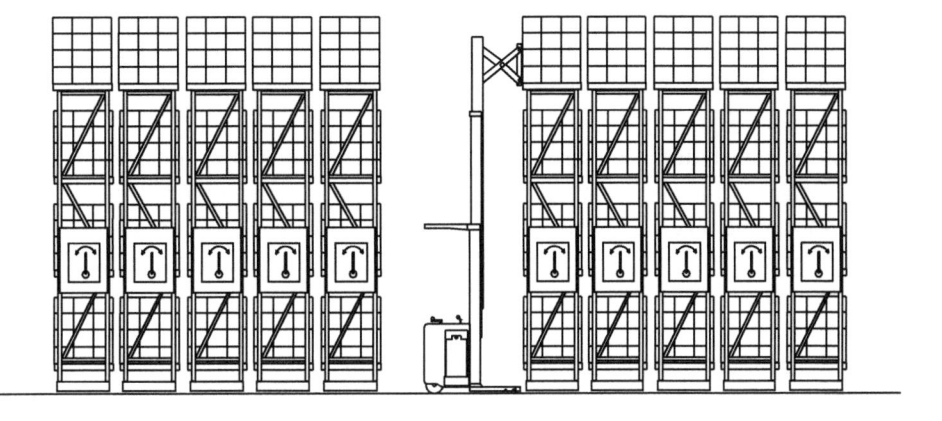

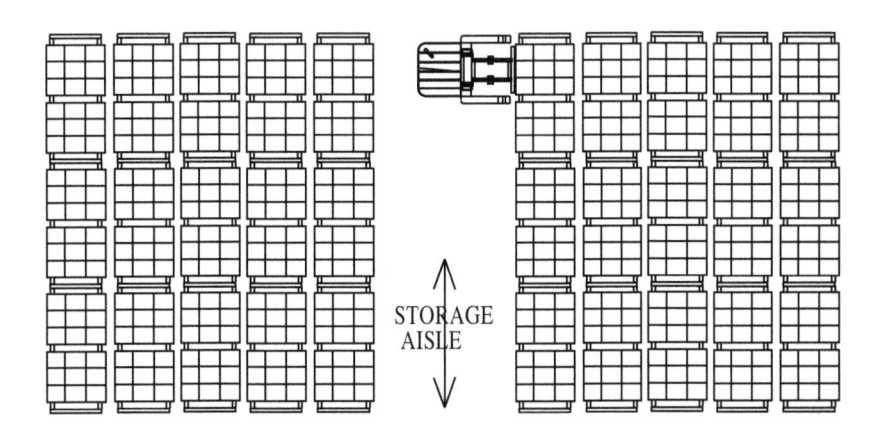

SHOWN WITH THE STORAGE AISLE OPENED
IN THE CENTER OF 10 ROWS OF SELECTIVE RACKS

CANTILEVER RACKS

CANTILEVER RACKS have load support arms which cantilever out from a column mounted on a base. The arms may be on only one side of the column, termed single-sided, or on both sides, termed double-sided. Columns are offered with a very large range of capacities and arms with a range of lengths and capacities.

These racks are typically used to store long loads such as lumber, pipes or structural steel. They may also be used for other awkward shapes.

Columns may be constructed of structural steel or formed metal and should allow vertical adjustment of the load arms. Because of the heavy weights often stored on this type of rack the columns should be placed on a firm base, preferably concrete. When placed directly on the ground they may sink and tilt off vertical. The same thing can happen if placed on an asphalt surface which softens in hot weather.

Spacing of columns depends on load weights, lengths and number of storage levels. For a mixture of load types, sizes and weights the storage requirement should be carefully reviewed with the supplier, to be sure none of the load arms will be overloaded.

Wide aisles are necessary to store long loads unless a specialty forklift is used. (see section 7)

A number of accessories are available to increase the storage capabilities and safety.

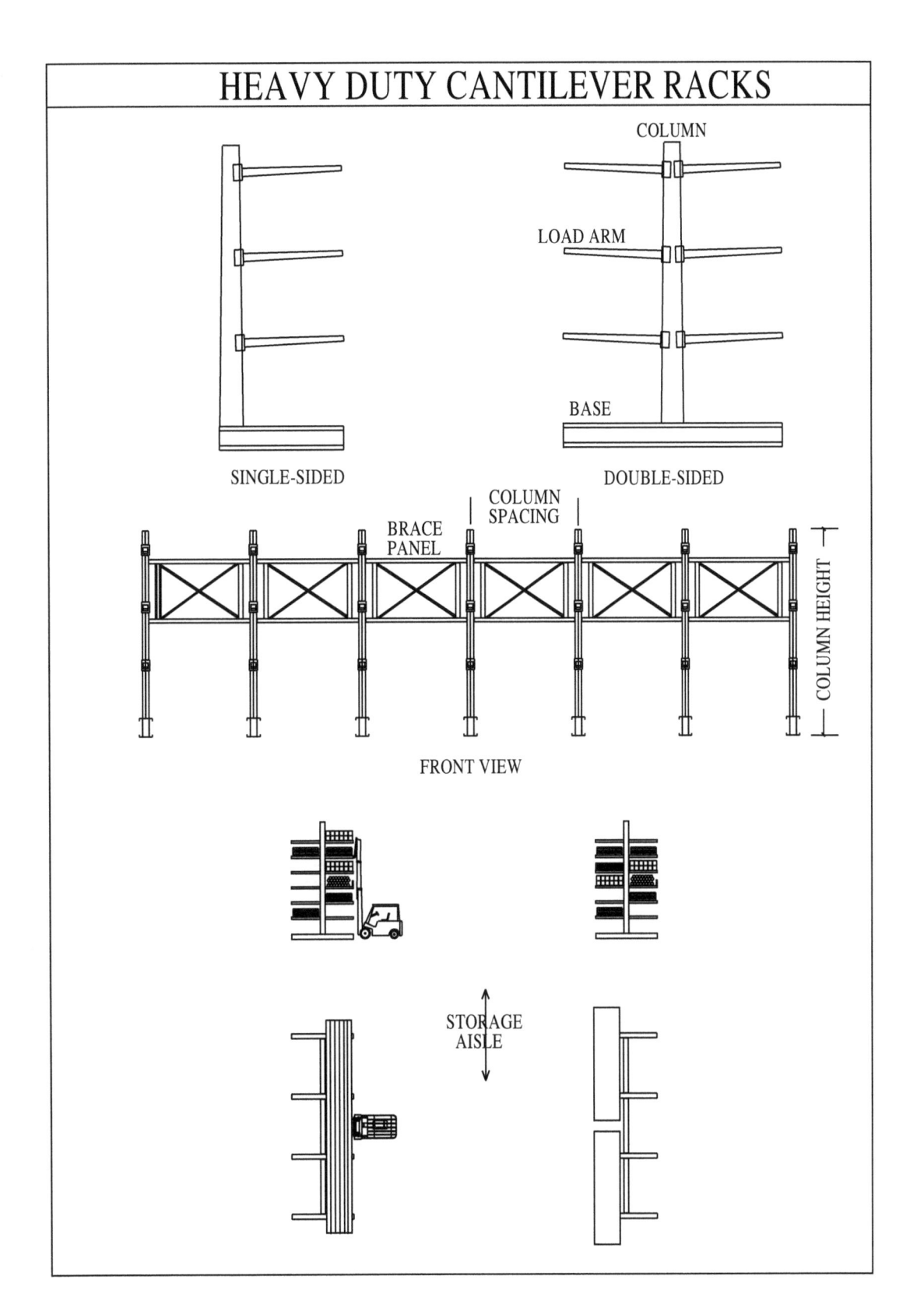

HEAVY DUTY CANTILEVER RACKS

COLUMN

LOAD ARM

BASE

SINGLE-SIDED DOUBLE-SIDED

BRACE PANEL COLUMN SPACING

COLUMN HEIGHT

FRONT VIEW

STORAGE AISLE

STORAGE RACKS

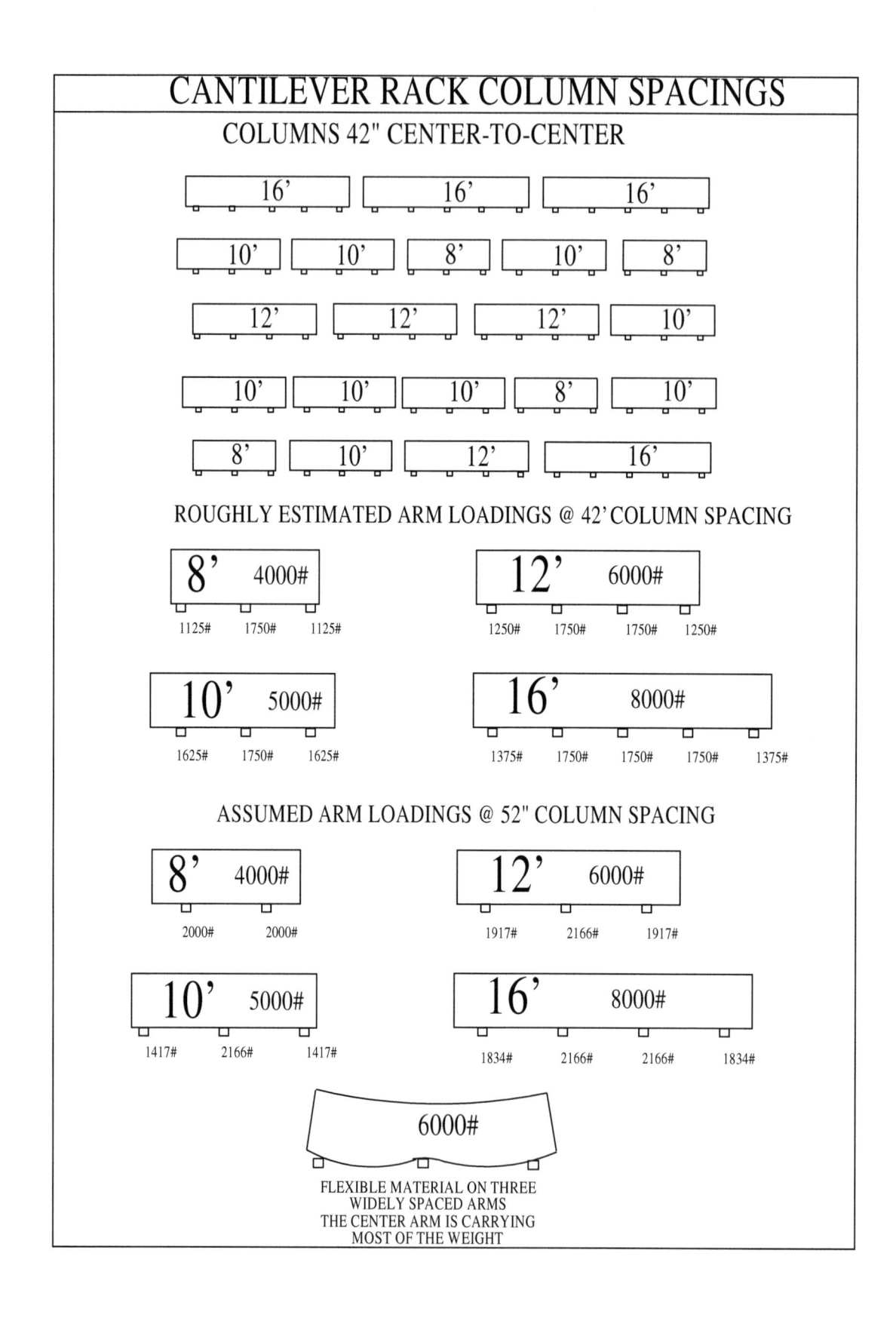

CANTILEVER RACK COLUMN SPACINGS
COLUMNS 42" CENTER-TO-CENTER

| 16' | 16' | 16' |

| 10' | 10' | 8' | 10' | 8' |

| 12' | 12' | 12' | 10' |

| 10' | 10' | 10' | 8' | 10' |

| 8' | 10' | 12' | 16' |

ROUGHLY ESTIMATED ARM LOADINGS @ 42' COLUMN SPACING

8' 4000#
1125# 1750# 1125#

12' 6000#
1250# 1750# 1750# 1250#

10' 5000#
1625# 1750# 1625#

16' 8000#
1375# 1750# 1750# 1750# 1375#

ASSUMED ARM LOADINGS @ 52" COLUMN SPACING

8' 4000#
2000# 2000#

12' 6000#
1917# 2166# 1917#

10' 5000#
1417# 2166# 1417#

16' 8000#
1834# 2166# 2166# 1834#

6000#

FLEXIBLE MATERIAL ON THREE
WIDELY SPACED ARMS
THE CENTER ARM IS CARRYING
MOST OF THE WEIGHT

HOW TO CONFIGURE AND EQUIP YOUR WAREHOUSE

THIS PAGE IS INTENTIONALLY BLANK IN ORDER TO KEEP RELAVENT TEXT AND DRAWINGS TOGETHER ON FOLLOWING PAGES.

A-FRAME RACKS

A-FRAME RACKS are another type of cantilever racks and may be single or double sided. The slope of the frames will vary between manufacturers and can also be made to order. Arms and accessories are available to suit many applications.

These racks are often used for long, hand loaded items but may be used for heavier items loaded by forklift or cranes. Frame slope allows a sling to be attached to the load. They are sometimes used beside production machines, where they may be only five or six feet high. Still another common use is for the support of vertically stored moldings, light tubing, etc. etc. This is a common sight in building supply outlets.

'A' FRAME CANTILEVER RACKS

188

SINGLE-SIDED

DOUBLE-SIDED

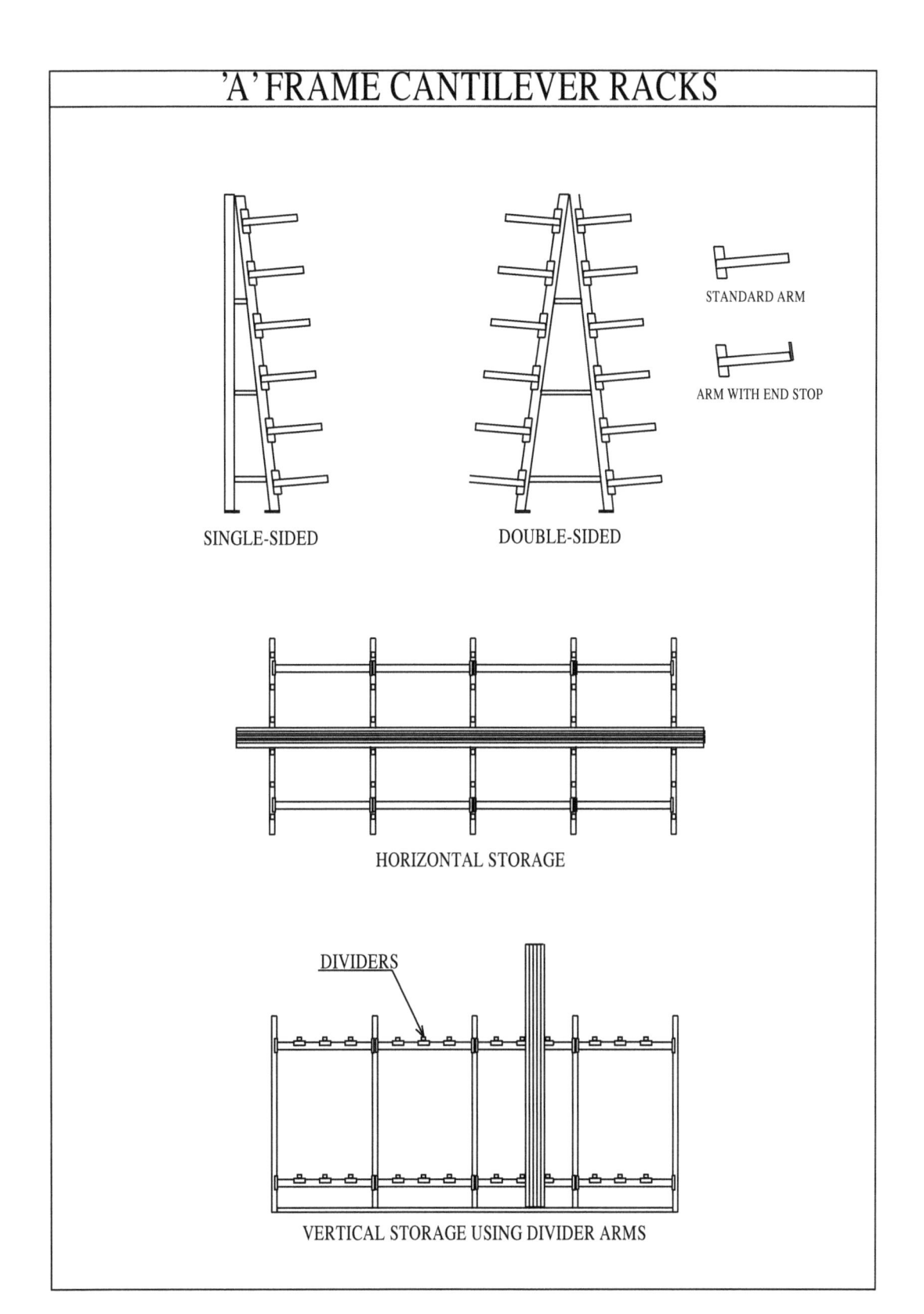

STANDARD ARM

ARM WITH END STOP

HORIZONTAL STORAGE

DIVIDERS

VERTICAL STORAGE USING DIVIDER ARMS

5 *STORAGE RACKS*

STACKING FRAMES

The next page shows two types of stacking frames. In the upper half of the drawing a stacking frame constructed from tubular metal is shown with optional fork entry channels, and to the right is the same frame with a plywood deck.

This type of frame can be used to good advantage in some situations. For instance, a plant stores may have many large castings, motors, gear boxes and other specialized items which must be on hand in the event of a machine breakdown. Some of these items may be in storage for years without being needed; they are therefore not stored in a prime location. Stored in stacking frames, sometimes only a few here and a few there in any space available, these items are accessible in just a few minutes. The frame can be transported to the point of use if desired. They can be ordered with dimensions and stacking capacities to suit.

The pallet stacking frame shown at the bottom can be used as a means to stack loads which hold easily crushed items. Seasonal storage, high and deep, can be in space which is used for other purposes at other times.

They can also be used to store and pick odd shaped or non-stackable items.

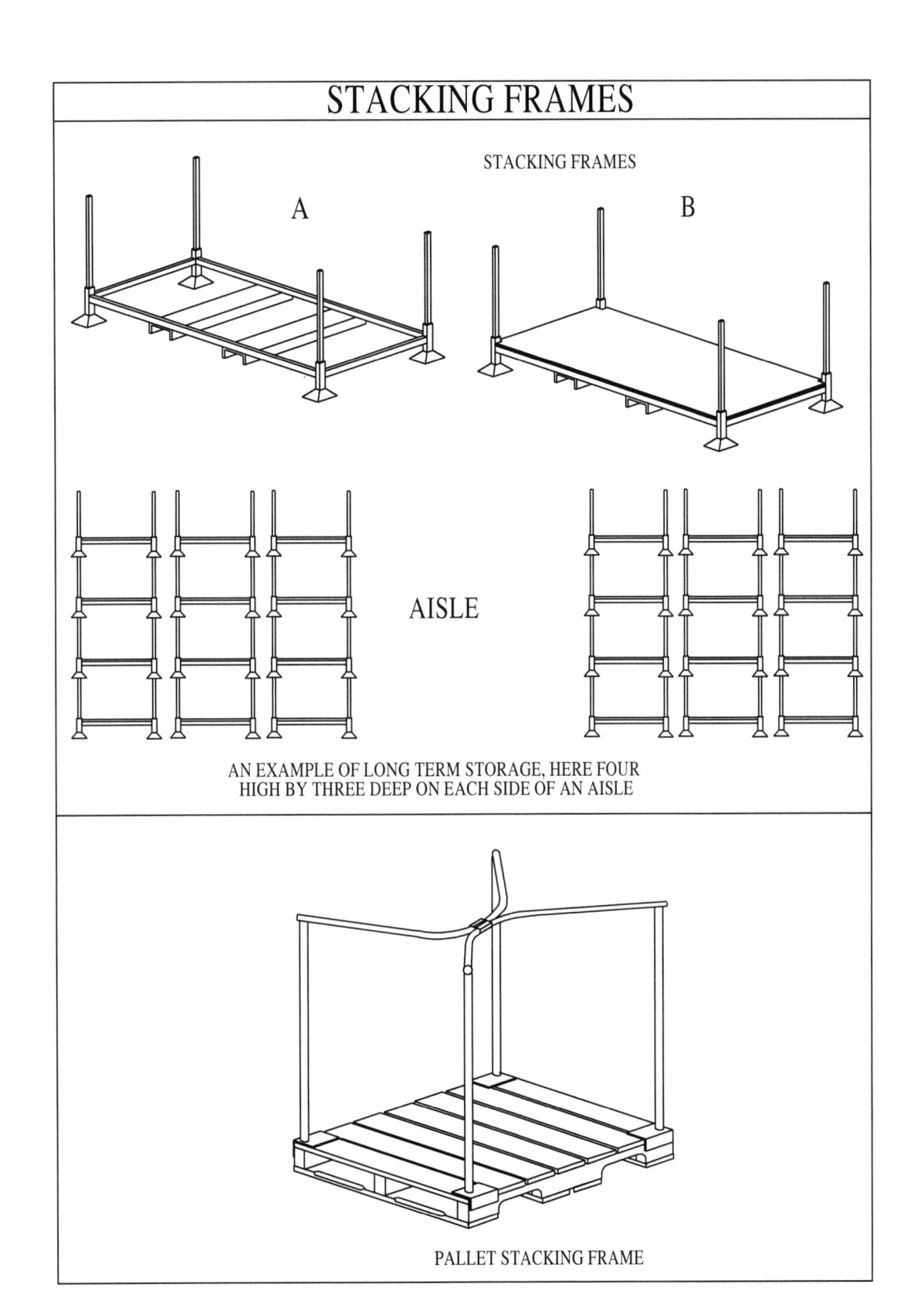

STACKING FRAMES

STACKING FRAMES

A   B

AISLE

AN EXAMPLE OF LONG TERM STORAGE, HERE FOUR
HIGH BY THREE DEEP ON EACH SIDE OF AN AISLE

PALLET STACKING FRAME

SECTION SIX
FORKLIFTS

General Information

THIS PAGE IS INTENTIONALLY BLANK IN ORDER TO KEEP RELEVANT TEXT AND DRAWINGS TOGETHER ON THE FOLLOWING PAGES.

FORKLIFTS

The subject of forklifts is divided into sections six and seven This section will first explain the two main components (**power tractor** and **forks**) joined to make a low lift pallet truck and the three components (**power tractor, mast**, and **forks or attachment**) which are combined to create any high lift truck. A number of variables are described.

The question of electric or gas power is important and some differences in operational factors are noted.

194

In section seven the many types and models on the market are described, with listings of their typical best uses and notable features. Additional comments are also included.

LOW LIFT PALLET TRUCKS

Low lift pallet trucks may be non-powered or battery powered. In either case they are equipped with forks which have a linkage to a cam. When the linkage is activated, by hand or powered hydraulic pump, the cam raises the forks enough to raise a pallet off of the floor so it can be moved. Movement is by manual or electric power.

HIGH LIFT PALLET TRUCKS

All trucks with a mast have three main components.

TRACTOR (may also be called the power tractor or power unit)

MAST (to elevate the forks)

FORKS OR OTHER ATTACHMENT (to lift and/or manipulate the load)

TRACTORS

The two most common types of forklift tractors are counterbalanced and outrigger supported. Counterbalanced forklifts may be powered by battery or by an internal combustion engine using gasoline, propane or diesel. They are available from small to huge and with tires for indoor or outdoor operation and with three or four wheels. The three wheel models have a shorter turning radius but can't lift as high as four-wheelers. Some smaller models with pneumatic tires can be effectively used for combined indoor-outdoor uses. The operator is in a sitting position except on some 3-wheel units, mostly battery powered, which are operated from a standing location at the rear. Counterbalanced trucks usually have a combination of large wheels and high under clearance, which is an asset at the docks. They do, however, require wider storage aisles than outrigger forklifts.

Outrigger equipped tractors are battery powered and have small load wheels, making them suitable for use only indoors, or on a dry paved surface when outdoors. Standard capacities range up to about 7000#. In general they will lift their maximum rated loads higher than counterbalanced trucks and some of these models are capable of very high lifts with reduced loads. Outrigger trucks have low to medium under clearance and must be considered carefully if intended to enter delivery trucks. The great advantages of these forklifts are the space savings they provide by working in narrow aisles, along with fume-free operations and very high lifts.

Walkie stackers, electric powered, also come in counterbalanced and outrigger models, with many of the same advantages and disadvantages.

A third model of forklift operates in very narrow storage aisles. These move up or down the aisle but do not turn within the aisle to deposit a load. They deposit the load by a combination of movements, which may include the use of a swinging mast or load carrying attachment, sideshifter, or side shuttle. These, and specialty long load handlers, are described in section seven.

SOME FORKLIFT CHARACTERISTICS

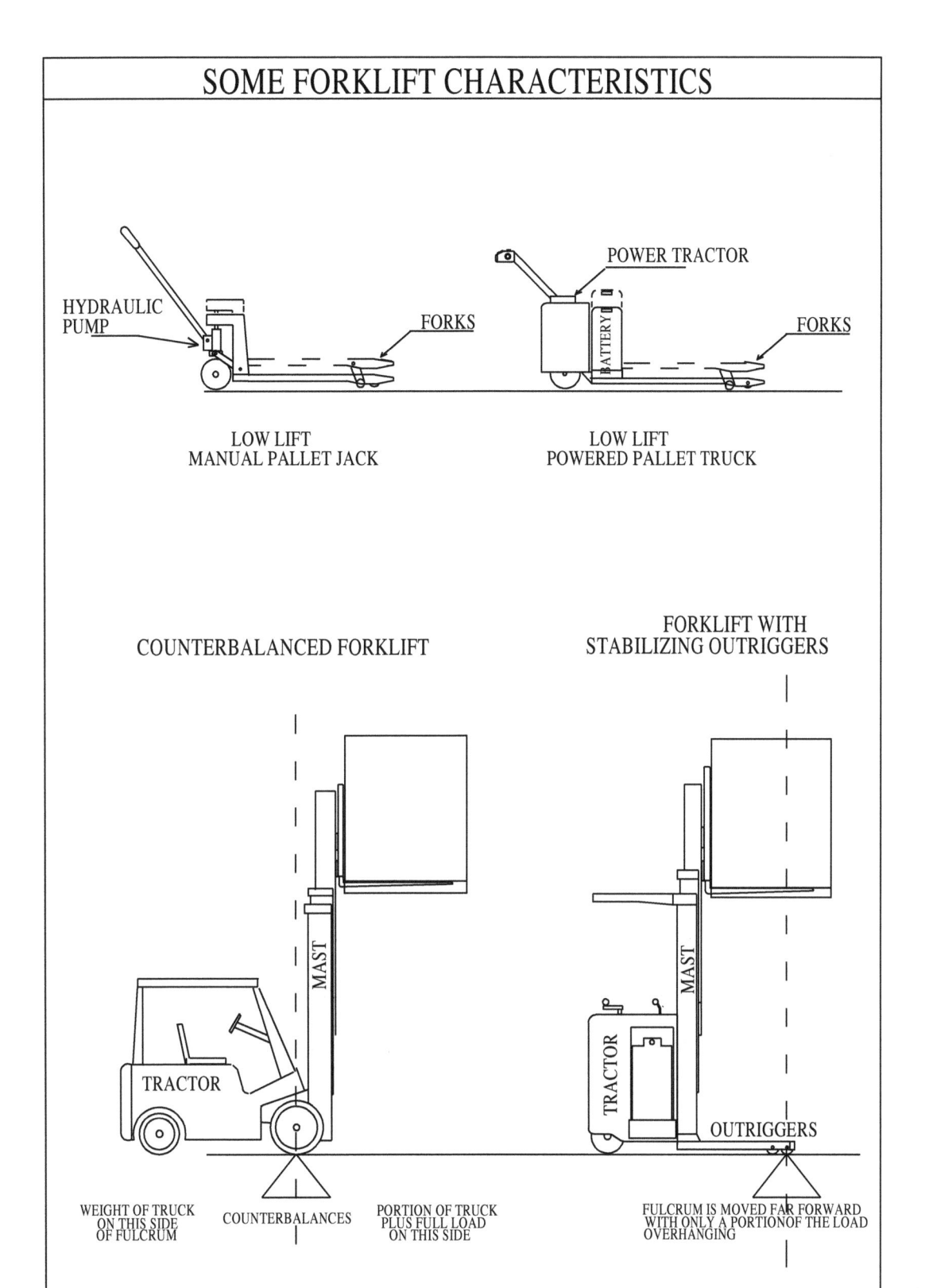

HYDRAULIC PUMP — FORKS

LOW LIFT
MANUAL PALLET JACK

POWER TRACTOR — BATTERY — FORKS

LOW LIFT
POWERED PALLET TRUCK

COUNTERBALANCED FORKLIFT

MAST
TRACTOR

WEIGHT OF TRUCK ON THIS SIDE OF FULCRUM | COUNTERBALANCES | PORTION OF TRUCK PLUS FULL LOAD ON THIS SIDE

FORKLIFT WITH STABILIZING OUTRIGGERS

MAST
TRACTOR
OUTRIGGERS

FULCRUM IS MOVED FAR FORWARD WITH ONLY A PORTION OF THE LOAD OVERHANGING

SOME COUNTERBALANCED CAPACITY VARIATIONS FROM THE SAME BASIC MODEL

Some manufacturers offer more than one model with the same rated load capacity. There will usually be a price difference and care should be taken to assure you get the one which will best suit your needs. There may be a three and a four wheel model. Some components, such as the engine or battery, motors, pumps, wheel sizes, lifting and travel speeds and overall vehicle weight and ruggedness may vary considerably. However the heavier built unit will usually be able to lift the same load to a higher height and, quite likely, have a longer life with less maintenance.

The four wheel forklifts in the top row on the next page are all based on a basic 3000# unit but by increasing the size of the counterweight or removing it completely the truck can have a variety of ratings and aisle widths. Some other components, such as the mast, may also be modified.

The forklifts in the lower row are all based on a basic 4000# unit and again the ratings are varied according to the weight of the counterweight and other affected components.

Assuming you want a 4000# truck and don't need a very high lift you have the choice of **D** in the top row or **G** in the bottom row. They both have the desired capacity. However the top unit will have a shorter wheelbase (possibly an advantage) but will likely also have smaller wheels, engine, etc. etc. than the lower unit. It may achieve the 4000# rating by adding counterweight and strengthening other parts as necessary.

The lower 4000# unit, with a larger wheelbase and tractor, will probably have all larger components. It will also need wider storage aisles. So the choice comes down to selecting a unit capable of a light, medium or heavy workload, and with an acceptable storage aisle width.

Another example: if the need is for a truck to lift 3000# to a considerable height you may compare **A**, **F**, or **E**, depending on the lift height and workload. **E** will be capable of lifting 3000# to a higher level. Storage aisle width will vary with each model.

These are not all the possible variances and some models will not have all the options shown. Three wheeled trucks also add to the possibilities.

The important thing is to be aware of the differences so the choice can be made based on the job to be done, always keeping future workload changes in mind.

Outrigger type forklifts may also come with designs for light, medium, or heavy duty workloads. Their differences may be less conspicuous than counterbalanced trucks but they do exist and it falls on the purchaser to determine the best value for his application. Check the maximum battery compartment size available; designers do not provide an extra-large compartment for a truck meant for light or medium duty. Once again such things as motor and pump sizes, drive wheel size and speeds are indicators. These specifications are on most literature. If not, ask for them and review them carefully.

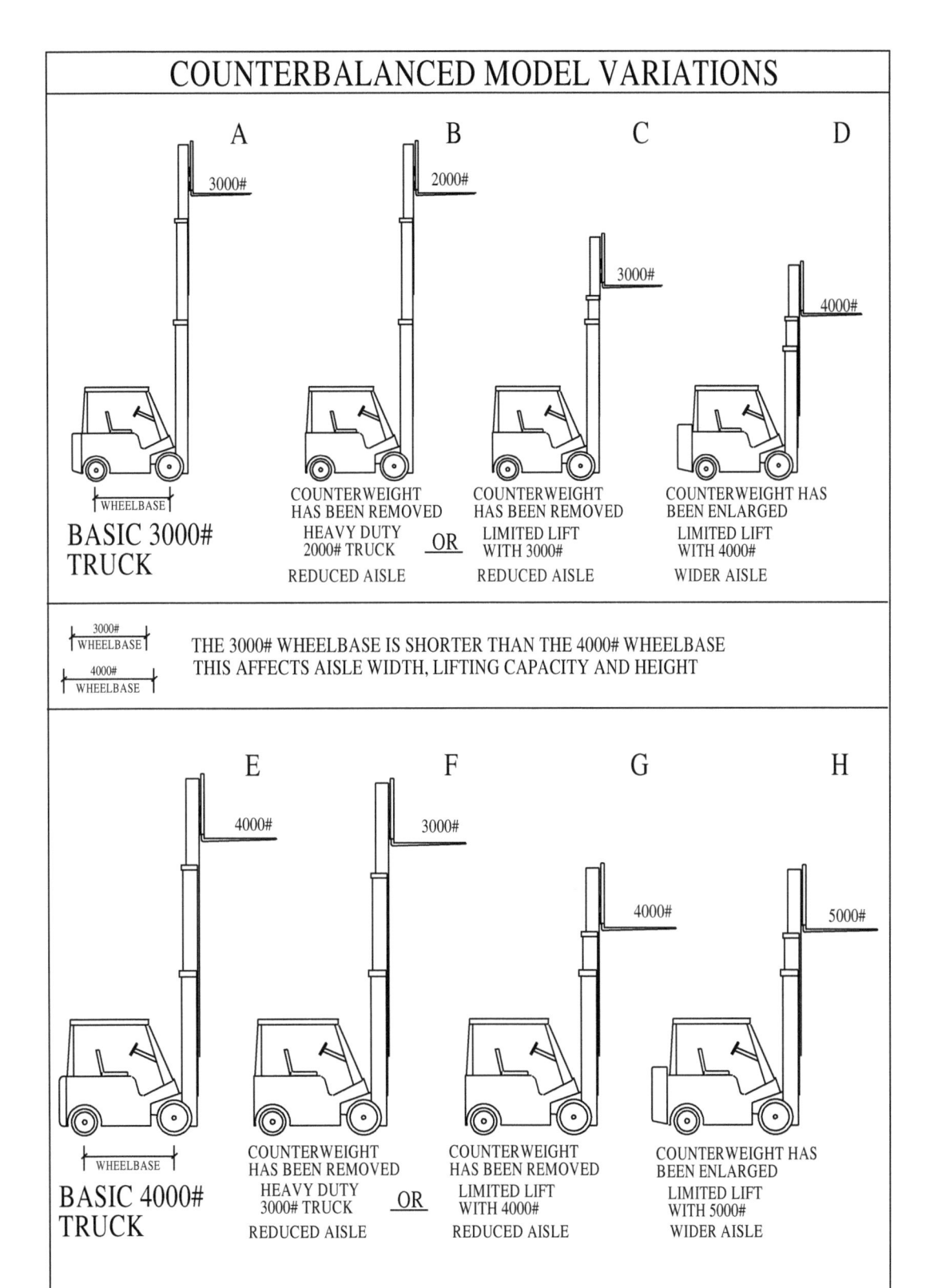

COUNTERBALANCED MODEL VARIATIONS

A — 3000#
WHEELBASE
BASIC 3000# TRUCK

B — 2000#
COUNTERWEIGHT HAS BEEN REMOVED
HEAVY DUTY 2000# TRUCK
REDUCED AISLE

OR

C — 3000#
COUNTERWEIGHT HAS BEEN REMOVED
LIMITED LIFT WITH 3000#
REDUCED AISLE

D — 4000#
COUNTERWEIGHT HAS BEEN ENLARGED
LIMITED LIFT WITH 4000#
WIDER AISLE

3000# WHEELBASE
4000# WHEELBASE

THE 3000# WHEELBASE IS SHORTER THAN THE 4000# WHEELBASE
THIS AFFECTS AISLE WIDTH, LIFTING CAPACITY AND HEIGHT

E — 4000#
WHEELBASE
BASIC 4000# TRUCK

F — 3000#
COUNTERWEIGHT HAS BEEN REMOVED
HEAVY DUTY 3000# TRUCK
REDUCED AISLE

OR

G — 4000#
COUNTERWEIGHT HAS BEEN REMOVED
LIMITED LIFT WITH 4000#
REDUCED AISLE

H — 5000#
COUNTERWEIGHT HAS BEEN ENLARGED
LIMITED LIFT WITH 5000#
WIDER AISLE

If, for example, a truck lift speed is 80 fpm when empty but is reduced to 40 fpm when lifting a full load it could be an indication of a pump and pump motor which are undersized for a heavy-duty workload. The ability to lift a load to a specified height is a factor of stability and does not necessarily mean that the maximum load can be lifted continuously for a full shift.

With all battery powered trucks always ask for the battery and charger specifications separately. Do not accept a "package price" which, unfortunately, may not make clear the size and quality of the battery and charger. The charger should be capable of recharging a fully discharged battery in eight hours or less, unless you are sure the truck will not be put on a two-shift operation. Otherwise adding a second battery will probably also mean adding a second charger. If there is one dominant piece of advice regarding battery powered trucks, it is that skimping on the battery and charger will be a costly decision in the great majority of applications. Buy what seems to be an overcapacity battery. As it ages it will produce less power and, with the built-in surplus, will still work a full shift when a lesser battery is not making it through the shift. Further, running an undersized battery down below its' recommended voltage can cause serious and expensive motor failures.

THIS PAGE IS INTENTIONALLY BLANK IN ORDER TO KEEP RELEVANT TEXT AND DRAWINGS TOGETHER ON THE FOLLOWING PAGES.

FORKLIFT MASTS

Forklift masts are not all the same! In addition to the lifting height there are a number of dimensional options which have been designed to meet varying requirements and restrictions.

There are two main categories of masts, NON-TELESCOPIC and TELESCOPIC. They are assembled from vertical steel channels, hydraulic cylinders and lift chains. A *fork carriage* attached to the chains moves up when the hydraulic cylinders are actuated to raise the chains.

Non-telescopic masts consist of only two outer channels while telescopic models have a number of additional inner channels, nested to extend in sequence as the forks are raised.

By varying the number and arrangement of channels, hydraulic cylinders and chains the mast features can be changed to fit many situations. Masts are commonly referred to based on the number of channels; simplex, duplex, triplex and quad. Five, and maybe more, sets of channels are available occasionally.

Here are some main specifications to be aware of:

OVERALL COLLAPSED HEIGHT (OACH) May also be called overall height lowered (OHL).
This is the height of the mast when it is fully lowered. This dimension is important when it is required to pass through doors or under other obstructions. Entering delivery vehicles or the tunnels of drive-in racks also must be considered. In fact, the mast height should be checked when the forks are raised at least eight inches because that's the minimum used to carry a pallet in or out of a delivery vehicle. This may involve *free lift*, explained shortly.

LIFT HEIGHT (LH) May also be called maximum fork height (MFH)
This is the height to the top surface of the forks when fully raised and in a level position. Lift height should be 10" to 12". higher than the top level of storage racks because the bottom of a pallet is below the forks and floor irregularities may further reduce the clearance by tilting the forklift.

OVERALL EXTENDED HEIGHT (OAEH)
This is the height of the highest point of the truck when the mast is fully elevated, with the forks at their maximum lift height. The fork carriage or load backrest very often extends higher than the mast itself and this should be carefully noted. Literature may or may not show the backrest or it may state the OAEH with and without the backrest. Damage to building fixtures and the forklift may result if the mast or backrest is too high.

FREE LIFT (FL)
This is the height the forks can be elevated before *any part of the truck or attachment* extends beyond the OACH. This includes the fork carriage and the backrest. Double stacking within a trailer is an example where this dimension can be very important. Once again the specifications should be read carefully so you will get what you expect, with no surprises.

MASTS

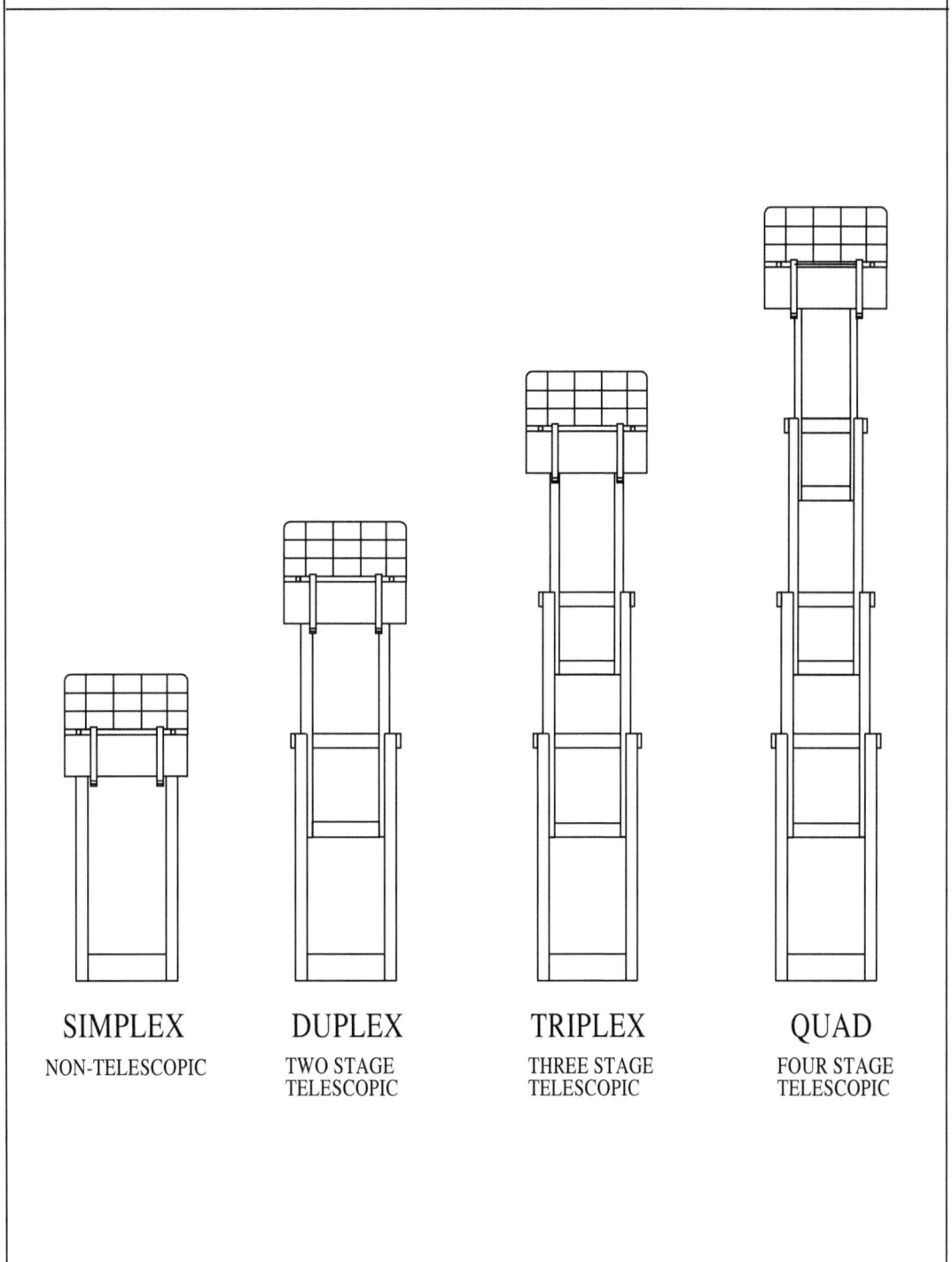

SIMPLEX	DUPLEX	TRIPLEX	QUAD
NON-TELESCOPIC	TWO STAGE TELESCOPIC	THREE STAGE TELESCOPIC	FOUR STAGE TELESCOPIC

MASTS

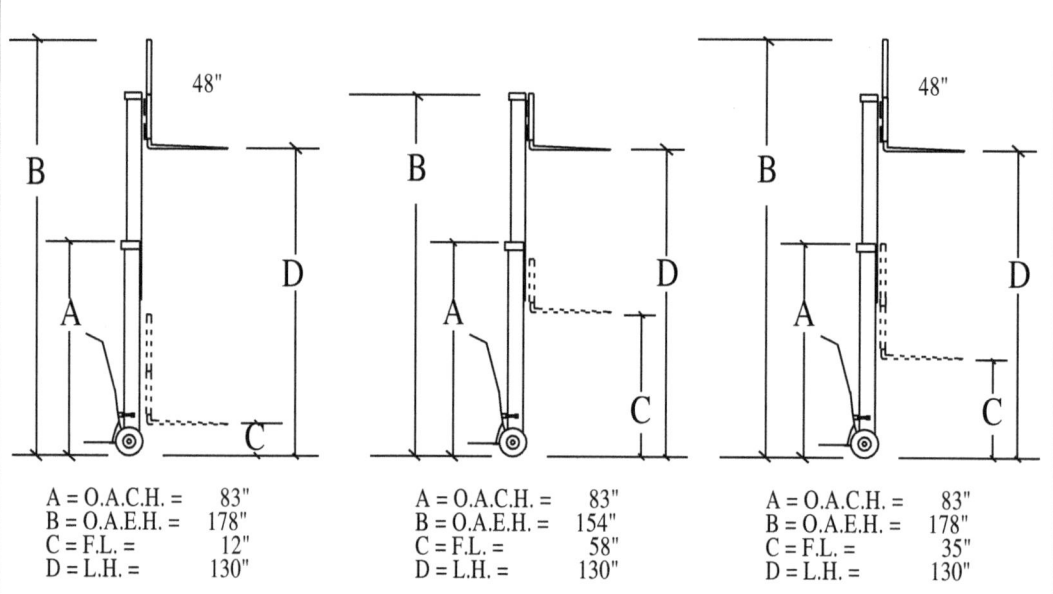

AND
EFFECTS OF LOAD BACKREST ON FREE LIFT AND OVERALL EXTENDED HEIGHT

O.A.C.H. = OVERALL COLLAPSED HEIGHT F.L. = FREE LIFT
O.A.E.H. = OVERALL EXTENDED HEIGHT L.H. = LIFT HEIGHT

SIMPLEX MAST WITHOUT LOAD BACKREST

A = O.A.C.H. = 78"
B = O.A.E.H. = 78"
C = F.L. = 66"
D = L.H. = 66"

SIMPLEX MAST WITH LOAD BACKREST

A = O.A.C.H. = 78"
B = O.A.E.H. = 102"
C = F.L. = 42"
D = L.H. = 66"

DUPLEX MAST WITH STANDARD (NOMINAL) FREE LIFT C/W LOAD BACKREST

A = O.A.C.H. = 83"
B = O.A.E.H. = 178"
C = F.L. = 12"
D = L.H. = 130"

DUPLEX MAST WITH FULL FREE LIFT WITHOUT LOAD BACKREST

A = O.A.C.H. = 83"
B = O.A.E.H. = 154"
C = F.L. = 58"
D = L.H. = 130"

DUPLEX MAST WITH FULL FREE LIFT C/W LOAD BACKREST

A = O.A.C.H. = 83"
B = O.A.E.H. = 178"
C = F.L. = 35"
D = L.H. = 130"

HOW TO CONFIGURE AND EQUIP YOUR WAREHOUSE

SOME EFFECTS OF A LOAD BACKREST

The load backrest is a safety device which is now standard equipment on most, or all forklifts, normally extending to a height of 48" above the top face of the forks. Some small stackers may have 36" backrests. There are instances where a backrest can create a problem. Examples could be, as mentioned, when stacking within a semi trailer or within drive-in racks when the backrest is higher than the loads. This short load scenario could also apply when the backrest will prevent lifting to the desired top rack level. Any such problem should be resolved from a safety point of view with any persons or agency involved.

The sketches on the previous page show the effects of a load backrest on free lift and overall extended height. The load backrest is not technically a part of the mast and although it is accounted for on most current literature there may still be some that do not make the effects clear.

The simplex mast shows a truck without a load backrest, having 66" of free lift with an overall extended height of 78", which equals the overall collapsed height. This simplex mast with a 36" backrest is limited to 42" of free lift because at that point the backrest starts to extend above the mast. When the forks are fully elevated to 66" the top of the backrest is at 102". In summary, when the backrest is added the free lift is often reduced and the extended height is increased.

These are examples only; not all simplex masts will have these exact dimensions.

The first sketch of a duplex mast shows a very small amount of free lift, often called "nominal" free lift. As the forks are raised the inner mast will soon extend above the outer mast, increasing the forklift height. Always try to have at least eight inches of free lift if there are any locations where the mast just clears a doorway or semi-trailer entrance. Then a pallet can be raised off of the floor without extending the mast. A load backrest will have no effect on free lift but will increase the extended height.

Next is a duplex mast with high or "full" free lift. A combination of additional lift cylinders and chains makes this extra free lift possible, lifting the fork carriage almost to the top of the mast before the second stage starts to extend. Again the situation and different dimensions are shown with and without a load backrest.

Most, but not all, triplex and quad masts provide high free lift as a built-in advantage of the design.

While checking the mast details take a look at the tilt specs, if any. Some trucks have no tilt available while others may offer it as an option and some provide tilt as a standard feature. Rearward and forward tilt are specified in degrees and vary considerably with different truck designs and lift heights. Tilt degrees are reduced on very high lifts. Tilt is a very important factor in many warehouse locations, including operations with dock levelers, storage racks and where chiseling under loads is required.

Read the literature carefully, and check with the supplier when indicated, to be sure of the mast and complete forklift specifications. Then provide the forklift specifications to others involved with the project, such as a rack supplier, and get their assurances that the forklift is compatible with their design and dimensions.

FORKS

Forks are attached to a *fork carriage* which raises and lowers on rollers within the inner mast channels. There is a selection of fork shapes, varied by length, thickness, taper, shape across the width of the tips and bevel of the tips.

Each combination of blade and tip shape is intended for a different application and some are more costly than others. So called "standard" forks are supplied with most trucks and they may be two or more inches thick near the heel, making them unsuitable for entry into the notches of 4-way notched pallets. They also will have fairly blunt tips, unsuitable for chiseling under a load sitting on the floor.

Fortunately there are a great many fork types designed and proven for specific applications. Talk over your requirements with the supplier, and get a recommendation. Occasionally two sets of forks are necessary, especially where load depth varies greatly, hopefully with one set used the majority of the time, and replaced by the second set only occasionally.

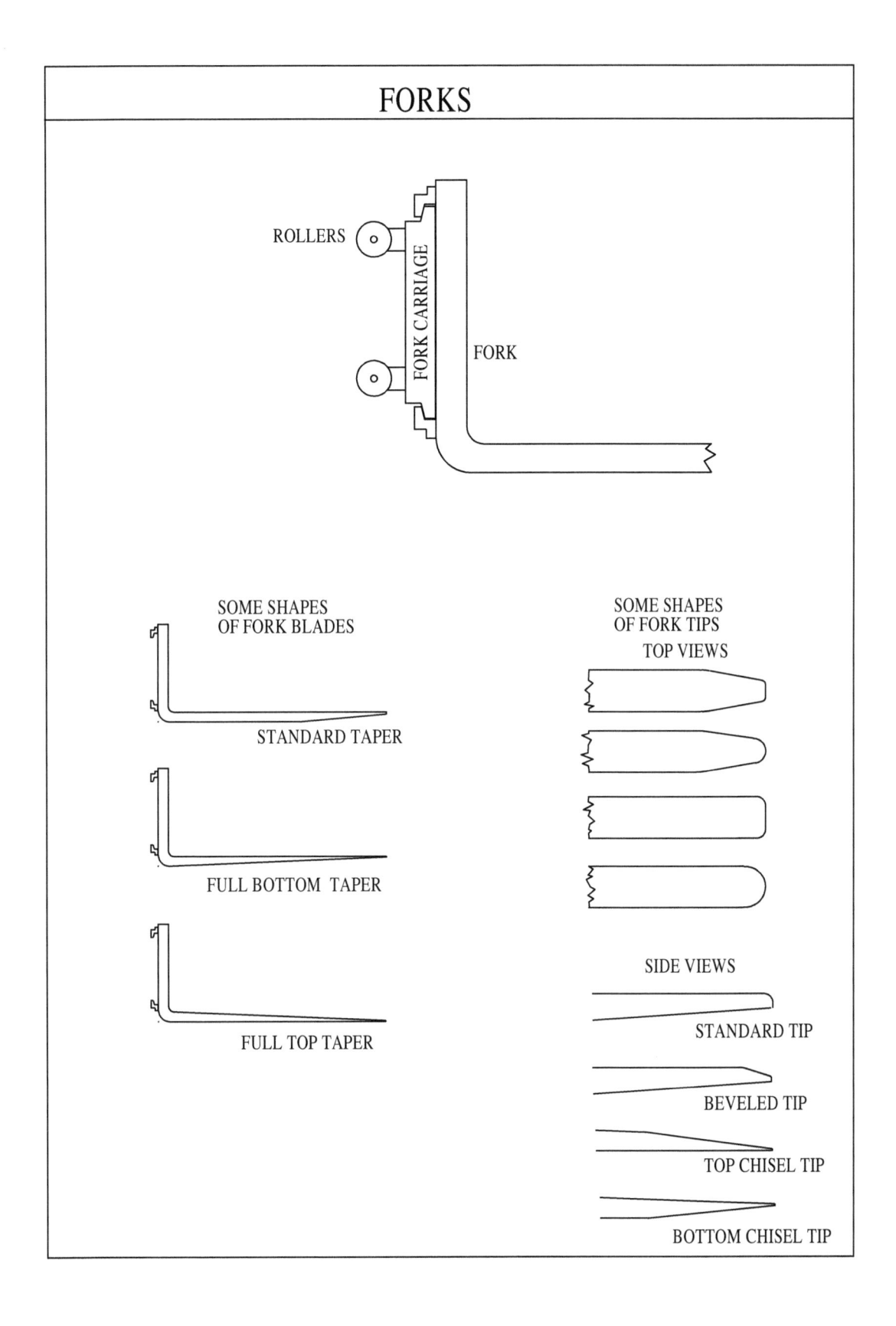

FORKS

ROLLERS

FORK CARRIAGE

FORK

SOME SHAPES
OF FORK BLADES

STANDARD TAPER

FULL BOTTOM TAPER

FULL TOP TAPER

SOME SHAPES
OF FORK TIPS
TOP VIEWS

SIDE VIEWS

STANDARD TIP

BEVELED TIP

TOP CHISEL TIP

BOTTOM CHISEL TIP

ATTACHMENTS

In many instances load handling is made easier and more efficient by the use of optional additional attachments. In some applications the forks are eliminated completely, with the load handled by the attachment only. Sometimes forks and attachments are used at alternate times on the same forklift, in which case a quick changeover design is essential.

The most commonly used attachment is a *sideshifter*. This feature allows the forks to be shifted to either side, usually up to 4" each side of center, allowing the operator to position the forks accurately to enter into a pallet or to shift the load for placement. These movements are especially useful for entering the notches of 4-way pallets or placing a load in drive-in racks or semi-trailers. In a great many applications this attachment will reduce damage and increase productivity and is highly recommended.

Attachments probably number in the hundreds, costing from very little to thousands of dollars. Once again the supplier should be made aware of all the duties of a forklift and asked for his recommendations.

A word of caution: in section nine there is a considerable explanation of the need to check all dimensions when combining forklifts and racks into a system. When doing so be sure any forklift attachments are accounted for, because they can change the forklift dimensions and reduce the lifting capacity.

A FEW ATTACHMENTS

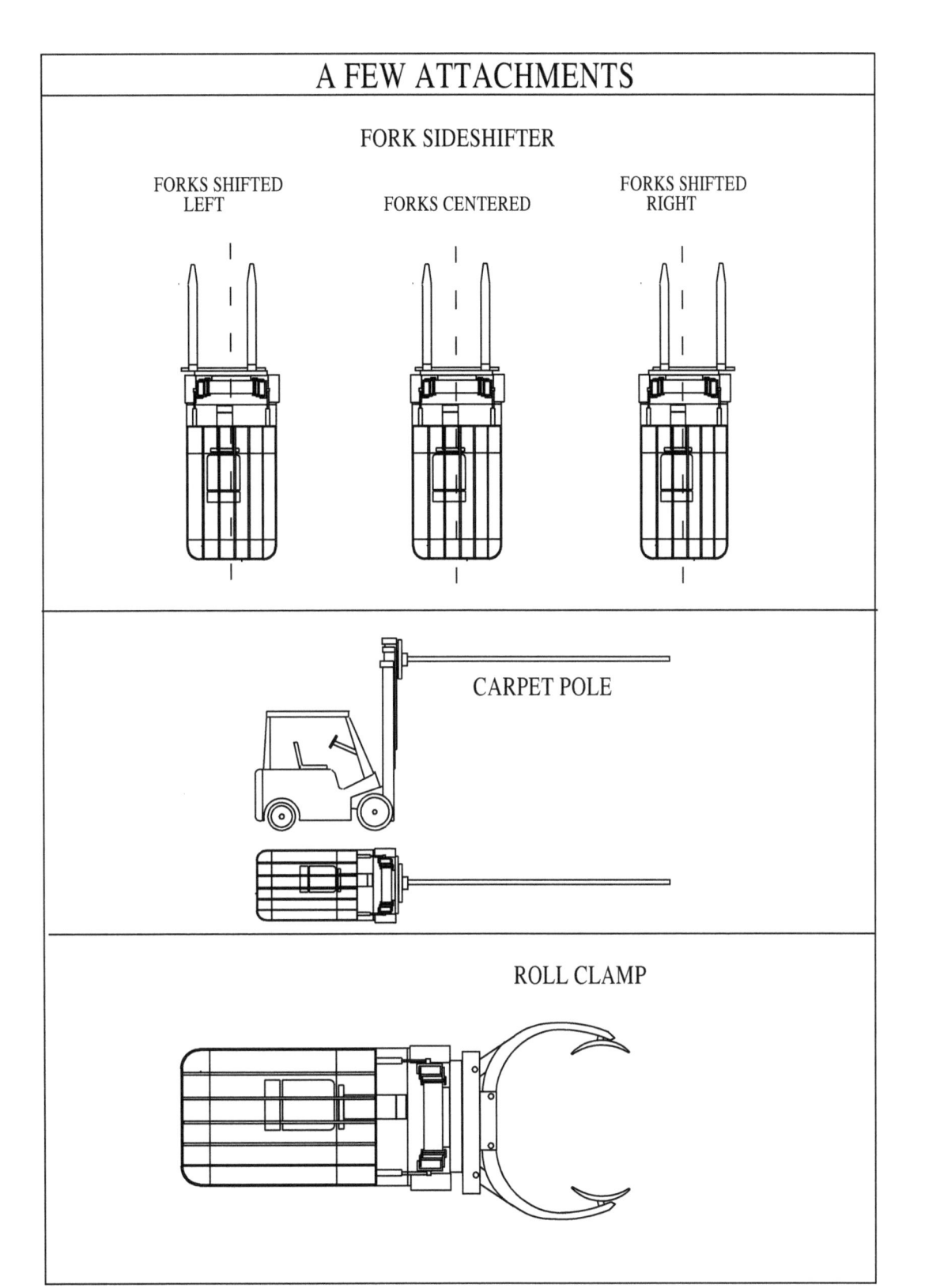

FORK SIDESHIFTER

FORKS SHIFTED LEFT   FORKS CENTERED   FORKS SHIFTED RIGHT

CARPET POLE

ROLL CLAMP

6   *FORKLIFTS*

ELECTRIC VS GAS

When it becomes time to select a counterbalanced forklift it is often necessary to choose between an internal combustion (IC) engine, powered by gasoline, LP gas or diesel, or an electric truck powered by battery. Narrow aisle and very narrow aisle trucks are usually battery powered, (although some very narrow aisle models operate from the building's electric supply), so the motive power choice is really only between sit-on counterbalanced trucks.

Each type of sit-on counterbalanced truck, internal combustion or electric, has distinct advantages in certain applications but in many other applications either type can be used successfully. In general an electric truck will be the best choice for indoor use, with an internal combustion unit for outdoors.

Use an engine powered truck indoors when the job requires maximum power on demand, such as on steep ramps or to chisel under heavy loads. They are often used for dock work. Fumes and noise must be expected. Steep ramps or long grades will quickly drain a battery unless it is very large. All outdoor applications favor I.C. trucks, preferably with pneumatic tires, although electric may work on a smooth, solid dry surface. Safe fuel storage is required.

Use an electric truck indoors where ramps are not a concern and fume/noise elimination is desirable. (Docklevelers are acceptable because they are short.) A higher initial cost is accepted with the probability of reduced long-term costs. A well-ventilated charging area must be provided and, if the unit is to be used on multiple shifts, a battery changing facility is needed to remove the battery and install a newly charged one.

With the purchase of a battery and charger the power cost for daily operation is reduced to a minimum while the I.C. truck has an ongoing fuel cost. Maintenance costs are also generally conceded to be less for electric trucks but some of the new high performance electronics on electric trucks are very expensive to replace, especially when available from only one source.

The manufacturers may have maintenance histories of each model. It is a good idea to check with some users of the exact model you are considering.

Unlike I.C. trucks, electric units do not give off a lot of heat and this factor, combined with the elimination of fumes and substantial reduction of noise, may lead to greater productivity from the forklift operator and all other workers in some areas.

A recent development in battery electric vehicles to overcome the long charge cycle normally required and the potential of having to change batteries for that reason between shifts, has been the advent of Rapid Charge systems, which enable the battery to be charged at a substantially higher rate of current for a shorter time, perhaps over lunch or coffee breaks, giving the battery enough power to power the forklift through more than one shift without the necessity of battery changes and the cost of additional batteries.

New battery developments include not only the normal lead acid battery, but also cadmium batteries, gel cells, high specific gravity batteries and lithium iron batteries. This subject needs to be discussed with your supplier and will depend on duty cycles etc.

SECTION SEVEN
FORKLIFTS

Comparative Specifications

7

FORKLIFTS

GENERAL SPECIFICATIONS

THERE ARE TWO ESSENTIAL REQUIREMENTS FOR ANY FORKLIFT:

1) IT MUST BE ABLE TO SAFELY LIFT SPECIFIED LOADS TO THE HEIGHTS YOU WANT TO LIFT THEM.

2) IT MUST BE ABLE TO OPERATE UNDER THE CONDITIONS PROVIDED FOR IT.

All other specifications are of your choice. There are models which can be powered by an internal combustion engine, battery, or electricity from your building supply, with a large variety of aisle widths and lift heights. The operator can be sitting, standing or walking and the forklift may be fitted with one or more optional attachments. The choices are many and sometimes difficult to wade through to arrive at the selection best for a specific application.

Forklifts types can be defined by a number of categories. A starting point is to differentiate between low lifts, having no lifting mast, and mast-equipped high lifts. A second major category considers whether the operator walks or rides on the truck, and a third distinction is non-powered or powered.

Non-powered low lift trucks are commonly called pallet jacks or pallet trucks. They consist of two main components; the *head*, with a pull handle and manually operated hydraulic pump to raise the second component, *forks*, and lift a pallet load slightly off of the floor so it can be moved. The lift height of various models varies, as does fork width and under clearance. Many specials are available for the handling of loads other than pallets.

Powered low lift trucks also consist of two main components, the *power tractor* and the *forks.* The range of options available for these models is very large. Battery size can vary according to the optional size of the battery compartment. Alternate speeds are often offered and the operator may walk, ride on a front platform or ride in a centrally positioned compartment. These trucks are very popular for low level case picking.

All high lifts fit into two general categories; counterbalanced and outrigger equipped.

Many other factors differentiate the trucks within each category. These include power source, lift capacity, operator location, three or four wheels, solid or pneumatic tires, travel and lift speeds, under clearance, aisle width required, guided or non-guided, etc.

This section is meant to make you aware of the many commonly used models and provide a means to compare some of their major specifications so you can quickly develop a short list of those that are of interest. The next four pages show the models which will be described in some detail in this section.

Orderpickers are separated into a distinct group in section 8, but since some unit load handling forklifts are also used for order picking there is a bit of duplication. This is done for those who want to skip the forklift descriptions and go directly to orderpickers.

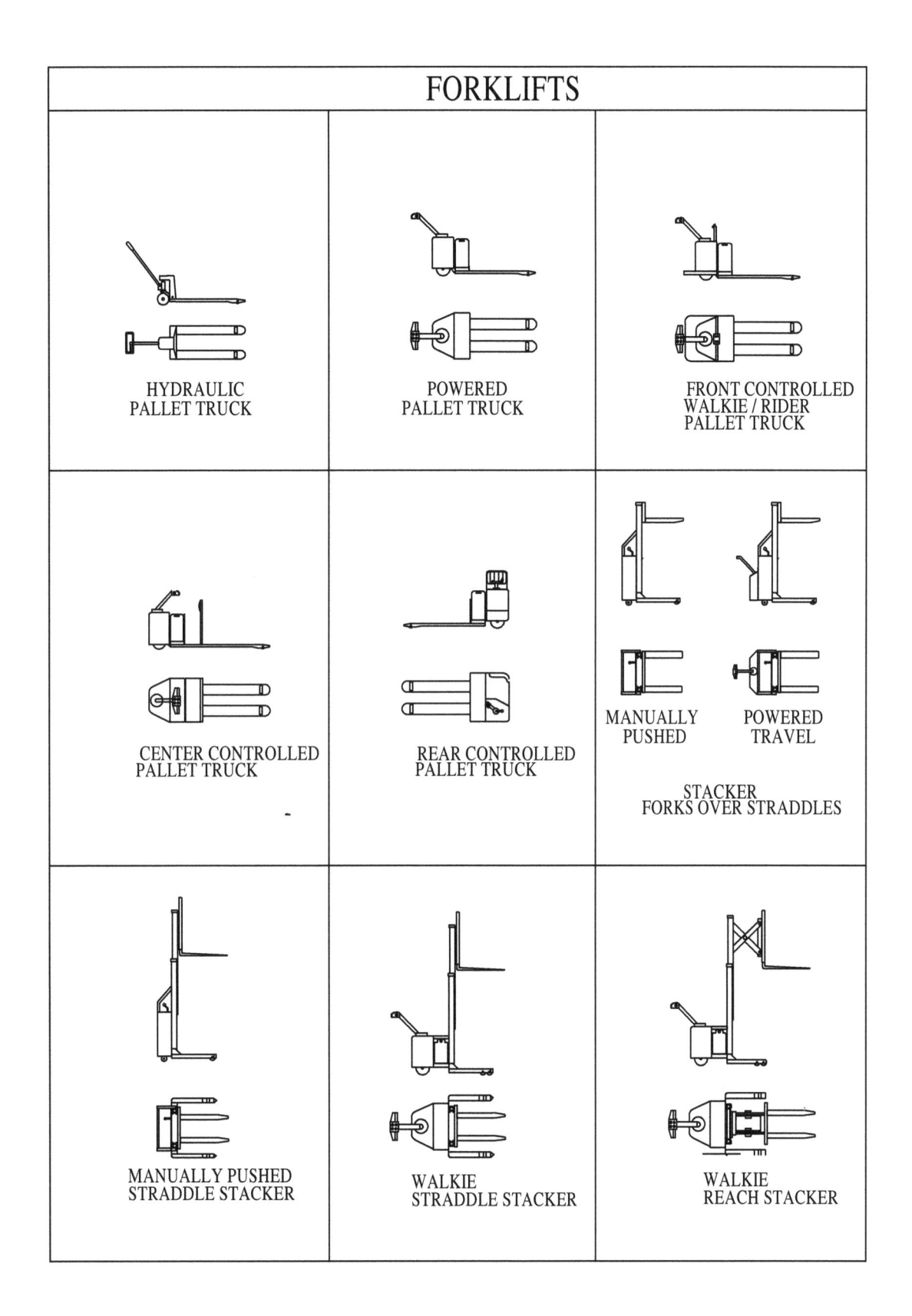

FORKLIFTS

HYDRAULIC PALLET TRUCK	POWERED PALLET TRUCK	FRONT CONTROLLED WALKIE / RIDER PALLET TRUCK
CENTER CONTROLLED PALLET TRUCK	REAR CONTROLLED PALLET TRUCK	MANUALLY PUSHED / POWERED TRAVEL — STACKER FORKS OVER STRADDLES
MANUALLY PUSHED STRADDLE STACKER	WALKIE STRADDLE STACKER	WALKIE REACH STACKER

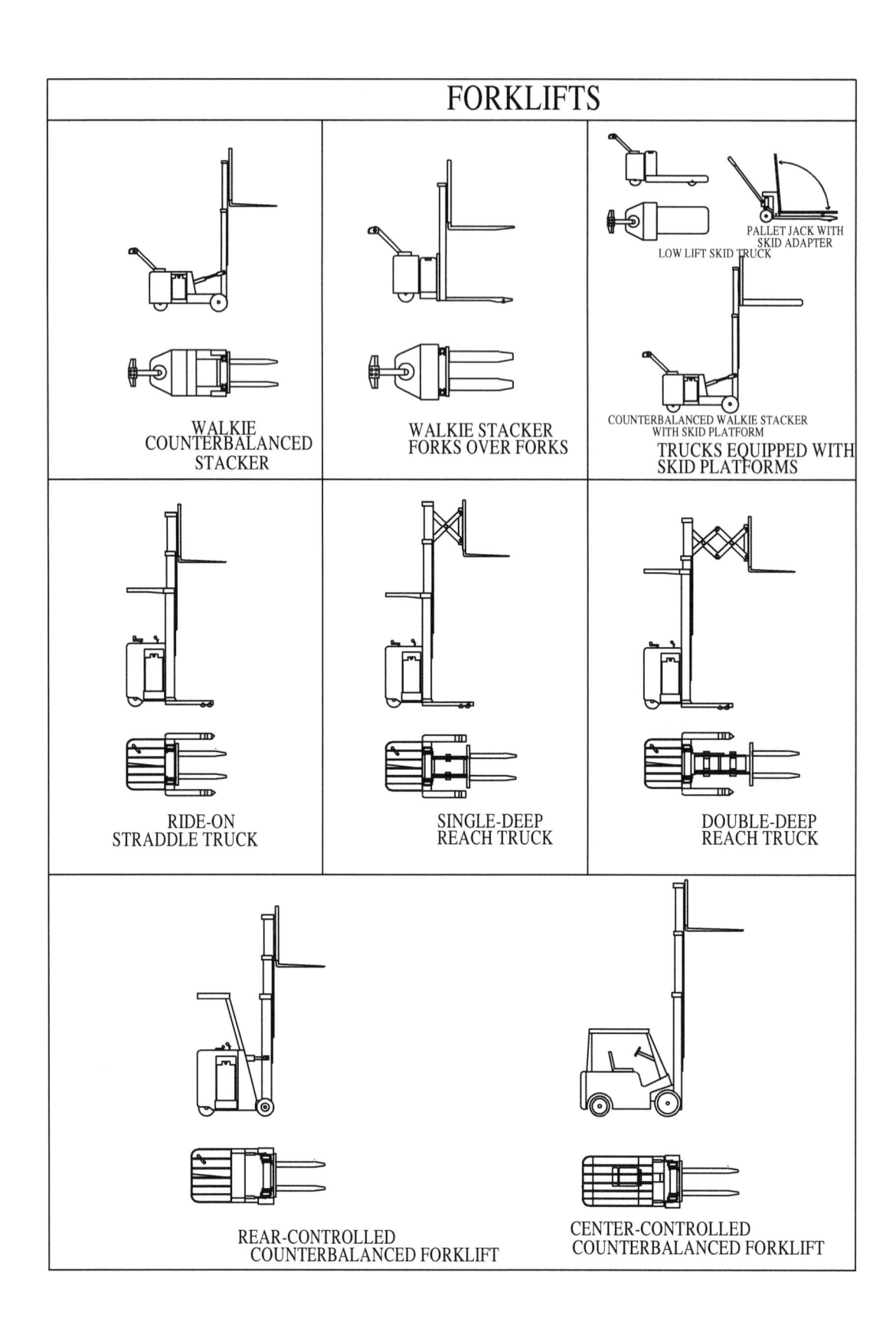

FORKLIFTS		
WALKIE COUNTERBALANCED STACKER	WALKIE STACKER FORKS OVER FORKS	PALLET JACK WITH SKID ADAPTER / LOW LIFT SKID TRUCK / COUNTERBALANCED WALKIE STACKER WITH SKID PLATFORM — TRUCKS EQUIPPED WITH SKID PLATFORMS
RIDE-ON STRADDLE TRUCK	SINGLE-DEEP REACH TRUCK	DOUBLE-DEEP REACH TRUCK
REAR-CONTROLLED COUNTERBALANCED FORKLIFT		CENTER-CONTROLLED COUNTERBALANCED FORKLIFT

HOW TO CONFIGURE AND EQUIP YOUR WAREHOUSE

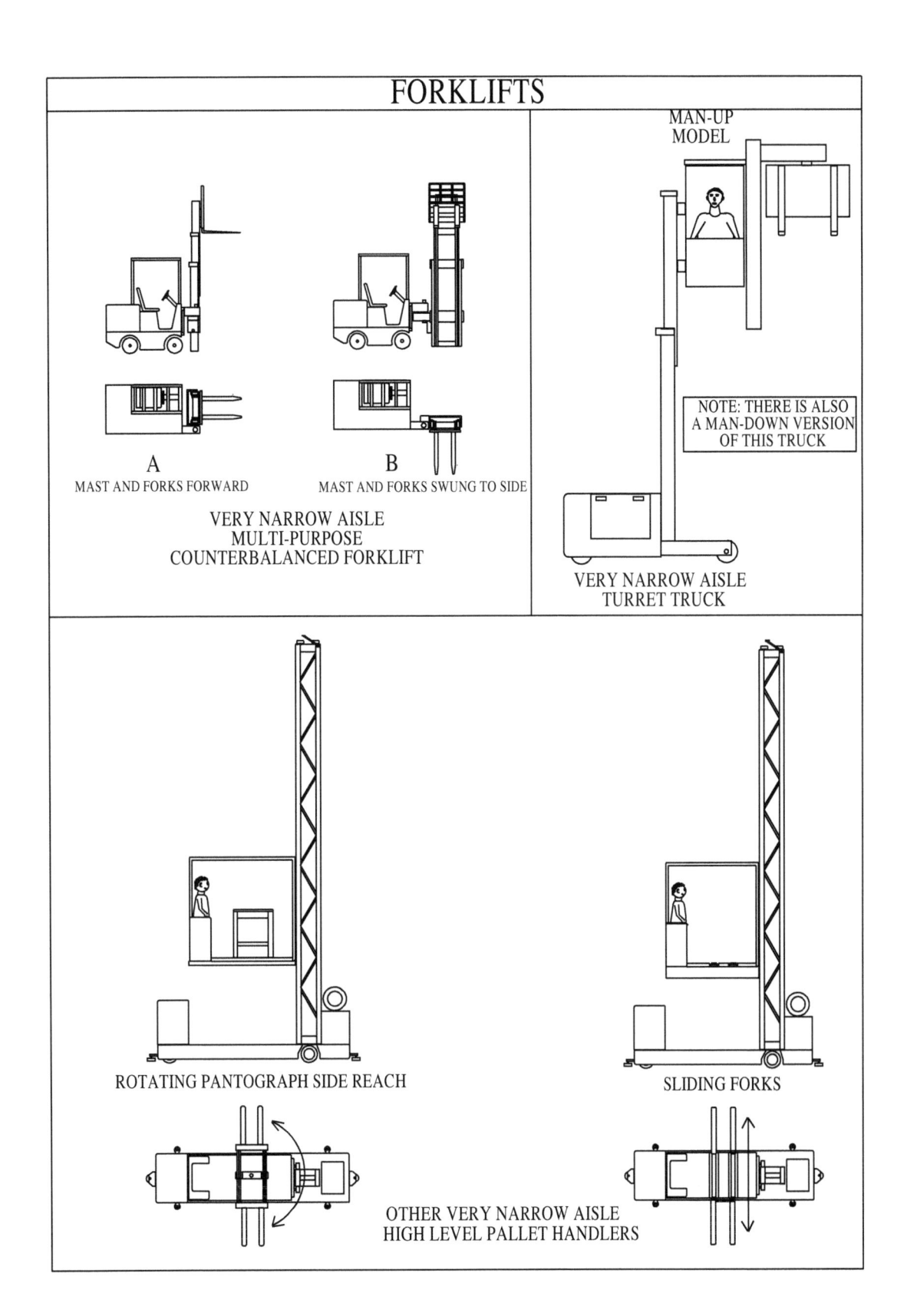

FORKLIFTS

A
MAST AND FORKS FORWARD

B
MAST AND FORKS SWUNG TO SIDE

**VERY NARROW AISLE
MULTI-PURPOSE
COUNTERBALANCED FORKLIFT**

MAN-UP MODEL

NOTE: THERE IS ALSO A MAN-DOWN VERSION OF THIS TRUCK

**VERY NARROW AISLE
TURRET TRUCK**

ROTATING PANTOGRAPH SIDE REACH

SLIDING FORKS

**OTHER VERY NARROW AISLE
HIGH LEVEL PALLET HANDLERS**

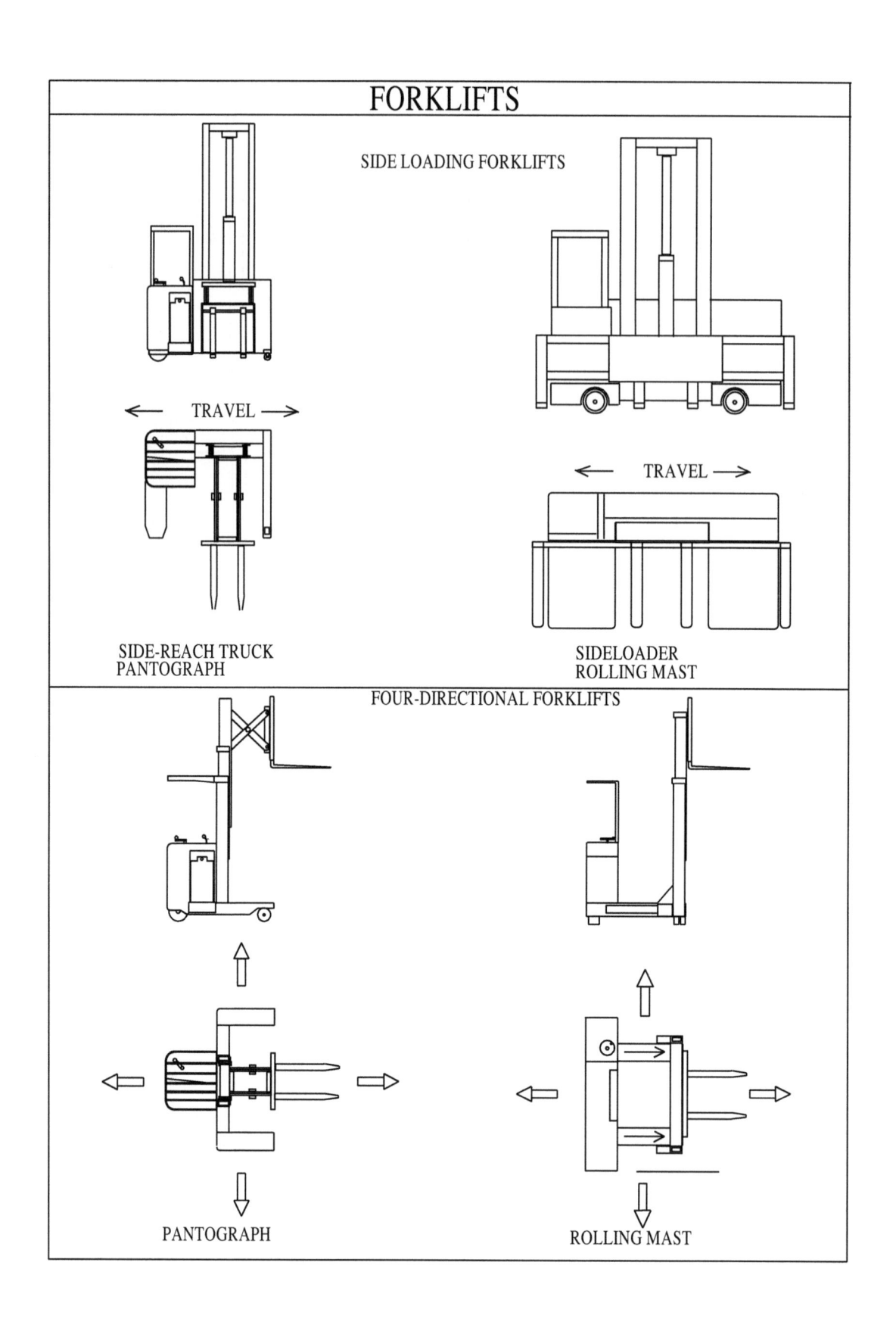

FORKLIFTS

SIDE LOADING FORKLIFTS

← TRAVEL →

← TRAVEL →

SIDE-REACH TRUCK
PANTOGRAPH

SIDELOADER
ROLLING MAST

FOUR-DIRECTIONAL FORKLIFTS

PANTOGRAPH

ROLLING MAST

HOW TO CONFIGURE AND EQUIP YOUR WAREHOUSE

FORKLIFT COMPARATIVE SPECIFICATIONS

When considering a new distribution center it is sometimes difficult to know where to start. Should you first determine what you would like to do and then search out a forklift and other equipment with the capabilities wanted, or is it better to first see what equipment is available and go from there? In most cases the answer will be to "go 'round the circle" a few times, adjusting the planned methods and available equipment to suit each other.

A good starting point might be to compare forklift types, with their enormous range of differences. Are you looking for a single forklift to perform many duties or a number of specialized trucks to work in different areas? Low, high or very high lift? Does aisle width matter? Etc., etc

On the following pages forklift sketches are accompanied with notes pertaining to *typical uses, notable features and some additional comments*. The notable features include standard load ranges, typical lift heights with full load, aisle widths, grade clearance and travel and lift speeds.

The next two pages list and show a range of classifications which are used here as guides to point out truck differences. These are "broad brush" classifications only, to let you quickly decide what models deserve further consideration.

Lift heights are the most difficult to determine because of the many forklift specifications which affect the lifting capacity to various heights. First there is the specified height to which the full rated load can be safely lifted. Then there are additional lift heights with reduced loads. These are termed downrated capacities and can be supplied by any manufacturer for any load and any height. See page 219.

Some forklifts can lift very high with reduced loads while others have limited ability to do so. If, for instance, you want to lift 3000# to 25 feet it may be necessary with some models to use a 4000# or 5000# truck and the resultant wider aisles may necessitate a revised layout. On the other hand there are trucks which can lift this high without any increase in aisle width.

The ability to lift higher with reduced loads may differ even within the range of a specific model. Many specifications come into play, such as battery weight, outrigger spread, amount of fork tilt, counterbalance weight, wheel base and wheel size, accessories, etc, etc. Therefore all downratings should be supplied by the manufacturer, and we have not attempted to do so.

Safety Note: Everyone who operates a forklift should be aware of its' lifting capacity at all heights and the weight being lifted. The ratings should be on the forklift where they can be clearly seen by the operator. A weight scale is highly recommended and is now standard or optional on many forklifts. Many jurisdictions now require certified training for all forklift operators. Such training is a wise move even when not mandatory.

Some very specialized forklift types, such as sideloaders or four-directional trucks may solve the problem of long load handling and, in some cases, may also handle standard pallets in a one- truck situation.

The following are guidelines used for rating each forklift on the drawings which follow shortly. Please note that these ratings are subjective, chosen by the authors as reasonable scales of qualification to allow comparisons.

AISLE WIDTH CLASSIFICATION

WIDE:	11' to 14'
MEDIUM:	9'-6" to 11'
NARROW:	7' to 9'-6"
VERY NARROW:	4'-8" to 6'-6"

GRADE CLEARANCES: Note that most literature shows the grade clearance by *percentage*. This is different form *degrees* of grade

1 to 10%	Low
11 to 20%	Medium
21 to 30%	Good
Over 30%	Very Good

TRAVEL SPEEDS:

NON-POWERED:	Very Slow
TO 3 ½ MPH	Slow
3 ½ to 6 MPH	Medium
6 to 8 ½ MPH	Fast
OVER 8 ½ MPH	Very Fast

LIFT SPEEDS:

1 to 20 FPM	Very Slow
20 to 40 FPM	Slow
40 to 60 FPM	Medium
60 to 80 FPM	Fast
OVER 80 FPM	Very Fast

Note, Grade Clearance should not be confused with Grade ability (grade climbing ability of a forklift). Operation of forklifts up and down slight grades may be acceptable but is extremely dangerous across grades as the truck will become unstable and could easily fall over sideways, especially if the load is elevated when cross aligned on a ramp. Always discuss ramp applications with your supplier. Never assume!

SOME COMPARATIVE SPECIFICATIONS

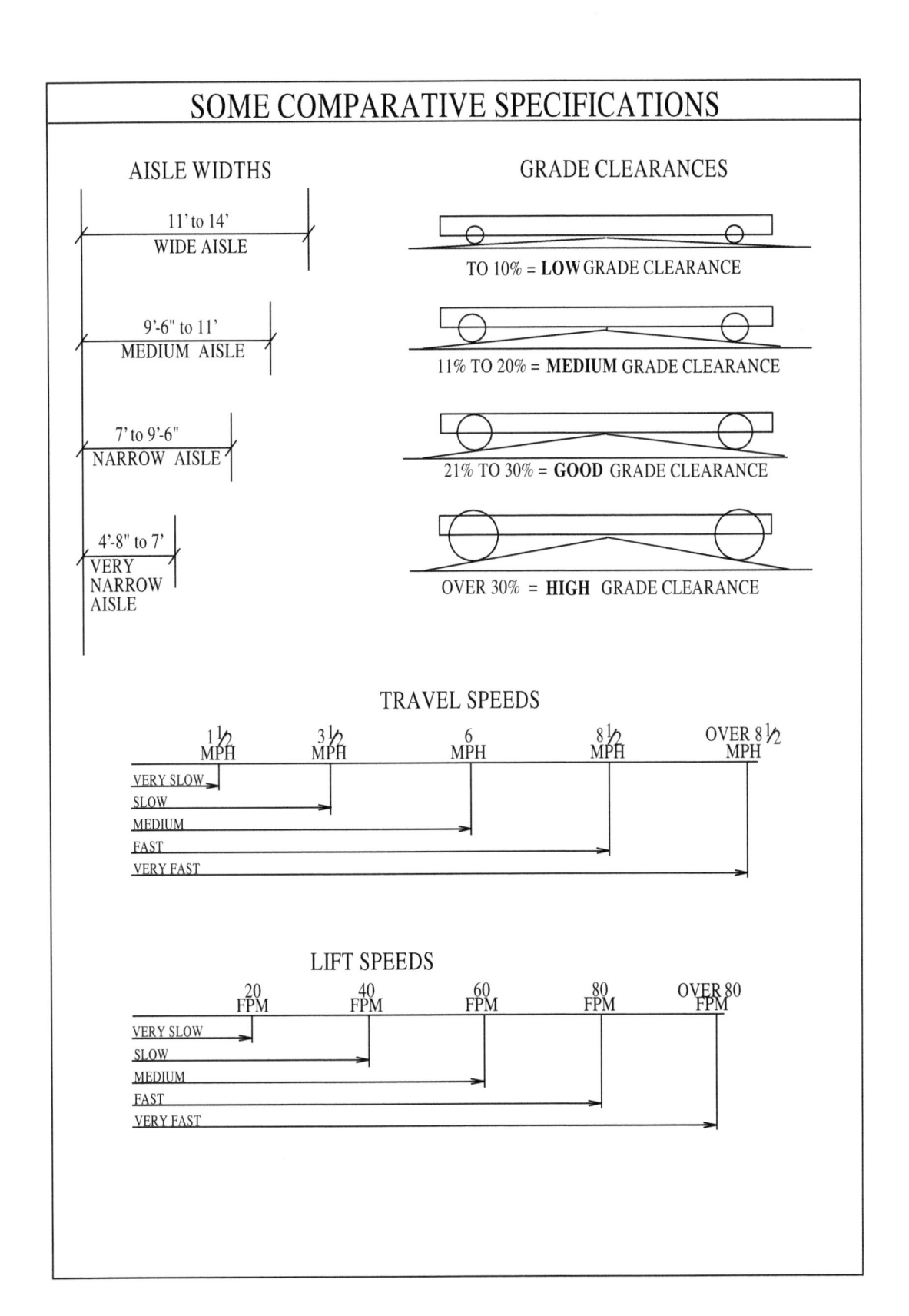

AISLE WIDTHS

11' to 14'
WIDE AISLE

9'-6" to 11'
MEDIUM AISLE

7' to 9'-6"
NARROW AISLE

4'-8" to 7'
VERY NARROW AISLE

GRADE CLEARANCES

TO 10% = **LOW** GRADE CLEARANCE

11% TO 20% = **MEDIUM** GRADE CLEARANCE

21% TO 30% = **GOOD** GRADE CLEARANCE

OVER 30% = **HIGH** GRADE CLEARANCE

TRAVEL SPEEDS

1½ MPH | 3½ MPH | 6 MPH | 8½ MPH | OVER 8½ MPH

VERY SLOW
SLOW
MEDIUM
FAST
VERY FAST

LIFT SPEEDS

20 FPM | 40 FPM | 60 FPM | 80 FPM | OVER 80 FPM

VERY SLOW
SLOW
MEDIUM
FAST
VERY FAST

7 FORKLIFTS

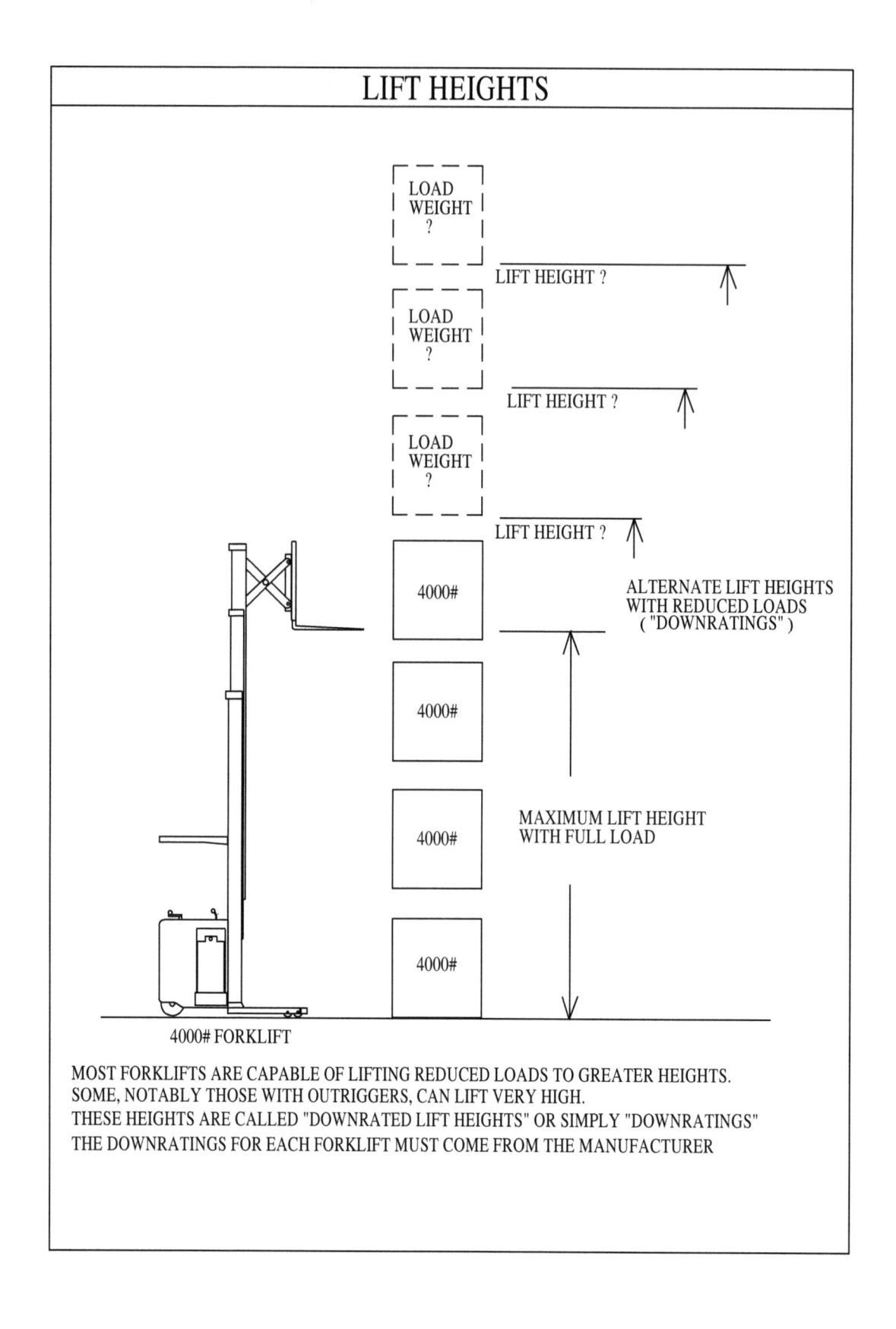

LIFT HEIGHTS

LOAD WEIGHT ?

LIFT HEIGHT ?

LOAD WEIGHT ?

LIFT HEIGHT ?

LOAD WEIGHT ?

LIFT HEIGHT ?

4000#

ALTERNATE LIFT HEIGHTS WITH REDUCED LOADS ("DOWNRATINGS")

4000#

4000#

MAXIMUM LIFT HEIGHT WITH FULL LOAD

4000#

4000# FORKLIFT

MOST FORKLIFTS ARE CAPABLE OF LIFTING REDUCED LOADS TO GREATER HEIGHTS.
SOME, NOTABLY THOSE WITH OUTRIGGERS, CAN LIFT VERY HIGH.
THESE HEIGHTS ARE CALLED "DOWNRATED LIFT HEIGHTS" OR SIMPLY "DOWNRATINGS"
THE DOWNRATINGS FOR EACH FORKLIFT MUST COME FROM THE MANUFACTURER

HOW TO CONFIGURE AND EQUIP YOUR WAREHOUSE

HYDRAULIC PALLET TRUCK

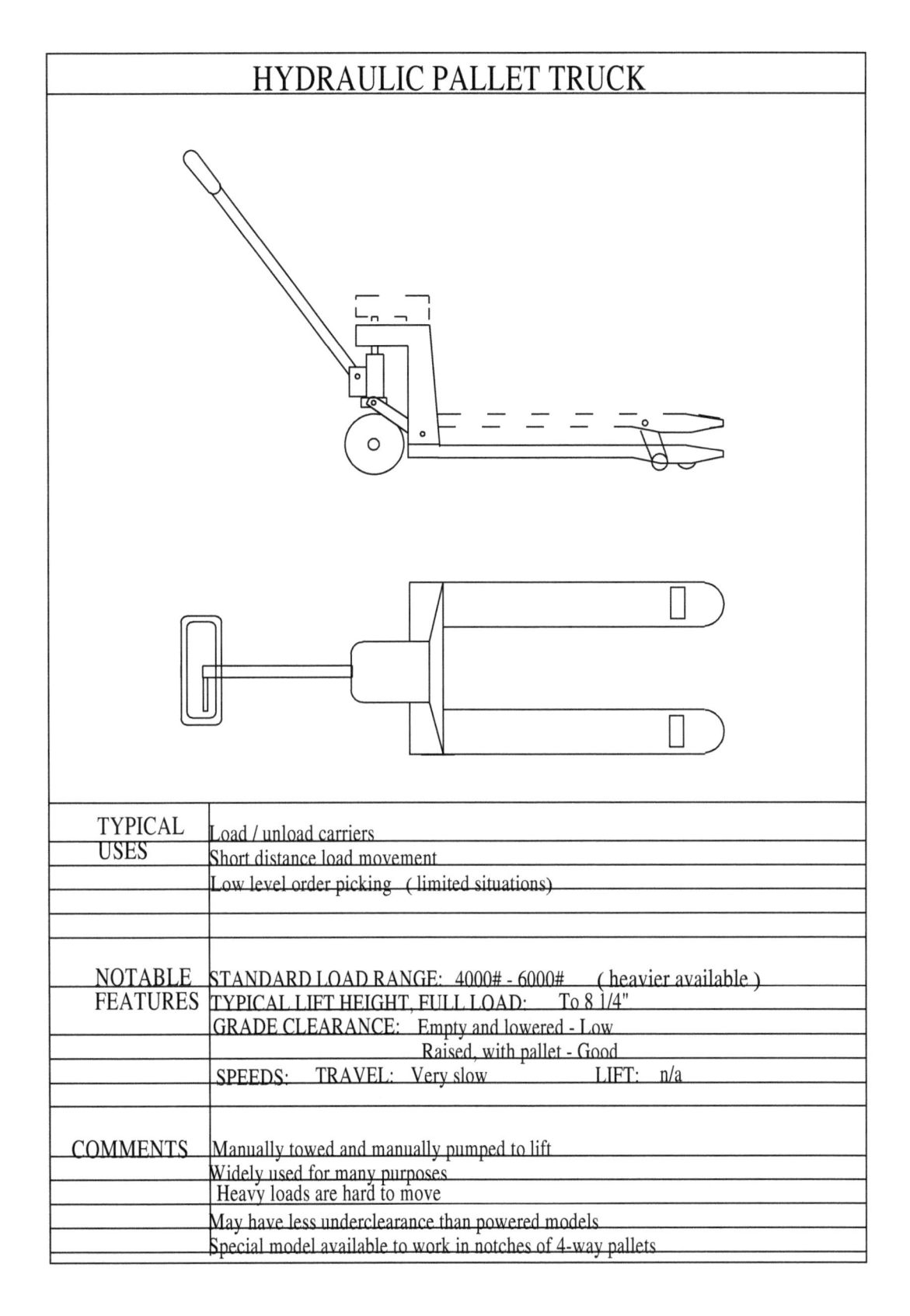

TYPICAL USES	Load / unload carriers
	Short distance load movement
	Low level order picking (limited situations)
NOTABLE FEATURES	STANDARD LOAD RANGE: 4000# - 6000# (heavier available)
	TYPICAL LIFT HEIGHT, FULL LOAD: To 8 1/4"
	GRADE CLEARANCE: Empty and lowered - Low
	Raised, with pallet - Good
	SPEEDS: TRAVEL: Very slow LIFT: n/a
COMMENTS	Manually towed and manually pumped to lift
	Widely used for many purposes
	Heavy loads are hard to move
	May have less underclearance than powered models
	Special model available to work in notches of 4-way pallets

220

7 FORKLIFTS

POWERED LOW LIFT PALLET TRUCK

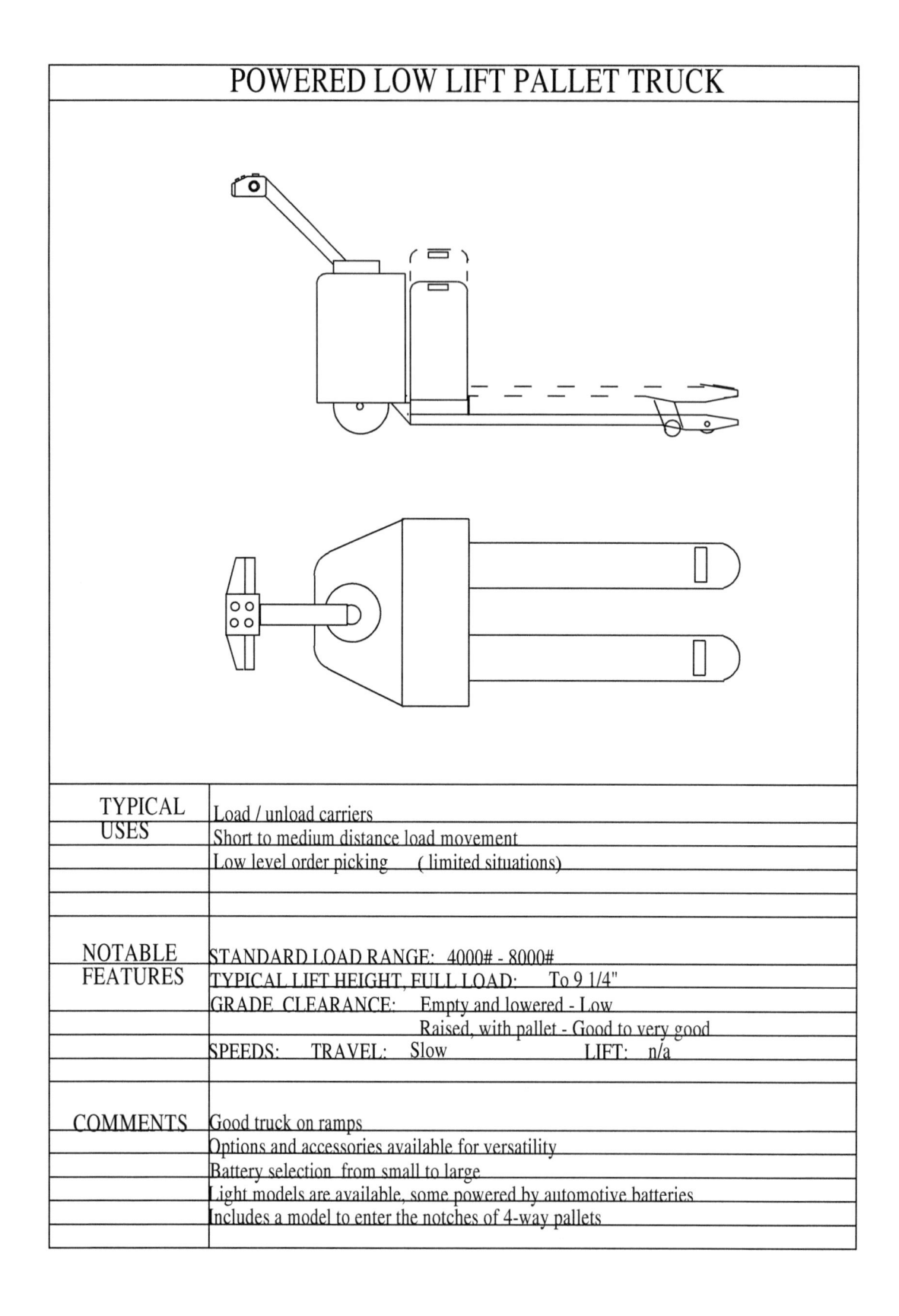

TYPICAL USES	Load / unload carriers
	Short to medium distance load movement
	Low level order picking (limited situations)
NOTABLE FEATURES	STANDARD LOAD RANGE: 4000# - 8000#
	TYPICAL LIFT HEIGHT, FULL LOAD: To 9 1/4"
	GRADE CLEARANCE: Empty and lowered - Low
	Raised, with pallet - Good to very good
	SPEEDS: TRAVEL: Slow LIFT: n/a
COMMENTS	Good truck on ramps
	Options and accessories available for versatility
	Battery selection from small to large
	Light models are available, some powered by automotive batteries
	Includes a model to enter the notches of 4-way pallets

HOW TO CONFIGURE AND EQUIP YOUR WAREHOUSE

FRONT CONTROLLED WALKIE / RIDER PALLET TRUCK

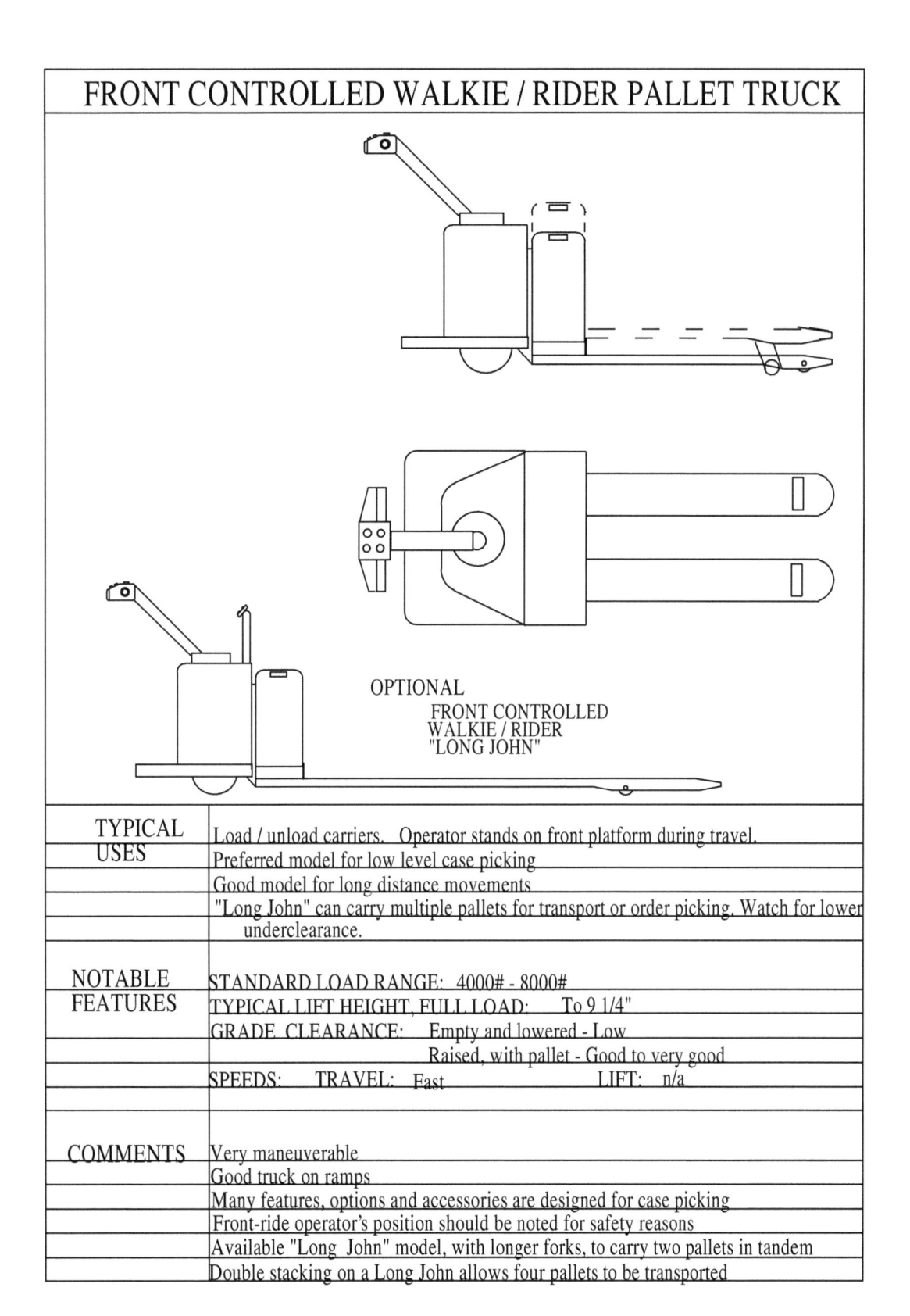

222

OPTIONAL
FRONT CONTROLLED
WALKIE / RIDER
"LONG JOHN"

TYPICAL USES	Load / unload carriers. Operator stands on front platform during travel.
	Preferred model for low level case picking
	Good model for long distance movements
	"Long John" can carry multiple pallets for transport or order picking. Watch for lower underclearance.
NOTABLE FEATURES	STANDARD LOAD RANGE: 4000# - 8000#
	TYPICAL LIFT HEIGHT, FULL LOAD: To 9 1/4"
	GRADE CLEARANCE: Empty and lowered - Low
	Raised, with pallet - Good to very good
	SPEEDS: TRAVEL: Fast LIFT: n/a
COMMENTS	Very maneuverable
	Good truck on ramps
	Many features, options and accessories are designed for case picking
	Front-ride operator's position should be noted for safety reasons
	Available "Long John" model, with longer forks, to carry two pallets in tandem
	Double stacking on a Long John allows four pallets to be transported

7 *FORKLIFTS*

CENTER CONTROLLED WALKIE / RIDER PALLET TRUCK

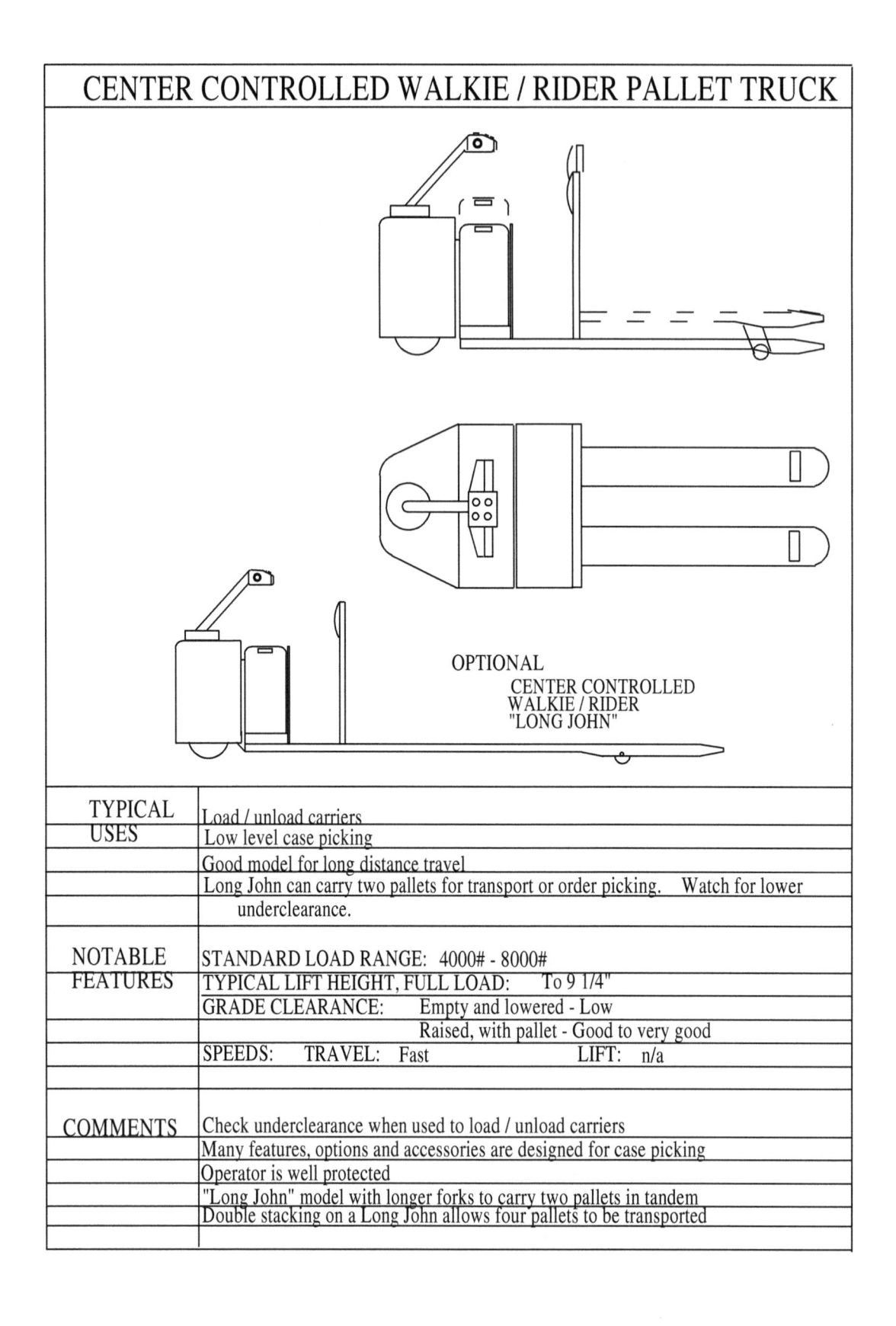

OPTIONAL
CENTER CONTROLLED
WALKIE / RIDER
"LONG JOHN"

TYPICAL USES	Load / unload carriers
	Low level case picking
	Good model for long distance travel
	Long John can carry two pallets for transport or order picking. Watch for lower underclearance.
NOTABLE FEATURES	STANDARD LOAD RANGE: 4000# - 8000#
	TYPICAL LIFT HEIGHT, FULL LOAD: To 9 1/4"
	GRADE CLEARANCE: Empty and lowered - Low
	Raised, with pallet - Good to very good
	SPEEDS: TRAVEL: Fast LIFT: n/a
COMMENTS	Check underclearance when used to load / unload carriers
	Many features, options and accessories are designed for case picking
	Operator is well protected
	"Long John" model with longer forks to carry two pallets in tandem
	Double stacking on a Long John allows four pallets to be transported

HOW TO CONFIGURE AND EQUIP YOUR WAREHOUSE

REAR RIDE-ON LOW LIFT PALLET TRUCK

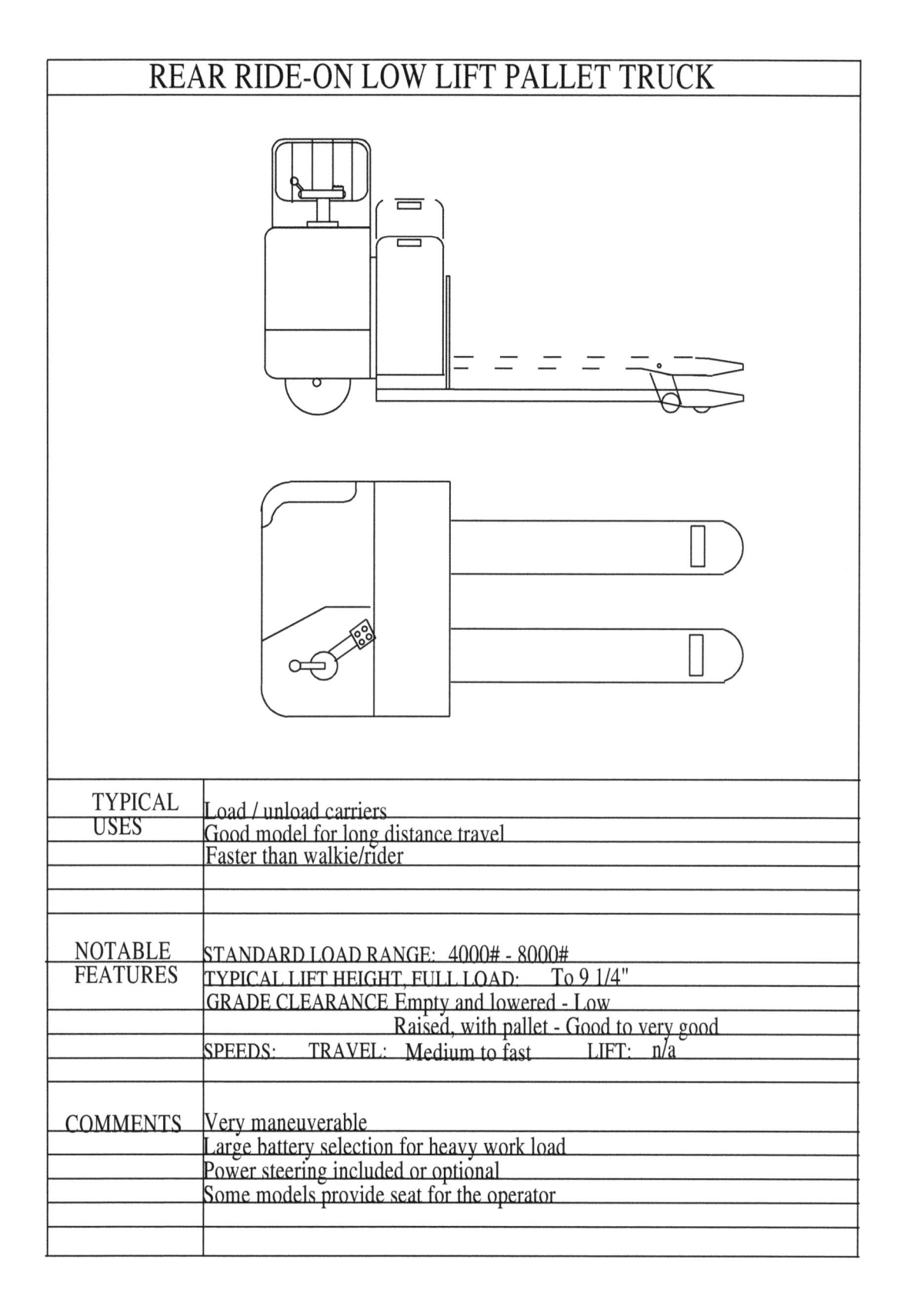

TYPICAL USES	Load / unload carriers
	Good model for long distance travel
	Faster than walkie/rider
NOTABLE FEATURES	STANDARD LOAD RANGE: 4000# - 8000#
	TYPICAL LIFT HEIGHT, FULL LOAD: To 9 1/4"
	GRADE CLEARANCE Empty and lowered - Low
	Raised, with pallet - Good to very good
	SPEEDS: TRAVEL: Medium to fast LIFT: n/a
COMMENTS	Very maneuverable
	Large battery selection for heavy work load
	Power steering included or optional
	Some models provide seat for the operator

7   *FORKLIFTS*

STACKERS WITH FORKS OVER STRADDLES

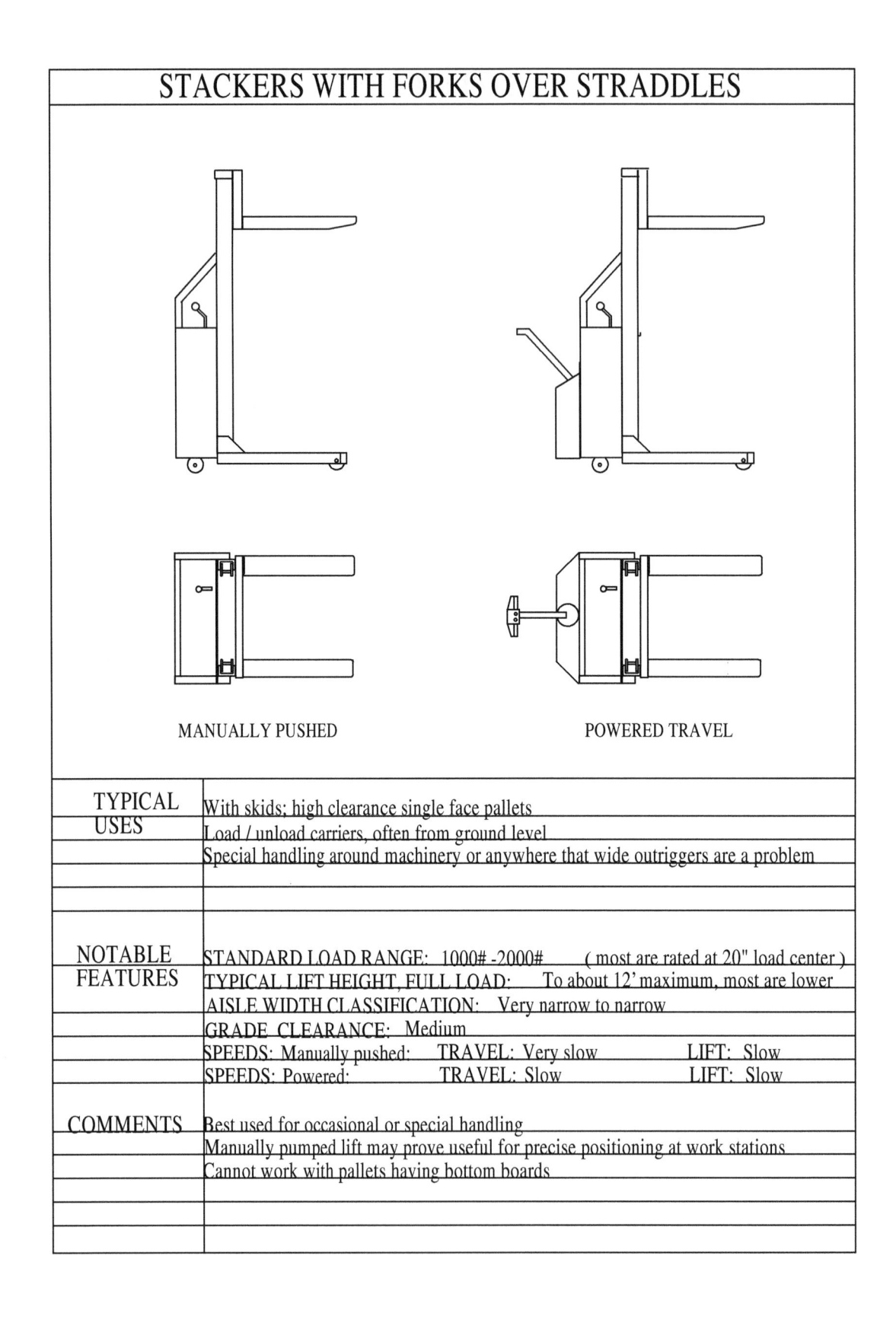

MANUALLY PUSHED   POWERED TRAVEL

TYPICAL USES	With skids; high clearance single face pallets
	Load / unload carriers, often from ground level
	Special handling around machinery or anywhere that wide outriggers are a problem

NOTABLE FEATURES	STANDARD LOAD RANGE: 1000# -2000# (most are rated at 20" load center)
	TYPICAL LIFT HEIGHT, FULL LOAD: To about 12' maximum, most are lower
	AISLE WIDTH CLASSIFICATION: Very narrow to narrow
	GRADE CLEARANCE: Medium
	SPEEDS: Manually pushed: TRAVEL: Very slow LIFT: Slow
	SPEEDS: Powered: TRAVEL: Slow LIFT: Slow

COMMENTS	Best used for occasional or special handling
	Manually pumped lift may prove useful for precise positioning at work stations
	Cannot work with pallets having bottom boards

HOW TO CONFIGURE AND EQUIP YOUR WAREHOUSE

STRADDLE STACKER, MANUALLY PUSHED

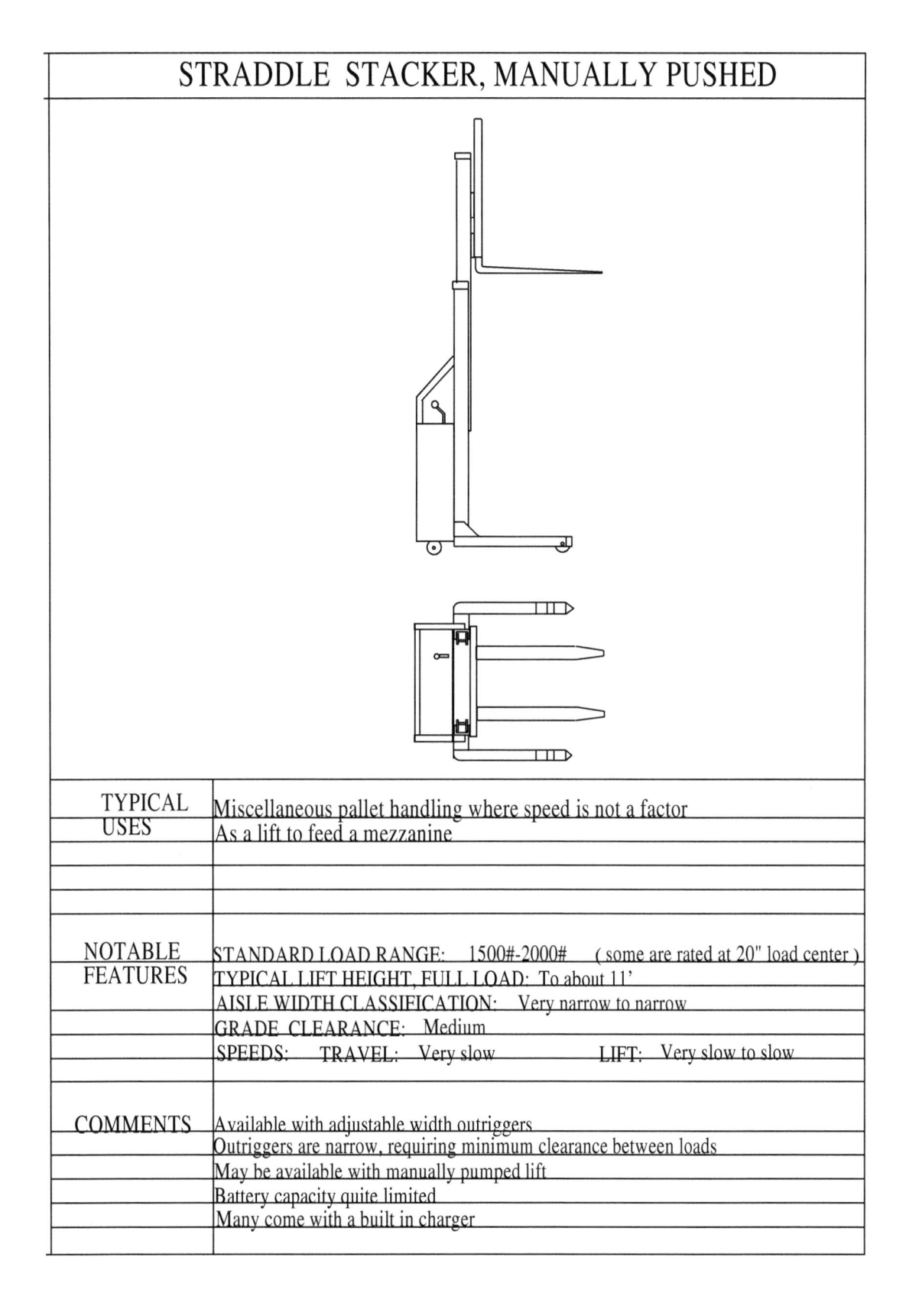

TYPICAL USES	Miscellaneous pallet handling where speed is not a factor
	As a lift to feed a mezzanine
NOTABLE FEATURES	STANDARD LOAD RANGE: 1500#-2000# (some are rated at 20" load center)
	TYPICAL LIFT HEIGHT, FULL LOAD: To about 11'
	AISLE WIDTH CLASSIFICATION: Very narrow to narrow
	GRADE CLEARANCE: Medium
	SPEEDS: TRAVEL: Very slow LIFT: Very slow to slow
COMMENTS	Available with adjustable width outriggers
	Outriggers are narrow, requiring minimum clearance between loads
	May be available with manually pumped lift
	Battery capacity quite limited
	Many come with a built in charger

HEAVY DUTY WALKIE STRADDLE STACKER

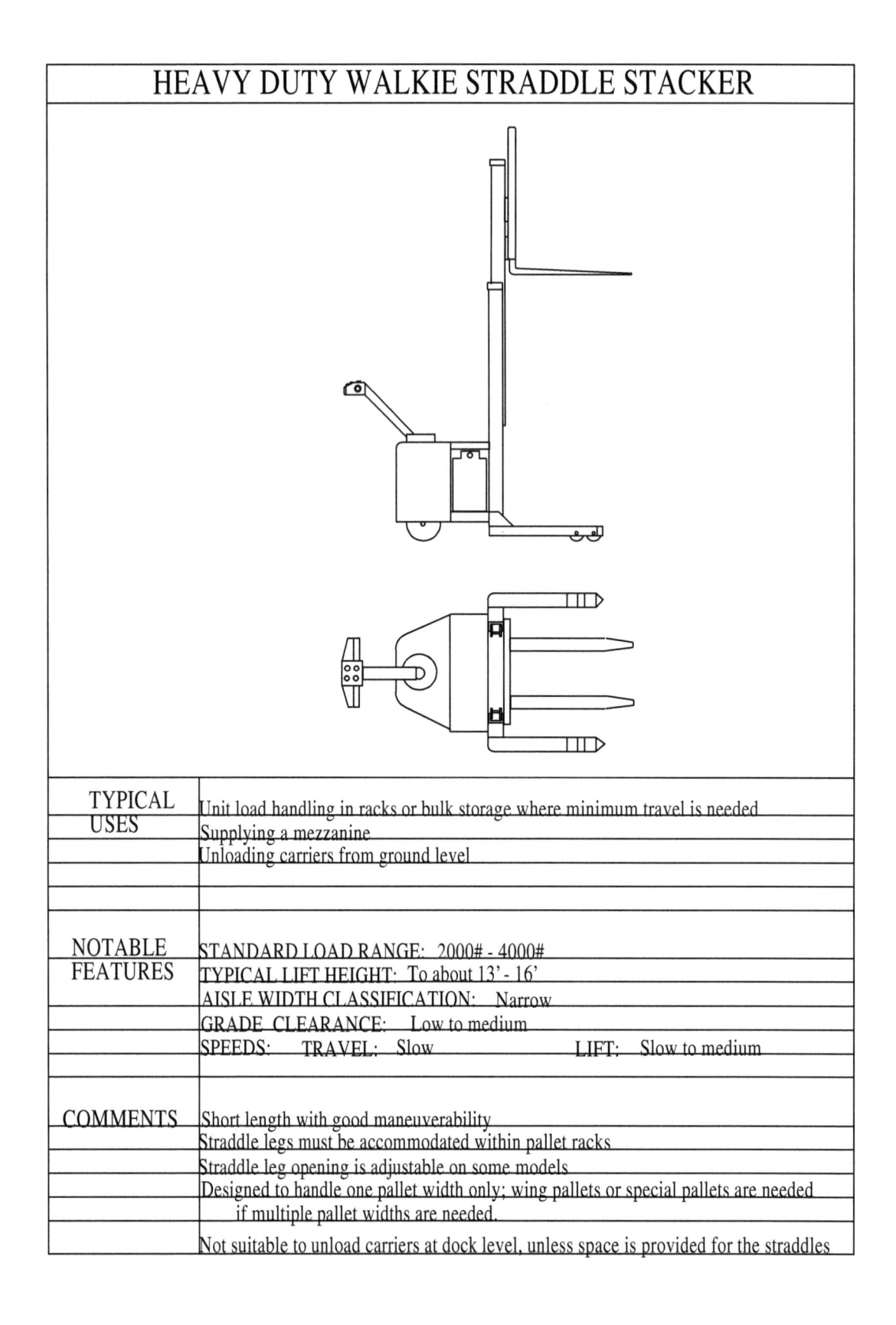

TYPICAL USES	Unit load handling in racks or bulk storage where minimum travel is needed
	Supplying a mezzanine
	Unloading carriers from ground level
NOTABLE FEATURES	STANDARD LOAD RANGE: 2000# - 4000#
	TYPICAL LIFT HEIGHT: To about 13' - 16'
	AISLE WIDTH CLASSIFICATION: Narrow
	GRADE CLEARANCE: Low to medium
	SPEEDS: TRAVEL: Slow LIFT: Slow to medium
COMMENTS	Short length with good maneuverability
	Straddle legs must be accommodated within pallet racks
	Straddle leg opening is adjustable on some models
	Designed to handle one pallet width only; wing pallets or special pallets are needed if multiple pallet widths are needed.
	Not suitable to unload carriers at dock level, unless space is provided for the straddles

HOW TO CONFIGURE AND EQUIP YOUR WAREHOUSE

HEAVY DUTY WALKIE REACH STACKER

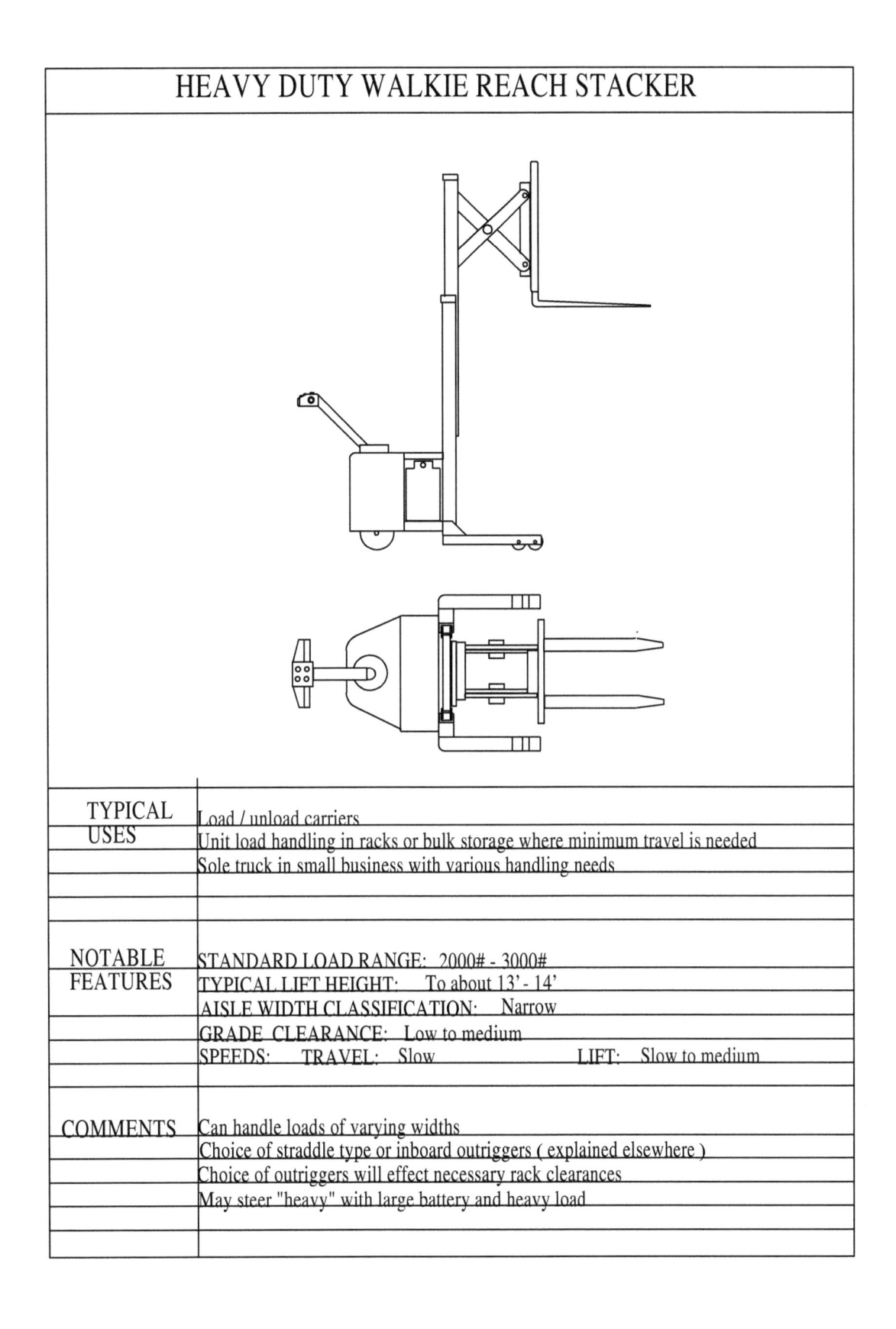

TYPICAL USES	Load / unload carriers
	Unit load handling in racks or bulk storage where minimum travel is needed
	Sole truck in small business with various handling needs
NOTABLE FEATURES	STANDARD LOAD RANGE: 2000# - 3000#
	TYPICAL LIFT HEIGHT: To about 13' - 14'
	AISLE WIDTH CLASSIFICATION: Narrow
	GRADE CLEARANCE: Low to medium
	SPEEDS: TRAVEL: Slow LIFT: Slow to medium
COMMENTS	Can handle loads of varying widths
	Choice of straddle type or inboard outriggers (explained elsewhere)
	Choice of outriggers will effect necessary rack clearances
	May steer "heavy" with large battery and heavy load

7 FORKLIFTS

HEAVY DUTY WALKIE COUNTERBALANCED STACKER

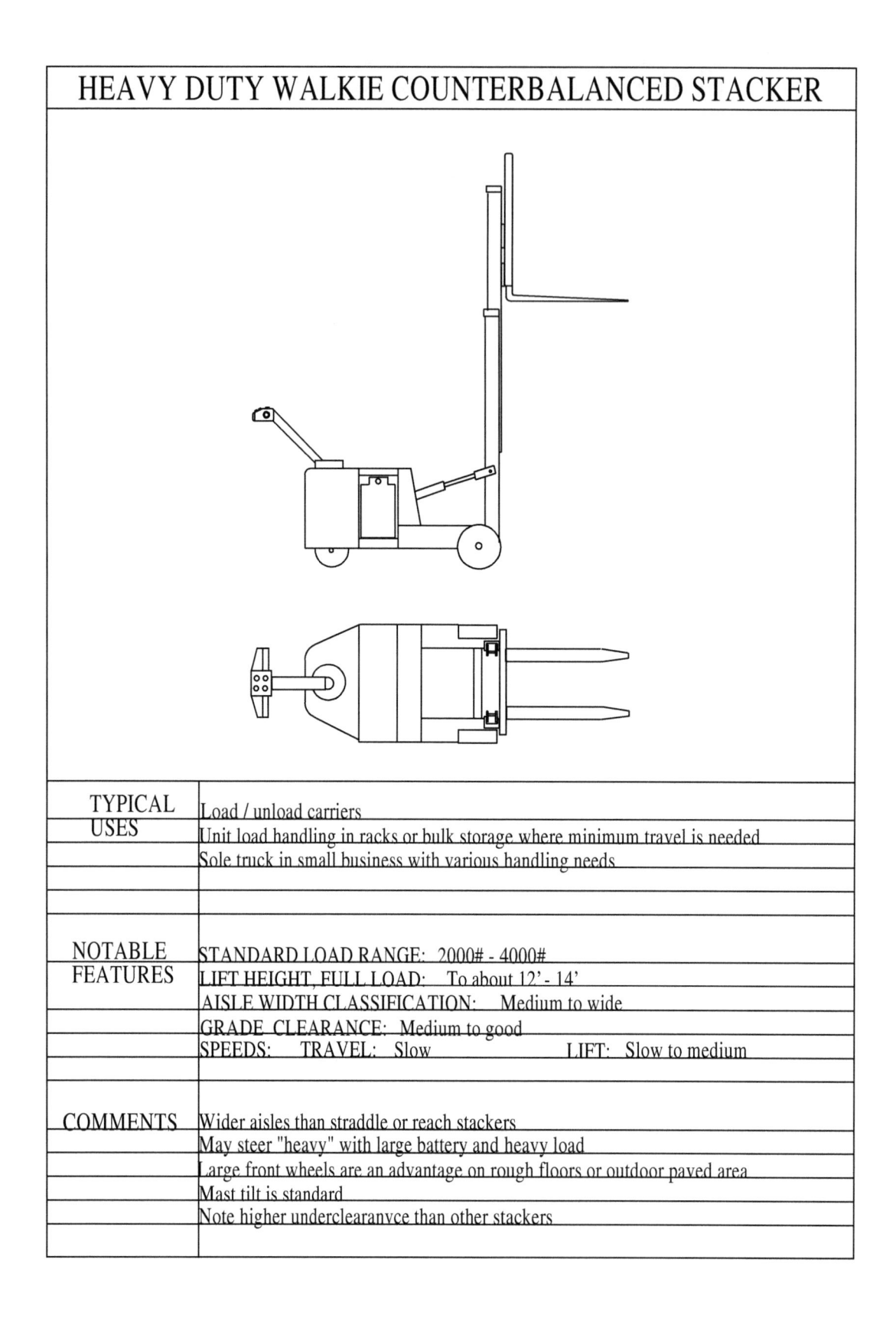

TYPICAL USES	Load / unload carriers
	Unit load handling in racks or bulk storage where minimum travel is needed
	Sole truck in small business with various handling needs

NOTABLE FEATURES	STANDARD LOAD RANGE: 2000# - 4000#
	LIFT HEIGHT, FULL LOAD: To about 12' - 14'
	AISLE WIDTH CLASSIFICATION: Medium to wide
	GRADE CLEARANCE: Medium to good
	SPEEDS: TRAVEL: Slow LIFT: Slow to medium

COMMENTS	Wider aisles than straddle or reach stackers
	May steer "heavy" with large battery and heavy load
	Large front wheels are an advantage on rough floors or outdoor paved area
	Mast tilt is standard
	Note higher underclearanvce than other stackers

WALKIE STACKER FORKS-OVER-FORKS

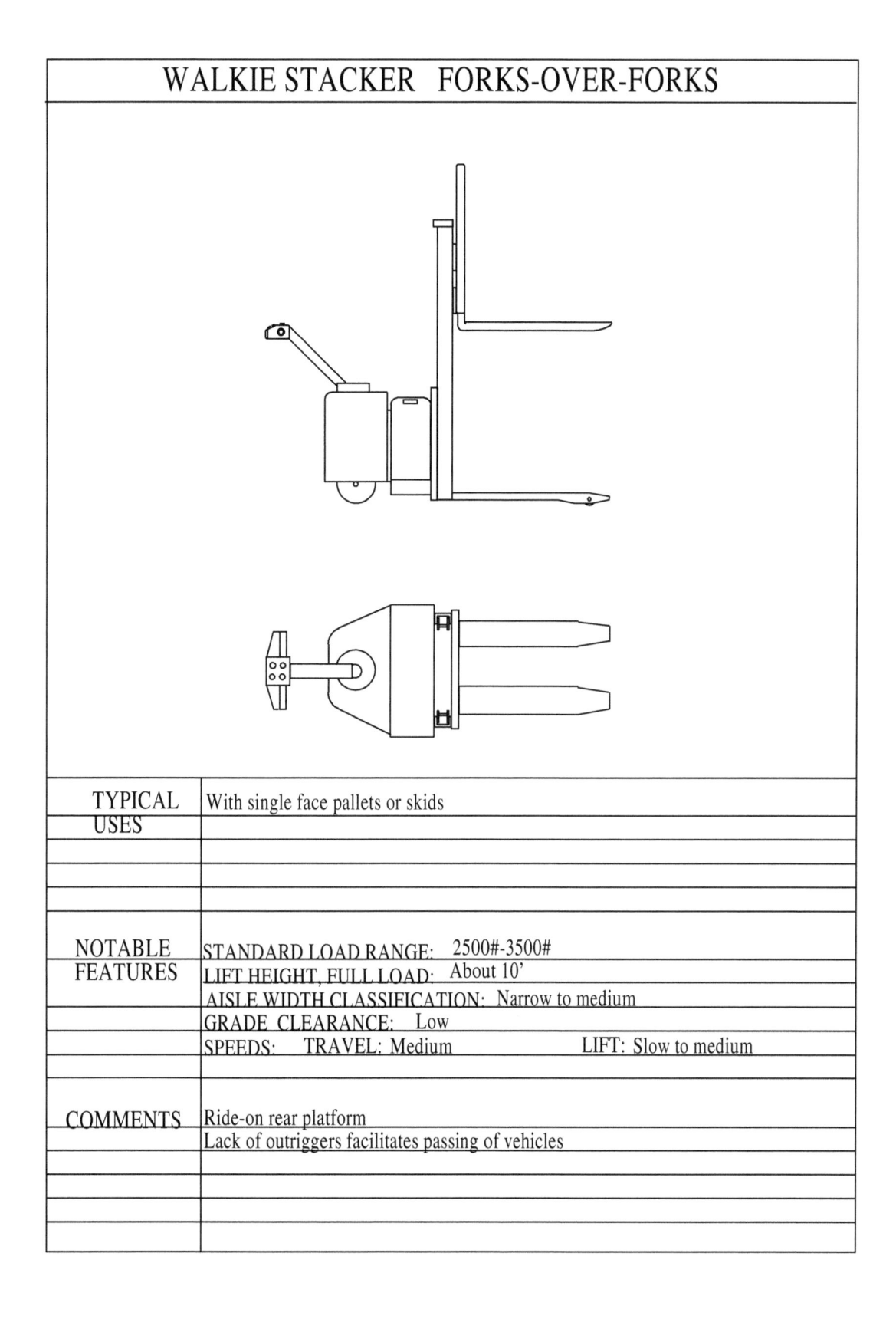

230

TYPICAL USES	With single face pallets or skids
NOTABLE FEATURES	STANDARD LOAD RANGE: 2500#-3500# LIFT HEIGHT, FULL LOAD: About 10' AISLE WIDTH CLASSIFICATION: Narrow to medium GRADE CLEARANCE: Low SPEEDS: TRAVEL: Medium LIFT: Slow to medium
COMMENTS	Ride-on rear platform Lack of outriggers facilitates passing of vehicles

7 *FORKLIFTS*

SKID TRUCKS

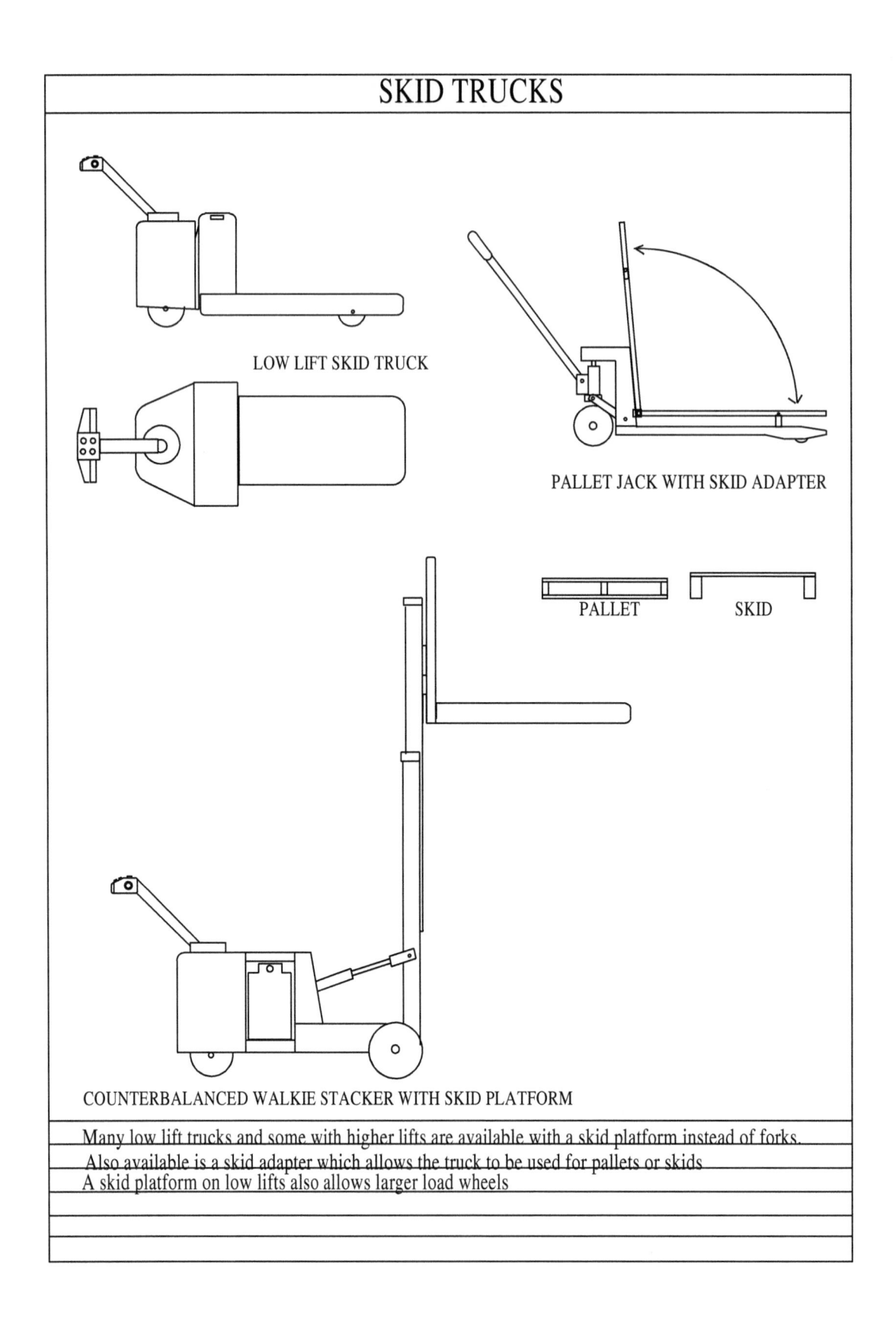

LOW LIFT SKID TRUCK

PALLET JACK WITH SKID ADAPTER

PALLET **SKID**

COUNTERBALANCED WALKIE STACKER WITH SKID PLATFORM

Many low lift trucks and some with higher lifts are available with a skid platform instead of forks.
Also available is a skid adapter which allows the truck to be used for pallets or skids.
A skid platform on low lifts also allows larger load wheels.

HOW TO CONFIGURE AND EQUIP YOUR WAREHOUSE

REAR RIDE-ON STRADDLE TRUCK

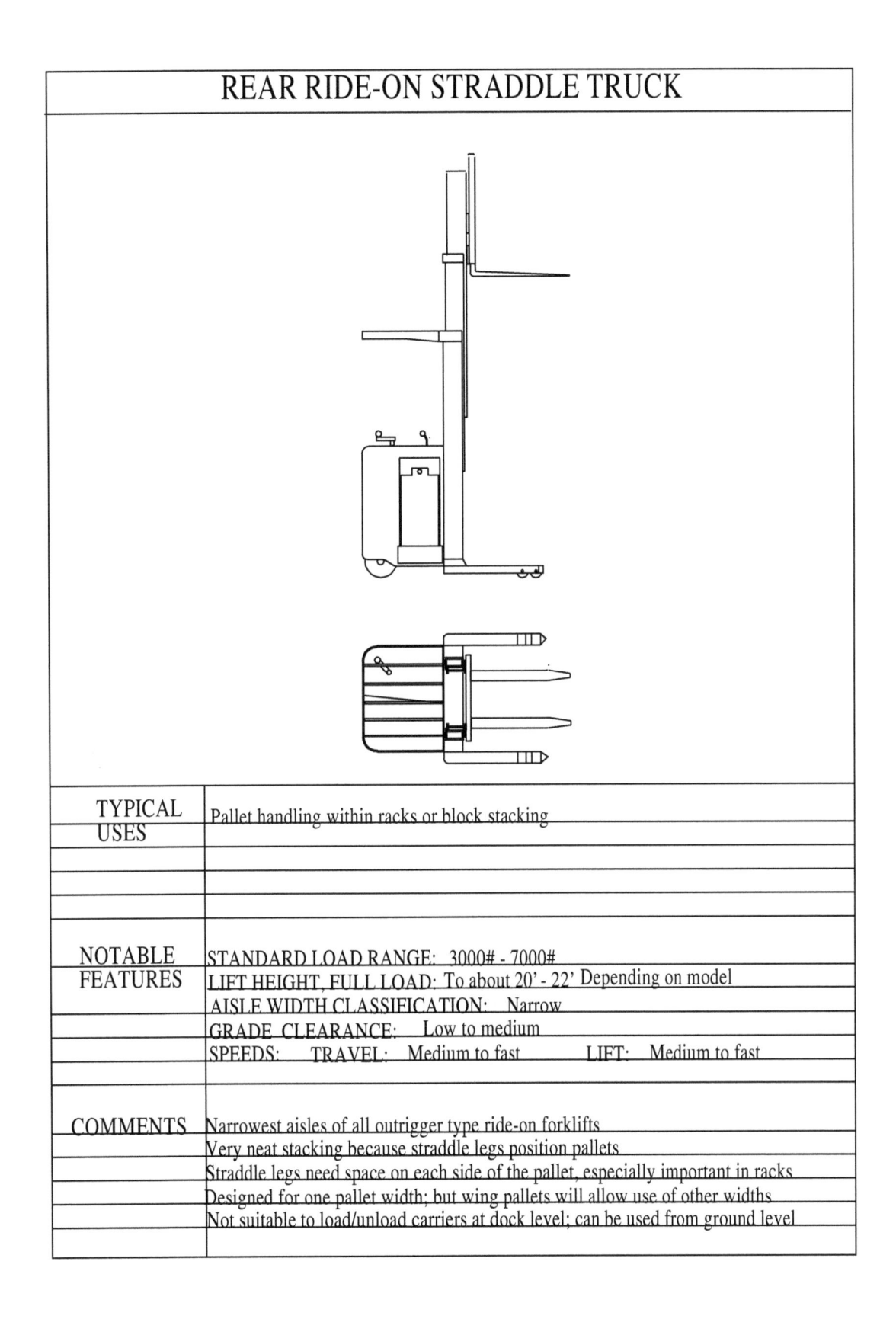

TYPICAL USES	Pallet handling within racks or block stacking
NOTABLE FEATURES	STANDARD LOAD RANGE: 3000# - 7000# LIFT HEIGHT, FULL LOAD: To about 20' - 22' Depending on model AISLE WIDTH CLASSIFICATION: Narrow GRADE CLEARANCE: Low to medium SPEEDS: TRAVEL: Medium to fast LIFT: Medium to fast
COMMENTS	Narrowest aisles of all outrigger type ride-on forklifts Very neat stacking because straddle legs position pallets Straddle legs need space on each side of the pallet, especially important in racks Designed for one pallet width; but wing pallets will allow use of other widths Not suitable to load/unload carriers at dock level; can be used from ground level

7 *FORKLIFTS*

REACH TRUCKS

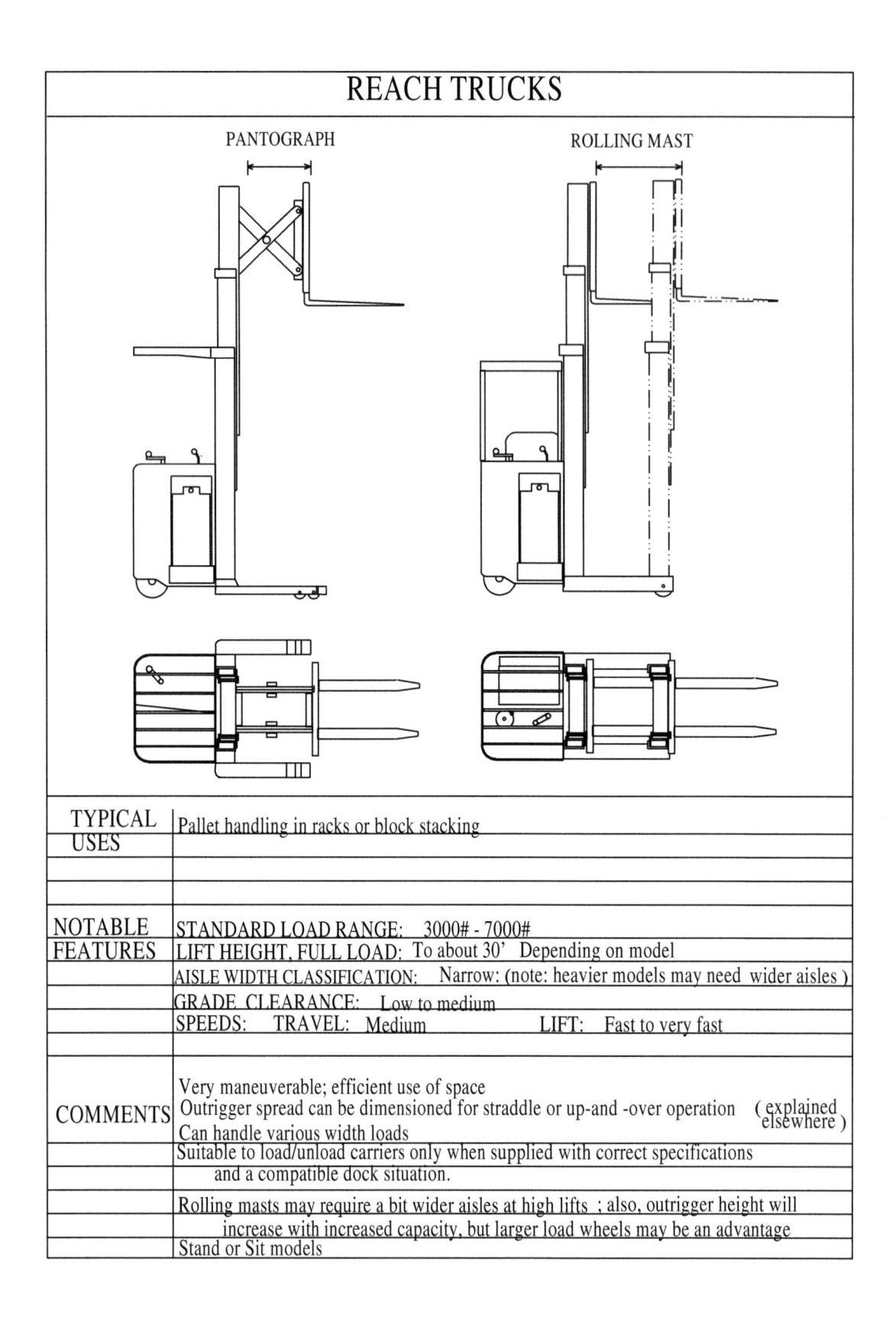

PANTOGRAPH ROLLING MAST

TYPICAL USES	Pallet handling in racks or block stacking
NOTABLE FEATURES	STANDARD LOAD RANGE: 3000# - 7000# LIFT HEIGHT, FULL LOAD: To about 30' Depending on model AISLE WIDTH CLASSIFICATION: Narrow: (note: heavier models may need wider aisles) GRADE CLEARANCE: Low to medium SPEEDS: TRAVEL: Medium LIFT: Fast to very fast
COMMENTS	Very maneuverable; efficient use of space Outrigger spread can be dimensioned for straddle or up-and-over operation (explained elsewhere) Can handle various width loads Suitable to load/unload carriers only when supplied with correct specifications and a compatible dock situation. Rolling masts may require a bit wider aisles at high lifts ; also, outrigger height will increase with increased capacity, but larger load wheels may be an advantage Stand or Sit models

HOW TO CONFIGURE AND EQUIP YOUR WAREHOUSE

DOUBLE-DEEP REACH TRUCK

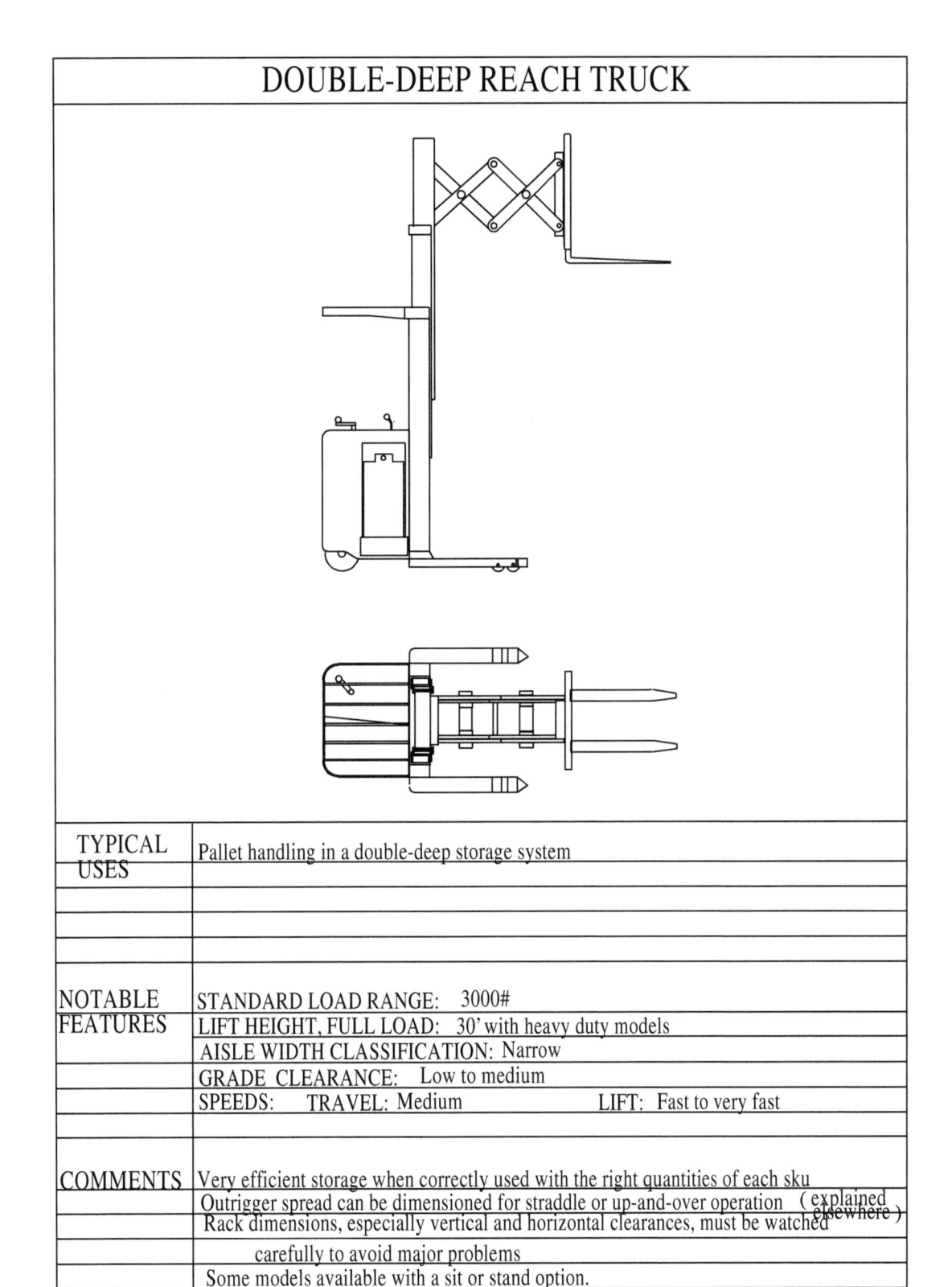

TYPICAL USES	Pallet handling in a double-deep storage system
NOTABLE FEATURES	STANDARD LOAD RANGE: 3000#
	LIFT HEIGHT, FULL LOAD: 30' with heavy duty models
	AISLE WIDTH CLASSIFICATION: Narrow
	GRADE CLEARANCE: Low to medium
	SPEEDS: TRAVEL: Medium LIFT: Fast to very fast
COMMENTS	Very efficient storage when correctly used with the right quantities of each sku
	Outrigger spread can be dimensioned for straddle or up-and-over operation (explained elsewhere)
	Rack dimensions, especially vertical and horizontal clearances, must be watched carefully to avoid major problems
	Some models available with a sit or stand option.

7   *FORKLIFTS*

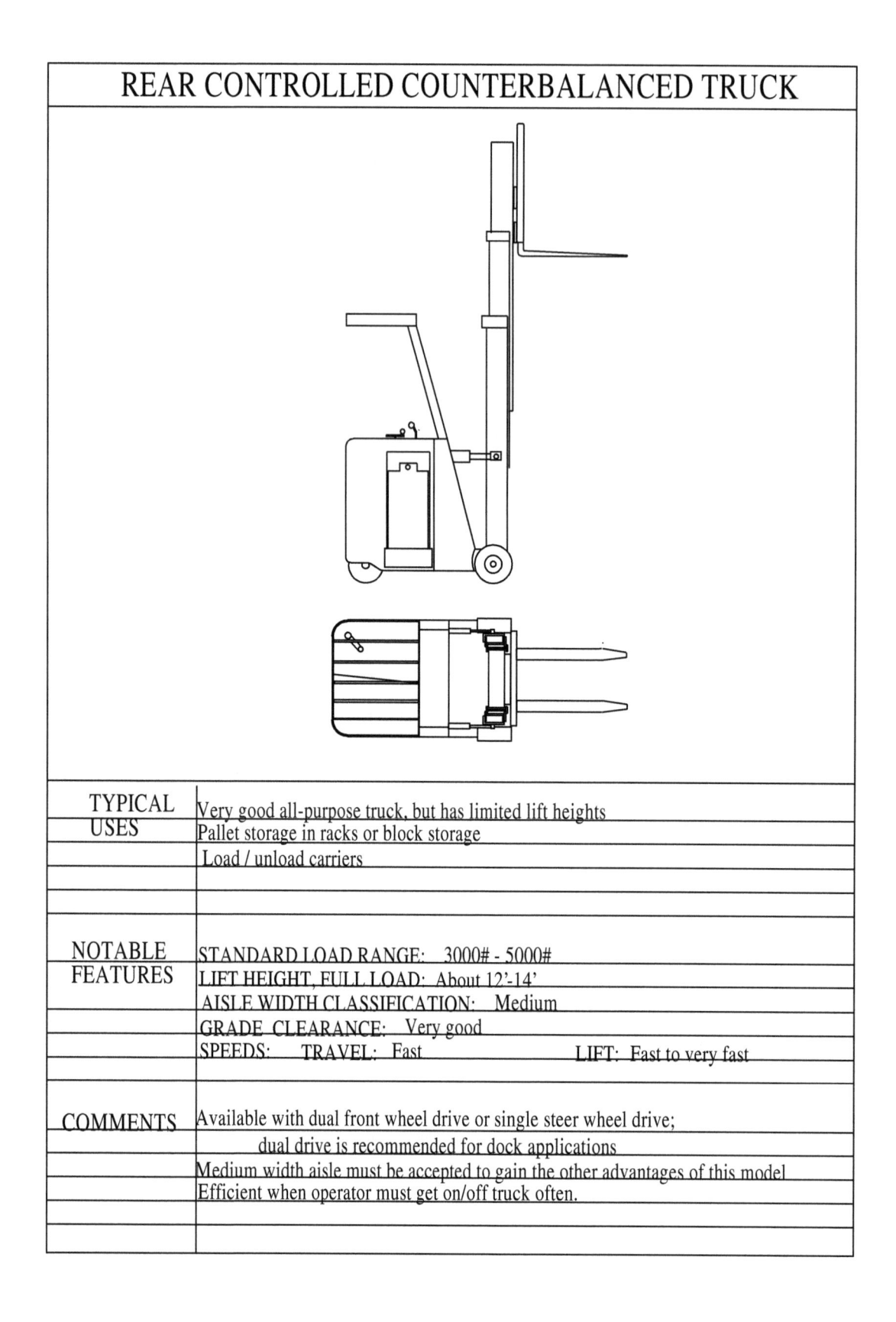

REAR CONTROLLED COUNTERBALANCED TRUCK

TYPICAL USES	Very good all-purpose truck, but has limited lift heights
	Pallet storage in racks or block storage
	Load / unload carriers
NOTABLE FEATURES	STANDARD LOAD RANGE: 3000# - 5000#
	LIFT HEIGHT, FULL LOAD: About 12'-14'
	AISLE WIDTH CLASSIFICATION: Medium
	GRADE CLEARANCE: Very good
	SPEEDS: TRAVEL: Fast LIFT: Fast to very fast
COMMENTS	Available with dual front wheel drive or single steer wheel drive; dual drive is recommended for dock applications
	Medium width aisle must be accepted to gain the other advantages of this model
	Efficient when operator must get on/off truck often.

HOW TO CONFIGURE AND EQUIP YOUR WAREHOUSE

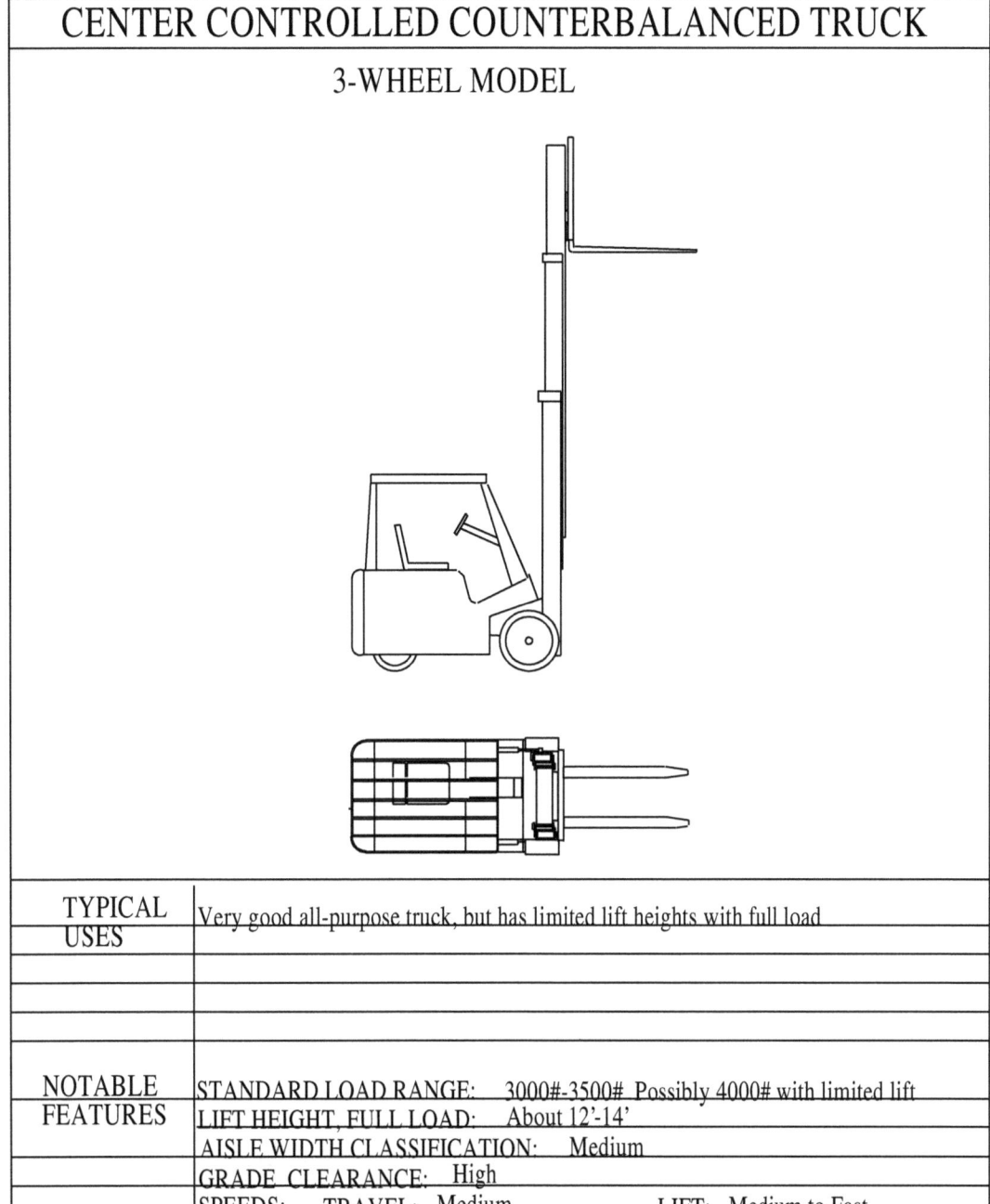

CENTER CONTROLLED COUNTERBALANCED TRUCK
3-WHEEL MODEL

TYPICAL USES	Very good all-purpose truck, but has limited lift heights with full load
NOTABLE FEATURES	STANDARD LOAD RANGE: 3000#-3500# Possibly 4000# with limited lift LIFT HEIGHT, FULL LOAD: About 12'-14' AISLE WIDTH CLASSIFICATION: Medium GRADE CLEARANCE: High SPEEDS: TRAVEL: Medium LIFT: Medium to Fast
COMMENTS	Narrower aisle than four wheel counterbalanced models Available with single rear wheel or dual front wheel drives. Dual front wheel drive is recommended when used to load/unload carriers Shown as battery powered. Internal combustion models also available

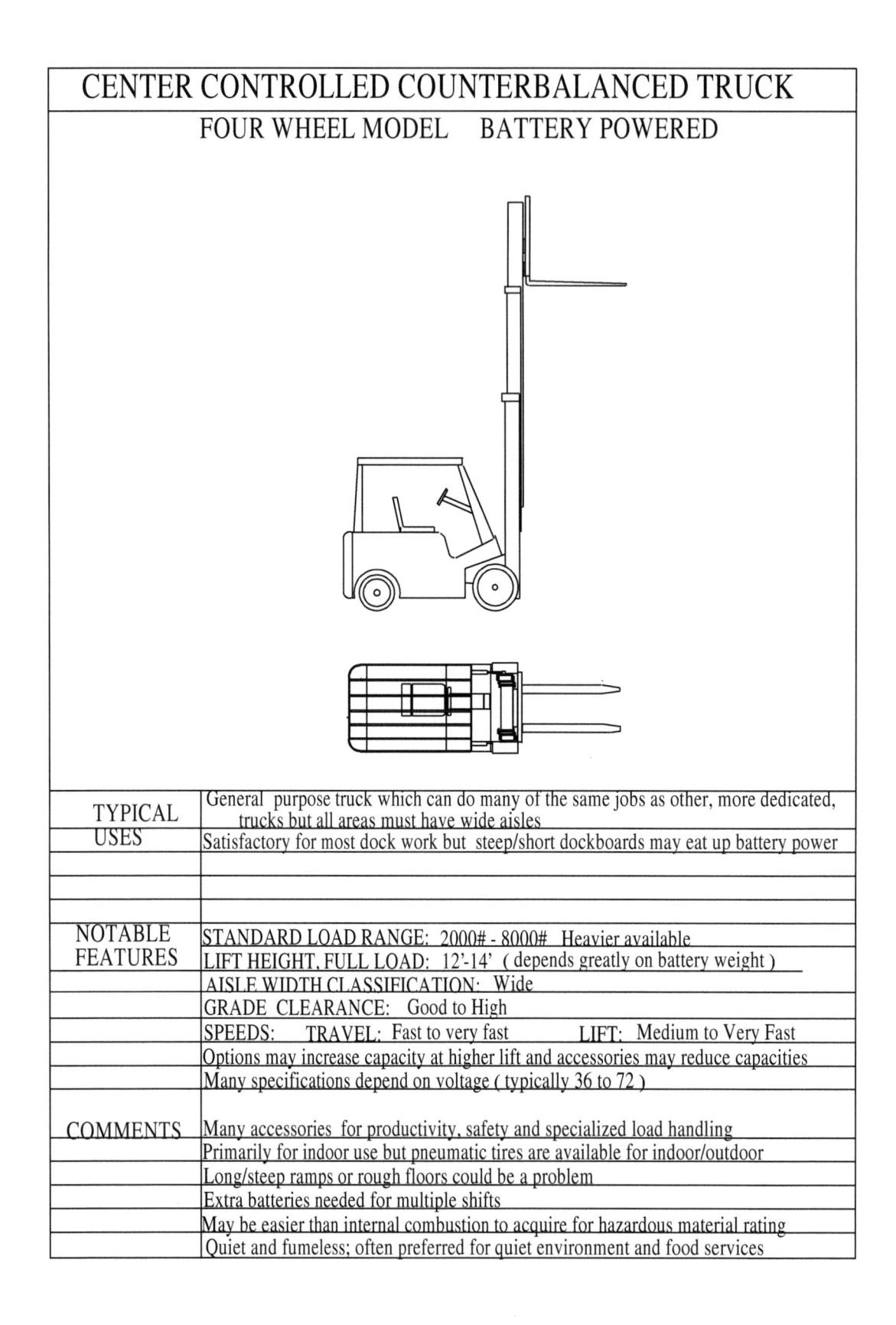

CENTER CONTROLLED COUNTERBALANCED TRUCK
FOUR WHEEL MODEL   BATTERY POWERED

TYPICAL USES	General purpose truck which can do many of the same jobs as other, more dedicated, trucks but all areas must have wide aisles
	Satisfactory for most dock work but steep/short dockboards may eat up battery power
NOTABLE FEATURES	STANDARD LOAD RANGE: 2000# - 8000# Heavier available
	LIFT HEIGHT, FULL LOAD: 12'-14' (depends greatly on battery weight)
	AISLE WIDTH CLASSIFICATION: Wide
	GRADE CLEARANCE: Good to High
	SPEEDS: TRAVEL: Fast to very fast LIFT: Medium to Very Fast
	Options may increase capacity at higher lift and accessories may reduce capacities
	Many specifications depend on voltage (typically 36 to 72)
COMMENTS	Many accessories for productivity, safety and specialized load handling
	Primarily for indoor use but pneumatic tires are available for indoor/outdoor
	Long/steep ramps or rough floors could be a problem
	Extra batteries needed for multiple shifts
	May be easier than internal combustion to acquire for hazardous material rating
	Quiet and fumeless; often preferred for quiet environment and food services

HOW TO CONFIGURE AND EQUIP YOUR WAREHOUSE

CENTER CONTROLLED COUNTERBALANCED TRUCK

FOUR WHEEL MODEL   INTERNAL COMBUSTION POWERED

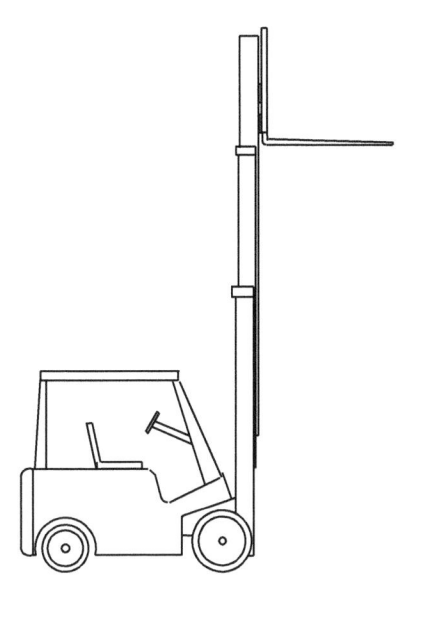

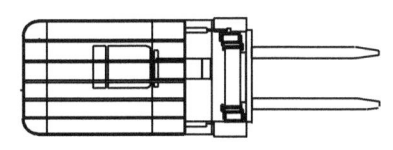

TYPICAL USES	Probably the most commonly used forklift; with a very wide range of sizes, options and accessories.
	General purpose truck which can do many of the jobs of other, more dedicated, trucks but all areas must have wide aisles
	Popular for dock work, long distance travel & " bull work" such as chiseling under loads
NOTABLE FEATURES	STANDARD LOAD RANGE: Weight capacities beyond most needs. Inquire.
	LIFT HEIGHT, FULL LOAD: About 12' to 14'
	AISLE WIDTH CLASSIFICATION: Wide
	GRADE CLEARANCE: Good to High
	SPEEDS: TRAVEL: Fast to Very Fast LIFT: Fast to Very Fast
COMMENTS	Fuel types include gas, lpg and diesel
	Fumes to be considered with internal combustion power
	Consider for ramps, rough floors or outdoors
	Solid rubber, pneumatic and special tires available
	Many accessories are available for productivity, safety and specialized load handling

SIDE-REACH TRUCK

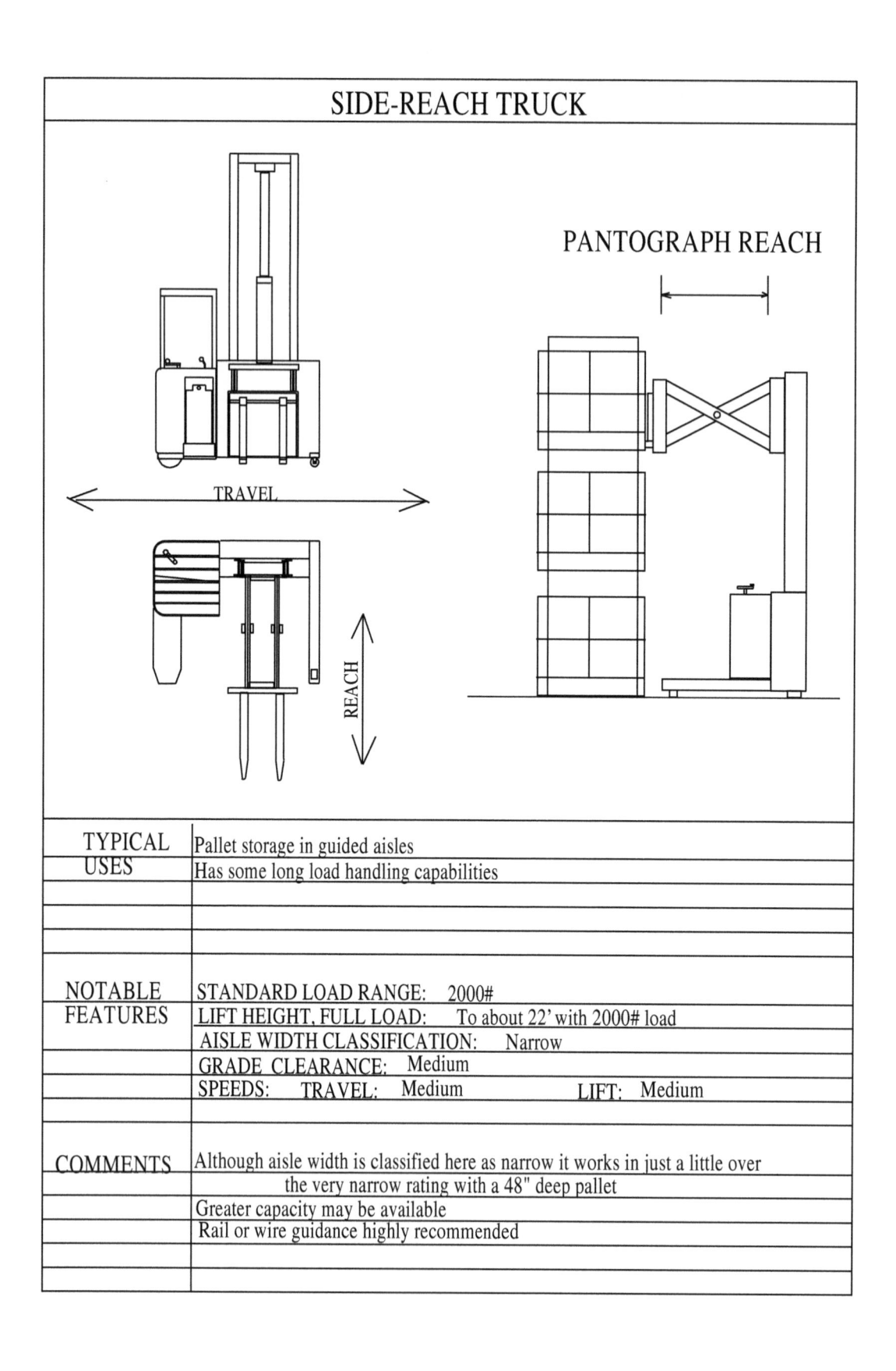

PANTOGRAPH REACH

TRAVEL

REACH

TYPICAL USES	Pallet storage in guided aisles
	Has some long load handling capabilities
NOTABLE FEATURES	STANDARD LOAD RANGE: 2000#
	LIFT HEIGHT, FULL LOAD: To about 22' with 2000# load
	AISLE WIDTH CLASSIFICATION: Narrow
	GRADE CLEARANCE: Medium
	SPEEDS: TRAVEL: Medium LIFT: Medium
COMMENTS	Although aisle width is classified here as narrow it works in just a little over the very narrow rating with a 48" deep pallet
	Greater capacity may be available
	Rail or wire guidance highly recommended

HOW TO CONFIGURE AND EQUIP YOUR WAREHOUSE

HEAVY DUTY SIDELOADER

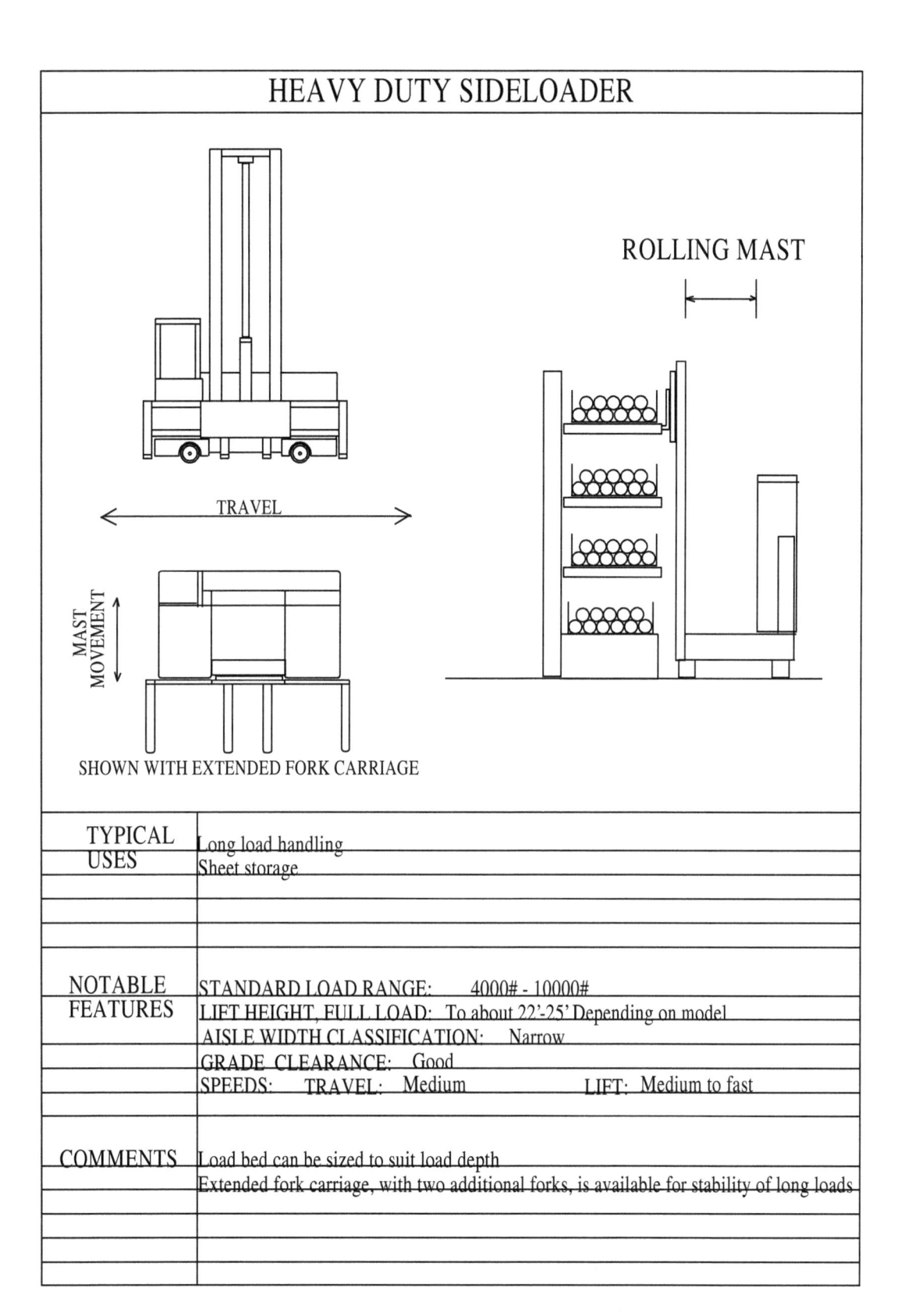

ROLLING MAST

TRAVEL

MAST MOVEMENT

SHOWN WITH EXTENDED FORK CARRIAGE

TYPICAL USES	Long load handling
	Sheet storage

NOTABLE FEATURES	STANDARD LOAD RANGE: 4000# - 10000#
	LIFT HEIGHT, FULL LOAD: To about 22'-25' Depending on model
	AISLE WIDTH CLASSIFICATION: Narrow
	GRADE CLEARANCE: Good
	SPEEDS: TRAVEL: Medium LIFT: Medium to fast

COMMENTS	Load bed can be sized to suit load depth
	Extended fork carriage, with two additional forks, is available for stability of long loads

7 FORKLIFTS

4-DIRECTIONAL REACH TRUCKS

4-DIRECTIONAL REACH TRUCK
PANTOGRAPH REACH
C/W SWIVEL WHEELS

4-DIRECTIONAL REACH TRUCK
ROLLING MAST
C/W SWIVEL WHEELS

TYPICAL USES	Single forklift to handle long loads or pallets.
NOTABLE FEATURES	STANDARD LOAD RANGE: 3500#-4500#
	LIFT HEIGHT, FULL LOAD: About 22'
	AISLE WIDTH CLASSIFICATION: Narrow to Medium depending on load depth
	GRADE CLEARANCE: Low
	SPEEDS: TRAVEL: Medium to Fast LIFT: Medium
COMMENTS	Narrower aisle than four wheel counterbalanced models
	Optional extended fork carriage for long loads is removable for pallet handling

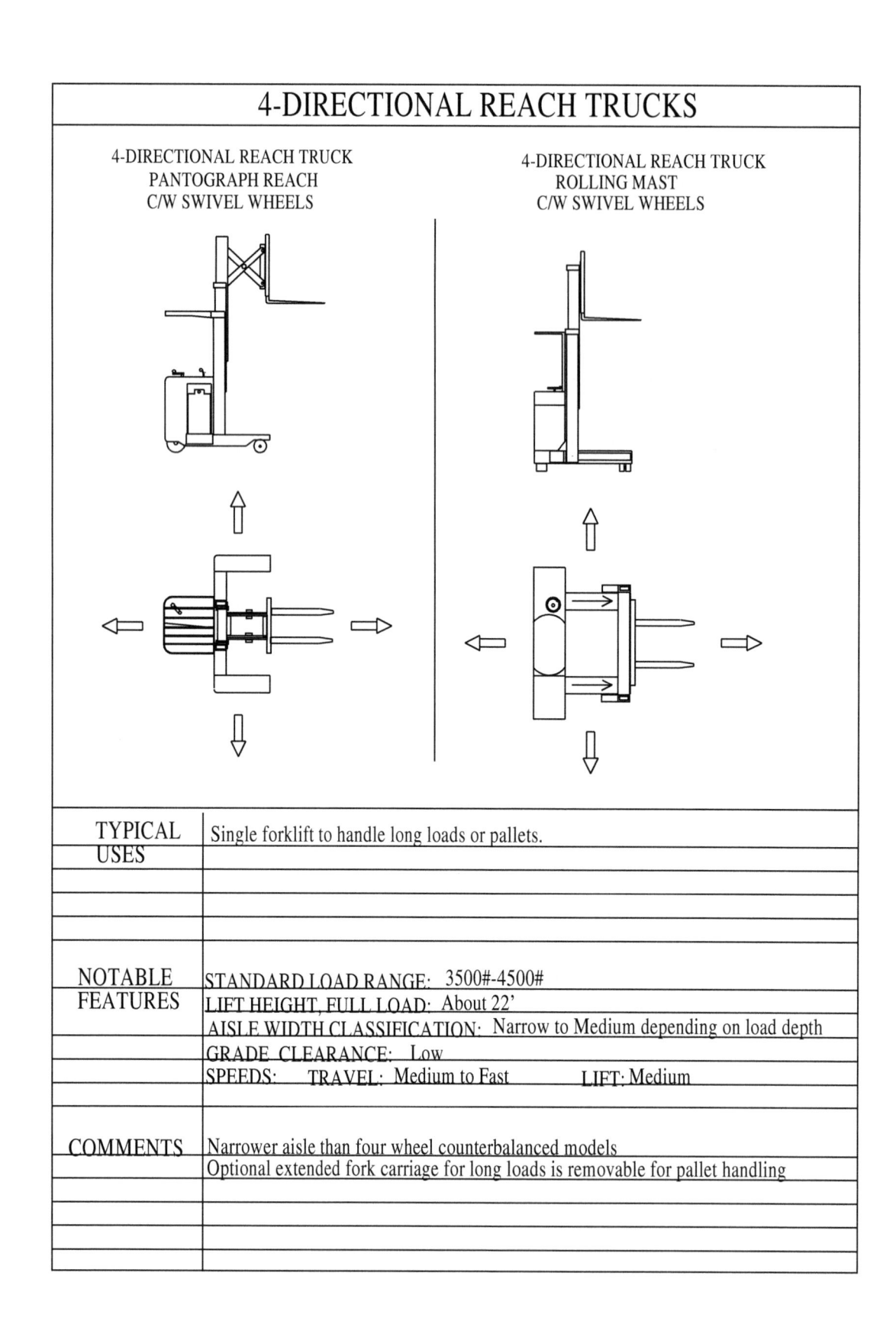

HOW TO CONFIGURE AND EQUIP YOUR WAREHOUSE

SWINGMAST VERY NARROW AISLE TRUCK

A: FORKS FORWARD

B: FORKS SWUNG TO THE SIDE

TYPICAL USES	Multi-purpose truck with many different capabilities
	With forks forward it is a center controlled counterbalanced truck
	When in a very narrow aisle the mast swings and the forks side shift
	Has some long load handling capability
SPECIAL NOTE	THE VERY WIDE RANGE OF THIS MODEL MAKES A SHORT SUMMARY IMPRACTICAL.
NOTABLE FEATURES	STANDARD LOAD RANGE: 3000#-12000#
	LIFT HEIGHT, FULL LOAD: Contact dealer re specific model.
	AISLE WIDTH CLASSIFICATION: Very narrow
	GRADE CLEARANCE: Good to very good
	SPEEDS: TRAVEL: Fast to very fast LIFT: Fast to very fast
COMMENTS	Very heavy; check carrier floors if using to load/unload
	Will operate better on rough or uneven floors than most other types of very narrow aisle machines
	There is a 6000# gas model available. Maybe others.

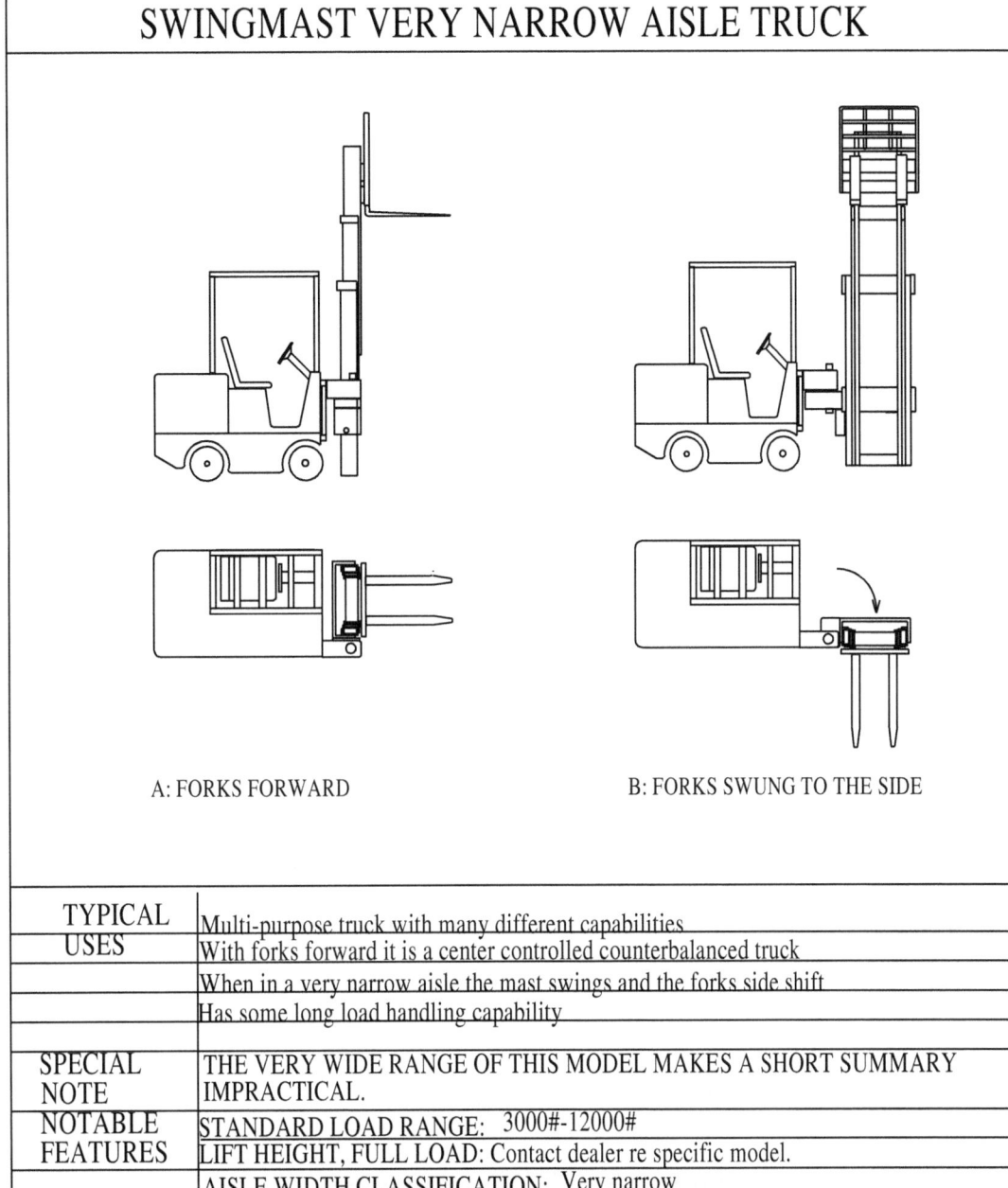

FORKLIFTS

MAN-UP VERY NARROW AISLE TRUCK

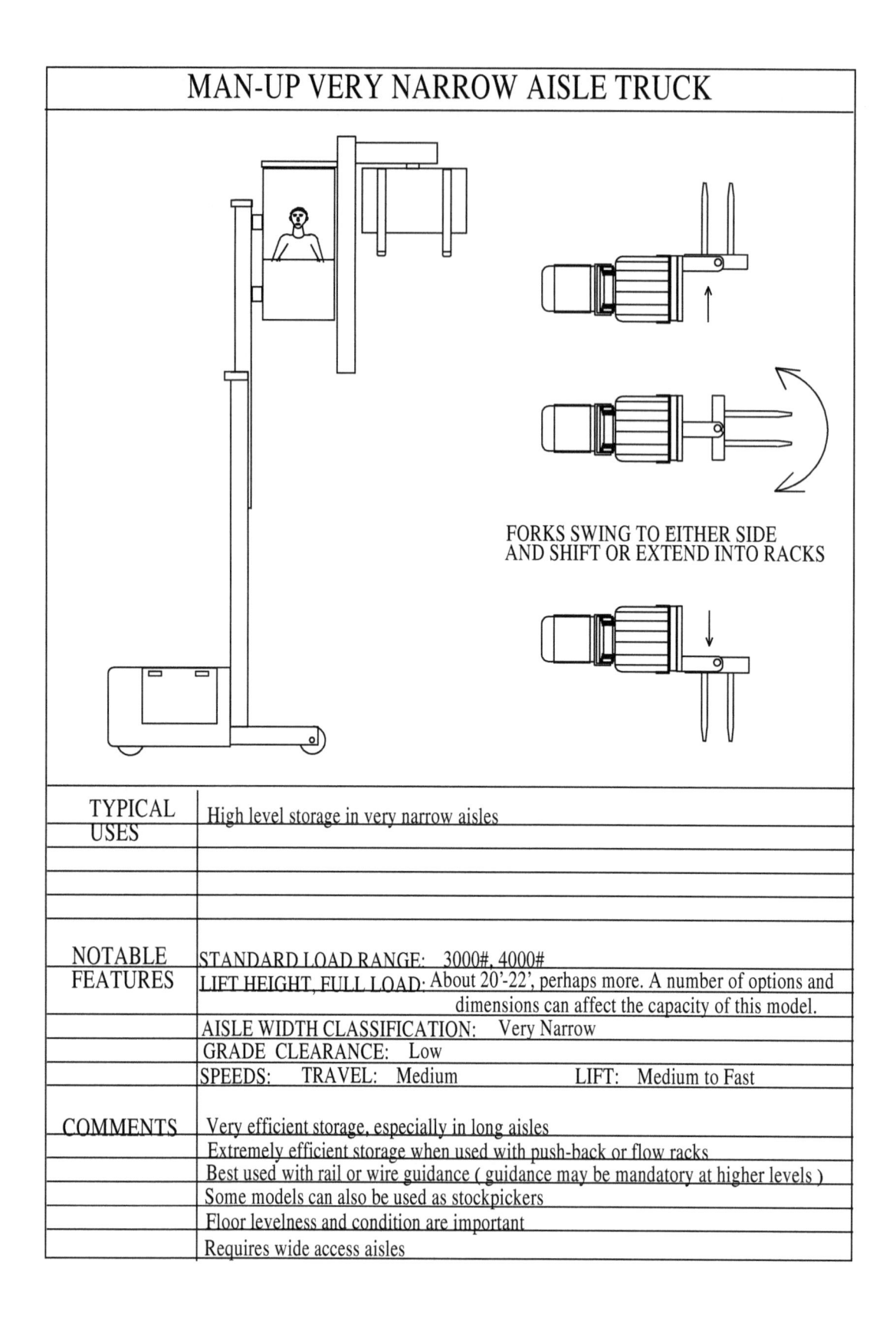

FORKS SWING TO EITHER SIDE
AND SHIFT OR EXTEND INTO RACKS

TYPICAL USES	High level storage in very narrow aisles
NOTABLE FEATURES	STANDARD LOAD RANGE: 3000#, 4000#
	LIFT HEIGHT, FULL LOAD: About 20'-22', perhaps more. A number of options and dimensions can affect the capacity of this model.
	AISLE WIDTH CLASSIFICATION: Very Narrow
	GRADE CLEARANCE: Low
	SPEEDS: TRAVEL: Medium LIFT: Medium to Fast
COMMENTS	Very efficient storage, especially in long aisles
	Extremely efficient storage when used with push-back or flow racks
	Best used with rail or wire guidance (guidance may be mandatory at higher levels)
	Some models can also be used as stockpickers
	Floor levelness and condition are important
	Requires wide access aisles

MAN-DOWN VERY NARROW AISLE TRUCK

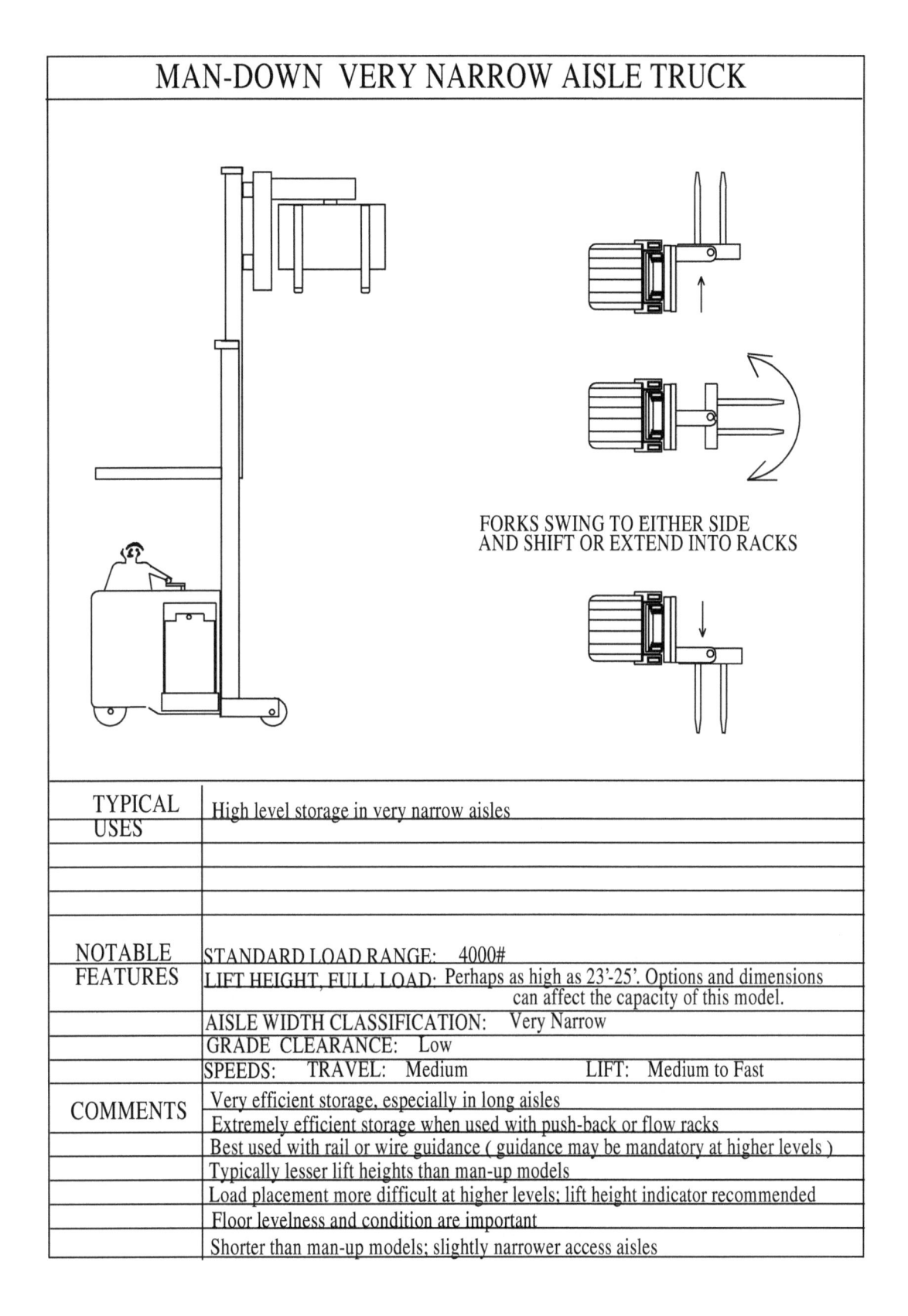

FORKS SWING TO EITHER SIDE
AND SHIFT OR EXTEND INTO RACKS

TYPICAL USES	High level storage in very narrow aisles
NOTABLE FEATURES	STANDARD LOAD RANGE: 4000#
	LIFT HEIGHT, FULL LOAD: Perhaps as high as 23'-25'. Options and dimensions can affect the capacity of this model.
	AISLE WIDTH CLASSIFICATION: Very Narrow
	GRADE CLEARANCE: Low
	SPEEDS: TRAVEL: Medium LIFT: Medium to Fast
COMMENTS	Very efficient storage, especially in long aisles
	Extremely efficient storage when used with push-back or flow racks
	Best used with rail or wire guidance (guidance may be mandatory at higher levels)
	Typically lesser lift heights than man-up models
	Load placement more difficult at higher levels; lift height indicator recommended
	Floor levelness and condition are important
	Shorter than man-up models; slightly narrower access aisles

7 FORKLIFTS

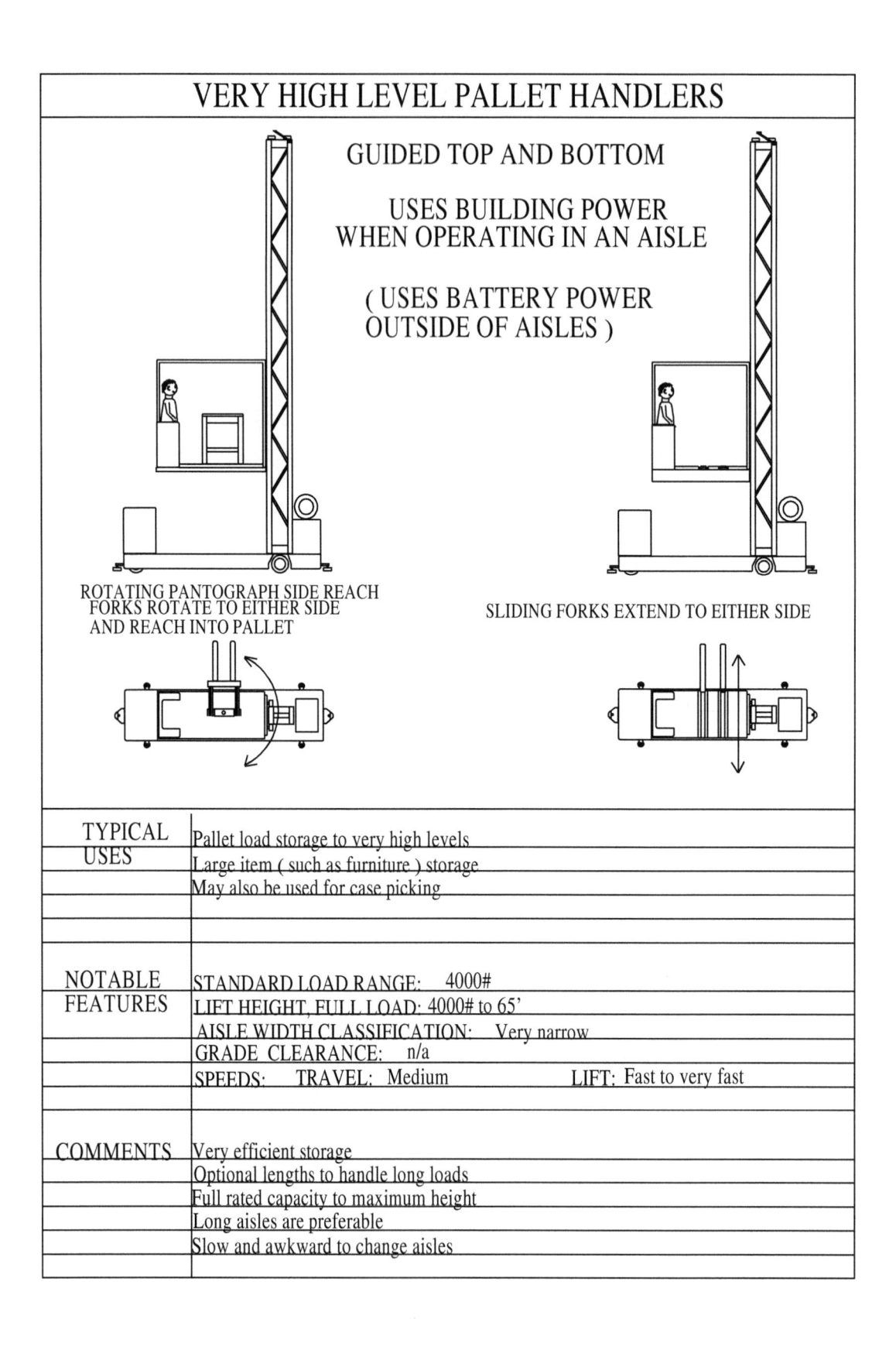

VERY HIGH LEVEL PALLET HANDLERS

GUIDED TOP AND BOTTOM

USES BUILDING POWER
WHEN OPERATING IN AN AISLE

(USES BATTERY POWER
OUTSIDE OF AISLES)

ROTATING PANTOGRAPH SIDE REACH
FORKS ROTATE TO EITHER SIDE
AND REACH INTO PALLET

SLIDING FORKS EXTEND TO EITHER SIDE

TYPICAL USES	Pallet load storage to very high levels
	Large item (such as furniture) storage
	May also be used for case picking

NOTABLE FEATURES	STANDARD LOAD RANGE: 4000#
	LIFT HEIGHT, FULL LOAD: 4000# to 65'
	AISLE WIDTH CLASSIFICATION: Very narrow
	GRADE CLEARANCE: n/a
	SPEEDS: TRAVEL: Medium LIFT: Fast to very fast

COMMENTS	Very efficient storage
	Optional lengths to handle long loads
	Full rated capacity to maximum height
	Long aisles are preferable
	Slow and awkward to change aisles

HOW TO CONFIGURE AND EQUIP YOUR WAREHOUSE

SECTION EIGHT
ORDERPICKERS

8

ORDERPICKERS — LOW LEVEL

THE STOCKPICKERS SHOWN WITH AN ASTERISK HAVE BEEN LISTED AND DESCRIBED IN THE PREVIOUS FORKLIFT SECTION. REFER THERE FOR DETAILS. THEY ARE SHOWN HERE AGAIN BECAUSE IN ADDITION TO PALLET HANDLING THEY ARE COMMONLY USED FOR PICKING OF CASES OR PIECES. THEY ARE CROSS REFERENCED ON THE NEXT PAGE

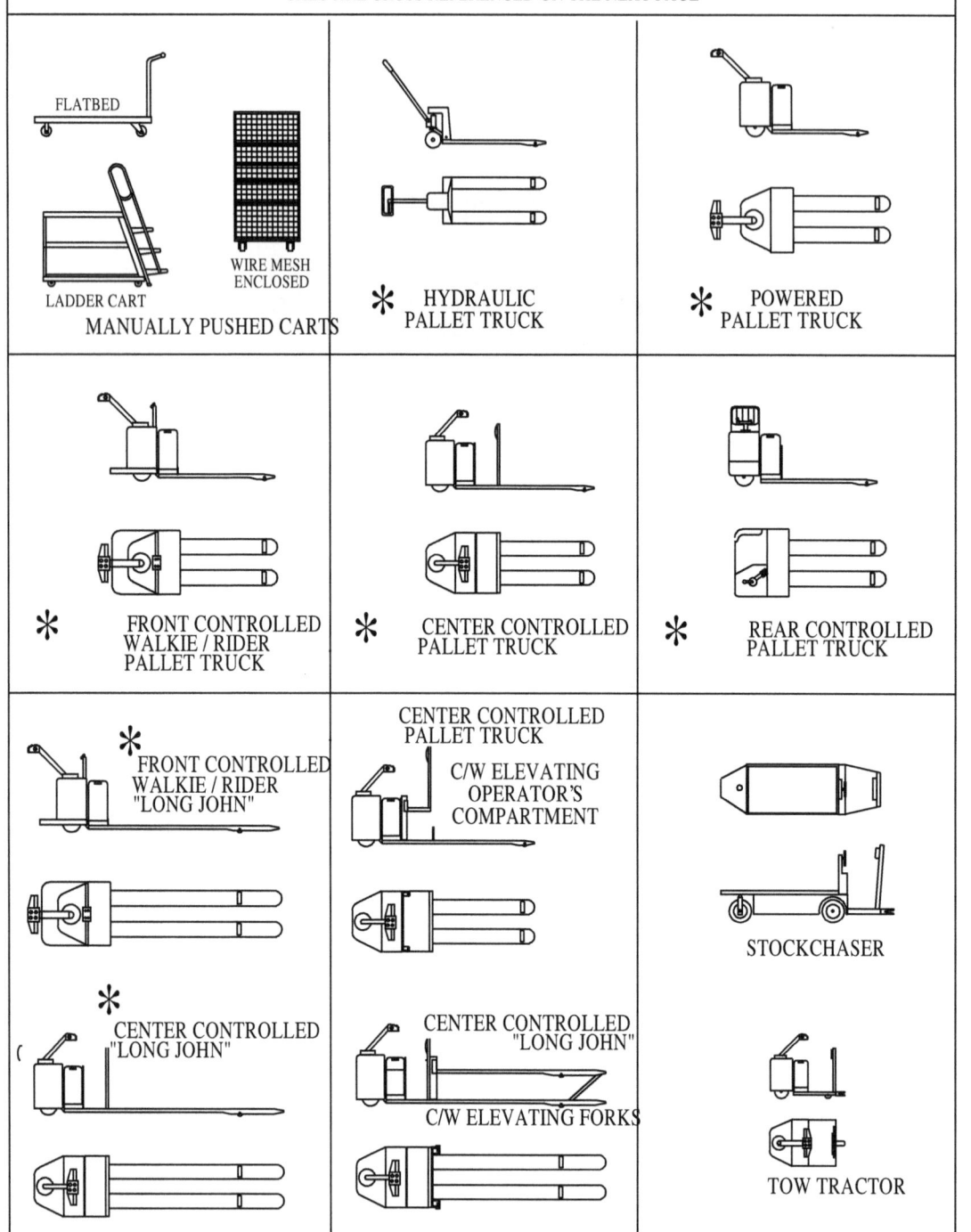

FLATBED / LADDER CART / WIRE MESH ENCLOSED — MANUALLY PUSHED CARTS	* HYDRAULIC PALLET TRUCK	* POWERED PALLET TRUCK
* FRONT CONTROLLED WALKIE / RIDER PALLET TRUCK	* CENTER CONTROLLED PALLET TRUCK	* REAR CONTROLLED PALLET TRUCK
* FRONT CONTROLLED WALKIE / RIDER "LONG JOHN" / * CENTER CONTROLLED "LONG JOHN"	CENTER CONTROLLED PALLET TRUCK C/W ELEVATING OPERATOR'S COMPARTMENT / CENTER CONTROLLED "LONG JOHN" C/W ELEVATING FORKS	STOCKCHASER / TOW TRACTOR

HOW TO CONFIGURE AND EQUIP YOUR WAREHOUSE

ORDERPICKERS

This section describes vehicles which are used for order picking. The selection is divided into four categories; those used for Low Level, Mid Level, High Level and Very High level picking.

There are no distinct lines between these levels but their ranges are approximated here as follows, based primarily on the equipment lift heights available.

Low Level: to about 7 or 8 feet.

Mid Level: to about 15 to 20 feet.

High Level: to about 30 feet.

Very High Level: above 30 feet; may be 60 feet or higher.

FORKLIFTS PREVIOUSLY DESCRIBED IN SECTION 7, AND WHICH ARE ALSO USED FOR ORDERPICKING, ARE LISTED BELOW AND ON THE DRAWINGS WITH ASTERISKS (*). REFER TO SECTION 7 FOR INFORMATION ABOUT THESE COMBINATION FORKLIFTS / ORDERPICKERS.

NAME

- HYDRAULIC PALLET TRUCK
- POWERED PALLET TRUCK
- FRONT CONTROLLED WALKIE/RIDER PALLET TRUCK
- CENTER CONTROLLED PALLET TRUCK
- REAR CONTROLLED PALLET TRUCK
- FRONT CONTROLLED WALKIE/RIDER "LONG JOHN"
- CENTER CONTROLLED "LONG JOHN"
- MAN-UP TURRET TRUCK
- ROTATING PANTOGRAPH SIDE REACH
- SLIDING FORKS SIDE REACH

PUSH CARTS

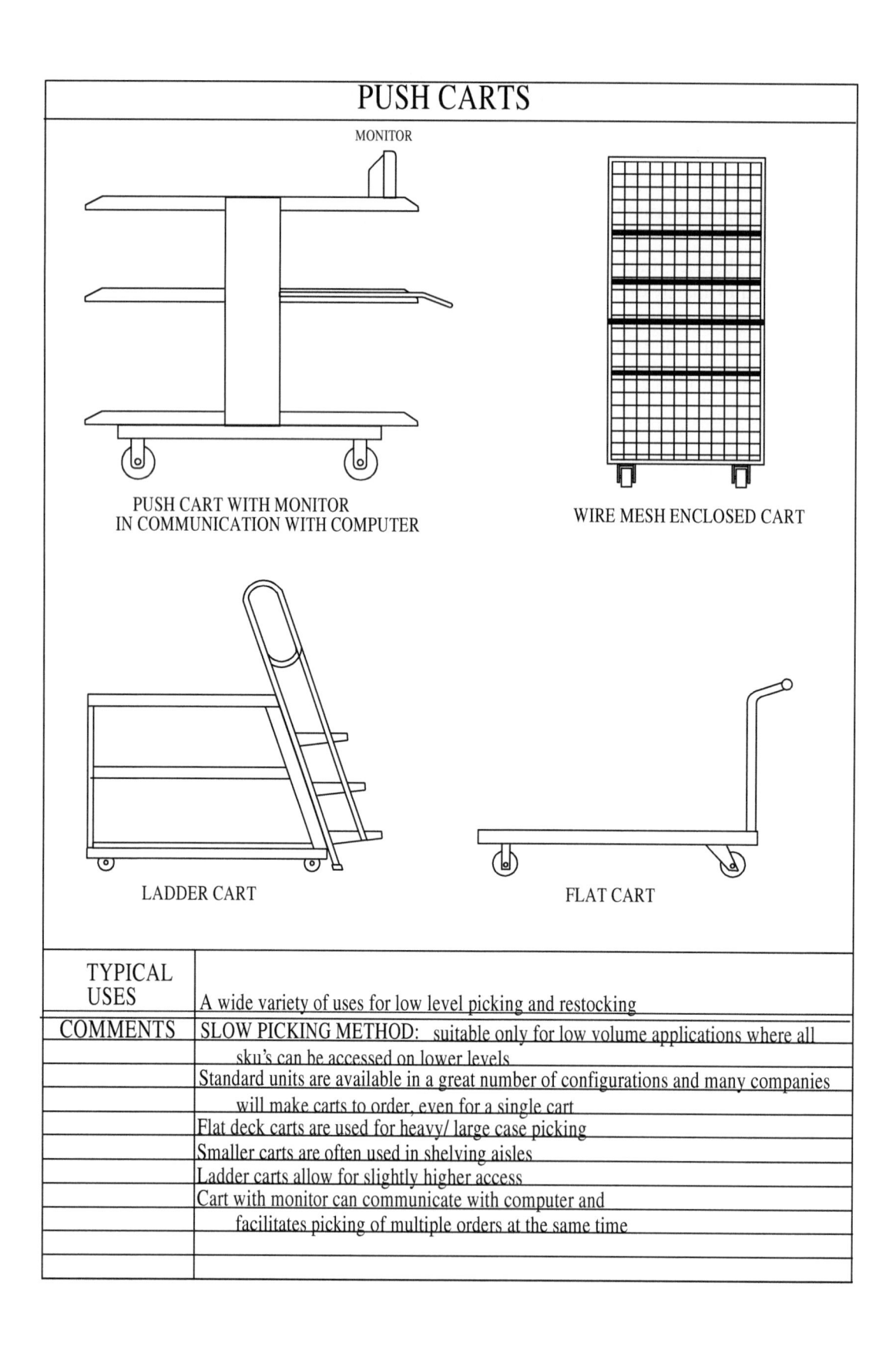

PUSH CART WITH MONITOR
IN COMMUNICATION WITH COMPUTER

WIRE MESH ENCLOSED CART

LADDER CART

FLAT CART

TYPICAL USES	A wide variety of uses for low level picking and restocking
COMMENTS	SLOW PICKING METHOD: suitable only for low volume applications where all sku's can be accessed on lower levels
	Standard units are available in a great number of configurations and many companies will make carts to order, even for a single cart
	Flat deck carts are used for heavy/ large case picking
	Smaller carts are often used in shelving aisles
	Ladder carts allow for slightly higher access
	Cart with monitor can communicate with computer and facilitates picking of multiple orders at the same time

LOW LIFT PALLET TRUCKS WITH PROVISION TO ELEVATE THE PICKER

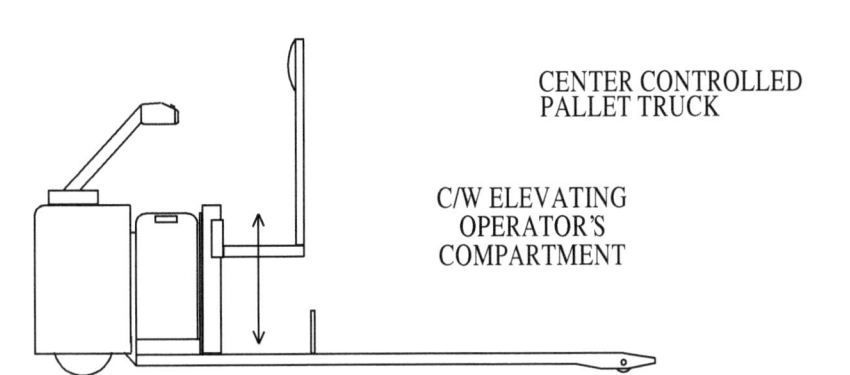

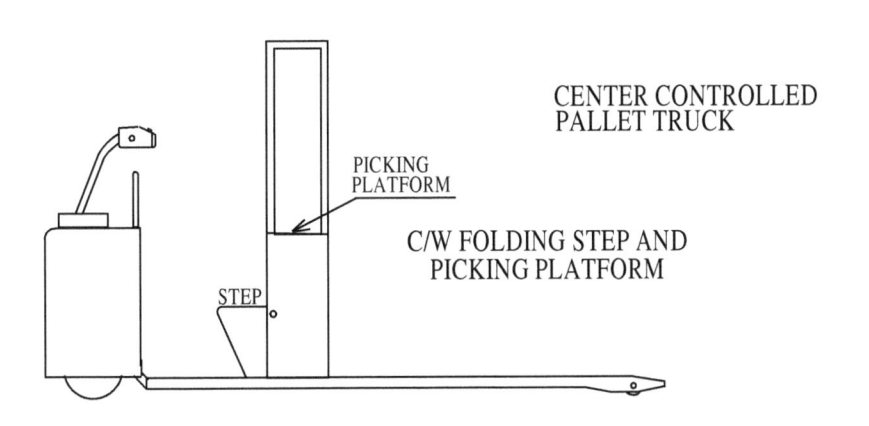

CENTER CONTROLLED PALLET TRUCK

C/W ELEVATING OPERATOR'S COMPARTMENT

CENTER CONTROLLED PALLET TRUCK

PICKING PLATFORM

C/W FOLDING STEP AND PICKING PLATFORM

STEP

TYPICAL USES	A wide variety of uses for low level picking and restocking
COMMENTS	Platforms raise picker about two feet, allowing higher picking.
	Using a step may be awkward with bulky or heavy items.

CENTER CONTROLLED LONG JOHN WITH ELEVATING FORKS

TYPICAL USES	A wide variety of uses for low level picking and re-stocking shelf items.
COMMENTS	Top forks raise 24", elevating the pallet to a more convenient level
	These forks can then be lowered as the load height is increased
	Typically carries two pallets for picking of large or multiple orders.

"STOCKCHASER"

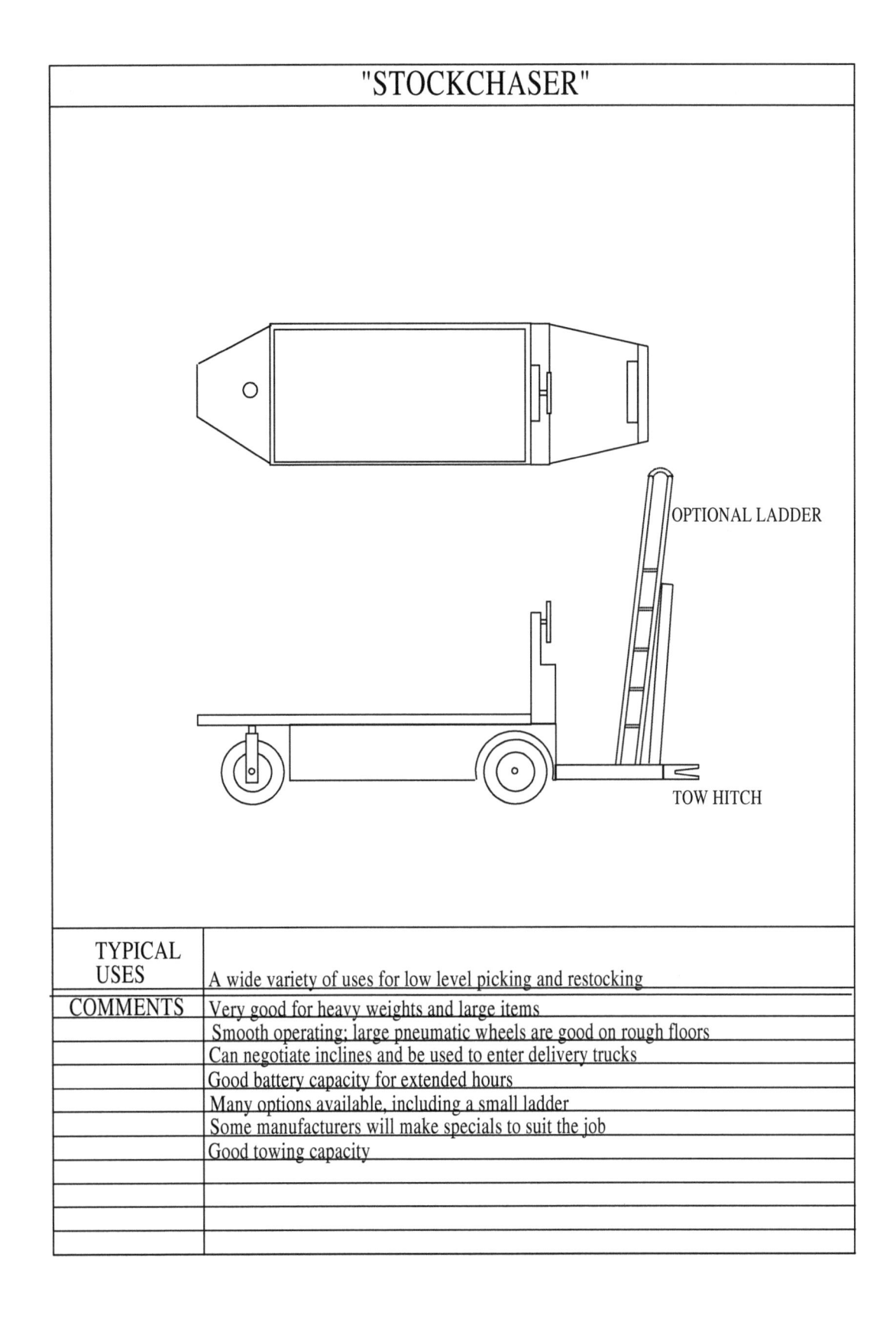

OPTIONAL LADDER

TOW HITCH

TYPICAL USES	A wide variety of uses for low level picking and restocking
COMMENTS	Very good for heavy weights and large items
	Smooth operating; large pneumatic wheels are good on rough floors
	Can negotiate inclines and be used to enter delivery trucks
	Good battery capacity for extended hours
	Many options available, including a small ladder
	Some manufacturers will make specials to suit the job
	Good towing capacity

TOW TRACTOR

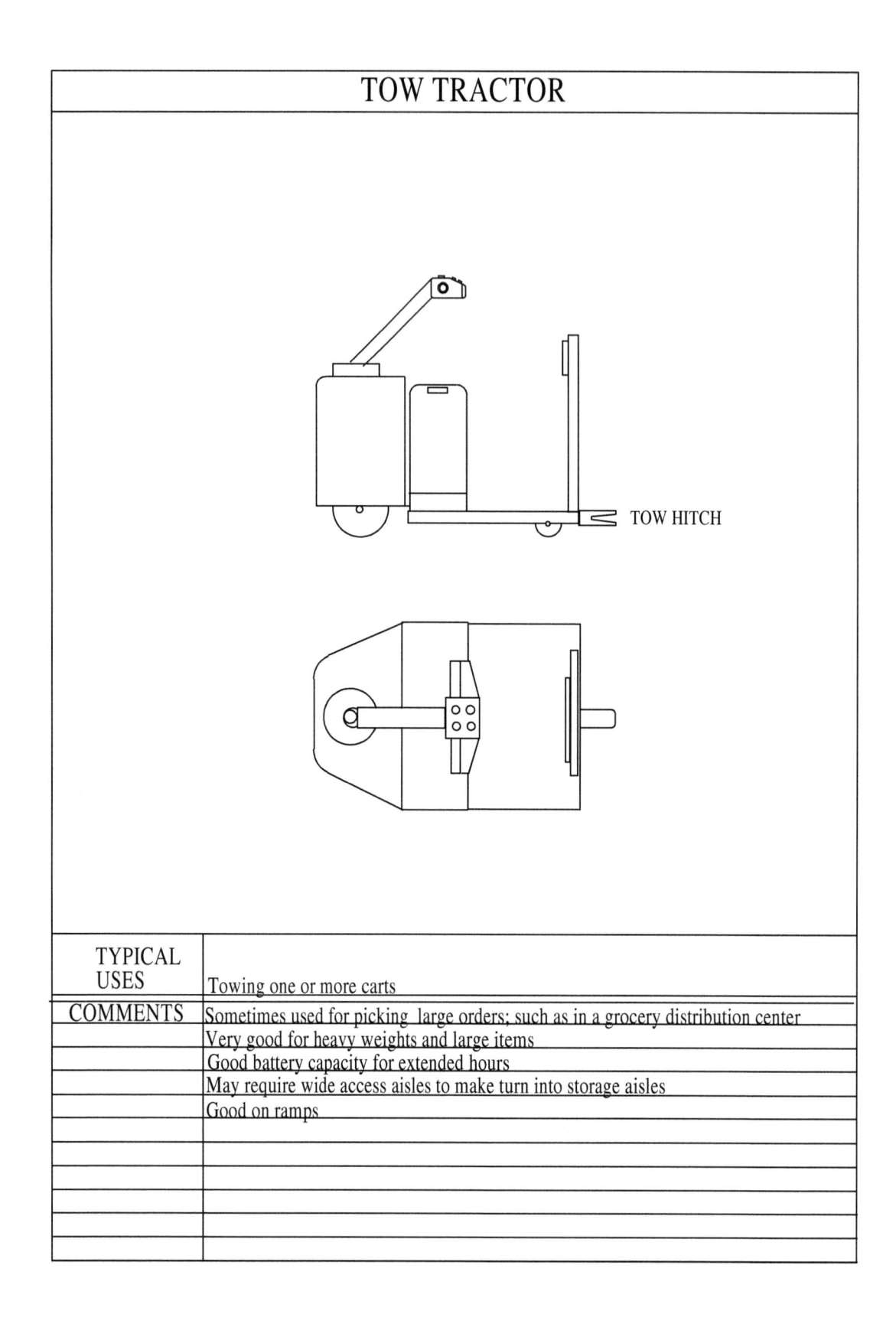

TOW HITCH

TYPICAL USES	Towing one or more carts
COMMENTS	Sometimes used for picking large orders; such as in a grocery distribution center
	Very good for heavy weights and large items
	Good battery capacity for extended hours
	May require wide access aisles to make turn into storage aisles
	Good on ramps

ORDERPICKERS   MID LEVEL

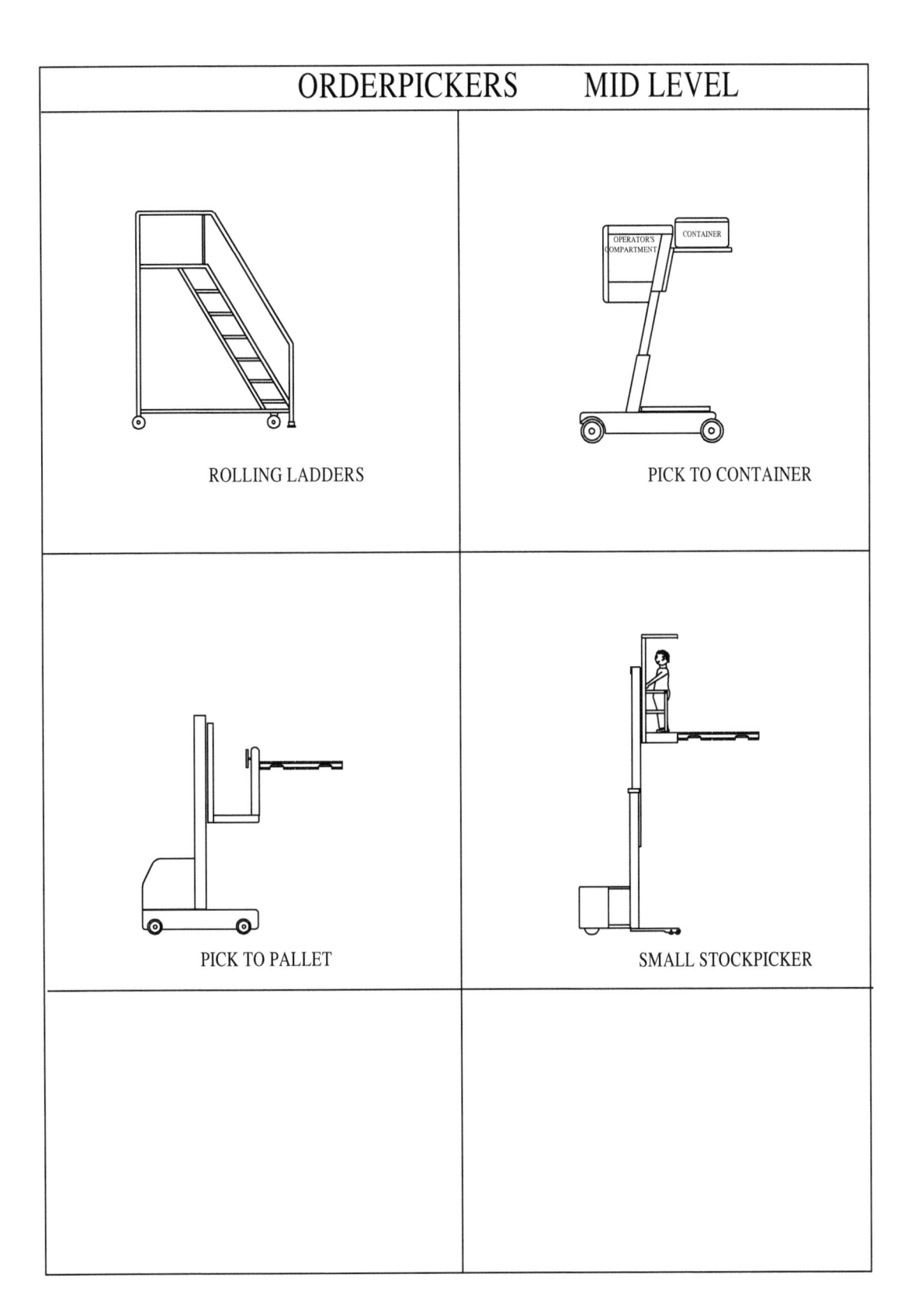

ROLLING LADDERS

PICK TO CONTAINER

PICK TO PALLET

SMALL STOCKPICKER

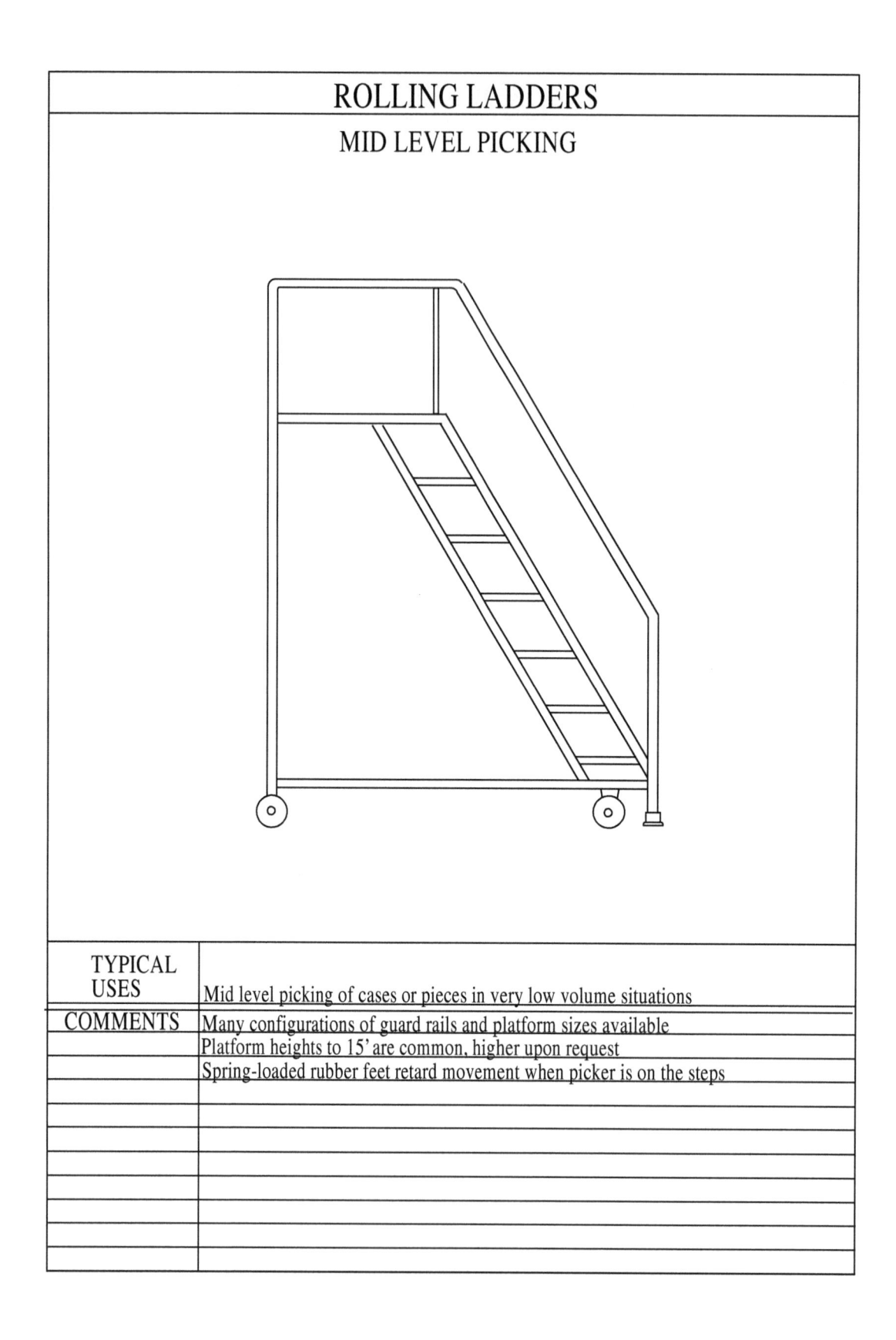

ROLLING LADDERS
MID LEVEL PICKING

TYPICAL USES	Mid level picking of cases or pieces in very low volume situations
COMMENTS	Many configurations of guard rails and platform sizes available
	Platform heights to 15' are common, higher upon request
	Spring-loaded rubber feet retard movement when picker is on the steps

HOW TO CONFIGURE AND EQUIP YOUR WAREHOUSE

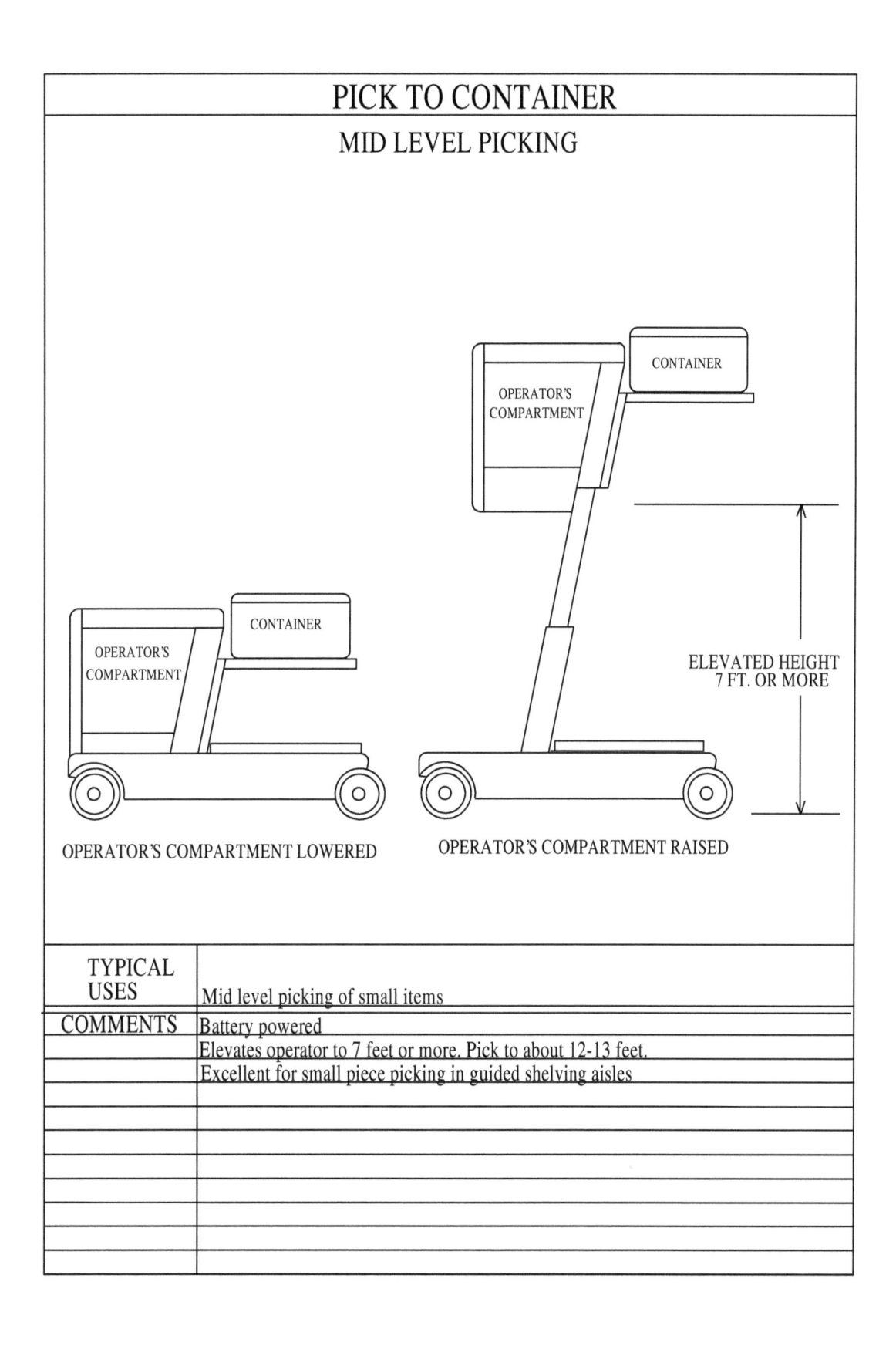

PICK TO CONTAINER
MID LEVEL PICKING

OPERATOR'S COMPARTMENT LOWERED

OPERATOR'S COMPARTMENT RAISED

CONTAINER

OPERATOR'S COMPARTMENT

ELEVATED HEIGHT 7 FT. OR MORE

TYPICAL USES	Mid level picking of small items
COMMENTS	Battery powered
	Elevates operator to 7 feet or more. Pick to about 12-13 feet.
	Excellent for small piece picking in guided shelving aisles

ORDERPICKERS

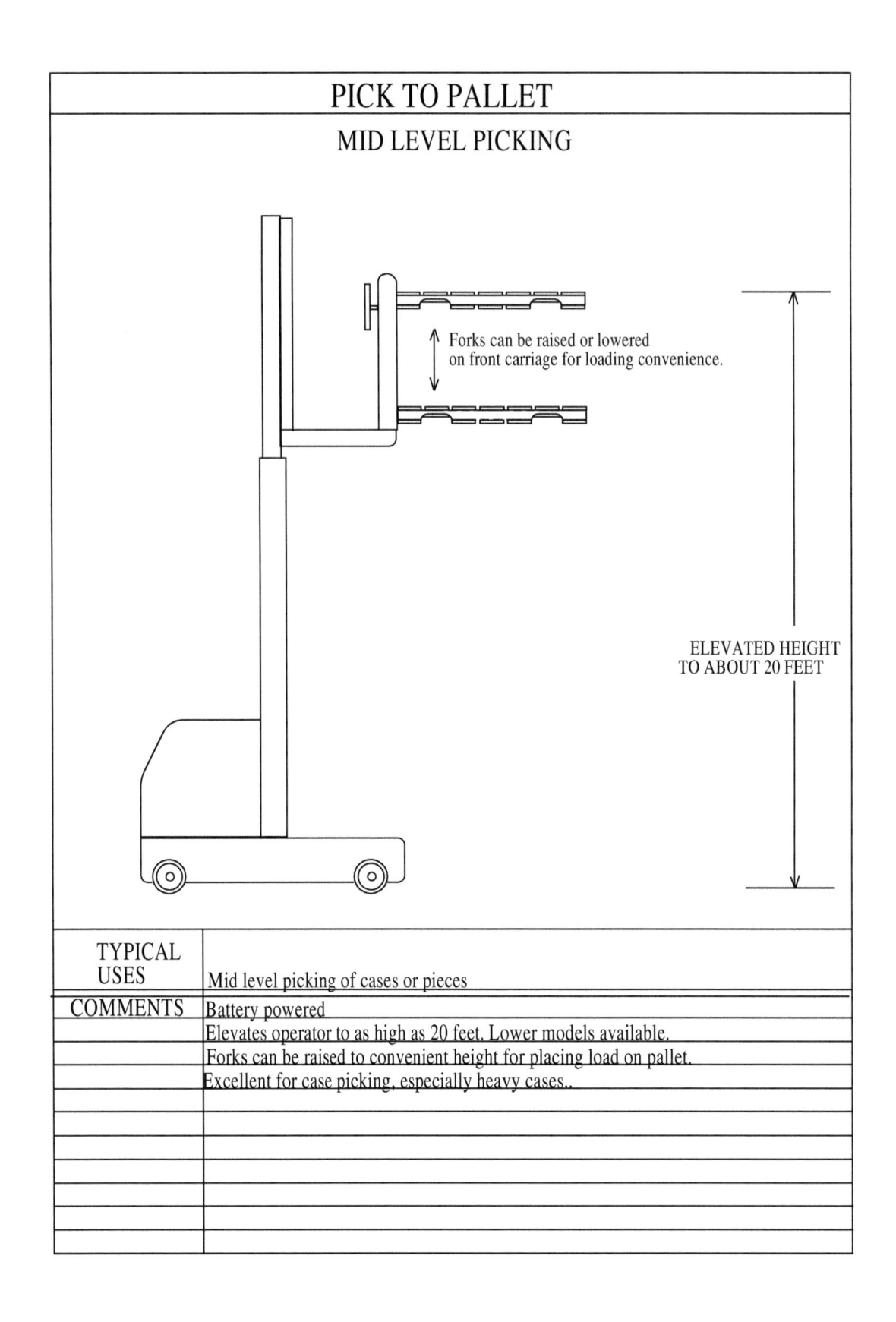

PICK TO PALLET
MID LEVEL PICKING

Forks can be raised or lowered on front carriage for loading convenience.

ELEVATED HEIGHT TO ABOUT 20 FEET

TYPICAL USES	Mid level picking of cases or pieces
COMMENTS	Battery powered
	Elevates operator to as high as 20 feet. Lower models available.
	Forks can be raised to convenient height for placing load on pallet.
	Excellent for case picking, especially heavy cases..

SMALL ORDERPICKER
MID LEVEL PICKING

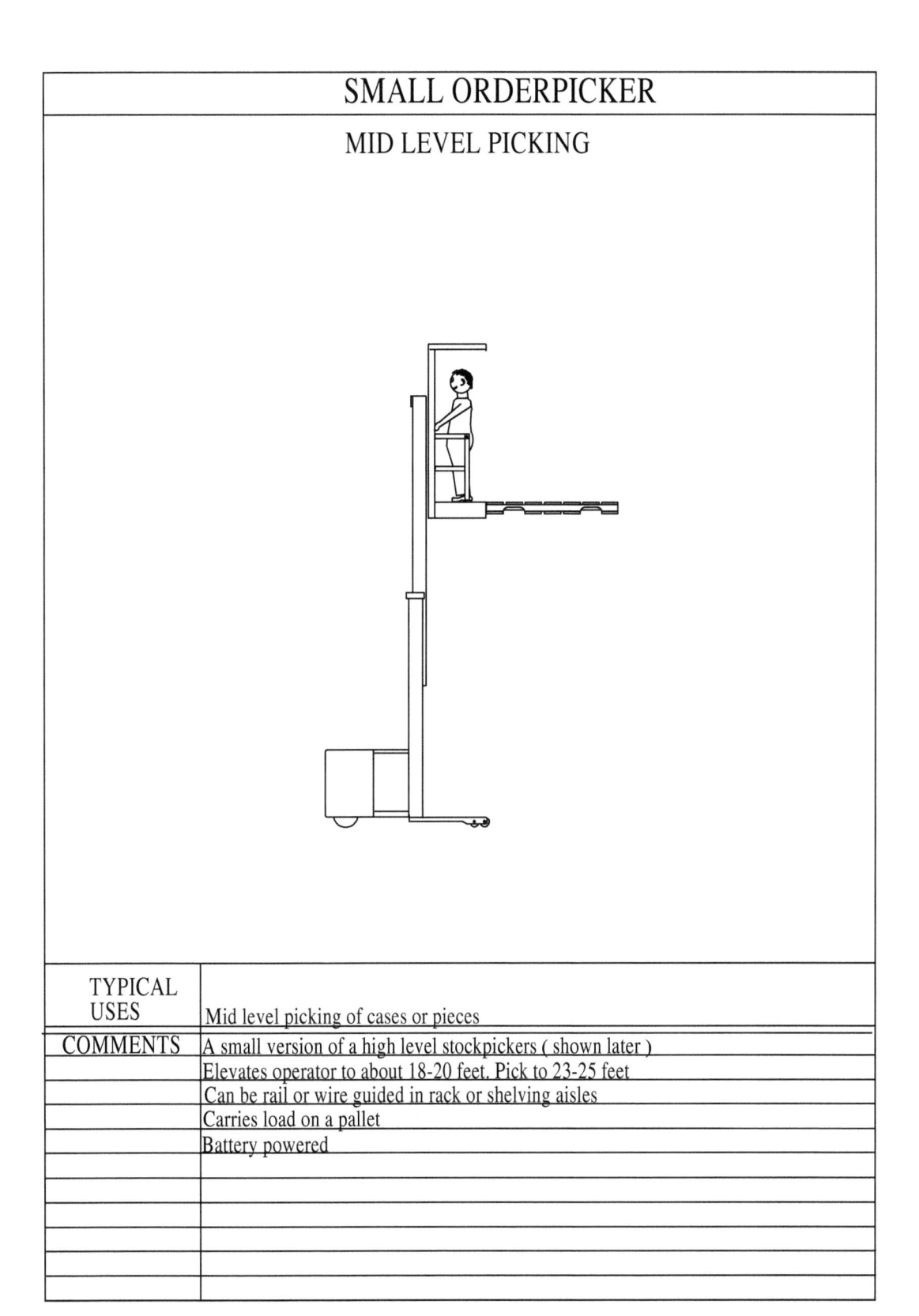

TYPICAL USES	Mid level picking of cases or pieces
COMMENTS	A small version of a high level stockpickers (shown later)
	Elevates operator to about 18-20 feet. Pick to 23-25 feet
	Can be rail or wire guided in rack or shelving aisles
	Carries load on a pallet
	Battery powered

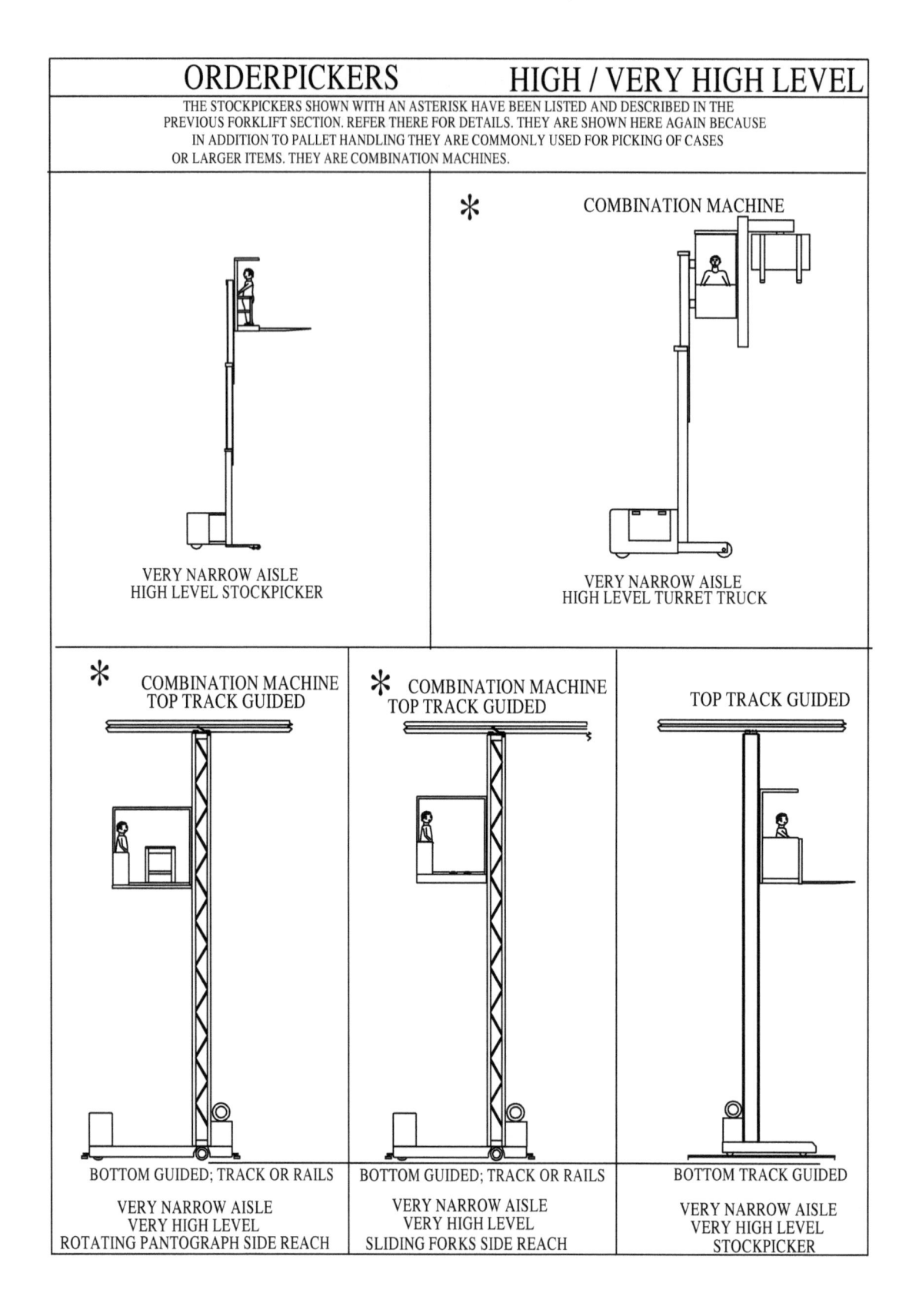

ORDERPICKERS — HIGH / VERY HIGH LEVEL

THE STOCKPICKERS SHOWN WITH AN ASTERISK HAVE BEEN LISTED AND DESCRIBED IN THE PREVIOUS FORKLIFT SECTION. REFER THERE FOR DETAILS. THEY ARE SHOWN HERE AGAIN BECAUSE IN ADDITION TO PALLET HANDLING THEY ARE COMMONLY USED FOR PICKING OF CASES OR LARGER ITEMS. THEY ARE COMBINATION MACHINES.

VERY NARROW AISLE HIGH LEVEL STOCKPICKER

* **COMBINATION MACHINE**
VERY NARROW AISLE HIGH LEVEL TURRET TRUCK

* **COMBINATION MACHINE TOP TRACK GUIDED**
BOTTOM GUIDED; TRACK OR RAILS
VERY NARROW AISLE VERY HIGH LEVEL ROTATING PANTOGRAPH SIDE REACH

* **COMBINATION MACHINE TOP TRACK GUIDED**
BOTTOM GUIDED; TRACK OR RAILS
VERY NARROW AISLE VERY HIGH LEVEL SLIDING FORKS SIDE REACH

TOP TRACK GUIDED
BOTTOM TRACK GUIDED
VERY NARROW AISLE VERY HIGH LEVEL STOCKPICKER

HOW TO CONFIGURE AND EQUIP YOUR WAREHOUSE

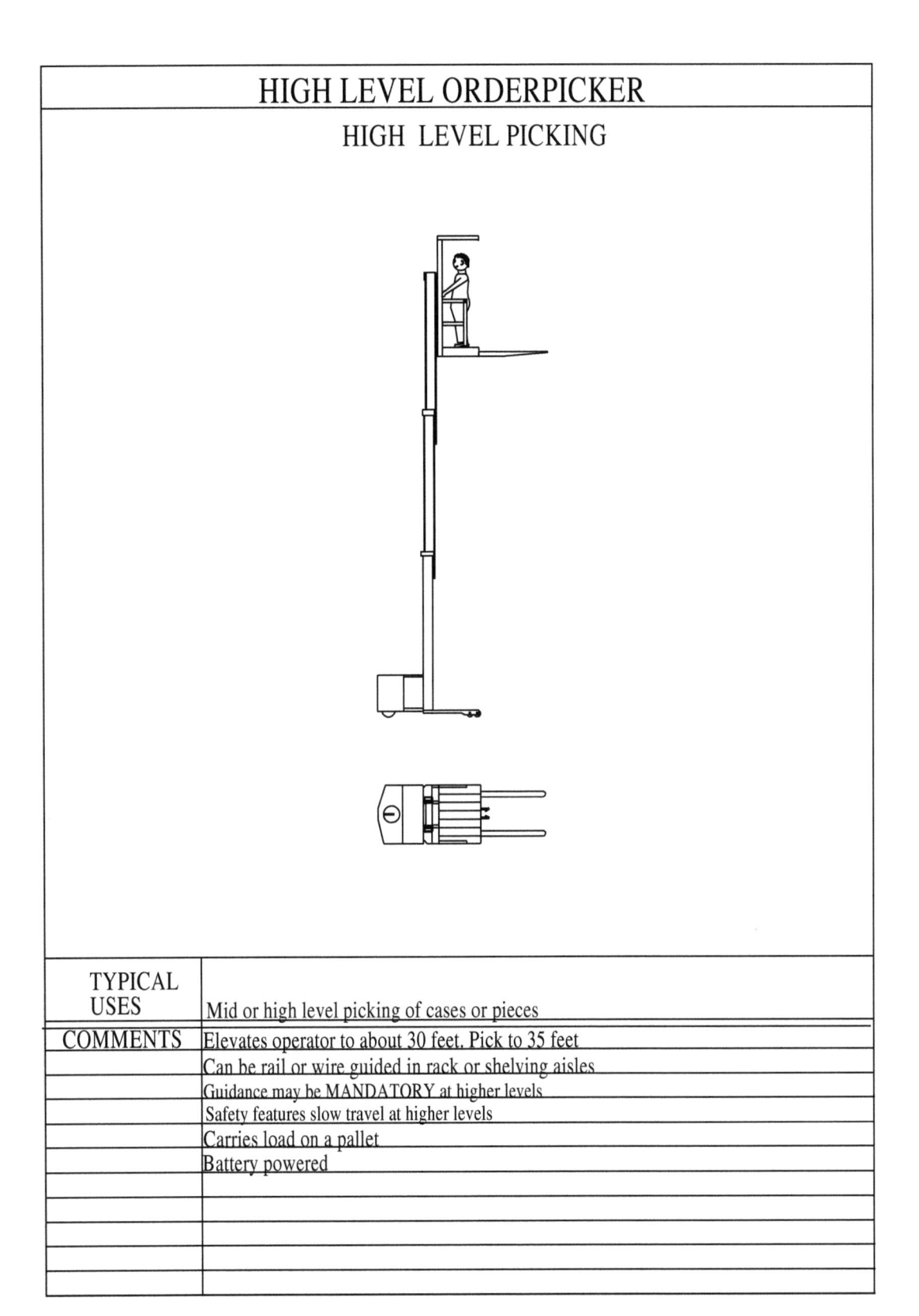

HIGH LEVEL ORDERPICKER
HIGH LEVEL PICKING

260

TYPICAL USES	Mid or high level picking of cases or pieces
COMMENTS	Elevates operator to about 30 feet. Pick to 35 feet
	Can be rail or wire guided in rack or shelving aisles
	Guidance may be MANDATORY at higher levels
	Safety features slow travel at higher levels
	Carries load on a pallet
	Battery powered

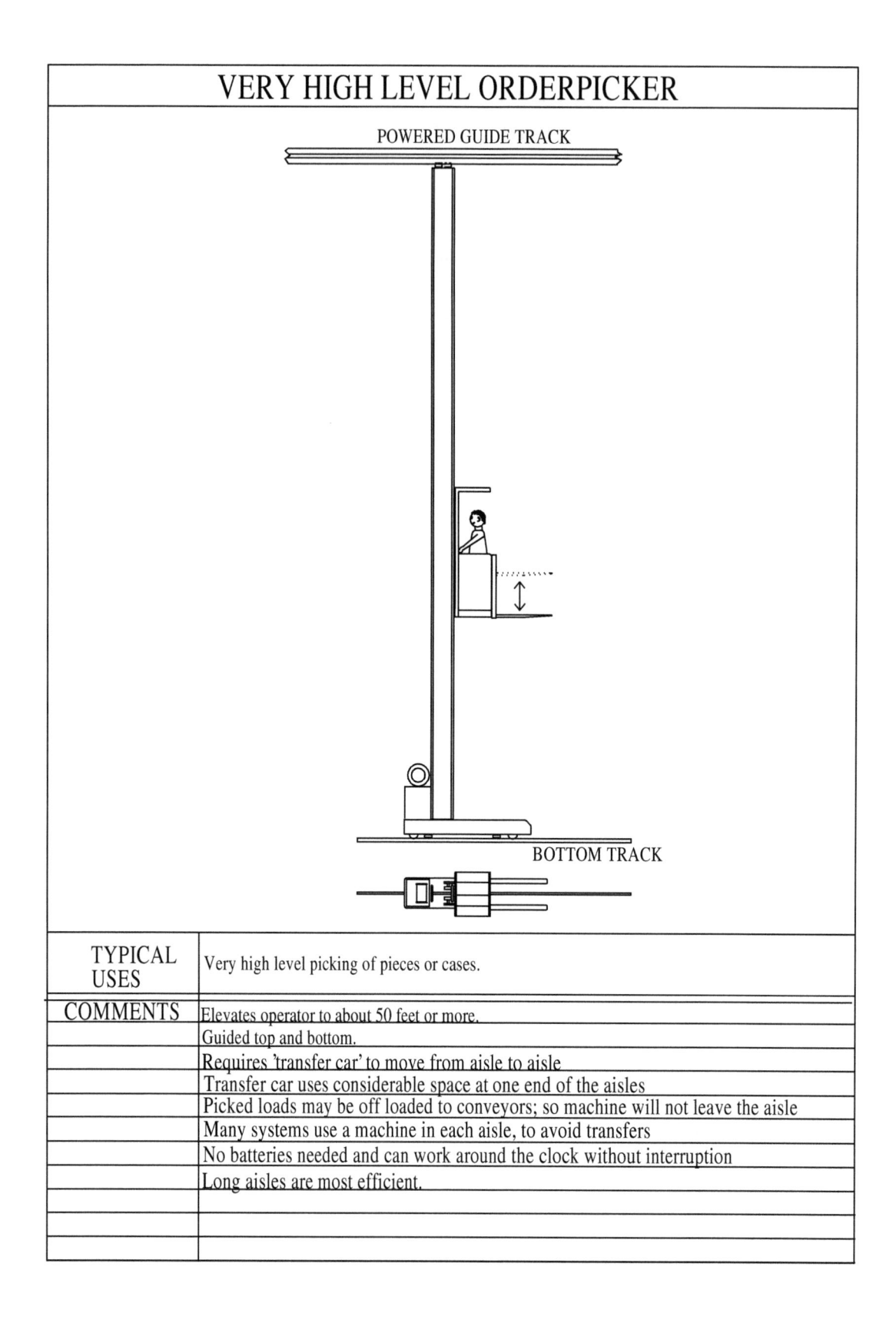

VERY HIGH LEVEL ORDERPICKER

POWERED GUIDE TRACK

BOTTOM TRACK

TYPICAL USES	Very high level picking of pieces or cases.
COMMENTS	Elevates operator to about 50 feet or more.
	Guided top and bottom.
	Requires 'transfer car' to move from aisle to aisle
	Transfer car uses considerable space at one end of the aisles
	Picked loads may be off loaded to conveyors; so machine will not leave the aisle
	Many systems use a machine in each aisle, to avoid transfers
	No batteries needed and can work around the clock without interruption
	Long aisles are most efficient.

HOW TO CONFIGURE AND EQUIP YOUR WAREHOUSE

SECTION NINE
COMBINING EQUIPMENT INTO A SYSTEM

9

The following are drawings and explanations of some situations when combining racks and forklifts into a system. The main message is that there are often a number of variables which should be considered and all dimensions of all equipment should be carefully checked and proven to be compatible with each other for the tasks expected of them.

However, racks and forklifts are only a small portion of the equipment combinations which can occur. It is strongly recommended that the supplier of each piece of equipment be made aware of its' intended use in the system and expected interfacing with other equipment.

Building permits, engineering and floor loading calculations may be necessary. We would also recommend a "Fire Code Consultant" be retained in the event the products stored are flammable in nature. Also checking with your insurance underwriter is recommended.

COMBINING EQUIPMENT INTO A SYSTEM

When the preferred types of equipment have been selected it is essential that their design and dimensions be checked to ensure their compatibility, so the system will function as expected. The number of times this is not done properly, and the very costly results, cannot be exaggerated.

Suppliers will quote on a forklift or rack which they understand to be what was requested, or what they are recommending based on their belief as to what is needed. Specifications and dimensions are provided, but possibly not all that are needed to ensure compatibility with the other types of equipment which will form the system. So all suppliers must be made aware of exactly where and how their product will be used. They cannot be expected to know all of the requirements as well as the end user.

Each supplier should then be expected to sign off on the application. For example where a forklift is to operate within drive-in racks the forklift supplier should be given all rack dimensions as furnished by the rack supplier and should then warrant the forklift compatibility to fit within the racks. The supplier of a dockleveler, having been given the forklift specifications along with dock and delivery truck heights, should warrant their compatibility. This should be done even if the suppliers are merely quoting as requested. Their knowledge of their products can help avoid errors and lead to many improvements in system design.

It would be impossible to examine here every forklift used with every storage rack and check for problems. So we will concentrate on full pallet storage, showing some major considerations. Use this same type of examination on all types of equipment and systems.

PALLET RACKS

The drawings on the following pages show sketches for discussion of the criteria for selecting and dimensioning pallet racks. These include *nominal* and *actual* load beam lengths, side clearances, beam shapes, capacity, deflection and some examples of overloaded situations. Next comes frame height and depth, row connectors, floorplates and anchors, post widths, post guards, frame capacity and effects of vertical spacing between beam levels.

Included in these basics are some important safety considerations which seem to be little known or simply ignored.

Also discussed are the options of storing bottom level loads directly on the floor or on load beams placed about a foot above the floor. The interface of forklifts for each of these alternates is then examined.

SELECTION OF LOAD BEAMS

First, the drawing on the next page shows sketches of racks with one, two and three pallets wide. The choice affects load beam length and capacity. Two-pallets wide is most popular. One-pallet wide is used for very heavy loads or to adjust a row of racks to a desired length. Three wide may be best for light loads but as weight increases so does the need for stronger, more costly beams. Heavier frames may also become necessary with long beams and heavy loads, so although fewer frames are needed the total rack cost may be increased. Beam length is determined by a total of all pallet or load widths (whichever is widest) plus side clearances.

SIDE CLEARANCES
For ease of storing and retrieving, and for controlling product damage, there should be at least 4" of side clearance between the pallets or, if products overhang the pallets, between the loads. Most forklift aisle charts are based on 4" of clearance but in some instances, covered later, the clearance must be more.

ACTUAL BEAM LENGTH
Some load beams include the thickness of the connecting bracket in the length and some do not. Thus on some racks a 96" beam means a distance of 96" between frame posts. On other racks the distance between frames may be as much as 96¼" or more as the thickness of the connectors is added on. This may seem like a picayune addition but in a long row it can mess up some layouts. And when combined with frame posts which are wider than expected the result can be a big problem. This effect is shown in a later sketch, after frames are explained.

TYPE OF LOAD BEAMS
Stepped load beams are preferred because they facilitate the use of less costly safety bars and other accessories. Wood safety bars are quite commonly used with this beam. Step beams also use up less frontage height, especially with heavy loads. Box or rectangular beams are often less costly and can be used when it is known that steps will not be needed, now or in the future. However safety bars are more costly because they must be metal and hook over the beams for support. The front face of the beam is higher than a step beam of the same capacity and this may be a factor in dimensioning frame height.

LENGTH AND TYPE OF LOAD BEAMS

CHECK FOR REQUIRED CLEARANCES BETWEEN PALLETS OR OVERHANGING LOADS

LOAD OVERHANGS PALLET

BEAM LENGTH STATED AS 96" AND IS 96" POST TO POST OF RACK FRAMES

THICKNESS OF CONNECTOR BRACKETS MAY NOT BE INCLUDED IN STATED BEAM LENGTH

BEAM LENGTH STATED AS 96" MAY BE AS MUCH AS 96 3/8" POST TO POST

FRAME POST

TOP OF LOAD BEAM

CONNECTOR BRACKET BEAM-TO-POST

DROP OVER SAFETY BAR

RECTANGULAR BEAM

FRONT FACE

DROP IN SAFETY BAR

STEP BEAM

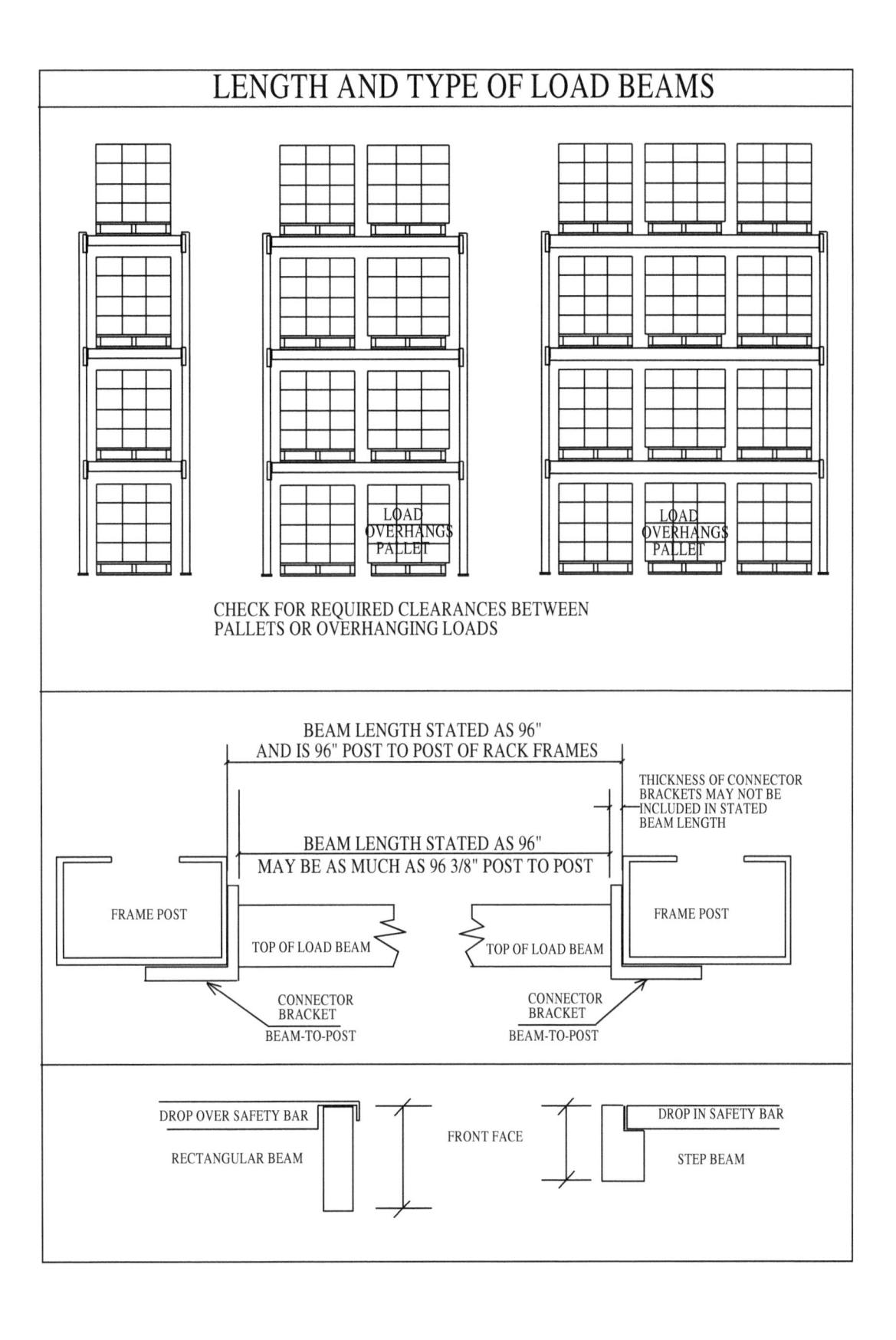

9 *COMBINING EQUIPMENT INTO A SYSTEM*

LOAD BEAM CAPACITY AND DEFLECTION

The capacity of load beams is stated as per pair, when uniformly loaded over their full length. The drawing on the next page shows two pallets of 3000# on a pair of beams with a 6000# capacity. This is so close to uniform loading that it would probably be approved by most manufacturers, however heavier load beams would be preferable here for safety and appearance.

Most manufacturers adhere to a deflection ratio of 1/180 of the beam length with a uniformly distributed load. With a length of 136" to hold three 40" wide pallets this amounts to ¾" deflection, which is quite noticeable. In a warehouse store, where customers can see the deflection, it may cause concern even though the racks are not being overloaded.

SOME OVERLOADING EXAMPLES

Above these two 3000# loads is a single 6000# load centered on the beams. These beams are being overloaded. In addition, the pallet is placed off center of the frame, overhanging the rear beam and placing a slightly disproportionate load on that already overloaded beam.

The top beam level is used to store sheets on three pieces of 4" x 4" wood stringers. Here the center stringer is carrying about 3000# directly on the center of the beams, again causing an overloaded situation. Once again the offset towards the rear of the frame overloads the rear beam even more than the front one. Unfortunately this is a situation seen quite often in the storage of metal sheets, plywood and lumber.

It is always wise to show your rack supplier what weights and storage methods you are planning to use.

UNIFORM AND NON-UNIFORM LOADING

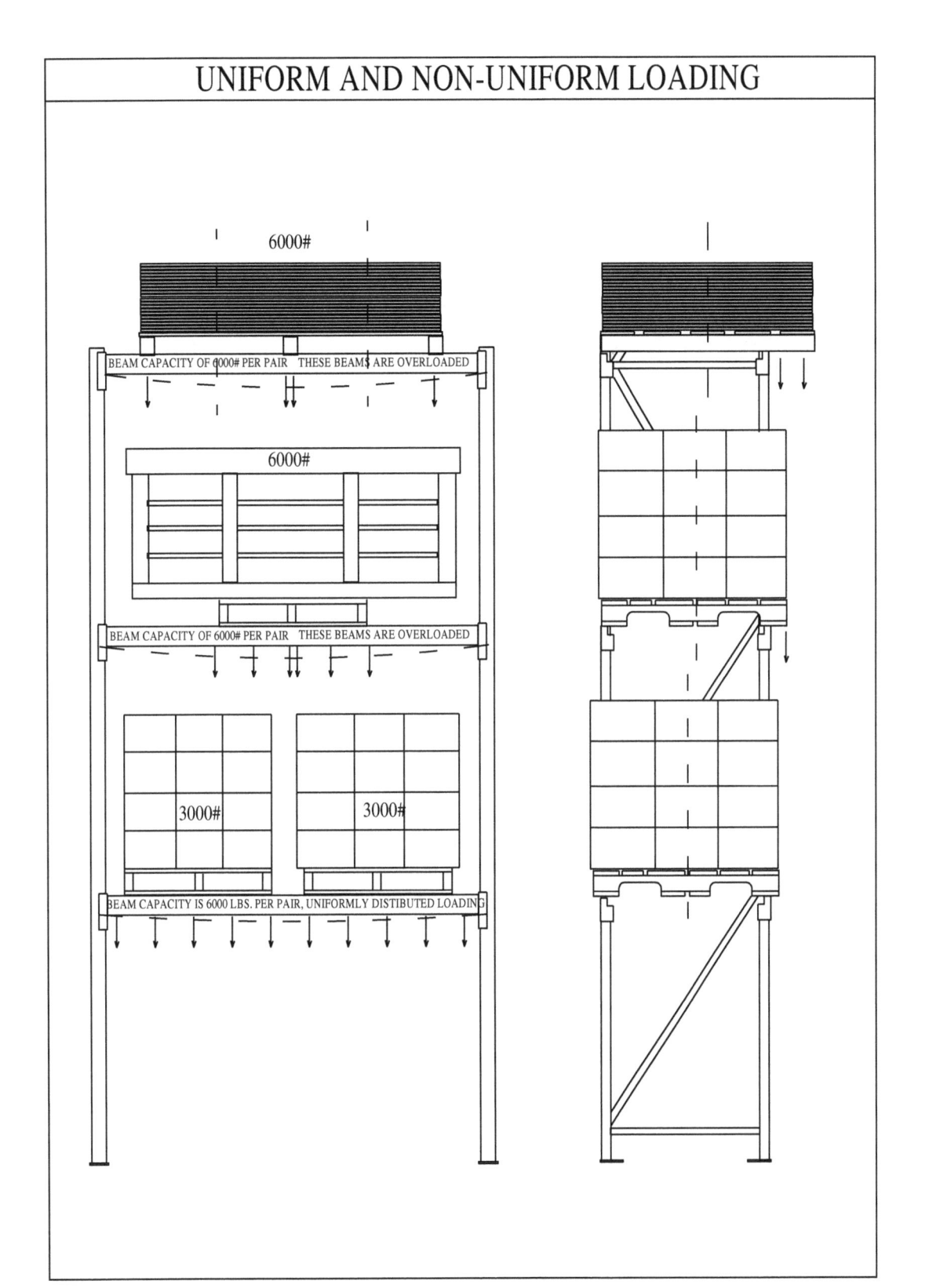

6000#

BEAM CAPACITY OF 6000# PER PAIR   THESE BEAMS ARE OVERLOADED

6000#

BEAM CAPACITY OF 6000# PER PAIR   THESE BEAMS ARE OVERLOADED

3000#   3000#

BEAM CAPACITY IS 6000 LBS. PER PAIR, UNIFORMLY DISTIBUTED LOADING

268

9 *COMBINING EQUIPMENT INTO A SYSTEM*

SELECTION OF FRAMES & ROW CONNECTORS

Refer to drawing on the next page.

FRAME HEIGHT

Frame height must include all vertical dimensions including pallet and load height, lift off clearance, beam face and the number of openings. Remember that the top of each beam can only be placed according to the adjustment increment allowed by the frame design; usually 2″, 3″ or 4″. Try to have all openings the same in each zone, or at least as few as practical. Notice the extended frame on the left side of the rack. This extension is often used for safety at row ends, to prevent cases from falling from the upper level.

FRAME DEPTH

Pallets may sit flush with the face of load beams, or they may overhang. Thus a 48″ deep frame will mean flush storage of a 48″ deep pallet but this same pallet will overhang the beams on a 42″ or 44″ frame. It is easier for a forklift operator to work with an overhanging pallet because placement does not have to be quite so accurate and the pallet is less likely to miss the beams.

BACK-TO-BACK ROW CONNECTORS

These can be a very important part of a rack system. They help keep rows aligned for anchoring, assist greatly for rack stability in high systems, and **may** be a factor in preventing a frame collapse if it is severely damaged. Row connectors should be substantial and well fastened to the frames.

The length of row connectors should be determined according to fire regulations and your insurer to arrive at a desired flue width. Money may be saved by early discussions with the insurer. Considerations to attain the flue width wanted are similar to the previous description of aisle width. Don't be confused between the rack-to-rack spacing and the actual clear flue space between loads. Sketch A in the right bottom of the drawing shows a flue based on flush pallet storage with no load overhang. Sketch B shows pallet overhang and the connector has been lengthened to maintain flue width. In C product overhangs the pallet and requires a still longer connector. Sketch D shows a much narrowed flue because the planning was for situation A but turned out having overhang as in C; without any lengthening of the connectors. Sprinklers may be rendered ineffective or unacceptable if this occurs.

Wall connectors are sometimes used on a single row near a wall but their use should be considered carefully, especially with cinder block walls and seismic conditions. Likewise, any connection to the building steel should be checked.

FLOORPLATES

Substantial floorplates with holes large enough for ½″ anchors are recommended. Floorplates are a factor in distributing weight of loaded racks to the floor and anchors are needed for safety and neatness. Very heavy loading, especially in a seismic zone, will require larger floorplates and anchors. **Rack loading and weight distribution to the floor should be checked at a very early stage, prior to designing the floor or leasing a building. Unpleasant surprises may lurk here, once again increased by seismic requirements.**

FRAME DIMENSIONS, ROW CONNECTORS, FLUE WIDTHS

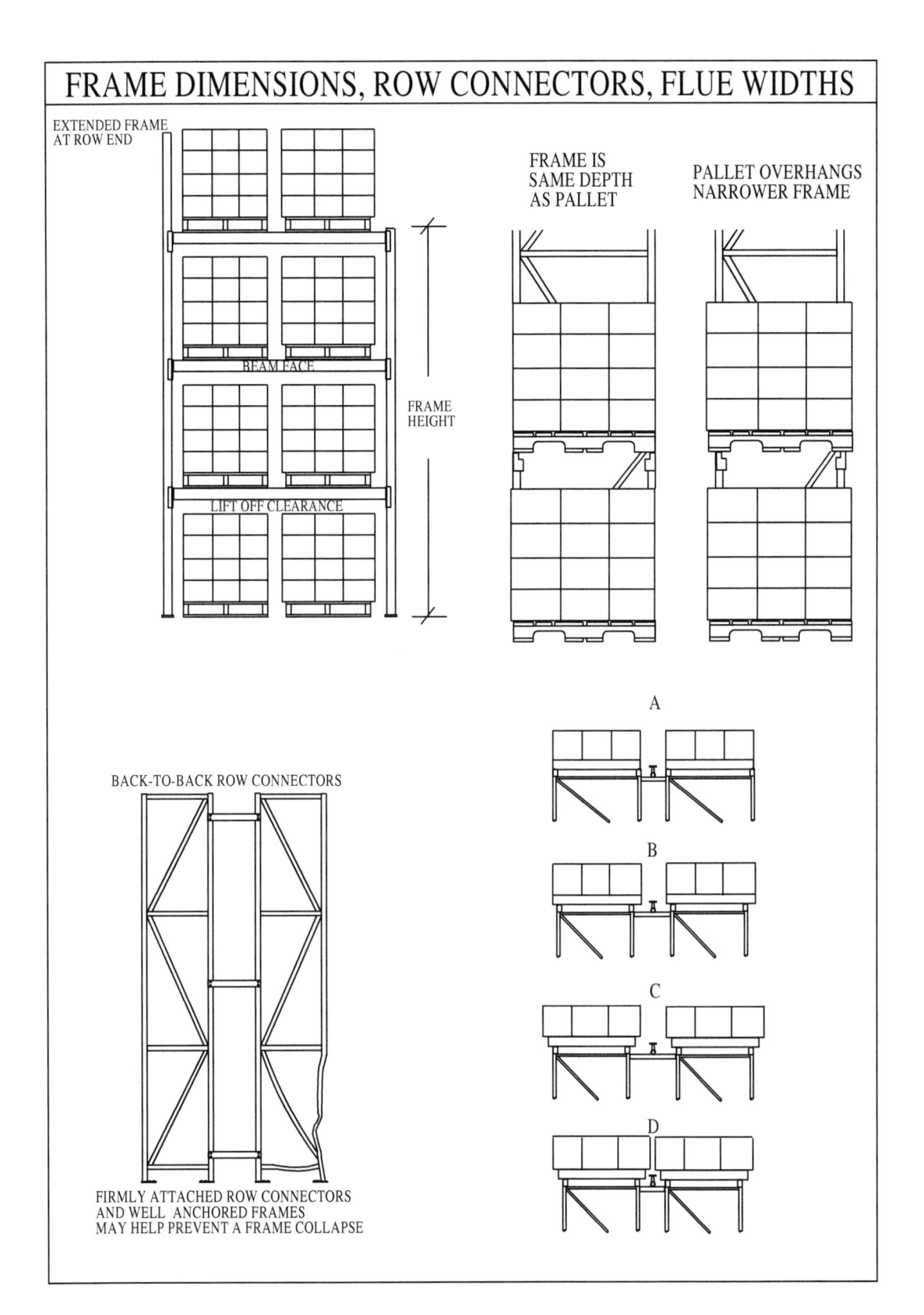

EXTENDED FRAME AT ROW END

BEAM FACE

FRAME HEIGHT

LIFT OFF CLEARANCE

FRAME IS SAME DEPTH AS PALLET

PALLET OVERHANGS NARROWER FRAME

BACK-TO-BACK ROW CONNECTORS

FIRMLY ATTACHED ROW CONNECTORS AND WELL ANCHORED FRAMES MAY HELP PREVENT A FRAME COLLAPSE

A

B

C

D

270

9 *COMBINING EQUIPMENT INTO A SYSTEM*

FLOOR ANCHORS

In many installations anchors are required for rack stability. Where not actually demanded they are recommended for safety and, when combined with post guards, reduce rack damage. Seismic installations may require an increased quantity of large, long anchors and, where possible, all rebar should be located to avoid the frame and anchor pattern. Doing so is not difficult and will save headaches and costs; hitting rebar with drills and trying to relocate anchors is expensive.

Always use two anchors on each front post. Most blows to the post will try to twist it and a single anchor will merely act as a fulcrum for the twist, perhaps being worse than no anchors.

POST WIDTH

It was previously mentioned that **stated beam length is nominal** and the actual dimension from post to post of frames may be longer than expected. This added length can cause problems at building columns or where the rack row was to be almost from wall to wall as shown on the following drawing, Also, the row length will grow even more if the frame posts are wider than planned, as shown on the same drawing. When combined, the two unexpected additions can cause costly problems, so the actual row length and frame locations should be confirmed by the supplier. In addition to any problems caused by a longer row the frames may be in unexpected locations relative to building columns; or suppliers of a sprinkler system could pre-cut pipes based on erroneous centers; etc., etc.

POST GUARDS

This is an accessory which should be seriously considered. Post guards add to safety and will usually more than justify their initial price. Most frame damage is done not by a heavy collision but by relatively small impacts repeated many times during daily operations. The guard should protect both sides of the post as well as the front. Sides are most often hit by pallets. Replacing a frame is costly because in addition to the frame cost there is the labor and disruption to unload the two adjoining bays, replace the frame and reload the bays. Post guards will prevent most of this cost.

ACCESSORIES

There are so many rack accessories available that only an experienced person can be knowledgeable of them all and the benefits of each. Talk it over with the supplier when he is fully aware of the application. Accessories can save time and damage to goods and racks but may require slight alterations to rack dimensions. Refer to section 5 for some examples.

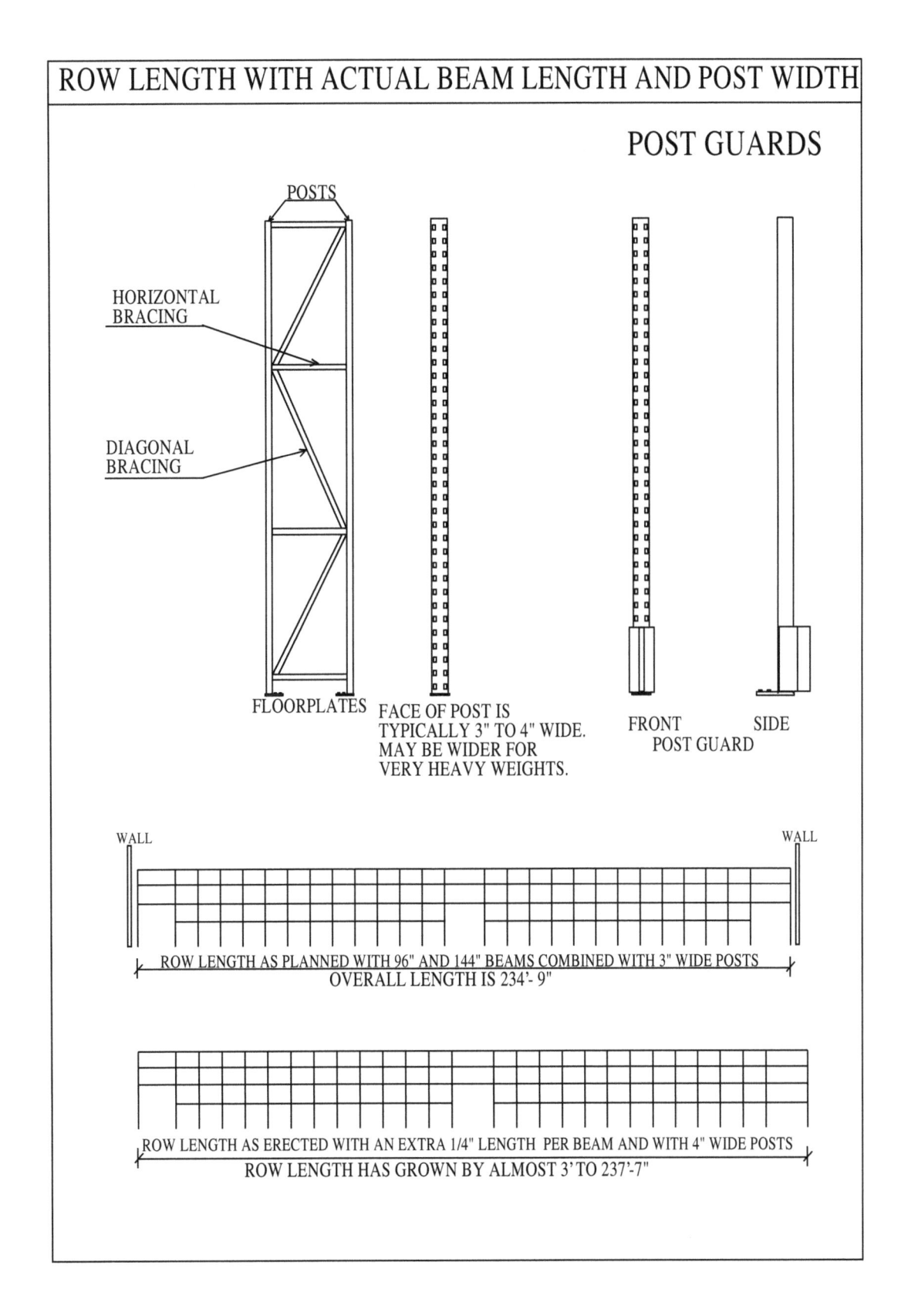

ROW LENGTH WITH ACTUAL BEAM LENGTH AND POST WIDTH

POST GUARDS

POSTS

HORIZONTAL BRACING

DIAGONAL BRACING

FLOORPLATES

FACE OF POST IS TYPICALLY 3" TO 4" WIDE. MAY BE WIDER FOR VERY HEAVY WEIGHTS.

FRONT   SIDE
POST GUARD

WALL   WALL

ROW LENGTH AS PLANNED WITH 96" AND 144" BEAMS COMBINED WITH 3" WIDE POSTS
OVERALL LENGTH IS 234'- 9"

ROW LENGTH AS ERECTED WITH AN EXTRA 1/4" LENGTH PER BEAM AND WITH 4" WIDE POSTS
ROW LENGTH HAS GROWN BY ALMOST 3' TO 237'-7"

9 *COMBINING EQUIPMENT INTO A SYSTEM*

SOME EXAMPLES OF SITUATIONS WHICH REDUCE FRAME CAPACITY

Like load beams, a frame has a stated capacity which applies only under specified conditions. The main specification calls for load beams to be installed with a maximum vertical spacing. This is referred to as the vertical pitch and is quite often designed as 4' or 5'. Load beams not only hold pallets but also act as braces for the frame posts which, by the way, are perforated for their full height to allow beam attachment. If beams levels are spaced beyond the design criteria they do not sufficiently support the posts and the frame capacity is reduced. So a 6' vertical spacing of beams on a frame designed for a 4' spacing will result in a reduced frame capacity.

The next drawing shows frames designed to have beams on a maximum pitch of four feet in order to maintain 30,000 lbs. frame capacity. Below it are shown some situations where the frame capacity is reduced because of a larger pitch and too few load beams. Racks are best used with two or more beam levels. Any time there is only one beam level great care should be taken to check out capacity **and** stability. Anchors will be especially important here.

In some cases the frame can be supplied with additional bracing to compensate for these deviations from standard usage; so always have your total plans reviewed and approved by the rack supplier.

RACK INSTALLATION

If the racks are to be installed by someone other than the supplier he should be involved at an early date. Experienced installers often have very pertinent suggestions to offer.

THE PREVIOUS PAGES HAVE LAID OUT THE BASICS OF SELECTIVE PALLET RACK DIMENSIONING AND CAPACITY CONSIDERATIONS. BUT DON'T FINALIZE ANYTHING UNTIL THE TYPE OF FORKLIFT HAS BEEN DECIDED. FORKLIFTS AND THEIR INTERFACE WITH VARIOUS TYPES OF RACKS ARE THE NEXT SUBJECT

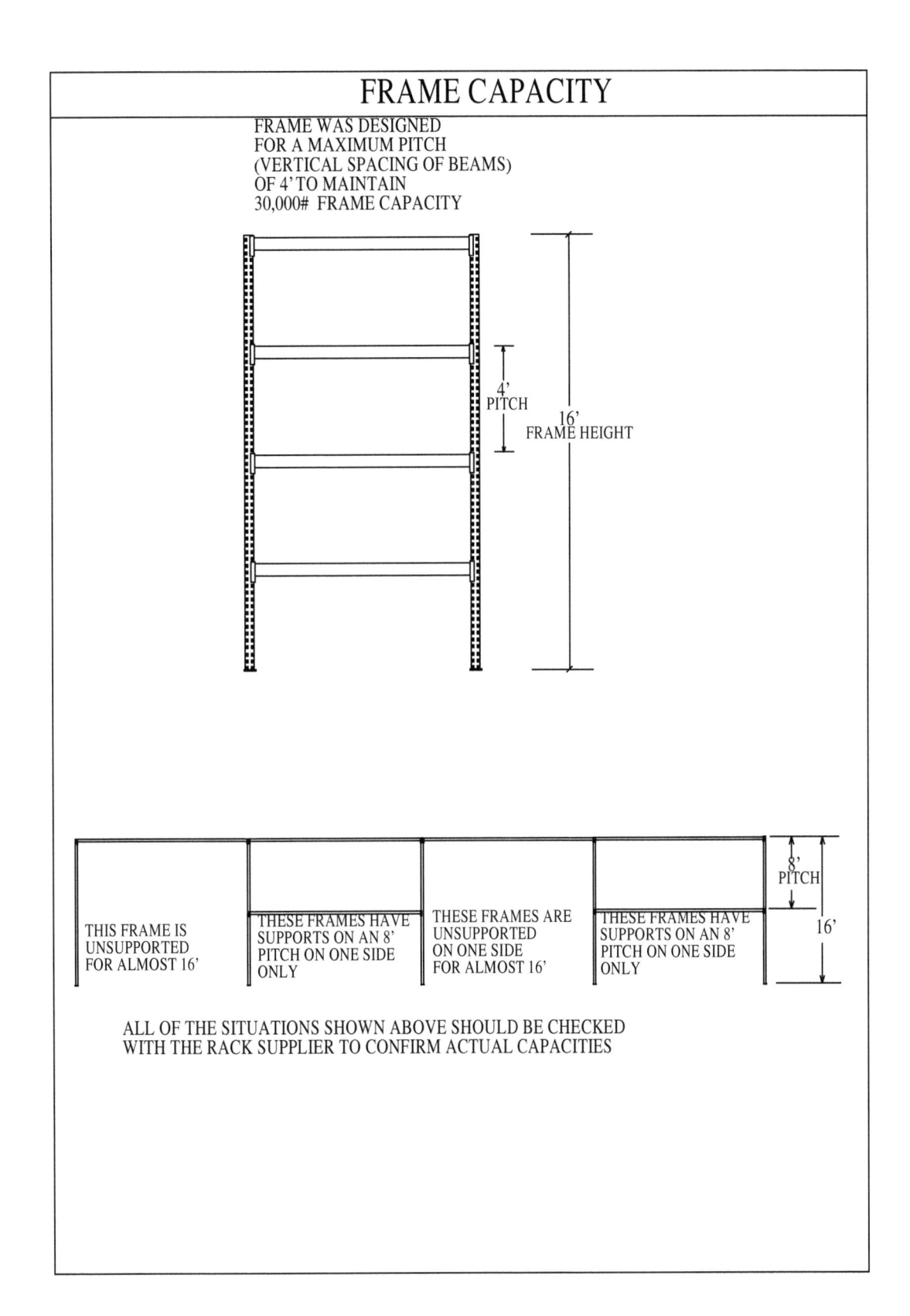

FRAME CAPACITY

FRAME WAS DESIGNED
FOR A MAXIMUM PITCH
(VERTICAL SPACING OF BEAMS)
OF 4' TO MAINTAIN
30,000# FRAME CAPACITY

4' PITCH

16' FRAME HEIGHT

8' PITCH

16'

THIS FRAME IS UNSUPPORTED FOR ALMOST 16'

THESE FRAMES HAVE SUPPORTS ON AN 8' PITCH ON ONE SIDE ONLY

THESE FRAMES ARE UNSUPPORTED ON ONE SIDE FOR ALMOST 16'

THESE FRAMES HAVE SUPPORTS ON AN 8' PITCH ON ONE SIDE ONLY

ALL OF THE SITUATIONS SHOWN ABOVE SHOULD BE CHECKED
WITH THE RACK SUPPLIER TO CONFIRM ACTUAL CAPACITIES

9 *COMBINING EQUIPMENT INTO A SYSTEM*

RACKS AND FORKLIFTS COMBINED WITHIN A SYSTEM

The basics of selective racks have just been outlined. Now we will cover the basics of forklifts to work with selective racks and then go on to look at other combinations. Perhaps the logical place to begin is with considerations common to all forklifts.

FORKLIFT CAPACITY
It was stated elsewhere that one of the three essential requirements of a forklift is "to be able to lift specified loads to the height you want to lift them". Be sure lift capacity is spelled out for all heights. **Don't assume** that because one 4000# model can lift 2000# to the height wanted that all other 4000# trucks can do the same.

LIFT HEIGHT
Elevated fork height should be about 10" to 12" higher than the top beam of the racks. This is especially important for very high lifts with heavy loads, because mast deflection increases with height, potentially reducing the actual fork height. The additional lift also allows for about 4" of pallet underhang, lift off from the load beam and deflection caused by floor unevenness. Where lifts are not especially high, the extra lift can be less, if necessary (due to improved visibility) but be careful.

MAST LOWERED HEIGHT
This may or may not be a consideration for the system itself but be sure it can pass through any doors or tunnels on its' route and, if needed, traverse a dockleveler and enter a carrier.

OVERHEAD OBSTRUCTIONS
With the forks raised to serve the top rack level will the load or load backrest (whichever is higher) clear any overhead obstruction such as building steel or lights?

FORK TYPE AND LENGTH
Many fork types are available for specific applications, such as entering the notches of four-way pallets or chiseling under crates. 4-way pallets may require slightly longer forks, as explained previously.

WHEEL SIZE
Many outrigger forklifts, especially reach trucks, have a selection of wheel sizes and the choice can be an important factor in rack dimensioning; affecting beam length, lift off requirements and frame height.

LIFT AND TRAVEL SPEEDS
Slow lifts can be costly in a high lift system. Travel speeds also affect throughput and there can be a big difference in these speeds among the many suppliers of the same model.

MAST AND LIFT HEIGHTS

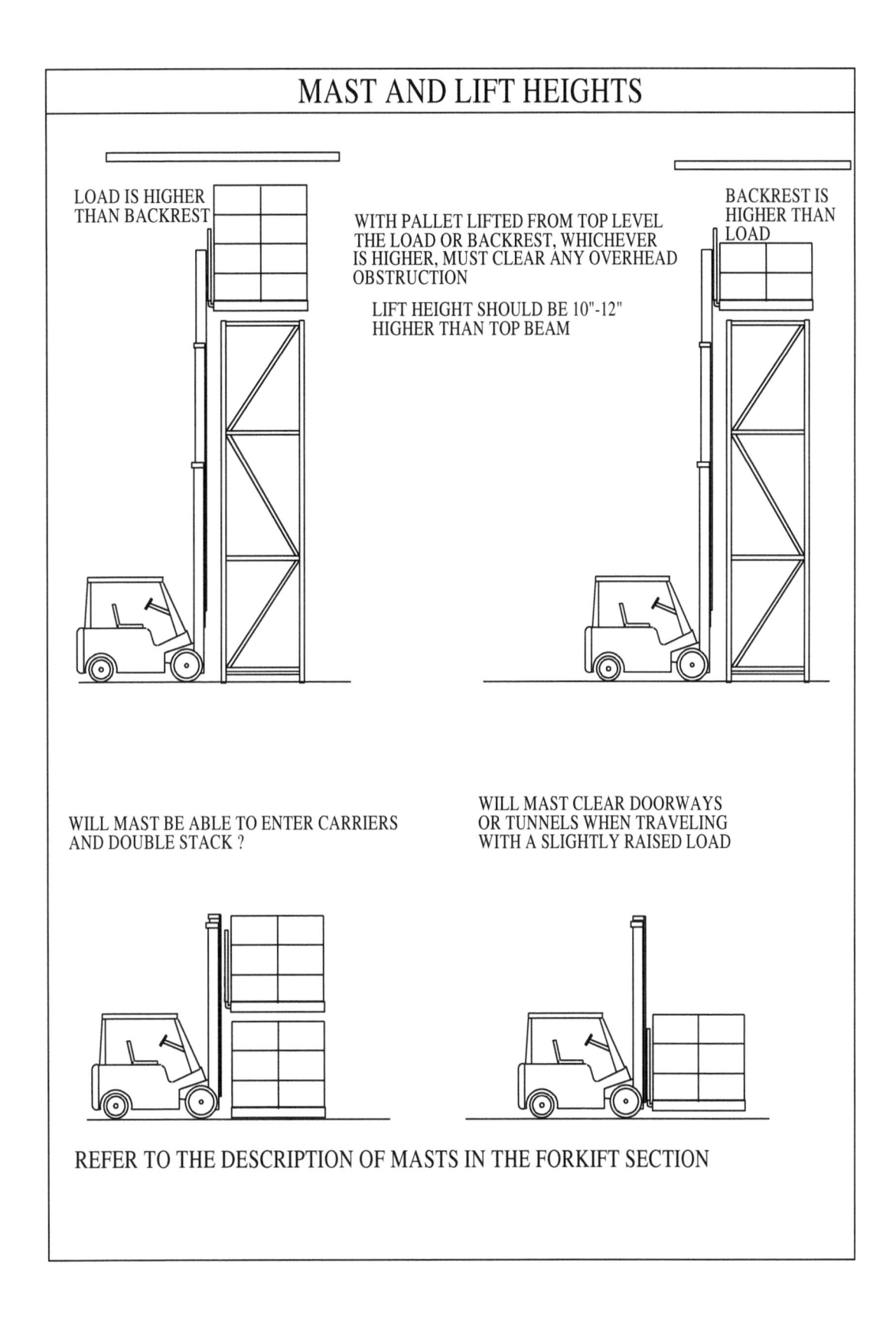

LOAD IS HIGHER THAN BACKREST

WITH PALLET LIFTED FROM TOP LEVEL THE LOAD OR BACKREST, WHICHEVER IS HIGHER, MUST CLEAR ANY OVERHEAD OBSTRUCTION

LIFT HEIGHT SHOULD BE 10"-12" HIGHER THAN TOP BEAM

BACKREST IS HIGHER THAN LOAD

WILL MAST BE ABLE TO ENTER CARRIERS AND DOUBLE STACK ?

WILL MAST CLEAR DOORWAYS OR TUNNELS WHEN TRAVELING WITH A SLIGHTLY RAISED LOAD

REFER TO THE DESCRIPTION OF MASTS IN THE FORKIFT SECTION

9   COMBINING EQUIPMENT INTO A SYSTEM

For purposes of the following explanations forklifts are divided into only two types; those without outriggers (counterbalanced) and those with outriggers (straddle and reach models).

Rack dimensions are not affected by counterbalanced forklifts *except* when the truck must enter into the rack; a situation to be covered shortly. On the other hand, trucks with outriggers have a direct bearing on rack dimensioning. The outriggers can be accommodated in a variety of ways and the choice factors are the subject of the next pages.

Rack dimensions are also influenced by the options of storing the lowest level of pallets directly on the floor or on beams placed about a foot above the floor. There are advantages and disadvantages for each method.

FLOOR STORAGE

ADVANTAGES:
Pallets can be handled with a low lift pallet truck.

Avoids the cost of extra beams and higher frames.

Holds the storage and building height to a minimum.

DISADVANTAGES:
Will, with some outrigger forklifts, need up to 7" or 8" between loads, affecting beam length.

More difficult to keep the floor clean.

BOTTOM BEAM STORAGE

ADVANTAGES:
May be preferable for floor cleanliness.

Will, under some conditions, allow for less side clearance between loads, for shorter beams.

DISADVANTAGES:
Pallets cannot be stored or retrieved with a low lift pallet truck.

There is an additional cost for extra beams and higher frames.

Raises the system and building height by a foot.

When using an outrigger forklift there are two very different methods of pallet handling, termed the **straddle** and **up-and-over** methods. When combined with the alternates of floor, or bottom beam storage, it becomes apparent that extreme caution is needed to assure satisfactory results.

So the rack and total storage height can have three alternates as shown in the drawing on the next page and beam length can be varied to suit. These options, along with aisle width selection, may provide the ability to fit a system into a less than ideal existing building.

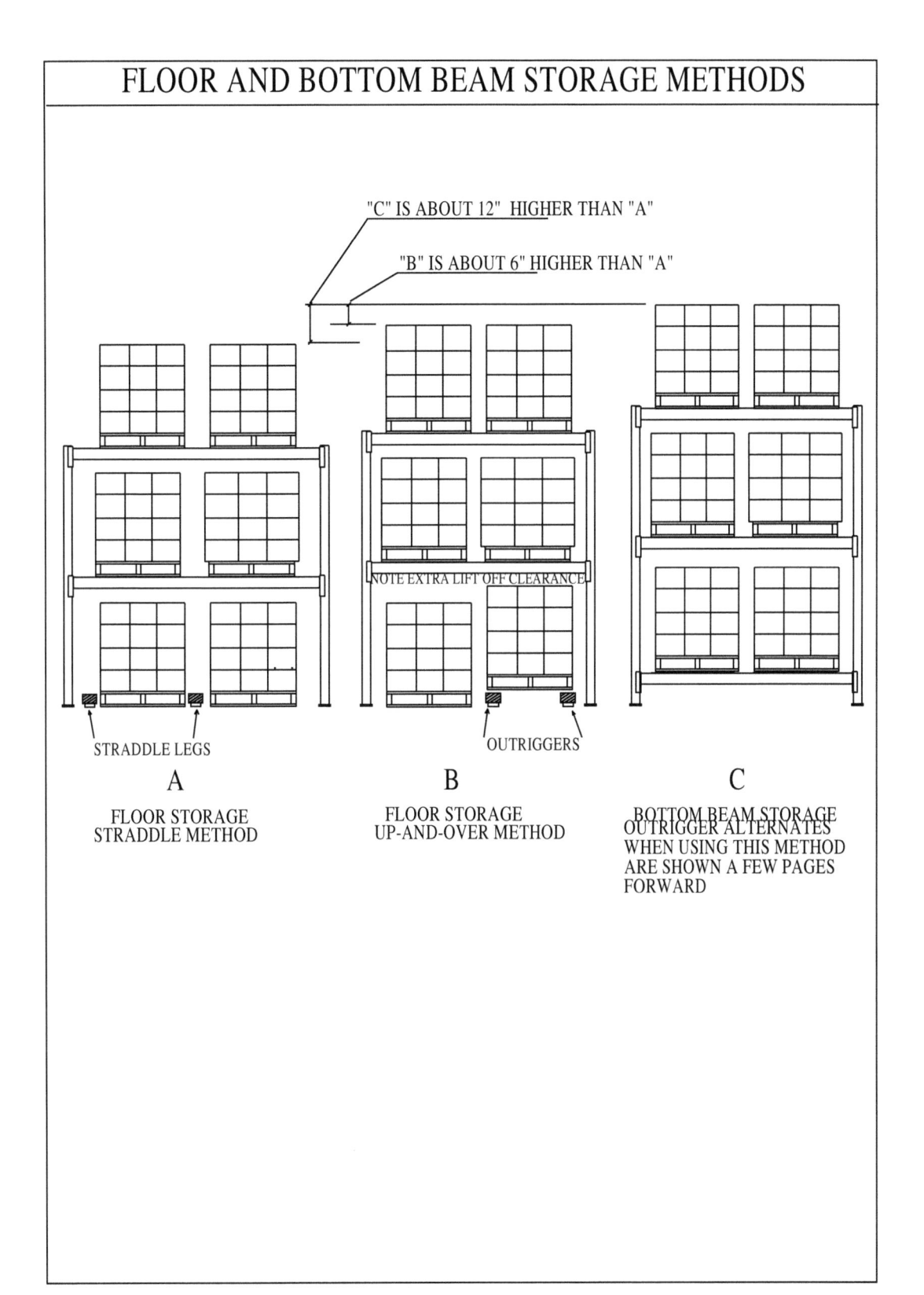

FLOOR AND BOTTOM BEAM STORAGE METHODS

"C" IS ABOUT 12" HIGHER THAN "A"

"B" IS ABOUT 6" HIGHER THAN "A"

NOTE EXTRA LIFT OFF CLEARANCE

STRADDLE LEGS

OUTRIGGERS

A
FLOOR STORAGE
STRADDLE METHOD

B
FLOOR STORAGE
UP-AND-OVER METHOD

C
BOTTOM BEAM STORAGE
OUTRIGGER ALTERNATES
WHEN USING THIS METHOD
ARE SHOWN A FEW PAGES
FORWARD

FLOOR STORAGE USING AN OUTRIGGER OPENING **WIDER** THAN THE PALLET

STRADDLE OR RETRACT METHOD

The outriggers on narrow aisle forklifts are referred to with a number of names; and this can become confusing. They may be called outriggers, base legs, straddle legs and even straddle-reach legs.

The term "outriggers" is rather generic but most often refers to base legs which are not meant to enter into the racks to straddle the pallet. They typically have blunt fronts and are wider than straddle legs with load wheels which are as large as practical. They may be spaced to allow a pallet to fit within them or they may have a narrower width for other reasons, such as for passing traffic in a narrow aisle.

"Base legs" is a term which may sometimes be used alternately for any for any type of outriggers or legs.

"Straddle legs" are dimensioned to straddle a specific width of pallet. They are typically narrower than non-straddle legs so they can straddle a pallet within racks while keeping the space between pallets, and therefore the beam length, to a minimum. They have tapered fronts to help line up the pallet as it is straddled. This is a faster operation than operating the reach mechanism. But straddle legs, with small load wheels and low underclearance, are a poor choice for entering delivery trucks.

"Straddle-reach legs" use straddle legs on a reach truck to attain the speed of straddling while having a reach mechanism for other uses, such as handling wider pallets.

The next drawing shows two different situations when storing on the floor. "A" depicts a truck with straddle type outriggers. These outriggers are designed to enter the racks, straddling the pallet in spaces wide enough to accept them. The spaces are increased from the minimum 4" to a typical 6", or as much as 8" for very wide outriggers. The extra 2" to 4" will, in extreme cases, lengthen the load beams by up to 12" in a two pallet wide bay and 16" in a three wide bay.

Lift off clearance is held to a minimum because a pallet has to be lifted only about an inch off of the floor; so rack frames and total storage height of the system will be kept to a minimum.

If the lengthened load beams cause a layout problem due to row length they can be shortened as in "B". Here a reach truck has an opening which is wider than the pallet but the outriggers are not intended to enter into the racks, allowing pallets to have less space between them. The truck is positioned in front of a pallet, forks are extended into the pallet and it is lifted a bit off of the floor and retracted back between the outriggers. Minimum height is maintained and load beams are shortened.

Each of these methods has an overall outrigger width of over four feet when designed for a 40" wide pallet, and this should be considered for passing in aisles or other narrow locations.

Choice of outrigger/leg type and overall width is obviously a major consideration.

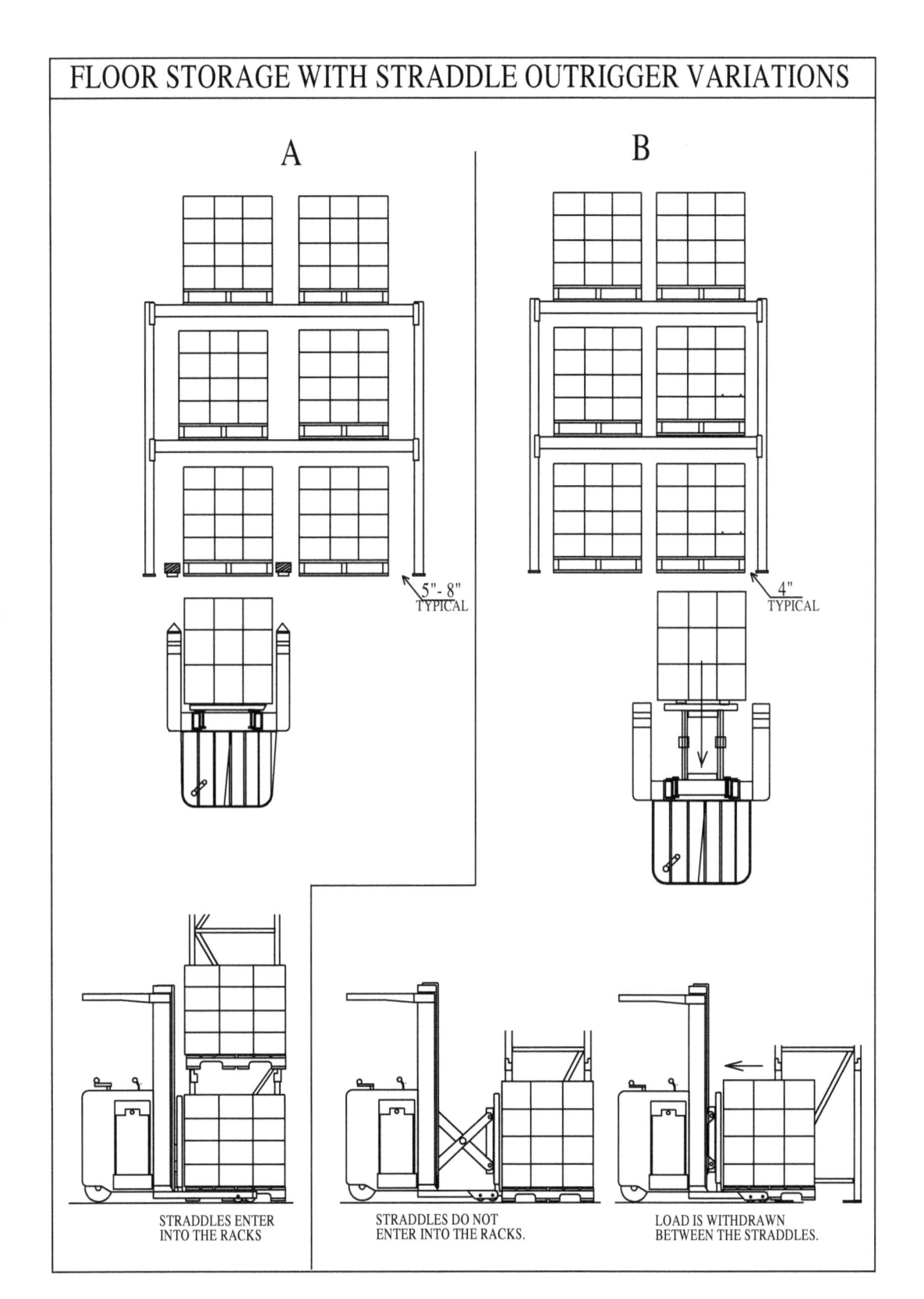

FLOOR STORAGE WITH STRADDLE OUTRIGGER VARIATIONS

A

B

5"- 8" TYPICAL

4" TYPICAL

STRADDLES ENTER INTO THE RACKS

STRADDLES DO NOT ENTER INTO THE RACKS.

LOAD IS WITHDRAWN BETWEEN THE STRADDLES.

9 *COMBINING EQUIPMENT INTO A SYSTEM*

FLOOR STORAGE USING AN OUTRIGGER OPENING **NARROWER** THAN THE PALLET

UP-AND-OVER METHOD

Floor storage is the most common method in use.

The next drawing shows a reach truck with a narrow outrigger opening. Here, because the pallet won't fit between the outriggers, they are positioned in front of a floor pallet, forks are extended into the pallet and it is lifted enough to clear the outriggers. This is typically a 6" or 7" lift, and requires extra lift-off space, requiring the first level of beams to be raised. This, in turn, means higher frames and a higher overall storage height.

The advantages are shorter load beams and a forklift with a narrow overall outrigger width.

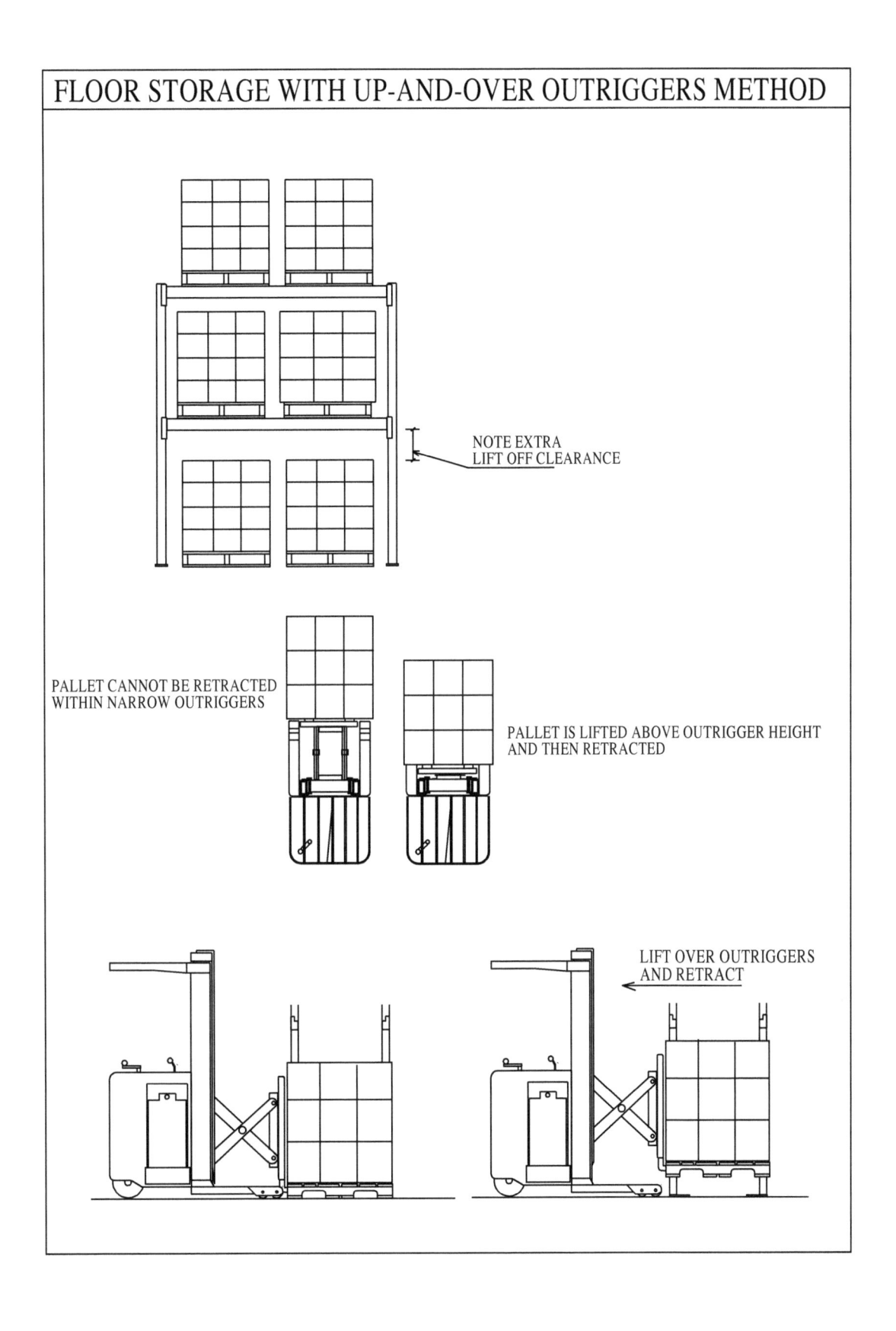

FLOOR STORAGE WITH UP-AND-OVER OUTRIGGERS METHOD

NOTE EXTRA LIFT OFF CLEARANCE

PALLET CANNOT BE RETRACTED WITHIN NARROW OUTRIGGERS

PALLET IS LIFTED ABOVE OUTRIGGER HEIGHT AND THEN RETRACTED

LIFT OVER OUTRIGGERS AND RETRACT

9 COMBINING EQUIPMENT INTO A SYSTEM

STORAGE USING A BOTTOM LOAD BEAM LEVEL

This method *may be chosen* for the reasons given previously *or it may be required* for systems with flow-through or push-back racks. In any case there is still the choice of outrigger type and width to be considered and also the preferred height of the beams.

The drawing on the next page shows a truck with an inside dimension meant to straddle the pallet and a truck with narrower outriggers. Despite using a bottom beam it may be necessary on high lifts to have a wide outrigger opening for stability. Once again the beam length must be dimensioned to suit the truck and layout preference.

Frames and the overall system, including the building, become about a foot higher than a straddle type floor storage system and 6" higher than the up-and-over floor storage method.

With a bottom beam system there are two other important considerations. If the outriggers are to go under the bottom beams as shown below there must be sufficient clearance, including an allowance for beam deflection.

Also, post guards cannot be welded to the frames because they will prevent beam placement. But the beam connectors will supply considerable protection if they are low enough on the frame.

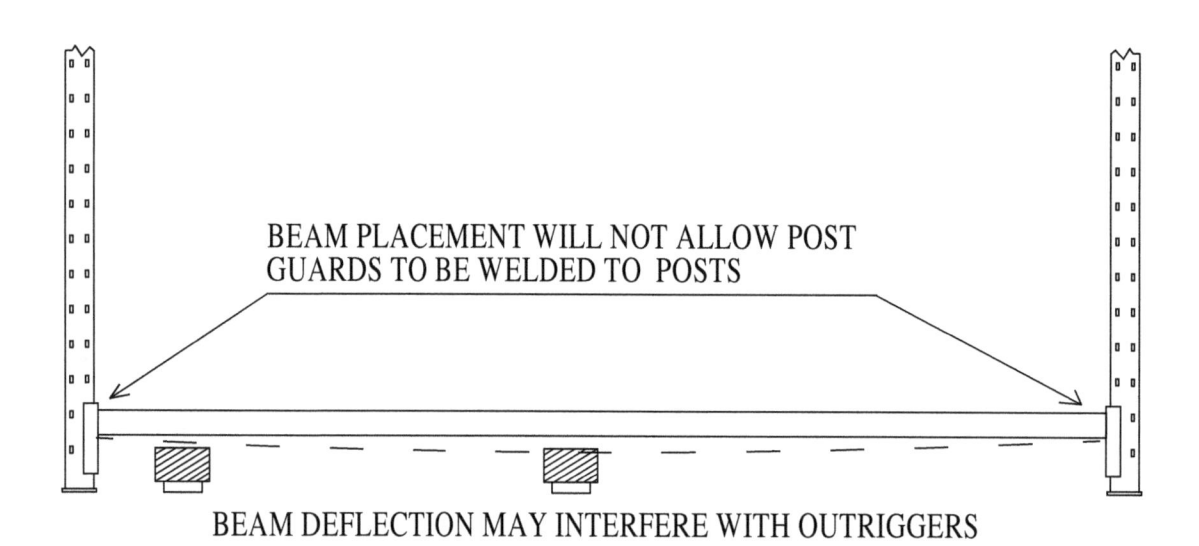

BEAM PLACEMENT WILL NOT ALLOW POST GUARDS TO BE WELDED TO POSTS

BEAM DEFLECTION MAY INTERFERE WITH OUTRIGGERS

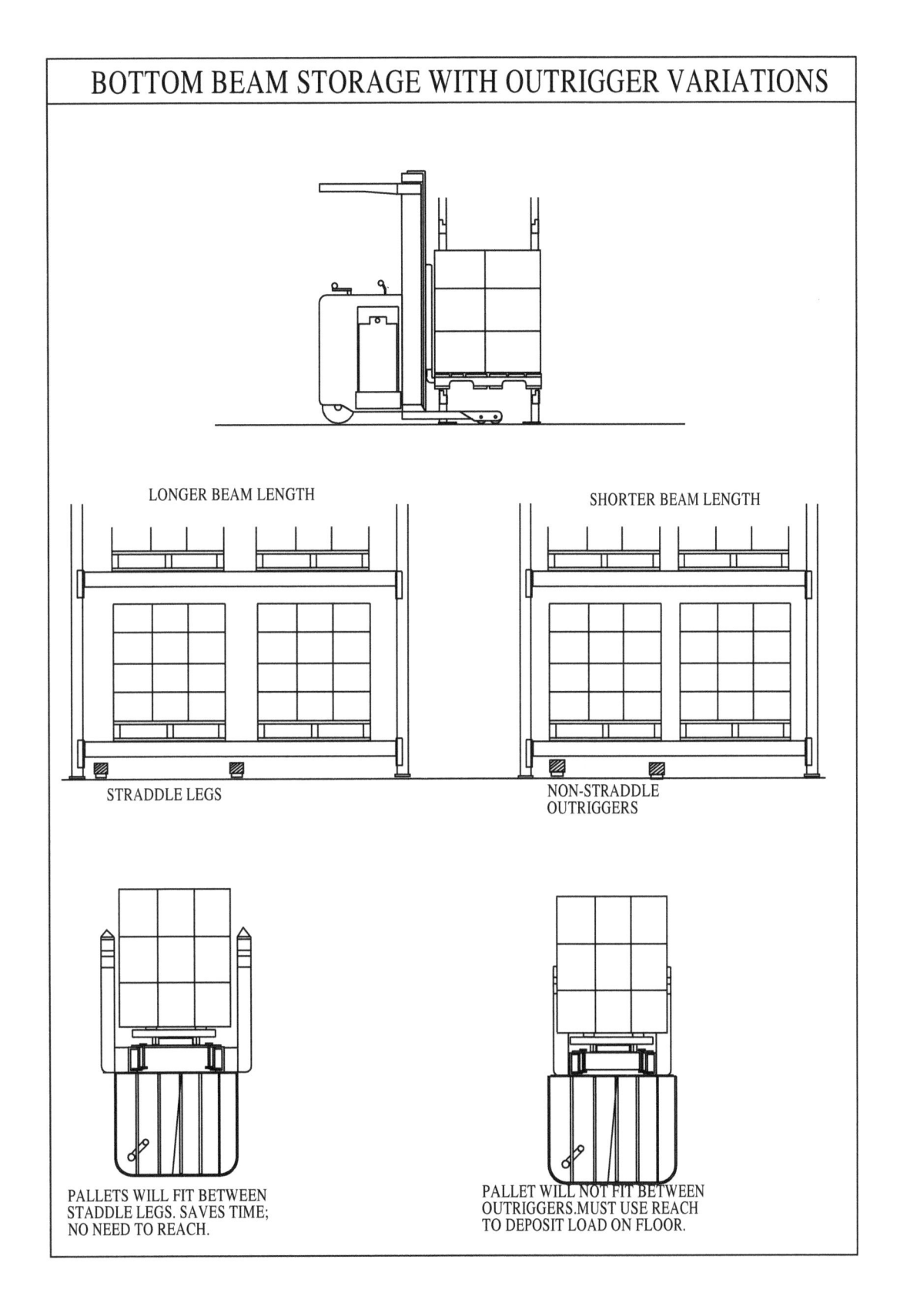

BOTTOM BEAM STORAGE WITH OUTRIGGER VARIATIONS

LONGER BEAM LENGTH

SHORTER BEAM LENGTH

STRADDLE LEGS

NON-STRADDLE OUTRIGGERS

PALLETS WILL FIT BETWEEN STADDLE LEGS. SAVES TIME; NO NEED TO REACH.

PALLET WILL NOT FIT BETWEEN OUTRIGGERS. MUST USE REACH TO DEPOSIT LOAD ON FLOOR.

9 COMBINING EQUIPMENT INTO A SYSTEM

A SPECIAL CONSIDERATION FOR DEEP-REACH TRUCKS

With a deep-reach truck, the outriggers *must* enter into the racks. This is inherent in the design, so the forks can reach fully into the inboard pallets. But also notice in the drawing on the next page that the **reach mechanism, complete with load backrest, must pass through the front rack.** To do so requires a minimum clear vertical opening which is governed by the height of the backrest or load, *whichever is higher.*

Only the straddle method of floor storage or the bottom beam methods are applicable here. Each of these methods will allow the outriggers into the front racks so the deep reach mechanism can extend to the rear row. Floor storage using the up-and-over method with narrow outriggers will not work because the front pallets on the floor will not allow the outriggers to enter the racks, which is necessary in order to access pallets on higher levels.

DEEP-REACH STORAGE METHODS

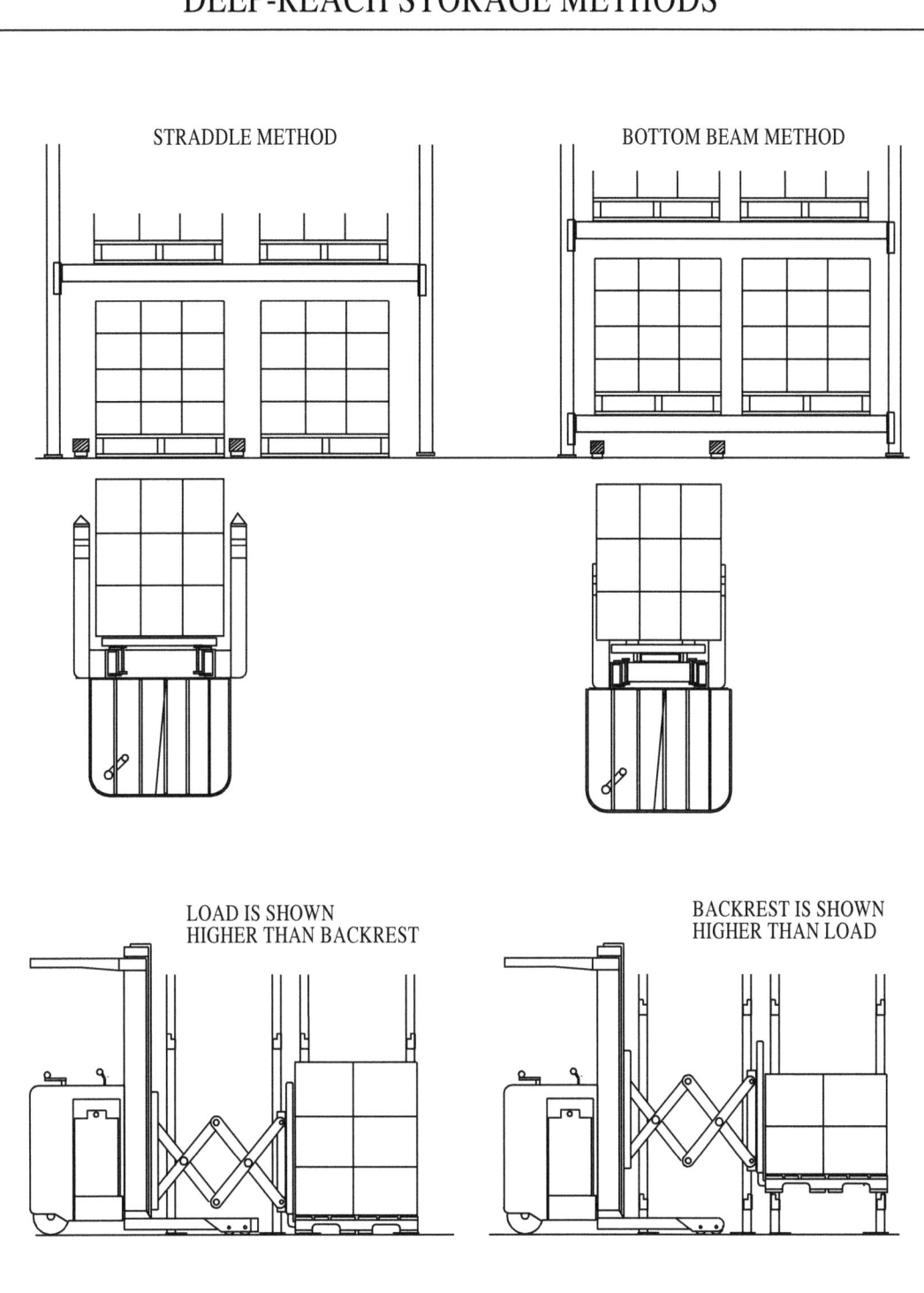

STRADDLE METHOD

BOTTOM BEAM METHOD

LOAD IS SHOWN HIGHER THAN BACKREST

BACKREST IS SHOWN HIGHER THAN LOAD

9 *COMBINING EQUIPMENT INTO A SYSTEM*

PUSH-BACK AND FLOW-THROUGH RACKS

Push-back and flow-through racks require careful consideration of the opening height between levels because the loads are angled upward as they are handled in and out of the system and must also be lifted over a pallet stop. Refer to the lower sketch on drawing on the next page.

Both types slant forward using rollers or wheels under the pallets. Push-Back racks are filled and retrieved from the front, while Flow-Through racks are loaded from the rear and retrieved from the front face.

Push-Back racks are FILO and Flow-Through racks are FIFO

These racks have a bottom rail level near the floor, usually supported on load beams. However, the rails may be placed directly on the floor if it is not necessary for outriggers to fit beneath them.

Manufacturers have various methods of supporting the rails on the front beam. Simply fastening the rails on top of the beam is wasteful of vertical space; sitting them on a ledge behind the beam is more efficient. If you have limited height look for the second method.

For push-backs be sure your lift truck supplier confirms the truck is capable of pushing the accumulated weight of all the loads in a lane. Forks should have enough tilt rearward to match the slope of the rails.

Flow-through racks are the most difficult to specify because of factors which don't exist in other rack systems. Different load weights and storage depths will have an effect on degrees of rail slope and control accessories needed. In fact it may be necessary to adjust lanes differently for various products or to accommodate changes over time; so choose this rack very carefully. Accessories include velocity retarders to control the speed of moving loads and a method to relieve the pressure on the front pallet. To do this a mechanism is used to create a gap between the front pallet and those behind it, thus making it free to be lifted

Always calculate the storage height, lift off clearance, fire regulation clearance and elevated fork height from the rear of the system and be sure the forks have sufficient tilt up and down to match the rail slope.

There are many designs of flow-through racks, including movement controlled by air flow, with few mechanical parts. Work closely with potential suppliers to determine what is the best design for your application, with the ability to accommodate variances, expected or unexpected.

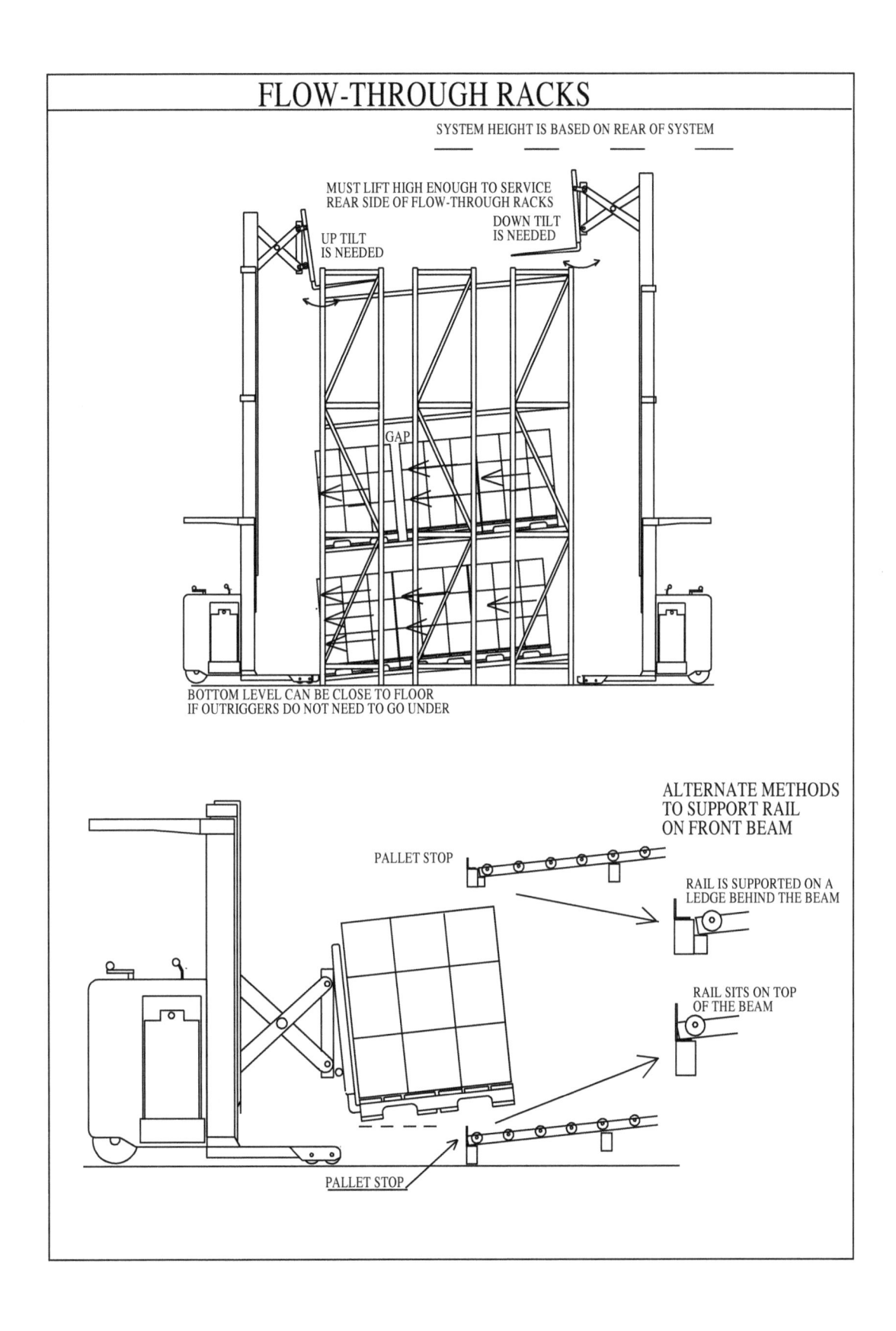

FLOW-THROUGH RACKS

SYSTEM HEIGHT IS BASED ON REAR OF SYSTEM

MUST LIFT HIGH ENOUGH TO SERVICE REAR SIDE OF FLOW-THROUGH RACKS

UP TILT IS NEEDED

DOWN TILT IS NEEDED

GAP

BOTTOM LEVEL CAN BE CLOSE TO FLOOR IF OUTRIGGERS DO NOT NEED TO GO UNDER

ALTERNATE METHODS TO SUPPORT RAIL ON FRONT BEAM

PALLET STOP

RAIL IS SUPPORTED ON A LEDGE BEHIND THE BEAM

RAIL SITS ON TOP OF THE BEAM

PALLET STOP

9 *COMBINING EQUIPMENT INTO A SYSTEM*

DRIVE-IN RACKS

Drive-in and drive-through racks require very close attention to dimensional and safety details, because the forklift and operator enter into the tunnels, sometimes with tons of product above.

The next few drawings show some of the details which should be considered. Beginning with the drawing on the next page the question of rail supports, their type and length, is examined.

Four types of rail supports, "A" through "D", are shown. Type "A" uses an angle iron rail fixed to the end of a short support. This design is very good because while allowing the distance between rails to be any width wanted it also provides safety (the load cannot fall through) and uses only ¼" of vertical. The top sketch shows a 36" clear opening with a 40" wide pallet in a 48" wide tunnel. The lower sketch shows a 44" clear opening with a 48" wide pallet in a 56" wide tunnel.

The top sketch on the next page shows a 36" clear opening with a 40" wide pallet when using a type "B" support. Note that this is unsafe because the pallet has been placed off center and could easily be dislodged if it is somehow shifted a bit more to the left. Additionally, this support is using 3" of vertical. Four rail levels will increase the system height by a foot.

The center sketch shows the support length increased to 9" with the clear opening reduced to 30". The pallet can no longer fall through but the narrow opening will be a problem for many forklifts.

The lower sketch shows type "C", with an angle stop added to prevent pallets from falling through while maintaining a wide opening. It is similar to type "A" but still uses 3" of vertical.

Type "D" has the problems of "B" and uses even more vertical, about 5".

There are some applications where types "B" and "C" may offer an advantage. Refer to page 292. The upper sketch shows a "B" used to extend under the very large wing of a special use pallet. No vertical space is lost and excessive sag of a heavily loaded pallet may be avoided.

The lower sketch shows a type "C" used to support a 48" wide notched pallet. This type of pallet is weaker at the notch locations and reducing the unsupported span may be important with heavy loads. In this sketch the pallet has maximum support while maintaining a 36" clear opening and centering the pallet between guides.

Always consider the pallet type and load before selecting a rail support; make a test if in doubt.

The next drawings, of forklifts within the racks, will show the importance of support length and clear opening.

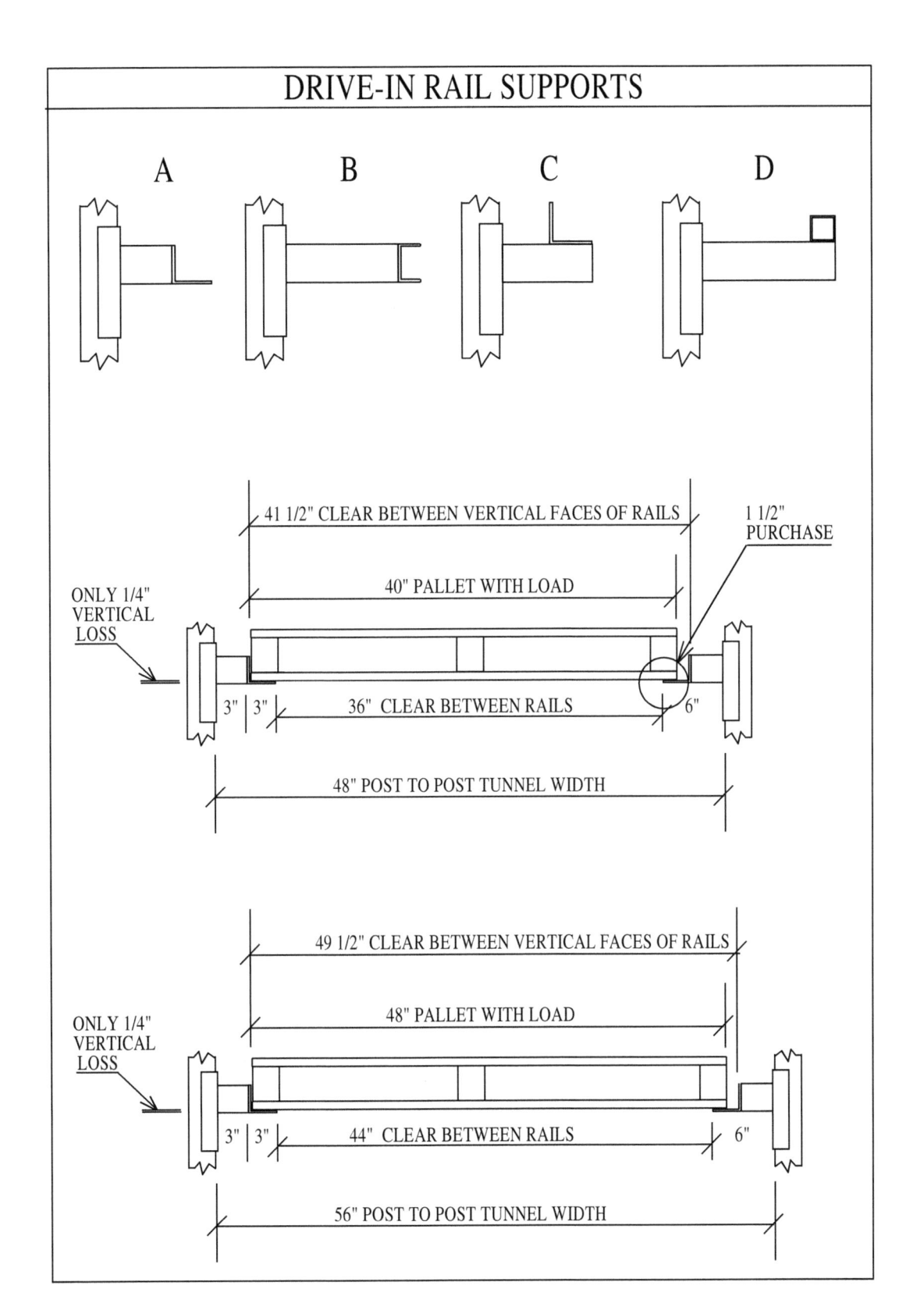

DRIVE-IN RAIL SUPPORTS

A   B   C   D

41 1/2" CLEAR BETWEEN VERTICAL FACES OF RAILS

1 1/2" PURCHASE

40" PALLET WITH LOAD

ONLY 1/4" VERTICAL LOSS

3" | 3"   36" CLEAR BETWEEN RAILS   6"

48" POST TO POST TUNNEL WIDTH

49 1/2" CLEAR BETWEEN VERTICAL FACES OF RAILS

48" PALLET WITH LOAD

ONLY 1/4" VERTICAL LOSS

3" | 3"   44" CLEAR BETWEEN RAILS   6"

56" POST TO POST TUNNEL WIDTH

9 *COMBINING EQUIPMENT INTO A SYSTEM*

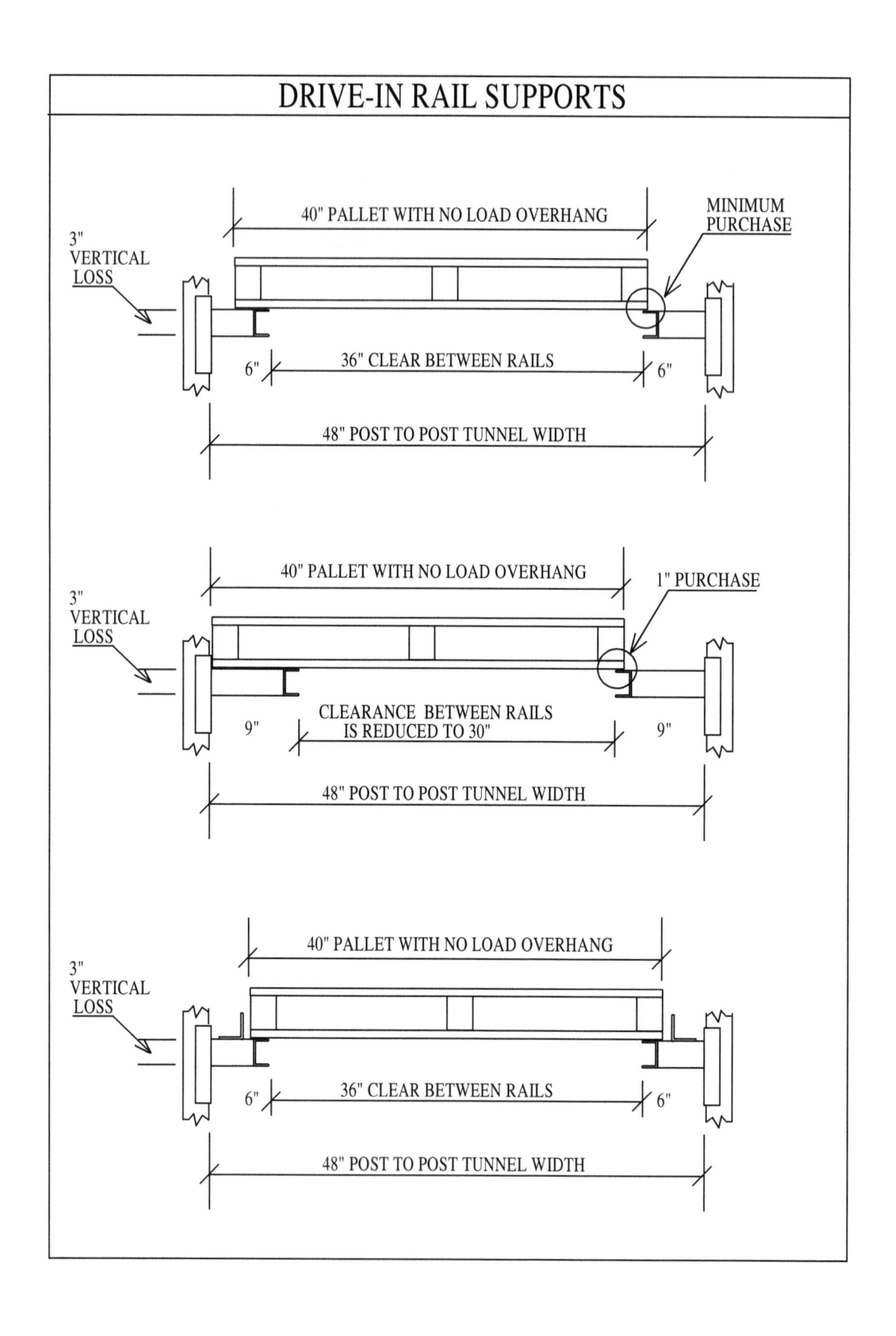

DRIVE-IN RAIL SUPPORTS

Top diagram:
- 40" PALLET WITH NO LOAD OVERHANG
- MINIMUM PURCHASE
- 3" VERTICAL LOSS
- 6" | 36" CLEAR BETWEEN RAILS | 6"
- 48" POST TO POST TUNNEL WIDTH

Middle diagram:
- 40" PALLET WITH NO LOAD OVERHANG
- 1" PURCHASE
- 3" VERTICAL LOSS
- 9" | CLEARANCE BETWEEN RAILS IS REDUCED TO 30" | 9"
- 48" POST TO POST TUNNEL WIDTH

Bottom diagram:
- 40" PALLET WITH NO LOAD OVERHANG
- 3" VERTICAL LOSS
- 6" | 36" CLEAR BETWEEN RAILS | 6"
- 48" POST TO POST TUNNEL WIDTH

HOW TO CONFIGURE AND EQUIP YOUR WAREHOUSE

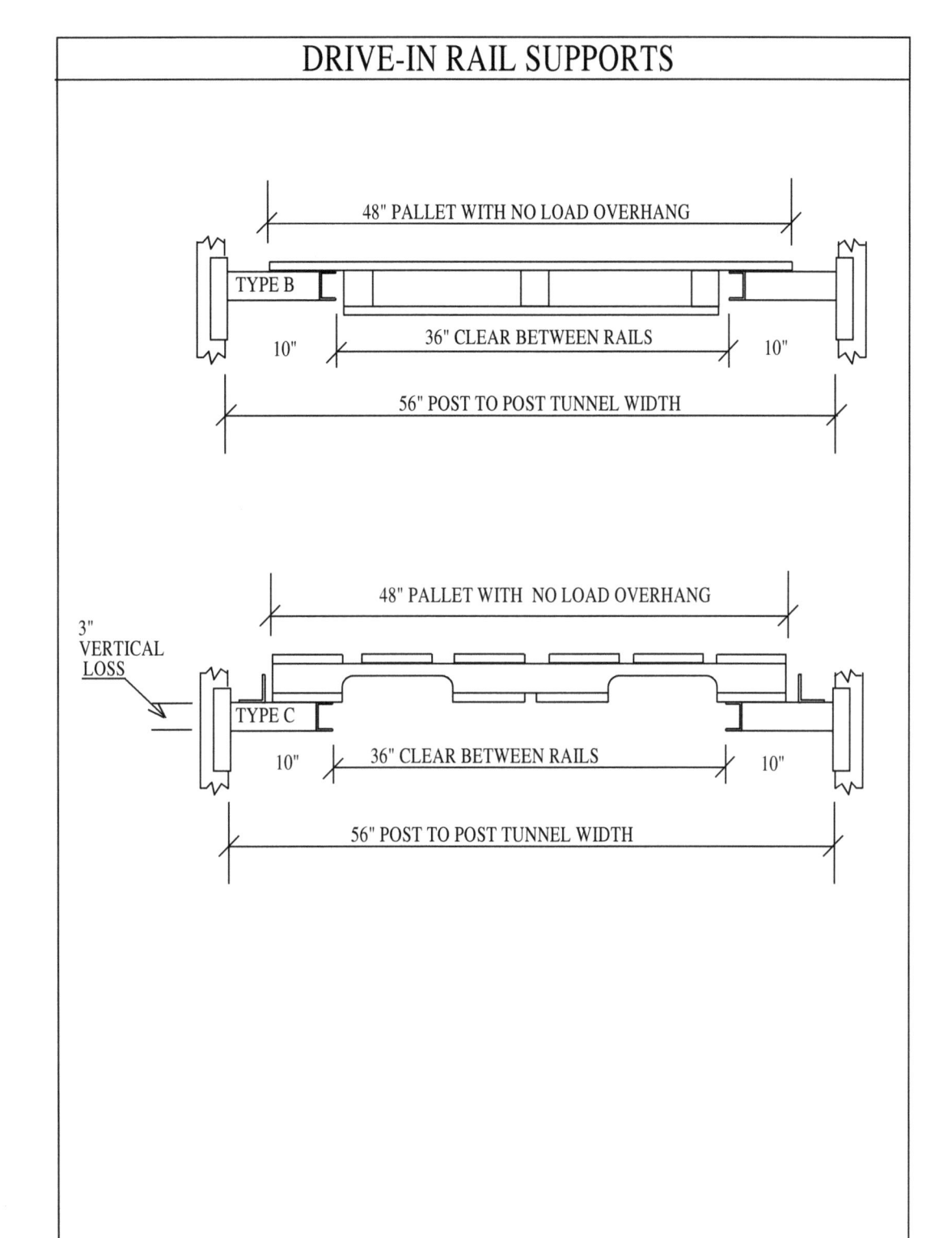

DRIVE-IN RAIL SUPPORTS

TYPE B

48" PALLET WITH NO LOAD OVERHANG
36" CLEAR BETWEEN RAILS
10" 10"
56" POST TO POST TUNNEL WIDTH

3" VERTICAL LOSS

TYPE C

48" PALLET WITH NO LOAD OVERHANG
36" CLEAR BETWEEN RAILS
10" 10"
56" POST TO POST TUNNEL WIDTH

Because forklifts must drive into the tunnels of drive-in and drive-through racks there are a number of clearances which must be checked. The next page shows a sit-on counterbalanced forklift in the racks. First check the body of the truck to be sure it fits under the first rail level and has sufficient clearance to the rack frames. Also, the overhead guard posts must fit between the rails or be modified to do so, as shown here.

The mast must fit between the rails at each level, again with sufficient clearance for forklift operation. Masts have strengthening cross members and will be widest at these points so allow for them if they happen to be at the same height as a rail.

As with all racks there must be a lift off clearance over the load or load backrest, whichever is higher.

In some instances pallets are stored two high on the floor, thus eliminating the lowest rail and any dimensional problems which it may cause. In fact, with light loads two pallets may be stored at every level.

The next page shows a rear stand-on reach truck in drive-ins. This type of truck can impose some additional cautions. Because the operator is standing to one side of the unit he is in proximity to any rail lower than his head. Be sure he is well protected by a side guard and/or posts from the truck body to the overhead guard. Another potential problem caused by a low rail is at the steering wheel. Be sure the operator's hand or wrist won't get jammed under the rail. These two factors make it desirable to avoid having a low rail with any rear stand-on forklift, perhaps double stacking on the floor, as per the previous drawing.

Some reach trucks may have hose reels with hoses extended to operate the reach mechanism, sideshifter or any other attachment. Check their position in relation to the rails.

The last drawing in this series is a reminder that extra lift off is needed at the lowest level for the up-and-over method, which is usually used with reach trucks in drive-in racks.

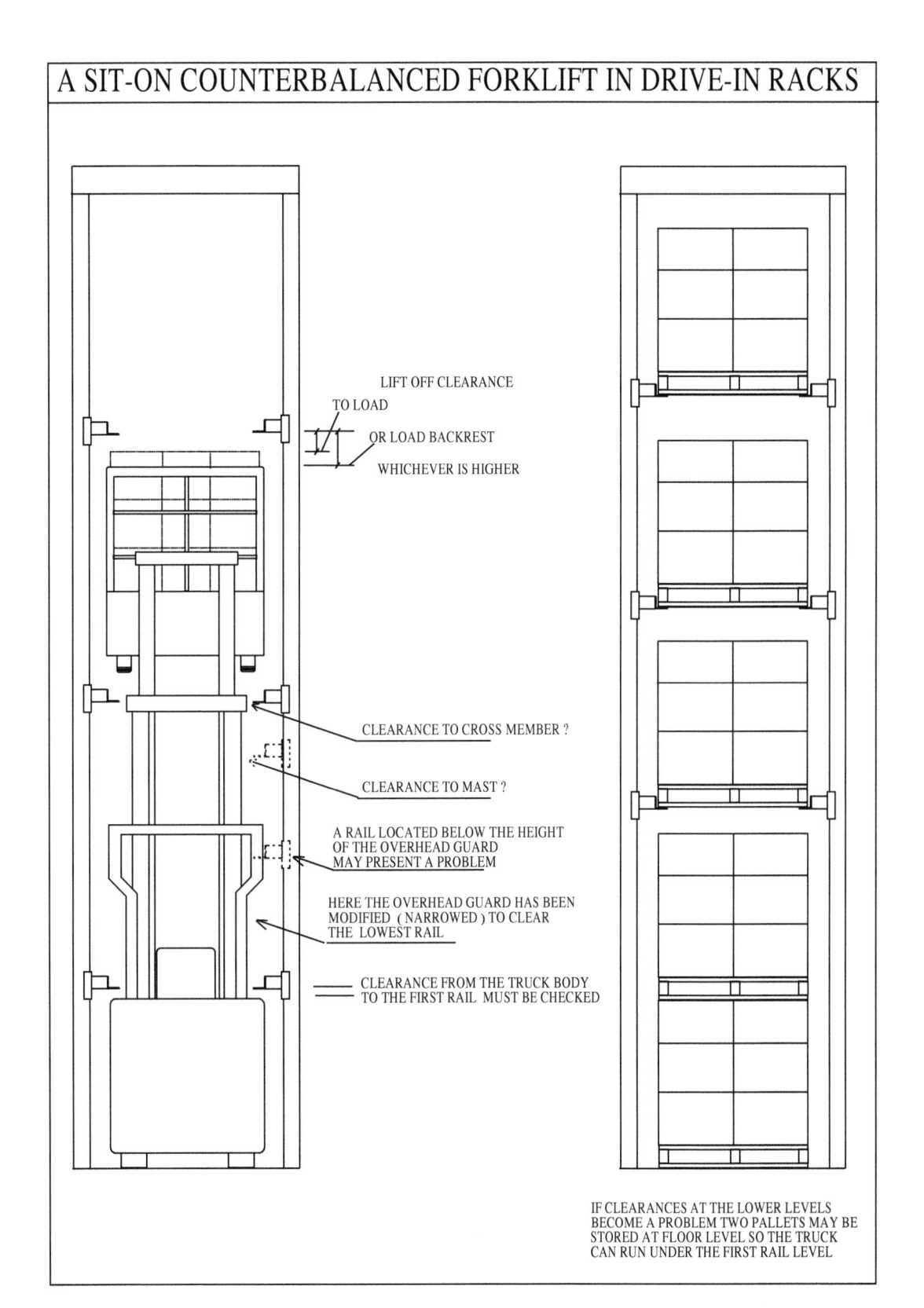

A SIT-ON COUNTERBALANCED FORKLIFT IN DRIVE-IN RACKS

LIFT OFF CLEARANCE
TO LOAD
OR LOAD BACKREST
WHICHEVER IS HIGHER

CLEARANCE TO CROSS MEMBER ?

CLEARANCE TO MAST ?

A RAIL LOCATED BELOW THE HEIGHT OF THE OVERHEAD GUARD MAY PRESENT A PROBLEM

HERE THE OVERHEAD GUARD HAS BEEN MODIFIED (NARROWED) TO CLEAR THE LOWEST RAIL

CLEARANCE FROM THE TRUCK BODY TO THE FIRST RAIL MUST BE CHECKED

IF CLEARANCES AT THE LOWER LEVELS BECOME A PROBLEM TWO PALLETS MAY BE STORED AT FLOOR LEVEL SO THE TRUCK CAN RUN UNDER THE FIRST RAIL LEVEL

COMBINING EQUIPMENT INTO A SYSTEM

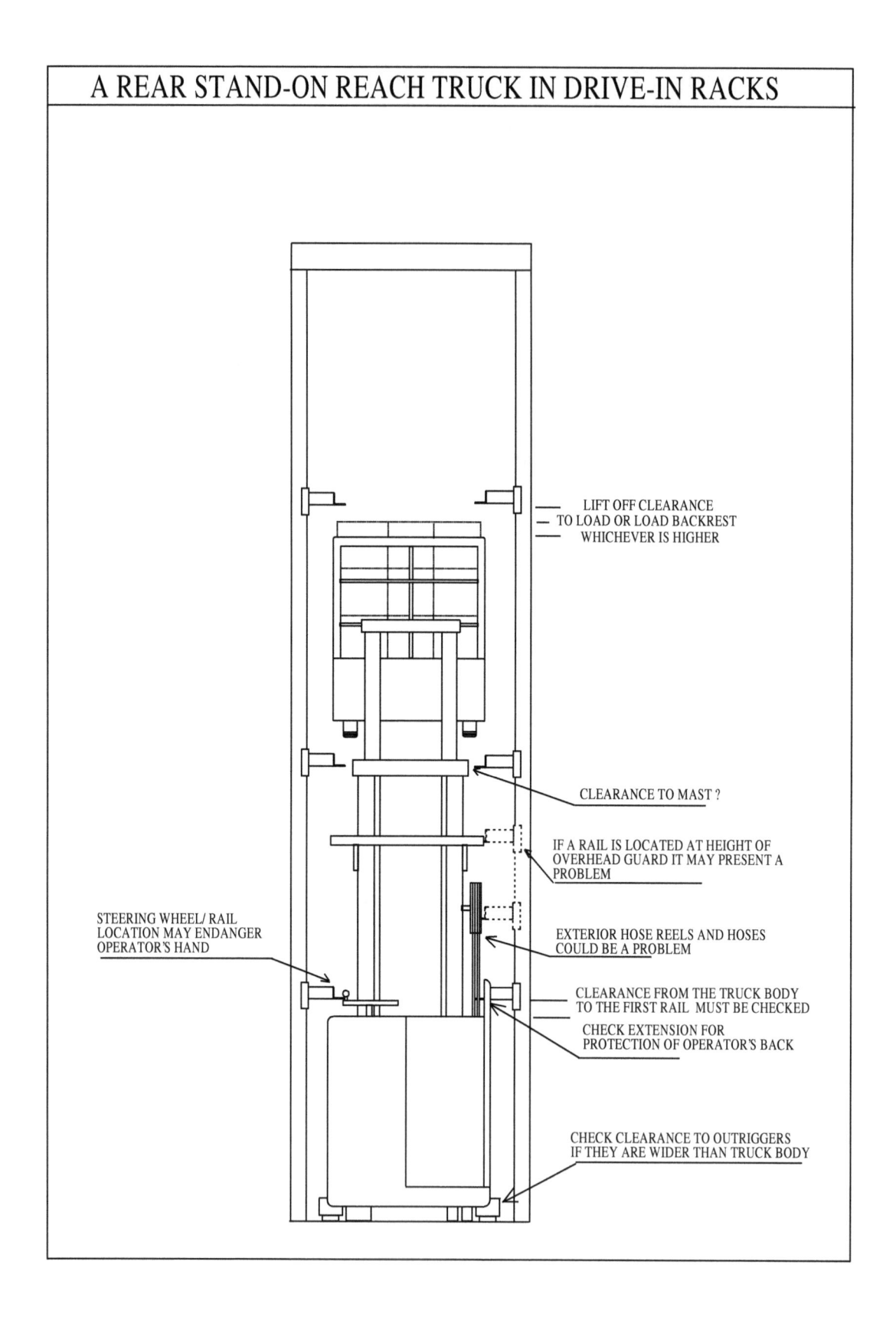

A REAR STAND-ON REACH TRUCK IN DRIVE-IN RACKS

- LIFT OFF CLEARANCE TO LOAD OR LOAD BACKREST WHICHEVER IS HIGHER
- CLEARANCE TO MAST ?
- IF A RAIL IS LOCATED AT HEIGHT OF OVERHEAD GUARD IT MAY PRESENT A PROBLEM
- STEERING WHEEL/ RAIL LOCATION MAY ENDANGER OPERATOR'S HAND
- EXTERIOR HOSE REELS AND HOSES COULD BE A PROBLEM
- CLEARANCE FROM THE TRUCK BODY TO THE FIRST RAIL MUST BE CHECKED
- CHECK EXTENSION FOR PROTECTION OF OPERATOR'S BACK
- CHECK CLEARANCE TO OUTRIGGERS IF THEY ARE WIDER THAN TRUCK BODY

HOW TO CONFIGURE AND EQUIP YOUR WAREHOUSE

SIDE VIEW OF A REACH TRUCK IN DRIVE-IN RACKS

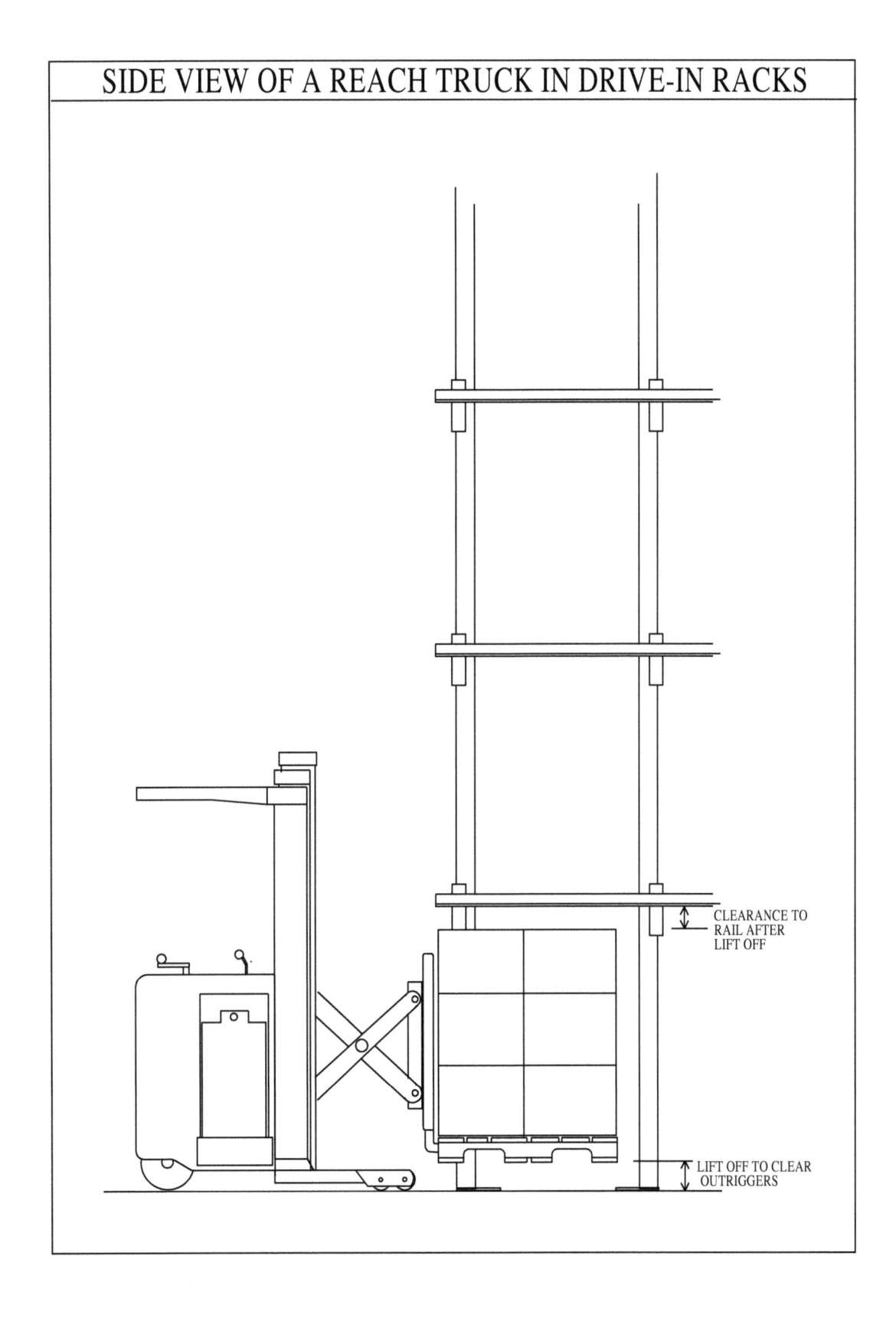

CLEARANCE TO RAIL AFTER LIFT OFF

LIFT OFF TO CLEAR OUTRIGGERS

The previous drawings and explanations of compatible dimensions cover some of the most common situations. However these are only a small portion of the equipment combinations which can occur. It is strongly recommended that the supplier of each piece of equipment be made aware of its' intended use in the system and, being provided with any pertinent information or drawings, confirm compatibility.

SECTION TEN
ORDER PICKING SYSTEMS
10

WHAT IS AN ORDER PICKING SYSTEM?

The word *"system"* is used in this manual to include any combinations of storage and handling equipment along with the methods and aisle width used to store and retrieve products.

This is a restricted definition; a broader definition might include all operations, from ordering through to re-ordering, as part of the system.

Three examples of *order picking systems* are as follows:

High level shelving is hand loaded from a high-level electric orderpicker truck and orders are assembled by retrieving the stored goods using the same orderpicker truck. Here you might want to consider guiding the orderpicker truck within the aisles to increase safety and efficiency while using the narrowest possible aisles. The operator can then easily pick from both sides while freed of the necessity to steer the machine. The guidance, shelving and orderpicker truck form the equipment combination while the hand storage and retrieval from both sides of the aisle is the method of use. Picking a single order or multiple orders on each cycle are options to consider.

Carousels are generally hand loaded with products and are subsequently programmed so the required parts for each order are brought to the pick station in a sequence requiring the least movement of the carousel carriers. At the pick station the picker selects the parts wanted for a number of orders and places them in separate containers. He then pushes a button to automatically rotate the carousel so the next desired parts stop in front of him. The carousels, along with the computer controls, form the equipment combination and the hand loading for storage along with picking of multiple orders on the same "run" comprise the method of use. This is a simple system for carousels; they can be automated far beyond this example and are discussed in more detail elsewhere.

A stand-on reach truck is used to load full pallets into selective racks; low lift pallet trucks are then used to pick cases from the pallets on the lower levels. When a pallet on the lower levels (the pick levels) becomes empty, it is replenished from the upper levels by the reach truck. The racks and two types of forklifts are the equipment combination and picking from the lower levels with reserve storage above is the method of use. Here you might want to consider an aisle width capable of allowing two loaded pallet trucks to pass, rather than using the narrowest possible aisle. An option to be decided is whether to allow each picker to traverse the whole system or to limit pickers to specified zones. Also there are some options to be decided for the rack configuration.

These are just a few examples of systems along with brief comments and cautions. The actual specifications and dimensions of a system must be done with great care if serious and costly errors are to be avoided. Some examples, using much more detail, are included elsewhere and it is recommended that this attention to detail be used for *each* system, regardless of how simple it might appear to be at first look. Remember to consider all aspects affected by the system you wish to institute; space, labor, replenishment, location management, picking, packing, shipping etc. and many more areas are all part of your system. Assure that you consider the effects of your new section and how it affects the other areas (positively or negatively).

ORDER PICKING

The term "order picking" is used here to define the process of selecting and retrieving cases or smaller pieces from their storage locations. Other commonly used terms for this process include "order selection" and "order assembly"; but order assembly might also refer to the merging of separately picked portions of the order or could refer to the gathering of full pallet loads in preparation for a large shipment.

Order picking is labor intensive and in many distribution centers will present the greatest opportunity for efficiencies and savings or, inversely, inefficiencies and high costs.

The choice of an **order picking system**, comprised of the best combination of equipment and methods, can be the most difficult of all your system planning. Many picking methods and a great diversification of equipment await your decisions.

Much consideration of basic statistics is needed if you are to get the results wanted. Here is an instance where the phrase "garbage-in, garbage-out" is applicable and expensive.

Before going into more detail of the many choices it must be mentioned that there are available a number of highly automated systems which are designed to reduce the labor content of manual picking and which will often also save space and increase accuracy of the filled orders. Each system requires an individual analysis for each application, which is beyond the general scope of this book, but should not be ignored if a potential exists for their use.

The following are lists of major choices to be made regarding **picking methods;** *equipment choices follow this section; with drawings and comments regarding machines suitable for the various methods and heights.* As with any combination of methods and equipment used to form a system it may be necessary to try various pairings, often resulting in different systems for different zones.

SOME VARIABLES IN ORDER PICKING METHODS

LOW LEVEL PICKING

MID LEVEL PICKING

HIGH LEVEL PICKING

VERY HIGH LEVEL PICKING

MULTI-LEVEL PICKING

SINGLE-ORDER PICKING

MULTIPLE-ORDER PICKING

HARD COPY PICK LISTS

ELECTRONIC (PAPERLESS) PICK LISTS

BATCH ORDER PICKING

COMPLETE ORDER PICKED BY ONE PICKER

ZONE PICKING

PICKER TRAVELS TO ITEMS

ITEMS ARE MOVED TO THE PICKER

Following are descriptions of each of these options.

ORDER PICKING LEVELS

For many years orderpickers were referred to simply as *low level pickers*, where the operator rode or walked but was not elevated beyond two or three feet, or *high level* where the operator was lifted higher. But with the tremendous lift capabilities and versatility of newer machines these designations now seem totally inadequate and you should be aware of the full range of options which are available. Consider these designations, arbitrarily chosen here to highlight the range:

LOW LEVEL   MID LEVEL   HIGH LEVEL   VERY HIGH LEVEL

LOW LEVEL   The order picker may walk with a push cart, non-powered pallet jack, an electric stock chaser cart or a powered low-lift walkie pallet truck; or he may ride on a powered walkie pallet truck. In either case he picks from the floor level, with the exception of a few specialized vehicles which may allow him to be elevated two or three feet.

MID LEVEL   Lifting to perhaps fifteen or twenty feet this would have been termed in previous years "high level". These machines are available for full case or individual piece picking and can be manually steered but generally are floor guided by guide rails on the floor or electronic wire guidance.

HIGH LEVEL   Lifts to perhaps as high as 30 feet with a dedicated orderpicking truck and 45 feet with a combination pallet handling/picking vehicle. They are almost always floor guided by rails or electronic wire and have additional safety features due to their high working levels. Because they are not supported by a top rail there will be capacity downratings at the highest levels.

VERY HIGH LEVEL   Lifting to 50 feet or higher these are available as combination pallet and picking machines or as dedicated orderpickers. They typically run on a bottom track or rail and are supported by an upper track or rail which often supplies power also to the vehicle. Typically these Very High Level machines are either aisle dedicated (one machine per aisle), or may require a special transfer car to switch them between aisles. Because these machines are rail supported top and bottom they do not suffer from downrating problems as the unit lifts, thus can be used to store and retrieve heavier loads to heights of 60′ and over.

PICKING LEVEL DESIGNATIONS

VERY HIGH LEVEL PICKING — ABOVE 45'

HIGH LEVEL PICKING — 20' - 45'

MID LEVEL PICKING — 8' - 20'

LOW LEVEL PICKING — 6' - 8'

MULTI-LEVEL PICKING

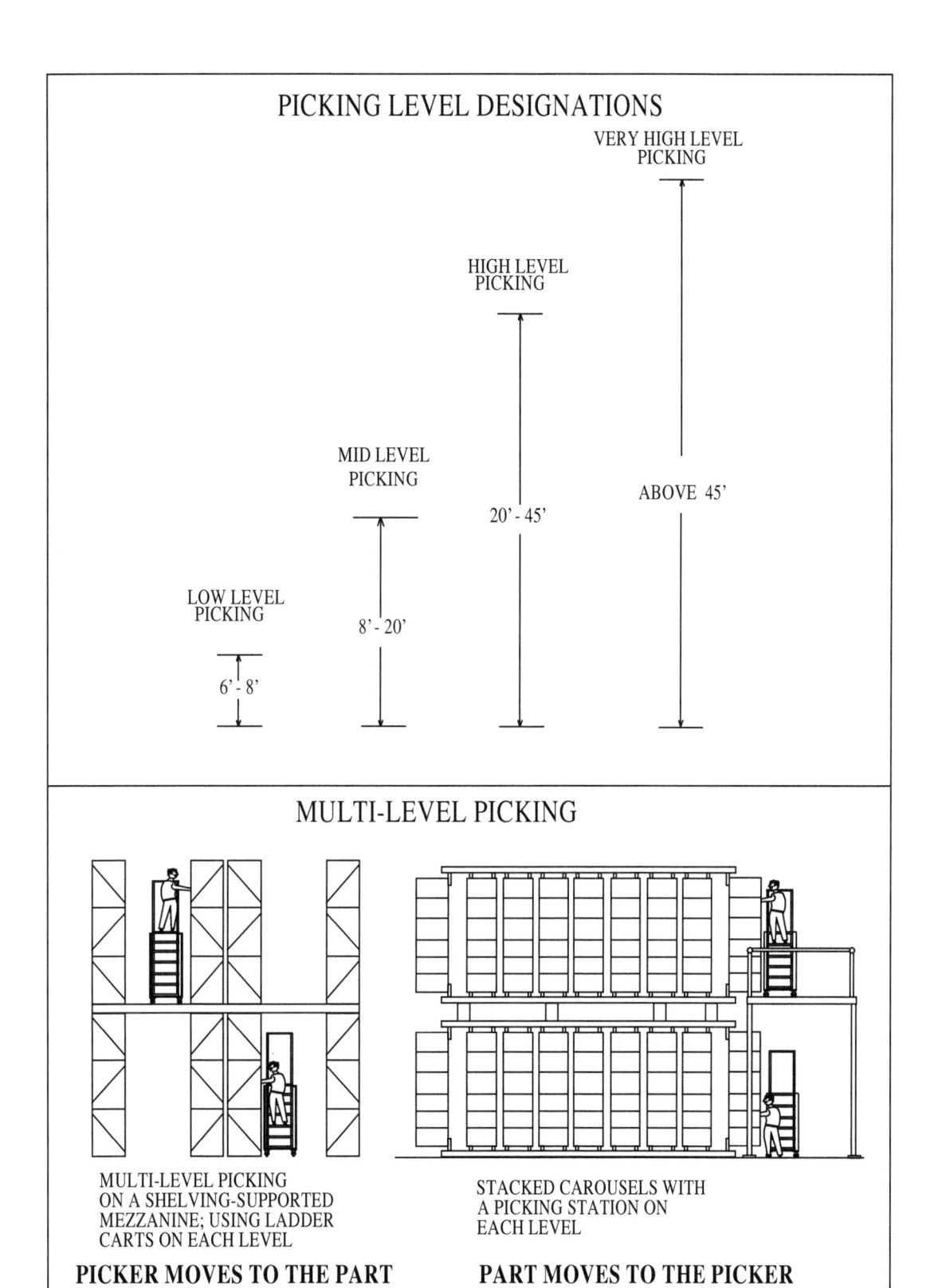

MULTI-LEVEL PICKING ON A SHELVING-SUPPORTED MEZZANINE; USING LADDER CARTS ON EACH LEVEL

PICKER MOVES TO THE PART

STACKED CAROUSELS WITH A PICKING STATION ON EACH LEVEL

PART MOVES TO THE PICKER

302

10 *ORDER PICKING SYSTEMS*

Design heights are almost continuously being extended and if you want extreme heights contact a supplier. When in an aisle they are usually powered by mains electricity from the building, perhaps as much as 600 volts. Some models are also battery powered to allow them to change aisles (while their load handler is fully lowered) while others require a specialized aisle transfer mechanism at one end of the system to allow movement between aisles. Most types are shown and explained immediately following this section. Unit load forklifts, order-pickers and machines which are used for both are covered in sections 6, 7 and 8.

MULTI-LEVEL PICKING

303

With this system portions of the pick line are on different levels of the building. The upper level may be on the second floor of a building but is more often on a mezzanine in order to use the full available height of the ground floor. More than two levels can be used if space permits. Mezzanines are quite often supported on storage racks or shelving which serve to store product on the lower level while also supporting a floor for the upper level. Some types of equipment, such as carousels, may be stacked directly one on the other. A fixed platform is located at the end of each level and the part is brought to the picker.

Each level can be considered as a separate zone utilizing low-level or mid-level picking. The order pick is typically started on the upper level with the container then transferred to the lower level for completion. But in some instances each level is picked into different containers, which are then merged for shipping. These may be termed Pick Towers and are discussed a bit later.

Specifics of the various picking methodologies are further clarified below.

PICKER TRAVELS TO ITEM OR ITEM TRAVELS TO PICKER

When stored in shelving or pallet racks the items required are accessed by walking or traveling to them on some type of machine. The pick vehicle may be a simple cart or an Orderpicker truck with lifting ability.

Machines such as horizontal or vertical carousels and conveyors may be used to bring the items to the picker. Most of these can be automated for very high pick rates and these also work well for batch or multiple-order picking with paperless pick lists.

SOME PICK CYCLE PATTERNS

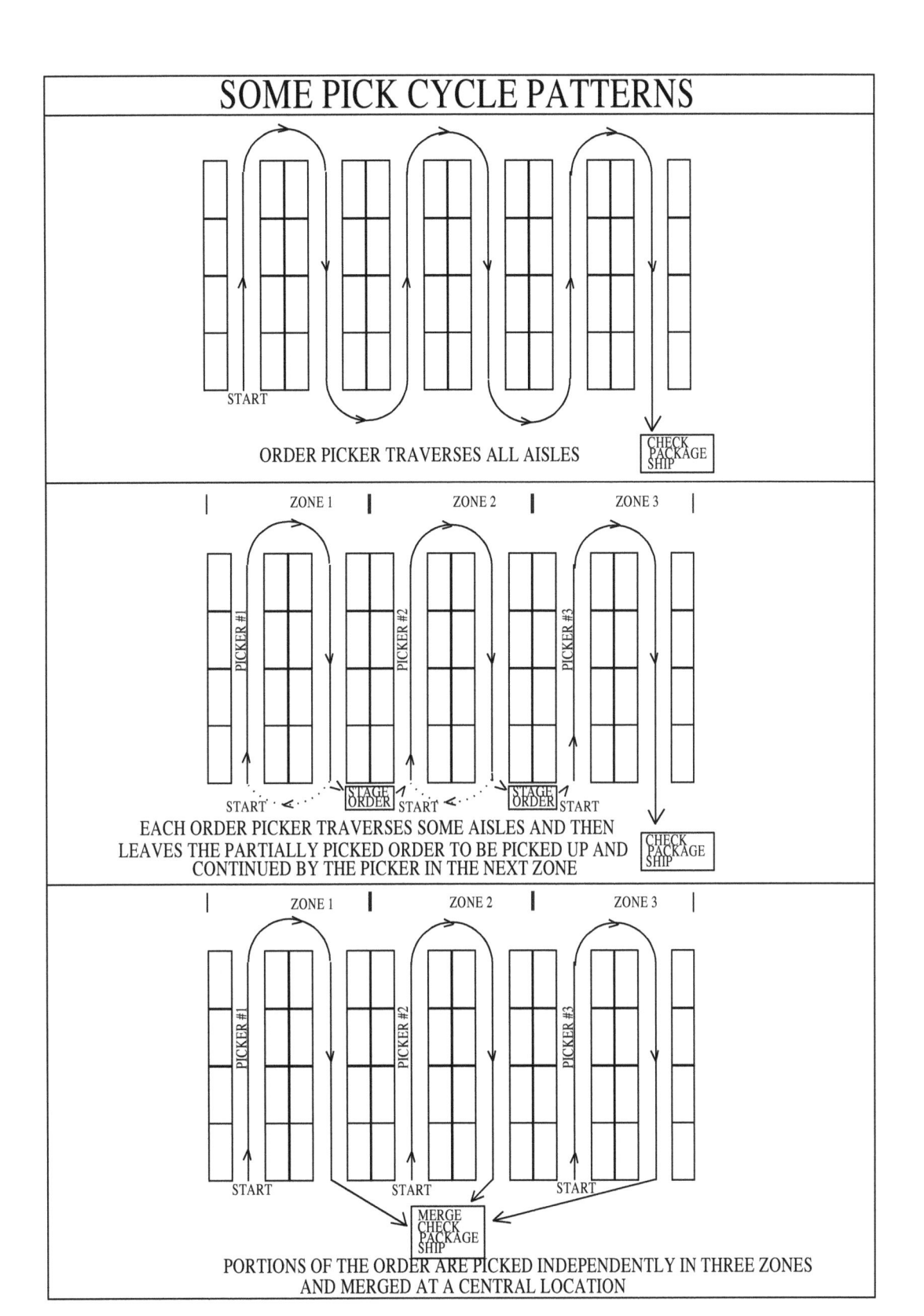

ORDER PICKER TRAVERSES ALL AISLES

EACH ORDER PICKER TRAVERSES SOME AISLES AND THEN LEAVES THE PARTIALLY PICKED ORDER TO BE PICKED UP AND CONTINUED BY THE PICKER IN THE NEXT ZONE

PORTIONS OF THE ORDER ARE PICKED INDEPENDENTLY IN THREE ZONES AND MERGED AT A CENTRAL LOCATION

SOME FACTORS IN DECIDING **YOUR** PICKING SYSTEMS

Since optimum picking systems are seldom identical to those of other companies, and even vary from zone to zone within the same distribution center, it is imperative that each zone be analyzed individually.

A "building block" method for estimating space requirements of different systems was outlined in a previous section. This should be referred to as one factor in selecting picking systems. However, space is only one part of the analysis; it may or may not be the primary concern.

This leads to the starting point of your considerations for each zone; *what is the primary goal for this zone and what are the other goals in order of their importance?* This simple listing will help greatly in your decisions.

Some goals, other than optimizing floor space, may include picking rates, picking accuracy, flexibility to add more pickers in peak periods, flexibility to change pick run patterns and change between single order or batch orders, FIFO control, multiple shift operation, provision for future growth in sales volume and increased SKUs, protection of fragile or valuable items, etc., etc. List all factors you can think of and then prioritize them.

When you are re-organizing, or leasing a building of known dimensions, the range of system choices may be fewer than those available when planning a new building. For instance, it may not be practical to use multi-level picking in an existing building of low height. If the intention is to lease an existing building it is recommended you plan as if a new facility is to be built to your specifications. In this way the ideal building can be determined and compared to any existing building being considered.

Once the list is prioritized, the selection of a system becomes much simpler. If, for instance, the first priority is to be able to double the number of order pickers during a peak season it may be found that a very narrow aisle system with high level orderpickers is too restrictive, even though it is very space efficient and satisfactory for most of the time. Here a low level zone picking system, where the length of the pick runs can be shortened and extra pickers inserted, may work better. Each picker may then have a zone of only one aisle, instead of multiple aisles, for the duration of the peak period. Having a zone for each picker will allow narrow or very narrow aisles while preventing the pickers from getting in each other's way, which, in the industry, is called "contention".

If this is a system which stores full pallet loads above the pick levels, the forklift will determine the minimum aisle width; but consideration should be given to making the aisle wide enough for two pickers to pass, allowing extra pickers to be used with a minimum of interference with each other.

In pallet storage, or hand loaded shelving, it is necessary to determine how many sku's will be in the system and how much shelf frontage is needed. Also, always have your growth potential in mind and include it in the planning.

In the shelving section a brief explanation showed the difference in shelving space utilization when storing randomly instead of in numeral sequence. Random storage is also very efficient in a picking system because it allows all SKUs to be stored in bands at different levels according to their activity. The fastest movers are at the most convenient levels with medium and slow movers at less desirable heights. There are a number of other factors in locating each sku; including size, weight, fifo, risk of contamination of other products etc. This is best done by computer programs used by professional consultants.

If you must store and pick in family groupings by numerical sequence a lot of space might still be saved by the simple process of storing all SKUs of exceptional size on lower shelves, just below the shelves holding smaller items. Notes placed in the locations from which the large items were removed will inform the picker of their lower locations. This is a method for small installations.

Selection of order picking systems is complex and it is highly recommended to seek help from people experienced with your industry and the range of options available. However, since each warehouse, stores area or distribution center has its own unique goals and problems it is hoped this manual will help you work more closely with any consultant. The following pages are designed to give you a better understanding of the options available, and how they may be able to assist in you controlling your picking costs.

Order Picking

As previously stated, there are many alternative methods available for your consideration, but before any of these methods can be fully appreciated, you must clearly understand the "elements" that the order picking process is made up of. They are as follows;

Process of **Receiving** the physical order, which can be from printed paper, to radio frequency to direct electronic interface.

Physical Order Selection. In most instances multiple unique customer orders will be made available to the picker, he must now go through the process of a specific single order, perhaps based on the urgency of the delivery requirement, or simply to pick the first of the pile, and separate it from the remainder. In many cases this process, if manual, can lead to order scanning and selecting based on the individual pickers preference, which may be towards smaller orders for example.

Read is the next function, the picker must understand the order and understand where the picks will begin, which could be based on aisle numbers, zones or multiple other concepts. Understanding the order, the picker now has to advance to the correct aisle or zone, this is called **Travel.**

Upon entering the aisle, zone etc, the picker advances to the first picking face via further **Travel**. The picker then **re-reads** the order again to confirm the exact down aisle location of the pick. Confirming this and completing his **Travel**, he again turns to the order. He physically **Finds** the pick location.

He **Reads** the order to double check the quantity required from this location. The picker **reaches** into the racking / shelving and selects the item.

Counting may be required, to assure the correct quantity is picked.

Place, the requested item(s) are placed into a box, pallet or compartment on a picking device.

Read to confirm order item(s) selected and check for the next picking location. The process then **Repeats** over and over until all the lines on the order are picked.

Picker then **Travels** back to the drop area, drops the orders off. Completes any required **paperwork** (such are discrepancies etc).

Travels back to the start area to pick up his next order

From the above elements of order picking the largest element by far is **travel** which frequently occupies up to 70% of the total picking cycle in many manual operations.

To develop the most suitable and cost effective picking method, you must therefore try to reduce the amount of travel which is present within your picking cycle, bearing in mind that the more complex the method the greater the initial cost in most cases, so you have to arrive at the best compromise for your particular requirements. Some of these methods worthy of consideration are as follows;

Single order selection

Zone Picking.

Cart picking devices

Powered equipment such as Battery Electric Pallet Trucks

Double (or triple) length pallet trucks.

Electric High Level order picking truck.

Batch picking several orders simultaneously.

Carton flow rack with pick to light (page310)

Pick towers.

Forward Picking.

Horizontal Carousels

Vertical Carousels & Shuttles (Vertical Lift Modules)

RF systems

Voice directed picking.

Single Order Selection.
This method is where one picker will pick one order to completion in the method as described above. The picking of one order at a time (per "pick cycle" or "pick run") is probably the most commonly used method. However in some circumstances, such as when there are only a few items on each order, it is practical to have more than one order picked on the same run to reduce travel per order.

Multiple Order Selection (Manual)
When using printed order forms to pick multiple orders on a pick cycle the picker will scan each order on a continuous basis and pick the specified items as he gets to them, usually placing each order in a separate container. This method puts a lot of responsibility on the picker and may lead to an increase in errors. Three or four orders at a time may be the maximum practical.

Zone Picking
On a pick run the order may traverse all necessary aisles to fill the whole order to completion, to reduce time each picker may only pick a portion of the order from a specified zone. The remainder of the order is picked by others in other zones. The picked portion of the order may be transferred from zone to zone until the order is completed; or each portion of the order may be sent directly to a location where all the portions are merged into the completed order.

This is where individual pickers are confined to specific areas (zones) of the warehouse which may be 2 or more aisles typically. The benefit here is familiarity and reduction in search time. This method also allows you to put all your fast movers in a common zone thus your picking in this zone is hitting a pick face far more frequently for picks to each order, thus travel is reduced in this zone.

Cart Picking.
This is the addition of a pushed cart or even a manual powered scooter with a carrier on the front which allows the picker to travel faster between picks, especially where there are some fairly large distances to cover, or where one picker is completing one order (such as a counter order) which often have very few lines per order, but the few items may well be scattered across the warehouse.

Powered Equipment such as Battery Electric Pallet Trucks.
These devices carry one pallet on their forks which are typically 42" or 48" long (forks). These pallet trucks, being powered, travel much faster than walking and are less fatiguing to the picker, thus travel time is reduced and the accuracy can be improved over manual travel.

Double (or Triple) length Electric Pallet Trucks.
Same as the single pallet truck with the advantage of additional space to build large orders without returning to drop off a full pallet and pick up an additional pallet. Over the course of a shift, double (or triple) pallet trucks can save a significant amount of "dead head" travelling to drop full pallets and retrieve empty pallets.

Electric High Level Order Picking trucks.
This is similar to a single pallet truck, but because it can lift the operator / picker to great heights, multiple rack or shelf levels are now available for regular picking which would not previously have been available from floor picking. Thus with twice (or more) of the picking height now available then you will effectively have reduced your travel by 50% (or more) to select the same items. This is obviously a time saver, and should be considered, if your volumes are sufficient. If a faster moving operation, be cautious of going too high with the order picker to select, as these kind of trucks typically start to be reduced in speed automatically above a certain lift height of the forks of say 6' to 10' typically. You should confirm these details with your potential hardware supplier.

Batch Picking several orders simultaneously
By this method you are now picking more than one order as the picker passes through a racking / shelving system. Thus, by selecting just 2 orders simultaneously, then in one pass through the system the picker has picked two orders, thus saving an entire additional pass through the entire system, thus a great time and travel saver. Obviously, you can add more that 2 orders into a batch, but care should be taken that the picker is not slowed down by scanning several hard copy orders, so, with the addition of some automation such as RF or Voice Pick, many of these issues can be addressed (see page 312). A multiple-order pick run becomes much more efficient with paperless orders. The pick list may be sent to a monitor mounted on a pick vehicle.

Carton Flow Rack with Pick-To-Light technology.

With this method, the cartons all flow towards the front of the flow rack which becomes the picking area. Reserve stock is held in the same flow lane behind the face pick cases, thus reducing the width required for each product sku face. By this method, the picker now passes in front of more SKUs with less travel. The system can be further enhanced with pick-to-light where all the length of several side by side carton flow rack frames have electronic indicators under each pick face. As the picker advances down the aisle all they have to do is read the quantity indicator under faces requiring that pick, pick the quantity, hit the complete button on the indicator and scan down the row for the next illuminated sku. This method is very fast and accurate, and ideal for certain smaller high volume items. Additional travel can be saved by the picker not having to return to the opposite end after completing an order pass, because the picker can just reverse direction and pick back to the opposite end. Repeating this function over and over until all orders are selected. Thus the picker does not have to be involved with anything except following the instructions on the indicators at each pick face.

Forward Picking.

Several very large distribution houses use this method, whereby they select the TOTAL quantity of each SKU required for today's picking, and move it up to a central area near the shipping docks. By doing this, only one pass is made through the entire warehouse, so wasted travel past unrequired SKUs is not required during the rest of the pick day. Also, travel to pick the forwarded pick items is shorter (only the required SKUs for today, so much less travel) and thus also faster. This method is frequently used in produce warehouses and some toy manufacturers distribution centers.

Pick Towers.

These are multi-level picking areas, usually rack supported, and in most cases have a conveyor belt system running down the center of the picking aisle. This system in a Pick Tower is interconnected with a conveyor system and orders progress through the various levels. The picker is usually working one zone within a level and feeds the picked product directly to the belt. The concept is very similar to that described above, but on multiple levels. Because the throughput can be enormous through these towers, normally the picking is done in "Waves" throughout the entire warehouse, so that orders can be kept in reasonable sequence as they travel to the sorting and staging area prior to shipping. With these systems consideration must also be given to "de-trashing", or the removal of master packs (once emptied of product). Many systems include a trash conveyor which runs overhead to take these empty cardboard boxes directly to a trash compactor.

Horizontal Carousels.

With this equipment, the items are transported to the picker automatically by a horizontally rotating series of hanging shelving units (typically 6′ to 12′ in height) rotating on an elongated track. By this method NO TRAVEL is required by the picker, just picking from the carrier shelf that is directed to the picker. While that operation is under way, the other horizontal carousels will rotate to their next pick location, so with correct management, the picker should never be waiting for a required shelf to move into position. Horizontal carousels represent one of the best cost per cubic foot stored aspects when measured against other fully automated systems. However, their disadvantage is utilizing the air space above them, which in a tall warehouse can become expensive, so they are not as cube efficient as some of the other methods. Also important consideration is that if the number of lines per order is very small, say 1 or 2 lines, then if you only pick one order at a time the potential pick rate will not be as high as you will be waiting for the carousel to index around. To overcome this limitation you can select several small orders simultaneously as described previously, this reduces the indexing travel between picks. Also recommend utilizing at least 2 carousels simultaneously as then one is indexing while the other unit is being picked. Typical carrier capacity is 600, 1000 and 2500 lbs available. Rotation speeds for indexing are usually in the 85 FPM range.

Vertical Carousels

These devises are similar to a horizontal carousel, except the Vertical Carousel is stood on end somewhat like a fairground Ferris wheel. They have multiple carriers travelling in a vertical motion, typically these carriers are 8' to 10' wide, but other options are available. The carriers are typically 24" deep as a maximum, with 16" and 18" depths being also fairly common, and typically allow for products of fixed maximum height to be stored of usually 19", this dimension when divided by 2 additional adjustable shelves giving say 6" for product height on each shelf, allowing for the shelf thickness. These units can better utilize the headroom available in a taller area, and typically most verticals are around 20' tall, but they are available up to over 40' in height. The height limitation stems from the fact that as the unit is like a "Ferris wheel" it is important to keep the load balanced throughout the machine carriers, otherwise if too much weight is combined on one series of carriers, the carousel drive system will not have the counterweight helping it, so the drive system must be powerful and able to prevent the unit from "freewheeling" as out of balance conditions occur. Verticals are very good at storing a huge number of smaller sized SKUs in a very small footprint, and the carriers on the carousel index vertically and can store to considerable heights. Thus the picker again has absolute minimum of travel across the typical 8' to 10' carrier face to select the required items. The carousel again automatically rotates to the next required location. In this case, accuracy is very high and losses due to theft etc of higher cost or risk items are substantially reduced as those items are not exposed to so many people and are considerably easier to secure within the steel enclosure of the vertical carousel. These units are very ergonomically correct, as the pickers are always picking from the perfect pick height, and never need to bend or reach above their shoulder height.

Shuttles or Vertical Lift Modules (VLMs)

The VLM is also storing in a vertical enclosed unit but utilizes flat trays often 6' to 10' wide and typically 32" to 34" deep to reduce reach requirements when picking. The trays are stored utilizing a "central elevating system" with a shuttle device to store the trays on rails in the front, or the rear, of the unit.

Because of the single lift device and no out of balance load consideration, and only one tray being handled at once, the VLM has higher weight capacity in the trays and units are typically 600 to 1000 lbs per tray with machines up to 2000 lbs per tray available. Typically the shuttles are 20' high and over, and become more cost effective as the height of the unit increases.

Product height on the trays is automatically measured as the tray is stored, the system assures the load is stored in a suitable clear height area between other stored trays, thus, the VLM can almost automatically maximize cube utilization in the system, by not wasting space vertically between trays.

Multiple access openings are available on the VLM to allow the unit stored trays to be accessed between multiple floors, further enhancing its advantages for many applications. Of course only one access opening can control the machine at one time.

RF systems.

Radio Frequency systems are manufactured by several suppliers and have been available for over 20 years. They have advanced over the years, but they are frequently combined with bar code scanners, and are hand held or gauntlet type devices. Although the weight of the unit has been improved over the years, many of these units are still quite heavy when worn on the wrist for 8 or more hours, plus the built in bar code scanners are not impregnable, and do not survive multiple hits as they have moving mirrors etc. built into them. So for reliability standby units are advisable. Cold storage applications need to be confirmed with the supplier to check suitability. These systems have a small screen which directs the picker from pick to pick, and displays the quantity to be picked, but of course this does require reading and confirming by the operator by button strokes.

Voice Directed Picking.

This technology has advanced massively in the last few years and is a wearable device (on the belt) typically weighing less than 2 lbs. It can be wired to a headset, but lately most units are Bluetooth to the headset the picker uses. The system prompts (verbally) the picker to travel to a specific location. The picker can ask the system to repeat any instruction. At the pick location the picker is asked to read back a 2 or 3 digit random check code (normally attached below the SKU on the rack beam) to assure they are in the correct location. If confirmed correctly, the system directs the picker to pick "X" quantity. Upon completion, the picker confirms and is verbally directed to the next pick location automatically. The advantage here is all transactions are recorded, so corrective action can be made if a picker is making multiple errors, or is performing below normal acceptable pick rates. All information up to the minute is available to the supervisor, which is a huge advantage and also allows management to congratulate productive employees, building morale. Pick routes are always the shortest route, and batch picking multiple orders can be built into the system. Having no moving parts, most Voice systems are ok in Cold Storage environments. If the optional bar code scanners are utilized, you should check acceptability to the environment with your supplier.

SECTION ELEVEN
GUIDANCE METHODS & AUTOMATED GUIDED VEHICLES - AGVS

11

FORKLIFT GUIDANCE METHODS

Forklifts and orderpickers can often gain significant advantages when guided within an aisle, rather than having the operator steer the vehicle. There are two common types of guidance; Rail and "wire". Either may guide in a very narrow aisle (VNA) or be placed on both sides of a wider aisle, as shown on the drawings which follow.

Some advantages of guidance are:

The operator does not have to steer the vehicle, thus freeing him to pay more attention to the main task, such as picking an order. Using a very narrow aisle allows the picker to access goods on both sides of the aisle. Raising or lowering the load or operating compartment while traveling is also safer when in guidance.

Less operating side clearance is needed and that leads to the narrowest aisle possible, thus saving a lot of space or getting more into the space available.

Safe lift heights may be increased considerably within the aisles.

Pallet loads will be stored more exactly because the forklift is in a position square to the racks.

All of the above will combine to result in less damage to products, racks and forklift; and may help in preventing injury to the operator.

Rail guidance typically consists of angle iron lengths anchored to the floor and welded at the joints, with rounded funnel entries at each end. When used in a very narrow aisle the distance between the rails must be very specific according to dimensions provided by the manufacturer.

With rail or wire guidance the operating side clearances may also be very specific or may leave a bit of choice, depending on the system equipment.

Wire guidance came after rails but it has been in use many years and is reliable. It consists of a wire embedded in the floor, with a signal from an electric current to activate a mechanism on the vehicle. This mechanism controls the vehicle steering and, typically, keeps it very close to being centered on the signal from the wire.

A slot for the wire path is cut into the floor and is then grouted over. So existing buildings can usually have this system installed. But in some instances the floor construction or other electric wires within the floor may cause malfunctions. Specialists should be consulted regarding the suitability of any floor for a wire guidance system, including a new one being planned.

Wire guidance is also used for Automated Guided Vehicles (AGV). These are explained in this section.

In addition to floor guidance there are some vehicles, often with a very high lift and full capacity, which also use a top guide rail. These can be pallet load handlers, orderpickers for case or piece picking or a combination of both operations.

RAIL GUIDANCE

DOUBLE SIDED GUIDANCE IN VERY NARROW AISLE

FLOOR BEAM

GUIDE WHEEL ATTACHED TO VEHICLE

ANGLE IRON GUIDE RAIL

SINGLE SIDED GUIDANCE IN WIDER AISLE

TWO GUIDE WHEELS ATTACHED TO VEHICLE

11 *GUIDANCE METHODS & AUTOMATED GUIDED VEHICLES - AGVS*

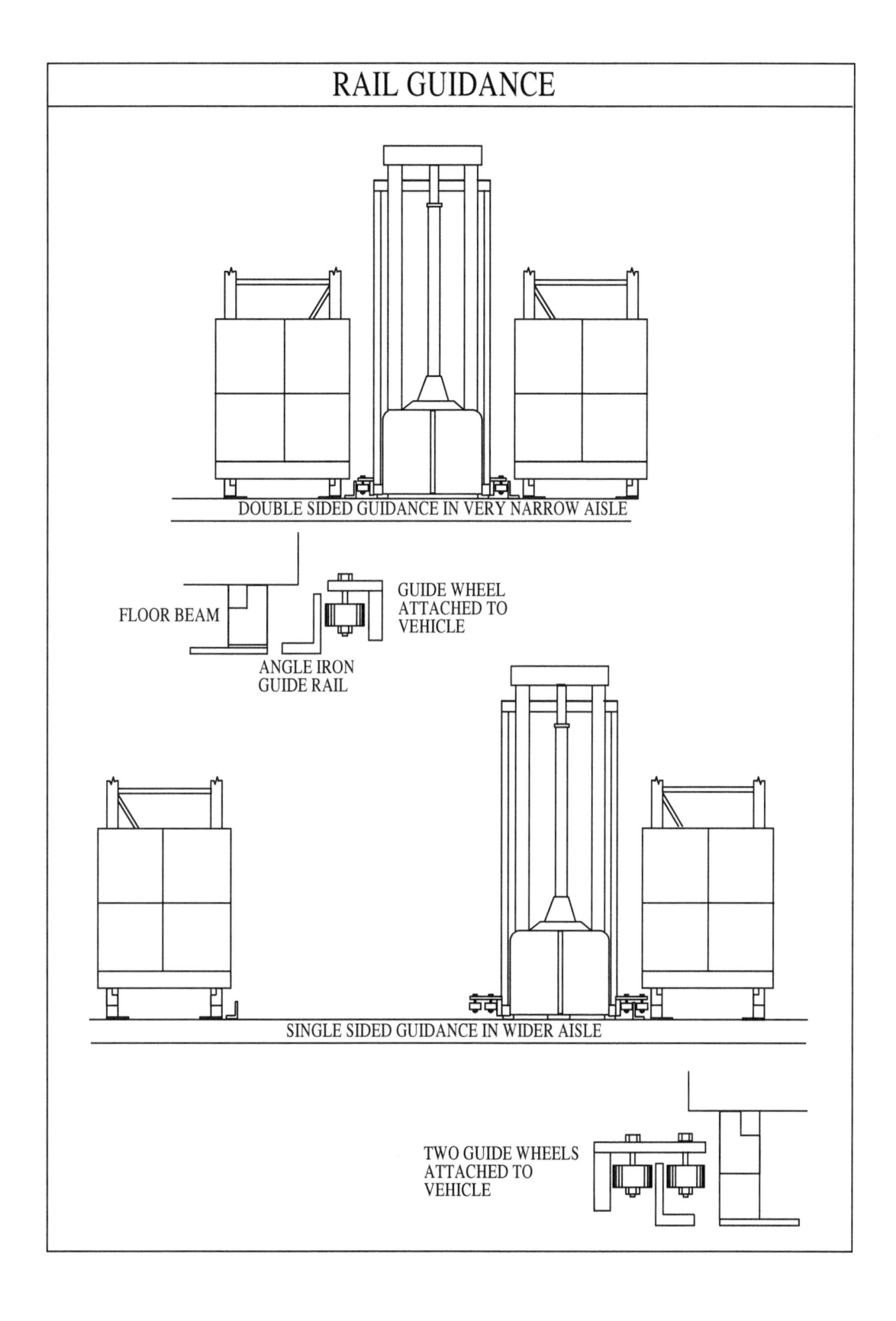

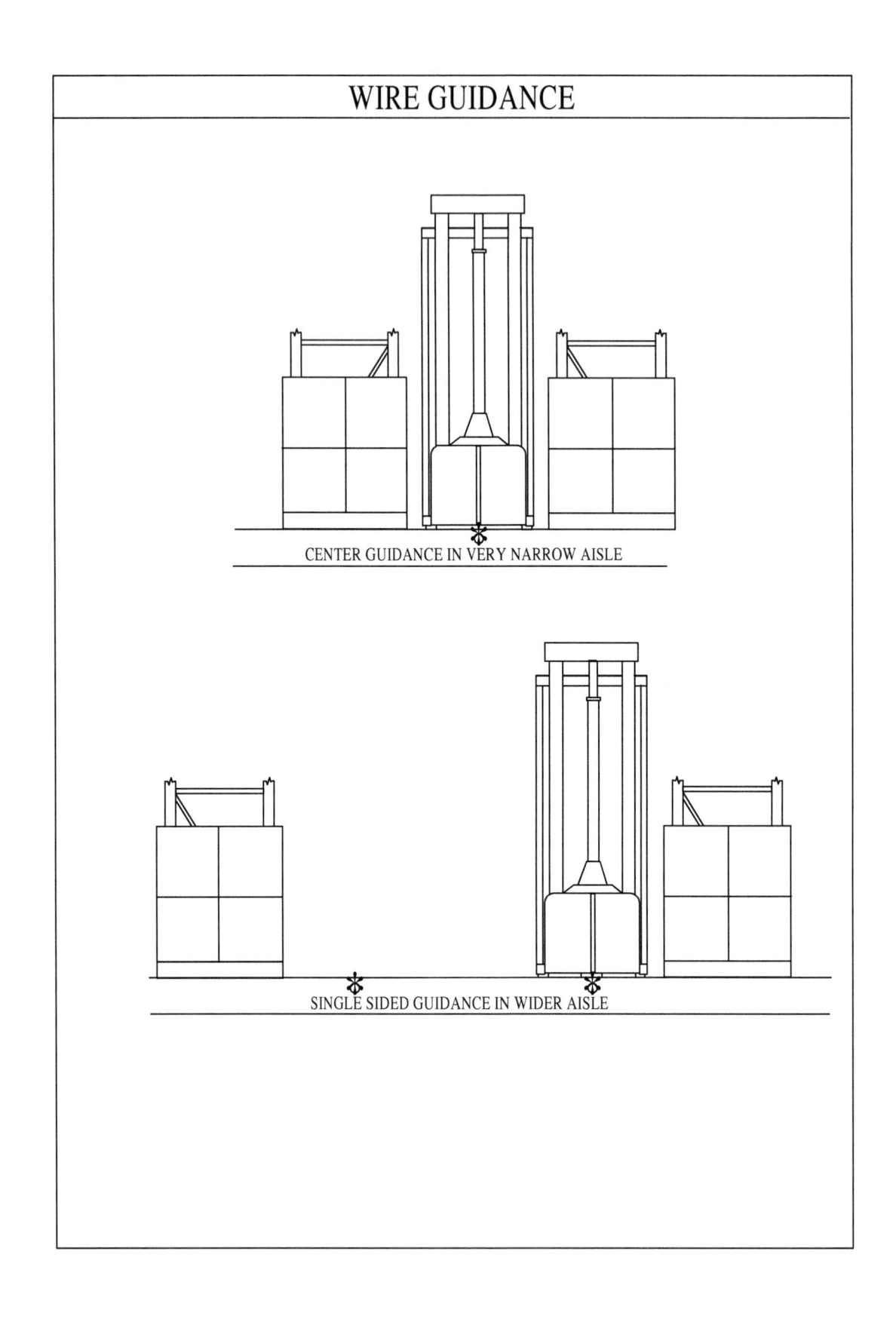

WIRE GUIDANCE

CENTER GUIDANCE IN VERY NARROW AISLE

SINGLE SIDED GUIDANCE IN WIDER AISLE

HOW TO CONFIGURE AND EQUIP YOUR WAREHOUSE

VEHICLES GUIDED TOP AND BOTTOM

TOP TRACK GUIDED

TOP TRACK GUIDED

BOTTOM GUIDED; TRACK OR RAILS

VERY NARROW AISLE
VERY HIGH LIFT
ROTATING PANTOGRAPH SIDE REACH

BOTTOM TRACK GUIDED

VERY NARROW AISLE
VERY HIGH LEVEL
STOCKPICKER

11 *GUIDANCE METHODS & AUTOMATED GUIDED VEHICLES - AGVS*

Automated Guided Vehicle

An AGV or Automatic Guided Vehicle is typically a wheeled burden carrier, self-propelled by an on-board battery. It travels a pre-determined guide path to programmed locations, often termed stations.

At each station where it is programmed to stop it may be loaded or unloaded, manually or automatically. The AGVs main purpose is to reduce, or eliminate, the labor cost of operators and forklifts to deliver products, horizontally, from one location to another on a repeated basis. It may be programmed for multiple station stops and is capable of other automated functions. The load deck can be customized to suit the materials being transported.

These vehicles are generally restricted to indoor use and became popular in the 1980's, initially using a wire guidance installed in the floor, as has been explained for forklifts. Large distribution centers and manufacturing plants quickly adapted to these systems because, despite an original high cost, they proved quite reliable; providing potential problems in the floor were first addressed.

Steel and high voltage wiring in the floor can affect the "field" created by the guidance wire and cause unexpected variation. Thus any building being considered for a wire guidance system should have its suitability checked.

As the acceptance of AGVs grew, the complexity of the guide paths also increased. Some limitations with the initial "dumb cart" technology became bothersome. Smarter carts where then developed, with more of the electronics and "smarts" built into the truck. This eliminated complex (and expensive) switching loops in the floor, required by the dumb carts. The Smart AGVs thus allowed more ability for choices of destinations, within multiple interlocking loop systems. The floor controls portion of these systems then became much less expensive and simpler to install and maintain.

In the 1990's a new guidance method became popular. These guide paths were made of tape or painted (perhaps fluorescent) on the floor, with optical sensors reading ability on each cart to keep it centered over the strip were developed. The very low initial cost and flexibility for changes of the guide path made this guidance path very popular based on cost. However some problems can develop if the guide path is not kept clean and intact; sometimes difficult to do in a busy facility.

Another guidance method was developed, primarily based on military developments in lasers. These systems scanned target bar coded plates hung in the building ceiling, and allowed the truck to triangulate its position very accurately. These systems could become very highly automated, but are considered as expensive initial investment and require much higher level technicians to keep them running well. These technicians can sometime prove hard to find, and retain.

The most recent guidance method was introduced in about 2012 and is "optical recognition" based. Basically the cart is driven though its desired path once, in "learn mode". The cart recognizes and follows programmed paths based on its surroundings, rather than a floor guide or target system. At the time of writing it is still not clear what, if any, weaknesses exist to be commented upon with this system.

AGVs regardless of which of the 4 types, can be fitted with various deck configurations including powered roller conveyors, able to automatically unload or load at pre-designated stations utilizing pallets, skids or other load devices.

AGVs can also be fitted with lifting masts enabling them to lift loads to substantial heights and stack pallet load on pallet load, enabling the possibility of a warehouse or distribution center without human operators. AGVs are frequently fitted with towing capabilities also, trailering several true-tracking trailers.

Safety is of course of paramount importance with AGVs. They are normally fitted with continuous non-contact object detection systems which slow or stop the AGV if an obstruction is sensed. Touch sensitive sensors also generally surround AGV's chassis and will stop the vehicle immediately if contacted.

Door openers, enabling units to pass between different environments within a facility are also available, and are usually also tied into the building fire alarm system, assuring the AGV never stops in the path of a fire door.

Recharging of the AGV battery or accumulators also needs to be considered, and many systems now incorporate high amperage pads in the floor that only become activated when the AGV is over them, these pads deliver a very fast charge enabling the unit to have enough power to return to the next charging point, even taking into account weekend or overnight shutdowns.

Your choice of AGV guiding system, guide path, stations, level of automation etc. etc. will take time, effort and expertise to determine. But if there are repetitive programmable movements within your facility, AGVs may be well justified.

Recent years has seen revived interest in the application of AGVs because technology has advanced rapidly in the control and circuitry involved. Manufacturing costs of these machines has generally become much more aggressively priced. The labor cost element of any warehouse or distribution center are a substantial portion of the overhead involved, and properly applied, AGV systems can substantially reduce horizontal transportation labor costs, especially in larger facilities. AGVs do not get distracted, and are frequently preferable when people also access transport aisles, as the safety record for AGVs is very good. They will detect pedestrians before contacting them, making for safer workplaces.

Always remember, AGVs can transport loads repeatedly over many routes, but you must address the loading process and the unloading process and assure it is not creating different problem areas for you.

AUTOMATIC GUIDED VEHICLE

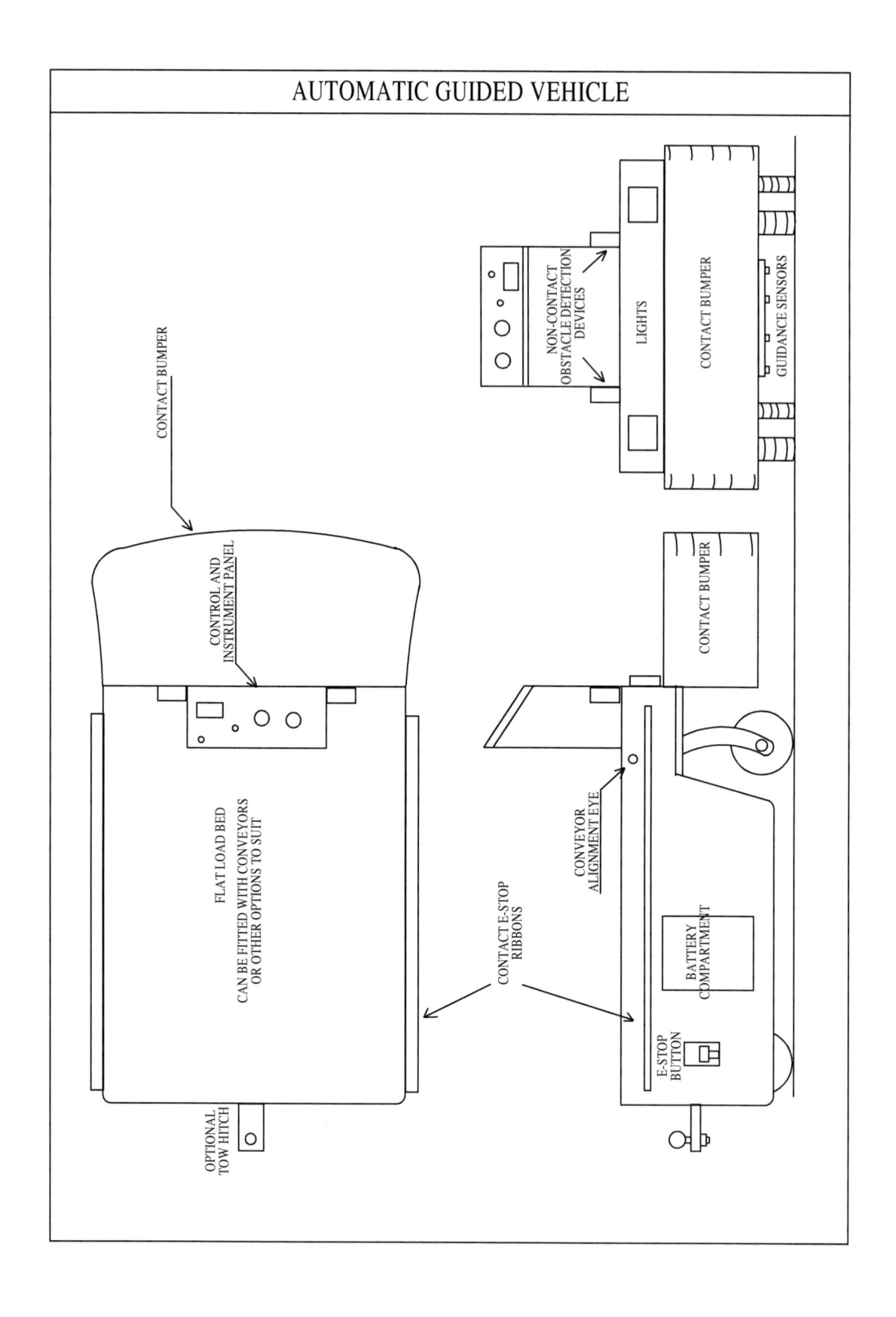

- CONTACT BUMPER
- NON-CONTACT OBSTACLE DETECTION DEVICES
- LIGHTS
- CONTACT BUMPER
- GUIDANCE SENSORS
- CONTROL AND INSTRUMENT PANEL
- CONTACT BUMPER
- FLAT LOAD BED CAN BE FITTED WITH CONVEYORS OR OTHER OPTIONS TO SUIT
- CONVEYOR ALIGNMENT EYE
- CONTACT E-STOP RIBBONS
- BATTERY COMPARTMENT
- E-STOP BUTTON
- OPTIONAL TOW HITCH

SECTION TWELVE
CONCLUSION

12

CONCLUSION

TRY, TRY, TRY AGAIN

The tasks of selecting warehouse equipment and configuring the storage area can be interlocked and contentious to such an extent that it is necessary to "go 'round the circle" a few times to review the best solutions for your specific needs.

The initially favored equipment and aisle widths may not yield the hoped for results.

Then it is time to try alternatives for any or all zones with various combinations of aisle widths, higher racking for more storage levels and/or deeper storage.

Thus it is desirable to be able to closely estimate the yields of any system, in any layout, without getting too deeply into them in time, drawings and cost. This is the main purpose of Sections 1 and 2, which contain Building Blocks and the DataForms. The 3rd block, a Segment, is a repeatable block with a known footprint and dimensions, as well as area and storage capacity. Changing any one or a combination of the segment components (length, width, storage depth, aisle width, area, height and capacity) will open up new chances for suitable systems within an efficient layout. Arranging and re-arranging them like plastic cubes in different configurations will result in a great deal of data on the DataForms.

*The simplicity of this selection process may have been obscured to some by the large amount of explanatory text, drawings, dimensioning and cautions which were mostly used to show the necessity of extreme attention to detail **after the preferred methods and layout are selected.***

In going around the circle again you may, for instance, without any specific forklifts in mind, try various applicable segments and then search out the equipment to suit. This method may work for you although some adjustments will probably be needed.

The contention between the narrowest possible aisles and the desire to have room for two forklifts or pickers to safely pass can be re-considered for each zone, as can the number and width of access aisles.

Also be aware that many consulting firms in this industry have computer programs and experience which can lead to easier, and probably more accurate, determination of the needs of each sku. They may also save time, money and frustration with their knowledge of national and local regulations.

It is our hope that a full understanding of the information presented in this manual will prove to be very beneficial to both one-time users and also to those with more exposure in the industry.

Remember to use the resources out there to assist you in your final solution configuration. Both racking and forklift equipment suppliers can provide a wealth of confirmation details to assist you once you have your initial plan concept in place.

SECTION THIRTEEN
TERMINOLOGY

13

Definitions of Anagrams & Technical Terms Used

Word	Definition
Address	An alpha numeric or just numeric used to designate a specific storage slot typically using Aisle, Bay, Height, slots down aisle run (segment)
FIFO	First In First Out (used to describe rotation method determined by storage method)
FILO	First In Last Out (used to describe rotation method determined by storage method)
FISHS	First In Still Here Somewhere (used to describe rotation method determined by storage method)
Turnover / Turns	Turnover is the number of times in a 12 month period that the inventory will be reordered to the original levels. One way of estimating this is to divide the average inventory level into the annual cost of sales. E.g. if an average inventory is 4 million dollars and the sales were thirty two million dollars, the inventory would be considered to turn eight times.
Cross Dock	Where a distribution center does not put stock into storage, but instead, immediately takes it from the receiving dock and places it directly in the shipping dock ready for shipping immediately to its new location.
Face	Pallet or Shelving space immediately accessible without moving other products
Pick Face	Pallet or Shelving space immediately accessible to a picker without moving other products
Slot	Space available for storing a pallet load (not necessarily occupied, but available)
SKU	Stock Keeping Unit (a specific product with unique identifier or part number / upc code
Bar Code	A machine readable code which can be quickly scanned to avoid having nondextrous pickers etc. from having to type in long part numbers or descriptions, saving time and avoiding errors.
UPC Code	Universal Product Code (code is unique and given to each different product / pack size etc.)
Aisle	Access space between rows of rack or shelving
Cross Aisle	Aisle which allows cross access between different storage aisles without travelling the full storage aisle length
Access Aisle	May also refer to Main or Cross Aisle. Usually a wider aisle allowing access to storage aisle or the dock etc.
Storage Aisle	As above, but usually limited to storage and retrieval of pallet loads or other good stored along either side.
Dedicated Aisle	Where specific products are confined to be stored and picked from a given storage aisle. This may be because of client demands to keep all their product together, or it could be relative to product cross contamination, where for instance soap powders, detergents etc. should not be stored within close proximity to bagged products such as sugar, flour etc. as the taste of the food stuffs can be contaminated.
Main Aisle	The principal access across several storage aisles, generally in front of the system, and frequently at both ends of the system. Usually alongside receiving and shipping areas.
Lane	A storage level within flow through racking or push back racks
Tunnel	Used in pallet mole type system, this is a single pallet face width by various numbers of pallets deep.
ANSI	American National Standards Institute

AGV	Automatic Guided Vehicle. Electric robot vehicle generally involved in horizontal transportation requirement without use of any manpower
AGV Lift Decks	Allows an AGV to drive under a load at the drive-in type station, elevate the deck lifting the load from the station, and then automatically taking and delivering the load by the same method to another work station.
AGV Conveyor Deck	As above, but instead of a lifting motion, the AGV is fitted with a powered conveyor deck which allows it to transfer loads from a conveyor load station, onto the AGV and then automatically travel to the assigned drop off location.
Traction Battery	Heavy Industrial Battery usually designed for deep cycling and typically lead acid or gel cell type. The weight of the lead is crucial in many cases to the stability of the forklift.
Reach Truck	Truck designed for narrow aisle use which retracts the load for travel and maneuverability within the front load wheels (wheel base) allowing for tighter turning radius, the reach mechanism (pantograph or moving mast) allows the truck to place loads into racking without straddling the bottom pallet or requiring raised bottom beam racking for the front wheels to pass under.
Counterbalance Truck	Where the capacity of the truck is substantially affected by the weight of a counter weight on the rear of the truck, helping to preventing the truck from tipping under normal conditions. However, when counterbalance trucks are increased in length to get more forward stability, ultimately the trucks lateral capacity can be adversely affected, especially with higher lift heights.
Deep Reach Truck	Similar to the reach truck, but this unit has an additional set of pantographs to allow the truck to store a second pallet deep into the racking. This typical reach from fork face to mast face is usually 53" for a truck handling 48" deep pallets.
FFL	Full Free Lift, means the fork carriage can be lifted all the way to the top of the first mast frame without the other stages of the mast rising up. This is especially important in trailer loading, drive in racks, low doorways etc. where the overhead clearance is limited.
OACH	Over All Collapsed Height usually referring to a lift truck mast, which is the lowest height the mast can be at to handle doorways etc
Dead man Brake	All electric and many IC powered lift trucks incorporate a dead man sensitized foot pedal or seat where by in the event the operator collapses for example and falls from the machine, it will immediately stop using emergency power. This brake is for emergencies only and NOT designed as a regular stopping brake.
Grade clearance	This is the angle at which two flat surfaces (ie Dock Plate and Warehouse floor) can be at before they will catch on the bottom of the forklift as it passes over. This angle is usually supplied by the forklift manufacturer for that particular model based on wheel base and ground clearance.
Grade ability	This is the maximum safe operating grade on which a forklift can be operated straight up or down. Stacking on a grade is never recommended.
Traverse	When the carriage of a VNA truck is moved across the width of the aisle to deposit / pick up a load or rotates a load to the other side of the aisle, this is a traverse motion.
SCR	Silicon Controlled Rectifier. This device allows power to flow through it, with no moving parts, when a small eddy current is applied to the bridge. This allows rapidly pulsed power to the drive motors so as to allow great speed and traction power control. Sometimes referred to a thyristors
Plugging	On most electric materials handling vehicles today, slowing down and stopping is accomplished by reversing the direction of travel selected on the vehicle. This process does not adversely affect the truck components, and with modern circuitry it in fact allows a slight charge to be built into the battery plates (like a capacitor), supplying a little extra power for the next function selected. In some cases a figure of up to 15% energy saving can be achieved with this process, and the right application.

Voltage	Battery electric vehicles are available in numerous voltages, most common is 36 volt, but 24 volt and 48, 72 and high voltages are available. In general a higher voltage does not ensure more power or speed, in fact by having more cells in a battery, a larger portion of the available active electrolyte area is reduced because of many more cell jar wall thicknesses. The reason most suppliers would switch to higher voltage is lighter, less expensive material costs for conductors etc, if you double the voltage, you half the current, so lighter components can be used to handle the same amperage (power).
Attachment	A device designed to fit onto a forklift to allow special handling features.
Chisel Forks	This is just one of numerous fork styles; in this case the bottom of the fork is tapered up evenly, all the way from heal to the tip, making for very thin fork tips which are ideal for chiseling under loads with just thin dunnage and no proper pallet.
Drawbar Pull	Is the load necessary when applied vertically over a pulley in front of the unit to be measured and is the weight where the unit starts to move without other external forces
Clamp	A forklift attachment, usually hydraulic, which allows for loads to be grasped between two hydraulically controlled arms
Pallet Clamp	Is used on order picking trucks to grip on the center board of a pallet to assure the pallet remains firmly in place while the truck is in operation.
Rotator	Forklift attachment, usually hydraulic allowing the forks or arms of the truck to be rotated. This is frequently used in paper roll handling to rotate the roll so that it can be stored on end, rather than on its side, which would be unstable.
Load Backrest	Mandated by law in many areas, is used to assure loads, when tilted back (up) will not be in danger of falling over the carriage height and onto the forklift operator below.
Overhead Guard	Overhead guards are mandatory in most jurisdictions and are designed to take a falling load, (maybe dislodged from a rack) through a given distance in free fall and not deflect more than a given amount. Thus protecting the operator
Battery cycle	On an industrial battery, it is the taking of a battery from the full charged state, through a work cycle, being put on charge until fully charged again, that is one cycle. Many industrial batteries are rated for 1560 cycles (i.e. 5 years on a daily basis). Avoid charging batteries half way through a shift, this deducts another cycle from the batteries life.
Fork Extensions	Never use fork extensions without first checking with the manufacturer of the forklift, as extensions ultimately move the load center forward and thus reduce the truck capacity, but built in safeties on the forklift can become inoperative in these situations
Yield Factors	This is the point where the deflection of a fork etc. has reached the point that additional increase in loading will cause the fork to take a permanent distortion (bend) from which it will not recover when the load is removed.
Specific Gravity	Of a battery is typically 1275 for a fully charged battery and down to 1100 for very flat. Some batteries have higher acid reading for "extra power" but still, the above rule should be a close approximation. Check with your supplier and with a hygrometer. Only add distilled water AFTER the battery is charged, as the liquid electrolyte will rise considerably during the charge cycle.
Rack End frame	The frame to which supporting rack beams are attached, always between at least two end frames creating a single racking bay.
Rack Bay	The storage space, horizontal and vertical between 2 rack end frames
Rack Beam	Beam mounted with clips between two rack end frames. Two beams, installed at the same level become a support for storing loads or pallets.
Flue	The distance between two back to back stored pallet loads (not necessarily the same as the distance between to 2 back to back frames because of load overhang)

Back to Back Spacer	This is a rack joiner used to help stabilize a racking system and secures the back to back frames together. Frequently there may be more than one back to back rack spacer dependent on racking height and stability calculations.
Pallet Support	A heavier duty bar fastened over and between two rack beams at the same level and designed to carry part of the pallet weight on a regular basis.
Racking Safety Bar	Lighter duty safety bar, put in to help prevent a misplaced pallet falling between the storage beam, however, it may be distorted in such an occurrence and should then be replaced. They are not of full load bearing design.
GPMC Pallet	Grocery type pallet, with 3 full stringers which have fork pockets grooved into the lower surface to allow 4 way entry with a fork lift with low profile forks
Slave Pallet	Used to place loads which have been received on a small or not standard pallet, the slave pallet then supports the load and original non-standard pallet when the load is placed into the storage system.
Rack Brace	Diagonal brace, in the end frame itself to give strength and stability to the frame, and also used "down Aisle" to brace the multi bay rack run from down aisle sway. Down aisle braces are typically within the flue space, when installed.
Rat Run	Required in many health regions for food / produce warehouses where an 18" or wider clearance may be required from all inside walls for cleaning / hygiene.
Footplates / Floorplates	At the bottom of each rack frame upright and designed to spread the load across more square inches of concrete, and also provides an anchoring location to anchor frame to the floor for stability.
P&D station	Put down and Dispatch station, used in high throughput applications where it is necessary to retain the lift truck in the aisle, lifting product into and out of racking. Other vehicles such as pallet trucks are used to move the product to and from the dock area, allowing the lift truck to remain at its prime purpose, and not doing the horizontal transportation function.
Staging Area	Where product is moved to or from trailers and is a temporary holding area while other equipment moves the product to and from the rack system.
Dock Seal	Used to keep rodents and cold weather out of warehouses and thus saving utility costs. Overhead seals also assure rain water does not fall on palletized products being loaded or unloaded from a covered trailer during inclement weather. Generally rubber, these seals seal the area between the back of the trailer and the warehouse itself.
Dock Lock	A mechanical hook generally mounted on the concrete which raises to lock onto the lower bar of the trailer bumper to assure the truck driver does not try to pull away from the dock when forklifts and personnel are still loading or unloading the trailer. Most frequently the hook lock is linked to a red and green signal light beside the loading door which indicates the current situation.
Dock Bumper	Dock bumpers are designed to reduce the sudden shock of the trailer backing up to the building. They are steel mounted rubber, and can be set forward from the dock / building wall to assure the trailer does not hit the building, especially important if the dock ramp the trailer is on leans toward the building, as the trailer top could contact the building long before the bumpers touch the dock, if incorrectly measured.
Cube Utilization	Expressed as a percentage of the occupied storage slots compared to the number of slots in the system
Pareto's Law	Often defined as 80/20 rule where 20% of a warehouse SKUs will account for 80% of the product movements within the facility.
Honeycombing	Empty slots, unused for a variety of reasons including LIFO storage systems
Floor Slot	A location of a single pallet load located on the building floor and not supported by racking.

Sprinkler Clearance	Fire regulations vary by location, and also by flammability of loads stored. You must check with your local fire department and underwriters of your insurance policy and we recommend using a fire code consultant as well, but in many current locations you may not sort any part of your highest loads to a height less than 18" clear of the sprinkler heads or building trusses. Frequently this increases to 24" or more.
Order Picker	Also called Order Selector, refers to the individual who is physically picking the order from racks or shelving. Unfortunately, this term is also used today to indicate the piece of equipment being used by the individual, so order picker can refer to a machine or the person using it.
Picking Order	File or printed document which is a unique order to one specific customer. It will frequently contain several "order detail lines"
Order Detail Line	Indicates the item to be picked, the quantity required, and the location the product is to be picked from.
Order header record	Defines which customer the order is for, their account number, address, ship to address, required date etc. There are NO picking detail lines in the header record.
Order priority	Indicates the urgency with which this order is required to be handled
Order Required Ship Date	Indicates the required date, so orders required today can take preference over orders required next week for instance.
Replenishment order	Received product needs to be stored into location within the system, grouping several received lines together will produce a "Replenishment Order"
Batch Picking	Combining multiple single orders into one large order, but keeping the line items discrete to each order.
Banding	Normally refers to a specific height location, or series of locations. By banding, floor based pick verses high level orderpicker picks can be dedicated to the most suitable machine, saving time and labor and improving efficiency.
PIR	A method still used, usually using dedicated high level picking trucks in a 8'6" aisle picking multiple order simultaneously onto picking carts on the forks and having the unit pick all upper levels going down the aisle and all lower levels returning to the beginning of the same aisle. Very fast for the right application, originally introduced by Barrett.
Hot Pick	A pick which jumps the queue of existing in-house orders because of its urgency.
Reorder Point	The inventory level at which a part must be reordered when it falls below that level.
Active Location	Is the preferred picking location for the product and is generally used where you have case / broken pallet picking where the backup stock is stored overhead in as close proximity as reasonably feasible.
Push system	Where stores do not order an item, but it is "pushed" out to them for a special sales item. This is frequently done by larger store groups driven by the marketing department.
Cold Storage	Typical of the food distribution business, where the product must be held within a certain temperature range to prevent premature spoilage. Produce warehouses are often at 3 degrees centigrade. Frozen food would be at -20 degrees centigrade, and flash freezing is at -40 degrees and is used to rapidly cool freshly manufactured product to assure the whole load reached -20 for long term storage, rapidly.
Shrinkage	An inventory adjustment because of pilferage, over or under shipment, or receiving errors.
RFID	Radio Frequency Identification. Utilizing a small disposable solid state circuits on pallets or individual products, and can be automatically scanned into and out of warehouses without any other manual input.
Voice Pick	Pickers wear a small computer on their waists and a set of Wi-Fi headphones and microphone so the system audibly directs pickers from location to location through an order, with no paperwork or manual keying.

DATAFORM EXAMPLE:

DATAFORM #1

THIS FORM IS PROVIDED FOR, AND LIMITED TO, THE SOLE USE OF THE PURCHASER OF THE MANUAL
" HOW TO CONFIGURE AND EQUIP YOUR WAREHOUSE"

DF128

PANEL ONE — INITIAL INPUT

- AREA _____
- FLOOR SLOTS / SEGMENT _____
- PICK FACES WANTED _____
- SLOTS WANTED _____
- TOTAL SLOTS / SEGMENT _____
- AISLE FACES WANTED _____
- # OF STORAGE LEVELS _____
- SEGMENTS NEEDED _____
- RESERVE SLOTS WANTED _____

AREA _____ ÷ SQ. FT. PER SEG. _____ = SEGMENTS _____

PANEL TWO — ALTERNATE STORAGE LEVELS ("STACK HEIGHTS")

# OF STORAGE LEVELS				
# OF FLOOR SLOTS				
SLOTS PER SEGMENT				
SEGS. FOR ____ SLOTS				
REVISED TOTAL SLOTS				

PANEL THREE

	PER SEG.	TOTAL	PER SEG.	TOTAL	PER SEG.	TOTAL	PER SEG.	TOTAL
AISLE FACES								
PICK FACES @ ____ HIGH								
AISLE FACE RESERVES								
REAR RESERVES								
TOTAL RESERVES								
PICK FACES @ ____ HIGH								
AISLE FACE RESERVES								
REAR RESERVES								
TOTAL RESERVES								
PICK FACES @ ____ HIGH								
AISLE FACE RESERVES								
REAR RESERVES								
TOTAL RESERVES								

PANEL FOUR — ALTERNATE CONFIGURATIONS OF LAYOUT WIDTHS AND LENGTHS.

TRIAL LAYOUTS	INITIAL # OF SEGS.	A (W X L)	ACTUAL SEGS. #	B (W X L)	ACTUAL SEGS. #	C (W X L)	ACTUAL SEGS. #
#1		X		X		X	
#2		X		X		X	
#3		X		X		X	
#4		X		X		X	

HOW TO CONFIGURE AND EQUIP YOUR WAREHOUSE

AREA DATA FOR DIFFERENT CONFIGURATIONS — DATAFORM #2

THIS FORM IS PROVIDED FOR, AND LIMITED TO, THE SOLE USE OF THE PURCHASER OF THE MANUAL "HOW TO CONFIGURE AND EQUIP YOUR WAREHOUSE"

DF129

ALTERNATE CONFIGURATIONS OF LAYOUT WIDTHS AND LENGTHS.

NOTE: SKETCHES WILL HELP DETERMINE THE NUMBER OF ACCCESS AISLES WANTED.

TRIALS FROM FORM #1	INITIAL # OF SEGS.	A W X L	ACTUAL SEGS. #	B W X L	ACTUAL SEGS. #	C W X L	ACTUAL SEGS. #
#1		X		X		X	
#2		X		X		X	
#3		X		X		X	
#4		X		X		X	

332

---

* TOTAL AREA ÷ ACTUAL # OF SEGMENTS

SEGMENTS — REF. TRIAL #

CROSS AISLE WIDTH | DOWN AISLE LENGTH | AREA DIMENSIONS | AREA (SQ.FT.) | ACTUAL # OF SEGS. | SEGMENT AREA INCL. ACCESS AISLES. SQ. FT. | FLOOR SLOTS PER SEG. | AREA PER FLOOR SLOT SQ. FT.

USE "STACK HEIGHT" CHARTS

AREA PER EACH SLOT @____ LEVELS | AREA PER EACH SLOT @____ LEVELS | AREA PER EACH SLOT @____ LEVELS | AREA PER EACH SLOT @____ LEVELS

___ X ___ = ___ FT.
___ X ___ = ___ FT.

ACCESS AISLE AREA FROM SKETCH
____ X ____ X ____

ACCESS AISLES ARE: ____ % ADD-ON

TOTAL AREA IS : ____ SQ. FT.

AND ____ % OF TOTAL AREA

REVISED LENGTH: ____ + ____ = ____ (ACCESS AISLES)

OVERALL DIMENSIONS:
WIDTH: _____ LENGTH: _____

---

* TOTAL AREA ÷ ACTUAL # OF SEGMENTS

SEGMENTS — REF. TRIAL #

CROSS AISLE WIDTH | DOWN AISLE LENGTH | AREA DIMENSIONS | AREA (SQ.FT.) | ACTUAL # OF SEGS. | SEGMENT AREA INCL. ACCESS AISLES. SQ. FT. | FLOOR SLOTS PER SEG. | AREA PER FLOOR SLOT SQ. FT.

USE "STACK HEIGHT" CHARTS

AREA PER EACH SLOT @____ LEVELS | AREA PER EACH SLOT @____ LEVELS | AREA PER EACH SLOT @____ LEVELS | AREA PER EACH SLOT @____ LEVELS

___ X ___ = ___ FT.
___ X ___ = ___ FT.

ACCESS AISLE AREA FROM SKETCH
____ X ____ X ____

ACCESS AISLES ARE: ____ % ADD-ON

TOTAL AREA IS : ____ SQ. FT.

AND ____ % OF TOTAL AREA

REVISED LENGTH: ____ + ____ = ____ (ACCESS AISLES)

OVERALL DIMENSIONS:
WIDTH: _____ LENGTH: _____

BLANK FORMS

Milton Keynes UK
Ingram Content Group UK Ltd.
UKHW052214050923
428087UK00014B/918